Teacher for Justice

LUCY WOODCOCK'S TRANSNATIONAL LIFE

Teacher for Justice

LUCY WOODCOCK'S TRANSNATIONAL LIFE

HEATHER GOODALL,
HELEN RANDERSON
AND DEVLEENA GHOSH

This book is dedicated to all the teachers who, every day,
go above and beyond the call of duty for their students

Published by ANU Press
The Australian National University
Acton ACT 2601, Australia
Email: anupress@anu.edu.au

Available to download for free at press.anu.edu.au

ISBN (print): 9781760463045
ISBN (online): 9781760463052

WorldCat (print): 1112676750
WorldCat (online): 1112676628

DOI: 10.22459/TJ.2019

This title is published under a Creative Commons Attribution-NonCommercial-NoDerivatives 4.0 International (CC BY-NC-ND 4.0).

The full licence terms are available at creativecommons.org/licenses/by-nc-nd/4.0/legalcode

Cover design and layout by ANU Press

This edition © 2019 ANU Press

Contents

Illustrations ix
Abbreviations xiii
Acknowledgements xv

Learning – Unions and the World: 1910s and 1920s
1. Introduction: A Transnational Life 3
2. Unions 17

Scars: 1930s
3. Hunger. 41
4. Love 59
5. Unity and Betrayal 89
6. Refugees and Hope. 107
7. What Sort of Australia? 1938 127

Expanding Visions: 1939–1946
8. Women and War 145
9. Recognising Race: Decolonisation 167

Crossing Borders: 1945–1960s
10. Red Scare 195
11. Into Asia. 223
12. Peace and Prejudice 241
13. Uniting Women 259
14. Bringing the World Back Home 283

Legacy
15. Young in Hope. 305

Bibliography. 317
Author Biographies. 335
Index 337

Illustrations

Figure 2.1: Lucy in her early days of teaching 34

Figure 3.1: This *Newcastle Sun* photo showed the soup kitchens for the children of locked-out and striking miners 44

Figure 3.2: Erskineville was a working-class industrial suburb that had been badly affected by the Depression 54

Figure 4.1: Class 2C, 1947, in which Beverley Bates (née Langley) is front row (marked with cross) and Virginia Watton is in the second row, just behind and to Beverley's right. 64

Figure 4.2: Elsie Rivett c. 1926, co-founder of the Erskineville Children's Club and Library and long-time Peace activist 70

Figure 4.3: The Children's Club and Library on Rochford St, Erskineville, which Lucy helped to establish and of which she was a co-director 72

Figure 4.4: Children at the Children's Library, including Beverley's friend Virginia Watton in the middle 73

Figure 4.5: Beverley Bates from the *Pix* story about the Children's Library 74

Figure 4.6: Beverley Bates (centre) shared her memories of Lucy and Erskineville in an interview for this project 80

Figure 5.1: Lucy c. 1930s, at the height of her union organising. . . . 100

Figure 5.2: Lucy Woodcock as caricatured (affectionately) in the Teachers Federation journal *Education* in January 1939 103

Figure 6.1: Photograph of Lotte Fink (on left) and Lucy, talking and smoking, in Lotte's back yard in Sydney in the 1930s 125

Figure 7.1: Lucy Woodcock on the executive of the Teachers Federation with her allies in the campaign for the role of education in a vision of Australia's democratic future 133

Figure 7.2: 'Sees New Vistas for Education'. Sketch of Lucy for article in *Smith's Weekly* about her election to the University of Sydney Senate 140

Figure 9.1: The shops in front of Lucy's flat in upper 215A George Street where she spent most of her time and where all her political activities were carried out – the NEF met there, the NSW Peace Council met there and the Aboriginal-Australian Fellowship was created there. 168

Figure 9.2: Kapila Khandvala and Mithan Lam at the 1946 Australian Woman's Charter meeting. 171

Figure 9.3: Lucy on the Teachers' Certification Committee 1943 – this shows both how she was often the only woman and how diminutive she was. 187

Figure 10.1: The women on the organising committee for this 1953 conference, including Lucy and Elsie Rivett, attempted to address women's interests and tailor communication strategies towards women who were not in unions or existing peace organisations. 205

Figure 10.2: A photograph of the only known remaining poster for the NSW Convention on Peace and War in November 1953. 209

Figure 10.3: Front page of *Tribune*, 7 October 1953, shows one of the earliest recognitions by Australia's Communist Party that living Aboriginal people were threatened by atomic testing, rather than an isolated culture 213

Figure 11.1: Jessie and Lucy sharing a drink and a laugh during this 1954–55 trip. 226

Figure 11.2: The focus of Jessie's reports: the high-level diplomatic meetings during the trip. 227

Figure 11.3: Lucy, Jessie Street and Anasuya Gyan Chand, Maharashtrian NFIW leader and cooperative advocate, in Lodhi Gardens, New Delhi, 1954 233

Figure 11.4: Jessie Street, Lucy and Padma Narasimhan, Madras women's activist, (possibly) during the Madras Peace Conference, 25 December 1954. 236

Figure 11.5: Visiting Kapila Khandvala in Bombay, 1955. 240

Figure 12.1: Helsinki Peace Conference, June 1955, program cover 244

Figure 12.2: Teachers Federation executive group, c. 1953 253

Figure 14.1: Lucy at International Women's Day outdoor rally with Enid Hampson (Union of Australian Women, in striped dress) with Tom Wright (Sheet Metal Workers Union) speaking, IWD 1962 at Wynyard Park. 290

Figure 14.2: Lucy on delegation to China late in 1964 as guest of the National Chinese Women's Council. 294

Figure 14.3: Portrait of Lucy in the sunny sitting room of her George Street flat, overlooking the Quay, Sydney Harbour. . . . 298

Figure 15.1: Lucy Woodcock with Sam Lewis, Ethel Teerman Lewis and a friend at Sam's farewell event 306

Figure 15.2: Opening of the Lucy Woodcock Hall, Erskineville Public School. Heather Goodall with Kit Edwards, 2016. 313

Abbreviations

AAF	Aboriginal-Australian Fellowship
ABC	Australian Broadcasting Commission/Corporation
ACTU	Australian Council of Trade Unions
AFWV	Australian Federation of Women Voters
AIWC	All India Women's Conference
ALP	Australian Labor Party
ASIO	Australian Security Intelligence Organisation
ATF	Australian Teachers' Federation
CAEP	Council for Action on Equal Pay
CIC	Chinese Industrial Co-operative Movement
CICD	Campaign for International Cooperation and Disarmament
CND	Campaign for Nuclear Disarmament
CPA	Communist Party of Australia
CPI	Communist Party of India
EWL	Educational Workers' League
FSSTA	Federated State School Teachers' Association
IFTA	International Federation of Teachers' Associations
ILO	International Labour Organization
IPC	International Peace Campaign
IWD	International Women's Day
IWW	Industrial Workers of the World (also known as the Wobblies)
NATO	North Atlantic Treaty Organization

NCJW	National Council of Jewish Women
NCW	National Council of Women
NEF	New Education Fellowship
NFIW	National Federation of Indian Women
NSW	New South Wales
OC	Opportunity Classes
PNG	Papua New Guinea
SRC	Students' Representative Council
TLC	NSW Trades and Labor Council
UA	United Associations of Women
UAW	Union of Australian Women
UK	United Kingdom
UN	United Nations
UNESCO	United Nations Educational, Scientific and Cultural Organization
US	United States of America
USSR	Union of Soviet Socialist Republics
VPC	Victorian Peace Council
WFF	World Fellowship of Faiths
WFTU	World Federation of Trade Unions
WIA	Women's Indian Association
WIDF	Women's International Democratic Federation
WILPF	Women's International League for Peace and Freedom
YWCA	Young Women's Christian Association

Acknowledgements

This story, about a woman who took major public positions yet was reserved and even elusive about her personal life, posed many challenges. So there are many people to thank who have been generous with their time, their encouragement and their suggestions. We particularly want to thank our interviewees: Audrey McDonald, Jean Lewis, Beverley Bates, Kit Edwards, Ruth Fink Latukefu, Judith Emmett, Cathy Bloch, Clare Anderson, Lilon Bandler, Bob Makinson, Bruce McFarlane and Wendy and Allan Scarfe (who passed away last year and is missed by us all).

The Erskineville Public School community, from its principal and teachers to the parents of its students – and particularly Sean Macken and Angel Nunley – have all been enthusiastic participants in the exciting search for Lucy's work. We have been greatly assisted by analysts who have offered insights, critical readings and valuable resources: Phillip Deery, Meredith Burgmann, James Beattie, Lisa Milner, Martin Sullivan and Julia Horne. One of the least well-known areas of Lucy's tireless work was in support of refugees fleeing Nazism in Europe. We turned to community members like Ron Witton and to Nola Symonds and Phillip Moses of the Australian Jewish Historical Society to learn about her work in this area. We were fortunate to have great research done beyond what we could do ourselves by Jayne Reagan in Canberra in the National Library of Australia and the Noel Butlin Archives.

Lucy Woodcock was a committed unionist and, although much of her work, such as her contribution to the women's movement, the Peace movement and working-class and progressive education, was outside the unions, she remained anchored in her commitment to cooperative industrial organisation through unions. She aimed to strengthen all these movements by building alliances between them. Neale Towart, from Unions Australia (previously the NSW Trades and Labor Council), has been most helpful. We are deeply grateful for the support and assistance of the NSW Teachers Federation,[1] and, in particular, its president, Maurie Mulheron, along with Kerri Carr, Graeme Smart, Mary Schmidt and the Anna Stewart Fellow working on Lucy's contribution, Sharron Talbot.

Finally, the book would not have come to fruition without the work and patience of Geoff Hunt and Venetia Somerset and ANU Press' Christine Huber and Emily Hazlewood.

Our families have encouraged us, put up with us and generally humoured each of us and we are all grateful. So this is a collective call out to them all!

---

[1] The NSW Teachers Federation has formally moved that there are to be no full stops or apostrophes used in the name of the Union.

Learning – Unions and the World: 1910s and 1920s

1
Introduction: A Transnational Life

Lucy Woodcock was a passionate and fearless campaigner for justice. Her long-time friend and ally Dymphna Cusack said that Lucy was 'well known as a fighter'. All her long life, from 1889 to 1968, Lucy worked for Equal Rights for women, for real access to good-quality and progressive education for girls and working-class children, and for an end to racism and international warmongering.[1]

These campaigns alone would make her life remarkable, but there are other, even more cogent reasons to explore her story. It challenges all the stereotypes about how organisations were built, where movements drew their support and how class intersected with commitment. Lucy's life demands that we consider how women might be involved in politics, not only in Australia but in the broader world. We argue her life was 'transnational' rather than 'international' and that her experience was shaped by gender and class. Her political commitments changed over time, according to the historical contexts in which she worked. She was a woman with a long career of activism, but she had distanced herself from the conventional and heterosexual world of many women activists on the Left. It was age and, perhaps, gender-orientation that have shaped

---

1   The term 'Equal Rights' has been capitalised where it was a political goal. Lucy expanded her understanding of this concept over her lifetime, as this book explains. By the end of her life, it meant for her equality of the sexes in income, opportunity and respect, regardless of class, race, religion, marital status or sexual orientation.

the way she is remembered. How would she herself have understood and engaged with the contemporary forms of the movements to which she was so committed?

Lucy's life was not transnational because she travelled widely. Born in 1889 and growing up in Sydney's Granville, Lucy worked first in rural Australia and then in inner Sydney. In fact, before World War II, she was only able to go overseas for a single year, in 1927, after which she was unable to travel internationally until she retired in 1953. Then, after a brief time in Europe, she travelled to China, Japan and India, before spending further time in Europe, including the socialist countries and finally at a Peace conference in Helsinki.[2] She went again later in the 1950s to socialist Europe as well as the United Kingdom and then in 1964 once again to China.

Yet even without extensive travel in her early life, Lucy Woodcock lived a transnational life because she framed all her understanding of politics – local, national and international – through transnational parameters and comparisons. Unlike the stereotypes of a Britain-focused Australia, Lucy was not particularly interested in European examples as models of achievement. On the contrary, she was acutely aware of European racism from the earliest years of her teaching career in the South Coast fishing village of Eden, where she was befriended by a family of refugees who had fled the Russian pogroms. Shaped by later experiences, Lucy worked ever harder to challenge racism as well as gender discrimination. Rather than turning to Europe, Lucy saw leadership in social justice and progress emerging not from the old colonisers but from the new and emerging countries of the formerly colonised world. She championed their independence and decolonisation movements but she was not interested in nationalist goals. Instead, she tried to build links between women and workers across borders, recognising the common ground that existed in spite of cultural differences. Her politics crossed the borders not only of old and new 'nations' but of organisations and movements. Analysing only one movement or another will not clarify the way Lucy – or many other activists – actually worked.

---

2   'Peace' is capitalised when used as the name of a political goal, as it is here, meaning the vision of an end to armed warfare. While for Lucy conflicts were inevitable – and even welcomed – conflict was best solved through negotiation and communication, a strategy she pursued all her life.

With these commitments to links across national borders, could Lucy be seen as a 'transnational activist'? Scalmer, Berger, Manjapra and others have written about activists they describe as 'transnational' because they took political stands in a number of different places, moving ideas and strategies from one area to another or, in the case of Gandhi, being the symbol mobilised by people in very different places.[3] There were, however, gendered constraints on activism. Access to travel and mobility was far easier for the men described by these analysts than for women. There *are* women identified as 'transnational activists' in the recent volume edited by Berger and Scalmer, notably the Australian Jessie Street.[4] Yet here is another key gendered constraint; it was Street's class position, her social and political status and wealth, from inheritance and marriage, which enabled her mobility. For working-class or professional women like Lucy Woodcock, physical mobility was far harder to access than for upper-class women, who were themselves more constrained than working-class men who might travel as seamen or soldiers.

To be able to move across borders, women needed either the resources of the upper classes or they needed employment or organisational networks that would set up the infrastructure that allowed mobility. Lucy was a young woman in the years before World War I, when one of the few jobs open to Australian women outside domestic labour was teaching. Education was to become one of the networks that allowed Lucy to be mobile in her later life, as well as expanding her knowledge of the wider world. Teaching had played an important role in the expansion of European colonialism throughout the nineteenth century in Australia and elsewhere – with Christian missionaries often establishing educational institutions in many colonies, including Australia. Yet there were also other women who travelled to take up roles in education who were not Christian missionaries at all. Education by the end of the nineteenth century had become a desired goal of modernisation among middle-class families in British colonies like India and in Dutch colonies like the East Indies, allowing women to travel and sustain employed lives without having the upper-class incomes or family connections of a Jessie Street.

---

3   This term has been used by Sean Scalmer in relation to Mohandas Gandhi and by Stefan Berger to describe E.P. Thomson in their edited volume, *The Transnational Activist* (New York: Springer, 2017), and this is the same concept developed by Kris Manjapra in talking about M.N. Roy, in his *M.N. Roy: Marxism and Colonial Cosmopolitanism* (Routledge, 2010).

4   Chloe Ward, 'Activism without Discrimination'. In *The Transnational Activist: Transformations and Comparisons from the Anglo-World since the Nineteenth Century*, ed. Stefan Berger and Sean Scalmer. Palgrave Studies in the History of Social Movements (New York: Springer, 2017), 227–56.

Educational work allowed Lucy to become aware of the wider world and, in the mid-1920s, to work for a year in working-class, inner-city schools in London, exploring innovative progressive education in challenging circumstances. Before that, however, it enabled Lucy to explore activism and leadership, building her organising skills as she mobilised her fellow women assistant teachers. Her abilities in negotiation were strengthened when she co-founded the New South Wales Teachers Federation in 1918, later taking leadership roles in this union as well as working towards building a national union in future decades. Lucy was to insist throughout her life that, although teaching demanded respect as a profession, in which women should have an equal place, nevertheless teachers were strongest when they united in collaboration and unionism. She insisted that teachers' organisations see themselves *as* industrial unions, taking an active role in the emerging politics of unionism in Australia.

Teaching also offered Lucy a way into tertiary studies. As a night student, she put herself through two Bachelor degrees at the University of Sydney in the early 1920s, first in arts and then in economics. Her humanities studies strengthened her orientation towards the wider world, as did her intense interest in economics. As a student and later close friend of left-wing economics academic Robert Francis (R.F.) Irvine (1861–1941), Lucy strengthened her view that capitalist accumulation happened at the expense of working people, which further confirmed her commitment to unionism and public education. At the same time, Lucy was exploring personal social networks, finding friends in the bohemian cultures of Sydney. Her links with visual artists like Irvine's daughter Ysobel and the painter and fellow teacher Rah Fizelle led her to make her home eventually in the same apartment block in The Rocks in which they and many other artists lived. It was a milieu where gender equality was championed as a way of life. Lucy saw herself as a member of this bohemian network until the end of her life.[5]

---

5   Lucy Woodcock hinted to Bruce McFarlane in his interview with her during the mid-1960s, concerning Robert Irvine, that she had mixed in bohemian circles, McFarlane, pers. comm., 8 August 2015; Kit Edwards, interview with Heather Goodall, 30 November 2017, at Kit's home at Hardy's Bay; Peter Kirkpatrick, *The Sea Coast of Bohemia: Literary Life in Sydney's Roaring Twenties* (St Lucia: University of Queensland Press, 1992); T. Moore, 'Australia's Bohemian Tradition' (PhD thesis, History, SOPHI, University of Sydney, 2007); John Docker, *Australian Cultural Elites: Intellectual Traditions in Sydney and Melbourne* (Sydney: Angus and Robertsons; 1974); Joy Damousi, *Women Come Rally* (Melbourne: Oxford University Press, 1994).

1. INTRODUCTION

There were two structures within which Lucy moved, education and unionism, as well as her personal 'bohemian' orientation. There were more dimensions as well. Lucy must have been interested in the political ferment of the 1920s and the political parties active in that ferment. Some social movements, which had gathered momentum previously, were interrupted by World War I. These included the union movement in Australia, which had already generated the Australian Labor Party (ALP). Just as important for Lucy were the women's movements, which were continuing their demands for a voice for women in parliament and policy. The Peace movement, however, expanded the scope of the social movements of the time. It drew opponents of war into the resistance to newly imposed conscription and then, as the conflict dragged on, it forced Lucy and others to recognise that the slaughter in Europe affected not only Europeans but soldiers and families in colonies around the world. In Russia, the Communist Party emerged from the carnage, defining itself as a revolutionary socialist party that offered visions of new worlds for working people and, sometimes, for women. Yet while such visions generated some hope, the massive displacement in Europe after the war only increased in the 1930s as dictatorships arose and persecutions accelerated. Again, refugees were forced to escape their homes. In Australia, the attempt to build a 'White Australia' through an exclusion policy was being challenged from the outside by Britain and India among many others, and, from the inside, through increasing Aboriginal assertion in the 1920s and 1930s.

Where did Lucy stand in this plethora of progressive movements? There have been important studies of each of these movements and parties. Tracing the life of one individual allows us to see how politically active people might have navigated their commitments in practice. Lucy in fact circulated within and across many of these movements, building strategic alliances and sometimes leveraging her involvement in one movement with her role in another.

Her commitments were not static – her evolving political activism was shaped as the context changed or as she gained knowledge. A very real constraint she faced was that the state had control over her movements while she was employed as a teacher in NSW. Lucy made no secret of her interest in left-wing causes and political activism. In the rising anti-communist hysteria in Australia after World War II, Lucy's desire to travel was seen as suspicious and she was refused permission to travel until her employment ended. Only when she retired, in December 1953, was she able to leave Australia to attend conferences organised by Peace movements, women's organisations and the United Nations, as well as visit China, Japan, the Soviet Union, the United Kingdom and western Europe.

***

The stories of the many activist women in the 1930s to 1960s period have remained untold. Jessie Street, who was certainly very involved with politicians, diplomats and international institutions, and who left the most extensive diaries, has received the most attention in histories of this period. Yet Jessie was unusual, as noted above, in being an affluent woman of high social status, despite her membership of the ALP and her sustained interest in the Soviet Union. Most other women activists in this period were either more unassuming or less affluent, and so did not attract the media or diplomatic attention that Jessie did.

This book attempts to remedy some of these gaps by tracing Lucy's activism across a number of fields, including her cross-border work in India, China and Japan, as well as her vigorous trade unionism and defence of public education. She insisted that working-class schools needed high-quality progressive educational methods while her refugee and peace advocacy allied her strategically with more bourgeois women's organisations. Lucy's life challenges a commonly held view that the 1950s was a period of conservatism and conformity, when any political expression at all – let alone left-wing expression – was stifled by threats of anti-communist persecution. Her sustained activism, across many movements, gives the lie to that myth.

We discovered Lucy as a transnational activist only because she travelled with Jessie Street to a Peace conference held in India in 1954. In our project, 'Countering the Cold War', we searched for connections between the left-wing women's movements in India and Australia, since archival and oral history evidence recorded these ongoing interactions during the mid-twentieth century. We found that Jessie Street had attended a conference in Madras (now Chennai) in December 1954 in the company of a Miss Lucy Woodcock. Our research into who 'Miss Woodcock' might have been, and why she was travelling in India, led us to the life of this extraordinary activist. While Lucy was very involved in many of the Australian movements we had been researching, she had seldom been the spokesperson until, in the later years of her life, she became president of the United Associations of Women and the NSW Coordinator of International Women's Day.

As this book demonstrates, Lucy Woodcock's life is evidence of the common and frequent contacts between Australians and Indians, more so than Jessie Street's, important though her work was. Lucy's life foregrounds the active role that non-missionary education took in these connections. We interviewed women in India and Australia and consulted newspapers and archives. The connections between Australian and Indian women have been multiple – political work through international organisations, whether communist, liberal or Christian, and the Peace movement. Education – particularly the teaching of girls and the teaching of literacy skills to adult working women – emerged as a crucial factor. Understanding how women in India and Australia became involved in secondary and tertiary education in this period emerged as an important theme, as did tracing the experience of those women who undertook such interactions as teachers or learners.

A major problem for our research is that Lucy Woodcock chose to leave no personal papers. She appears to have been very careful to conceal facts about her personal life. Most of the archives we have are those of the organisations in which she was active, like the NSW Teachers Federation or the New Education Fellowship, as well as the newspaper reports of her many political speeches. She wrote some political books, *Justice vs Tradition* (1925) and *The Lewis Case and You* (1956), but neither of these offers direct insight into her personal life.[6]

We can glean some ideas from those speeches and archives. They display her political passions, her tenacious campaigns, her energetic and practical contributions to organisations and alliances, and her trenchant, logical campaign writings. There is a caricature in the Teachers Federation journal from 1939 that depicts this tenacity. It shows her speaking energetically as she clutches a microphone – which the cartoonist draws as gasping: 'What? Again?'

---

6   Lucy's friend and biographer, Bruce Mitchell (in *Australian Dictionary of Biography*) understood Lucy to have been the principal author of the book *Justice vs Tradition*, published under the collective authorship of the Women's Propaganda Committee.

These give us little insight into Lucy's personal life. Lucy never married, and perhaps she may have become increasingly reticent about her private life because of the intensely scrutinised and policed moral world of public school teaching. Rebecca Jennings has discussed the challenges posed for historians by silences, which exist because many women living unconventional lives faced 'the continued impact of a culture of silence in discouraging women who became aware of their own same-sex desires in the 1930s, '40s and '50s from openly discussing them'.[7]

It was difficult to make unconventional lives public in any way. Women who were involved in same-sex relationships were unable to acknowledge their lovers or their lifestyle on pain of severe social ostracism and, in the case of teachers, the loss of jobs and income. Furthermore, the internalisation of silence may have led to fluidity in personal identification, and Jennings calls for recognition of the 'sophisticated ways that women forged lives for themselves' without making any definitive statements on their own personal lives.[8] Similarly, the people to whom historians turn for memories through oral histories are often silent about such aspects of other people's lives. Lucy always avoided discussing her personal life and was never explicit about her lifestyle, other than her reference to 'having bohemian friends'. Yet her lifelong relationships were with women and she left no children or immediate family.

This differentiated her from many women with whom she might have found common ground in political parties. There were few women leaders in the ALP at that time, and women's activism was marginalised. The constraints on women's activism were also disappointingly evident in the Communist Party of Australia (CPA), which promised liberation for women but was structured entirely on heteronormative assumptions.[9] Homosexual men and women were rarely visible in the party and faced patronising toleration. Women's work in the party was often narrowed to ostensible 'women's issues', such as the nurturing of children, the environment of working-class neighbourhoods and domestic economics like the Campaign Against Rising Prices. Women comrades were expected to be married with children and

---

7   Rebecca Jennings, *Unnamed Desires: A Sydney Lesbian History* (Clayton, Vic.: Monash University Publishing, 2015), xiv–xxii. Sally Newman had made a similar point about silences in analysing the diaries of Aileen Palmer, a woman to whose family Lucy was very close: 'Silent Witness? Aileen Palmer and the Problem of Evidence in Lesbian History', *Women's History Review* 11, no. 3 (2002): 505–30, doi.org/10.1080/09612020200200333.
8   Jennings, *Unnamed Desires*, 27.
9   Joy Damousi, *Women Come Rally* (Melbourne: Oxford University Press, 1994).

limit their activities to supporting their comrade husbands from the home. While this did not deter a number of strong women from demanding – and taking – an active role in the CPA, it was a difficult challenge. Betty Reilly, for example, devoted both to the CPA and to her organising work in Sydney textile factories, had left her husband in Melbourne to take up activist work in Sydney. She designed and made her own flamboyant clothes and took a sequence of men as lovers. While such sexual activity was tolerated among male CPA members, women members did not have the same latitude. Although, surprisingly, Reilly's devotion to the party remained undimmed, she faced harsh criticism from the CPA leadership for her sexual and lifestyle choices.[10]

Throughout the interwar period, Lucy took active leadership roles in the NSW Teachers Federation – as elected senior vice president from 1934 till her retirement in 1953 – and the Australian teachers' union (variously known as the Australian Teachers' Federation (ATF) and the Federated State School Teachers' Association (FSSTA) in different periods) in which she served a term as president in 1931–32. All these teachers' unions were deeply masculinist – not only were the state Education Departments committed to maintaining male leadership of schools, but male teachers took dominant roles in the various state teachers' unions. Lucy was bitterly frustrated by many of her male fellow unionists and, as this book demonstrates, she developed strategic alliances in the 1930s with more bourgeois women's movements in order to challenge male teachers' opposition to equal pay for women teachers.

Lucy eventually found some staunch male allies in the national and state teachers' unions. This enabled her to take policy initiatives to defend both married and unmarried women teachers and the implementation of progressive education for all working-class children in public schools. She promoted girls' education but refused to leave the working-class coeducational Erskineville Primary and lower secondary school to teach in more affluent suburbs in academically elite girls' high schools. Although her sympathies and political alliances were clearly in close alignment with those of her CPA teaching colleagues like Sam Lewis and Ethel Teerman in the 1930s, she does not appear to have joined the CPA or any other party.

---

10   Betty Reilly articles in *Communist Review*, March 1950, 465 and August 1951, 879; Betty Reilly Papers, AU NBAC N188, NBABL; Clare Anderson, Reilly's niece, interview with Heather Goodall, 2013.

There are, however, some more direct glimpses of the woman whom close friends like Sam Lewis remembered so warmly after her retirement from teaching. During her decade as president of the United Associations of Women, Lucy frequently contributed to the organisation's *Newsheet*. Her concise and often satirical entries show her as an effective polemicist: witty, insightful and hard hitting. Lucy formed a close working relationship with Vivienne Newson, the editor of the *Newsheet*; in Newson's reflections, Lucy becomes visible as the skilled negotiator, able to achieve the outcomes she wanted without leaving others feeling bruised or short-changed. Instead of cutting down her opponents, Lucy could nurture a shared sense of purpose and commitment. Lucy told Newson about many of the extraordinary episodes in her life of organising, struggles and travel. Newson explained in an obituary that she had begged Lucy to write a memoir to capture some of this diversity and drama. Lucy had shrugged off the request, saying she was too busy. Another friend, Kit Edwards, was tutored by Lucy for his matriculation in the early 1960s when he was a teenager. He remembers with some embarrassment that he had asked her directly why she had never married. Lucy had replied – as no doubt many women have to such intrusive questions – that she had 'never met the right man'.

There are as well a series of 18 letters from Lucy to Rewi Alley, the New Zealand socialist and cooperative activist, whom Lucy met in China during her first visit in 1954. Rewi asked her to keep him informed of politics and people in Australia and Lucy wrote to him at least twice a year over the next 10 years. Her letters were kept carefully – unknown to Lucy – in Alley's voluminous archive. They confirm Newson's impressions that Lucy was a witty and well-informed observer of national and international events and a strategic thinker, committed to seeking outcomes through conciliation and communication. She discussed, for example, the Suez conflict, pointing to its fundamental economic roots in the oil trade, and was scathing in her contempt for the 'trigger-happy fellows' on all sides who, she said, 'are always a menace to civilisation'.[11] In Lucy's long correspondence with Alley, her writing was always astute and politically informative, but was also always warm and affectionate, with each letter signed off with 'Much love, Lucy'.[12] Alley valued Lucy's letters, replying: 'I look forward very much to your accounts of how you find things as

---

11   Lucy G. Woodcock to Rewi Alley, 1 September 1956. Rewi Alley, Inward Correspondence – Lucy Woodcock, MS-Papers-6533–307, NLNZ.
12   Rewi Alley, Inward Correspondence – Lucy Woodcock, MS-Papers-6533–307, NLNZ.

you go around …', although mostly he sent pages of his diary and his poems, all later published.[13] Accounts of Rewi Alley's life in China have argued convincingly that he chose to remain in China not only because of his deep commitment to the Chinese people but because of the cultural freedom he found there for his homosexuality, a freedom he had not found in his homeland of New Zealand.[14] It may have been this dimension of Alley's lifestyle that had aligned him to Lucy, consistent with the traces in her writing and the memories of friends suggesting that Lucy may have been in a same-sex relationship for at least some time. This may have been why she was so reserved about her personal life. While there can never be certainty, nevertheless the memories in oral histories may give us insights into her bohemian friendships, her lifelong sorrows and her emotional vulnerabilities.

A final glimpse of Lucy may lie in the rare, unexpected – and now treasured – letters that colleagues received from Lucy when they were experiencing distress, illness, the loss of a loved one or a personal crisis. These warm letters voiced unexpected concern and a surprising degree of personal knowledge.[15] Lucy had clearly kept a nurturing eye on her younger colleagues, though she seldom allowed her concerns to show.

This book raises the issue of gendered constraints acting on all women – particularly working-class and lower middle-class women like Lucy – who engaged in political action. This includes the important constraints imposed on those who challenged the heteronormative privileging of marriage and heterosexual lifestyles across both left- and right-wing political attitudes in Australia. Lucy defied such constraints and carved out a life for herself; her tenacious activism was always both practical and conciliatory.

Lucy Woodcock's story challenges stereotypes about unionism, teachers, feminism and nationalism. It highlights the fact that an Australian woman in the postwar mid-twentieth century – at a time when there was supposedly little left-wing political activity, especially in the area of gender – could play a sustained role in union and women's politics.

---

13 Rewi Alley to Lucy G. Woodcock, 17 October 1955. From her belongings, which were gathered after her death and have been cared for by Kit Edwards.
14 Anne-Marie Brady, *Friend of China: The Myth of Rewi Alley* (Abingdon: Routledge Curzon, 2002).
15 See, for example, Lucy Woodcock to Audrey McDonald, 1962, when she took leave as secretary of the International Women's Day committee to give birth to her son, Darren.

It points to her transnational strategies in championing the hopes and possibilities offered to women and working people by social change in India and China. The narrative of her life enables questions about the impact of gender and sexual orientation on activism at home even more than activism in the transnational arena.

This book is organised around the key periods in Lucy's life. The first section, 'Learning – Unions and the World', has just two chapters, giving an overview of Lucy's developing interests as a young, working-class woman living in the shadow of World War I. She threw herself into teaching and immediately began to challenge the limits on women's role in it, taking an active part in forming an effective teachers' industrial union, and exploring bohemianism and economics during her hard-won university degrees.

The 'Scars' section follows, in which all five chapters trace different impacts of the hard Depression years on Lucy and on her strategies in working-class education, in union organisation for women's rights and Equal Pay, and in building alliances with feminist organisations to challenge the ambiguities in the teachers' unions. Yet those years also brought to Lucy the excitement of implementing progressive learning in public schools, the joys of love and community solidarity and the visions of new futures. Next there is another short section, 'Expanding Visions', charting in two chapters the intense impacts of World War II for Lucy – in undermining the rights of women still further but also in foregrounding racism and decolonisation, bringing into view the exciting advances in women's rights being promised in decolonising nations.

Characteristically, Lucy put her new insights into action. 'Crossing Borders' traces in five chapters the next major period of Lucy's life, from the end of World War II until her death in 1968. First, in her final decade as an employed teacher, she challenged the conventional teaching orthodoxies as she campaigned for Peace, for women's Equal Pay and for international communication in education. Then, retired and free from government obstruction, Lucy herself travelled to cross the borders she had seen retarding advances for women and damaging the chances for Peace. During the final years of her life, she worked perhaps even harder to cross cultural borders inside Australia – between settler Australians and Aboriginal Australians – and to continue the campaign for peace, for progressive and informed education in working-class public schools and for international communication. She brought the world back home to expand the vision of all Australians. The outcomes of these major periods of Lucy's life are charted in the final section, 'Legacy', when some of the continuing questions about her life can be raised, at the same time as reflecting on the great strengths of her visions and the endurance of her achievements.

2

Unions

Lucy Woodcock's international life began in what might seem the most unlikely of places – a small fishing town called Eden on the South Coast of New South Wales. This town had been the hub of Ben Boyd's transnational whaling empire. The Scotsman's ships, crewed by Aboriginal, Māori and Pacific Islander seamen alongside Englishmen and even the odd American, had crossed the Tasman, heading towards the Antarctic Circle. Perhaps it was not so surprising after all that Lucy discovered her wider world here.

Born in Granville, Lucy Godiva Woodcock had lived close to her parents' home during her five years as a 'pupil-teacher', her postings taking her only as far as Pitt Town and South Parramatta. Barely older than her students, she learnt 'on the job' from 1906 to early 1910. In her first real placement, in mid-1910, she was still an 'assistant teacher', but was far from home, in chilly – and lonely – Eden on the South Coast.

Lucy worked hard, as she was to do all her life, not only teaching in class but organising 'Empire Day' with a picnic for the whole community, a pageant and races for the children and a dance afterwards for the grown-ups. She felt a long way from home until she was welcomed into the warmth of the Robinovitz family, local storekeepers who knew what it felt like to miss their home.

For them, the little fishing town was an Eden, both in name and reality. It was a safe refuge after the terrifying persecution in Europe. Queenie Symonds, a child in the Robinovitz family, recalled her mother's warm welcome to all newcomers:

> Our house was always opened. And I must tell you, there was a pupil-teacher sent down from Sydney, it took her three days to come. Miss Woodcock. And she'd never been away from home in her life.
>
> As she passed our place, my mother said, 'Miss Woodcock, come in and have some afternoon tea'. And she looked and she saw my young sister and her eyes filled with tears. And she said, 'Do you know, we were a family of six or seven, and I left a baby at home, my youngest sister'. So my mother said, 'Come in every day after school and have something!' It wasn't so much a cup of tea, but my mother used to make her own ginger beer, it was like a beautiful soft drink. You couldn't go and buy lemonade in those days, no such thing! And Miss Woodcock became a very close friend of ours. And so much so, that … my younger sister (who unfortunately has just died) took up teaching on her account.[1]

In later years, Queenie came to Sydney and worked in a real estate office in Enfield, where she met Lucy again:

> Miss Woodcock, who we knew in Eden, came into the office one day and said they had bought some land and built a house there. And we kept up our relationship. And she was the one then that persuaded my sister who had just started to be a teacher.[2]

Over the shared home-made ginger beer in Eden, the Robinovitz family told Lucy their story. The elderly patriarch of the family, Isaac Robinovitz, had escaped as a young man from Odessa during the 1880s because of the rising religious persecution in Russia. His journey to Australia was difficult. He worked in various labouring jobs to make his way, via London and New Zealand, to Australia, eventually opening his 'Polytechnic Store' in Eden. He remained in touch with his family in Kishinev, Odessa. His decision to leave had been wise – the violence in Kishinev escalated to murderous proportions, with terrible massacres in 1903 – just a few years before Lucy met them. By then the news had circulated round the world.[3] The stories she heard were not just of one man's escape but of the terrible impact on the generations left trapped behind. The Robinovitz family was

---

1 Queenie Symonds, interviewed by Brenda Factor, NSW Bicentennial oral history collection [sound recording], 1987. Held in National Library of Australia (Session 1 of 2, 42:47–43:45), nla.gov.au/nla.obj-216364926/listen?searchTerm=Woodcock%20jewish%20refugees, accessed 15 October 2017.
2 Ibid.
3 *Bega Budget*, 27 May 1911, 2.

still not financially secure when Lucy arrived in Eden, but their warmth and generosity gave her great comfort. Their kindness stayed with her for the rest of her life, and so too did their story.[4]

Despite her hard work, Lucy was not interested in individual advancement. Her approach to work and learning was collective. She was interested in the early discussions about forming a teachers' union and, as an 'assistant teacher' after finishing her training as a 'pupil-teacher', she was particularly alert to the disadvantages these 'assistants' suffered. The first Assistants' Union was established briefly in 1897 but then reformed as the Women Assistant Teachers' Association' in 1907. Pressure from assistant teachers went some way towards improving their recognition and representation in the various emerging unions for teachers, but there was a long way to go. Lucy began to advocate on behalf of assistant teachers as well as fully employed or qualified teachers, long before the NSW Teachers Federation was eventually established in September 1918.[5]

Lucy's support for the NSW Women Assistant Teachers' Association was driven, in part, by her frustrations around the differences in pay and opportunity for women teachers, who formed the majority of 'assistants'. All teachers' pay had been cut during the 1890s Depression, but, in 1893 and 1896, women suffered specific disadvantage when the pay of girls' and infants' mistresses, the only senior positions available to women, were reduced by a much greater margin than those of male teachers. Although the wages of male teachers had been restored to their 1880 level by 1911, those of women had not.[6] Lucy had been a schoolgirl in 1906 when Peter Board, the NSW Director of Education, had made his support for a discriminatory wage system very clear. Annie Golding, one of the early advocates of decent wages for women teachers, challenged Board, ridiculing him in his own words that women should 'take the salaries of women'. Board stood by his belief, insisting that marriage was more

---

4   Isaac Robinovitz biography, courtesy Phillip Moses from the Australian Jewish Historical Society; *Hebrew Standard of Australasia*, 1 January 1942, 6; 25 June 1942, 8; 5 November 1942, 3; 26 November 1942, 6; 15 August 1946, 7; ChaeRan Y. Freeze and Jay M. Harris, eds, *Everyday Jewish Life in Imperial Russia: Select Documents, 1772–1914* (Lebanon, New Hampshire: Brandeis University Press, University of New England, 2013), 31.
5   Bruce Mitchell, *Teachers, Education and Politics: A History of Organisations of Public School Teachers in New South Wales* (St Lucia: University of Queensland Press, 1975), 23, 36.
6   Mitchell, *Teachers, Education and Politics*, 25–26.

important for any 'sensible' woman than the departmental representation demanded by Golding. 'Every true woman', he insisted, 'ought to think of getting married'.[7]

This attitude persisted. As Lucy was finishing her training in 1910, the NSW Teachers' Association passed a motion that women teachers must resign on marriage. This was carried with the support of many women teachers, particularly unmarried ones. Bruce Mitchell asserted that they were 'anxious to protect their career prospects'.[8] The following year, 1911, the new NSW Labor Education Minister, G.S. Beeby, said he would make married women resign from the teaching service. No Labor government in NSW actually took this threatened action, but the proposal remained a troubling possibility. In 1913, the Teachers' Association adopted a motion calling for 'Equal Pay for Equal Work', but this was not included in the constitution of the new Teachers Federation in 1918, discussed below. It was later added only as an objective in 1920, after a battle by Lucy and others at the Federation's conference.[9] Lucy entered her career as a fully qualified teacher receiving only a fraction of the wages paid to her male colleagues and facing the threat of dismissal if she were ever to marry.

In 1913, Lucy returned to Sydney to teach at Lidcombe Public. In 1914, she began a new endeavour; enrolling at the University of Sydney as a night student in arts, the first of her two university degrees. She graduated in 1922 and by then had begun a degree in economics, graduating in 1924. While doing her first degree, she was aware of discrimination. She spoke years later, in 1962, about one instance burnt into her memory, after a radio program in which Mungo MacCallum II defended women's rights:

> My mind went back to my own undergraduate days. His father, Sir Mungo, was no believer in women's rights. In his classes, he invariably addressed the mixed group as 'Gentlemen!' On one occasion, the women, tired of being ignored, planned to forego their customary places in the front of the lecture room and occupy the back benches. He had always looked over them to the back of the room.

---

7   Transcript of Teachers' Assoc deputation to Public Service Board, 15 December 1906, pp. 14, 34–36, 1907/00530, in 1906–1907 Bundle, Box P3952, NSW Archives; cited in Mitchell, *Teachers, Education and Politics*, 224.
8   Mitchell, *Teachers, Education and Politics*, 26.
9   Ibid., 57.

> But the changed position did not affect his opening remark, for although he was looking straight at some forty women students, we were still 'Gentlemen' and 'Gentlemen' we remained while present at English Lectures.
>
> As Vice chancellor of the University, Sir Mungo had no time for women speakers at public functions. At the famous meeting to launch the Carillon appeal, he would have denied us our right to put the point of view of the folk whose efforts in money raising built that Carillon. He had to be defied, and I know, because it was my maiden speech! Hot under the collar from being asked to forego the right of addressing the meeting, the speech was made. (It seems as if I have gone on making speeches ever since!)
>
> Maybe the opposition to full equality can still be bridged if only enough women can be made indignant at being overlooked.[10]

World War I turned Lucy's life upside down. Many years later, she told a young student about the day she found out that the war had started. She was at Sydney University and she met the paperboy at the gates, exchanging money for the paper. She was so shocked by the war news that she did not think to ask for change, having paid the lad two shillings not a threepence. Distressed, she made her way into the city centre, where she saw people dancing in the streets in celebration of the hostilities. This disturbed her even more[11] but there was worse news to come.

Lucy's family was shattered by the war. Thomas, her much loved brother, survived almost till the end, before dying in France in January 1918. For Lucy, this was a brutal demonstration of the futility and destructiveness of war, a lesson that imbued her later life. Her parents were too broken to cope. Lucy, as the eldest child in the family, became the executor of her brother's will. Despite, or perhaps because of, her family's tragedies, she intensified her union activity and so she was one of the people who pushed the Teachers' Association and others into forming an industrial union. In September 1918, the NSW Teachers Federation was finally established to bring all teachers' organisations into the NSW Arbitration process. Lucy was a key participant in the formation meeting and later described to Bruce Mitchell, for his history of the NSW Federation, the electric atmosphere as the motion's movers and seconders made powerful

---

10   United Associations of Women (UA) *Newsheet*, August 1962, 2–3.
11   Kit Edwards, interview, 30 December 2017.

speeches before the final decision.[12] The next goal was recognition in the federal Arbitration system, and this was to prove far more difficult.[13] Nevertheless, as discussed later, Lucy persisted, maintaining her focus on the national sphere throughout her teaching career, even as she took on senior roles in the NSW Teachers Federation.

Lucy had continued her studies, despite the war. In fact, she thrived in the university atmosphere, even as a night student. She majored in English and philosophy in her BA but drew most from her second degree, which was in economics. Enrolling in 1920, she learnt from a range of popular lecturers, including the left-leaning economist R.F. Irvine.[14] Later, she told friends that her studies had opened up ways to explore the issues she was passionate about since her first years of teaching – race, internationalism, social injustice and gender. Certainly this degree shaped the rest of her life – Lucy argued all her later campaign contributions on grounds that would today be understood as political economy, from her speeches during the Depression, to all her statements on gender equality in employment through to her incisive economic analyses in the United Associations of Women newsletters in the 1960s. All of Lucy's closest associates in the Teachers Federation had studied economics, including not only Sam Lewis but, later, Elizabeth Mattick. Lucy appears to have continued her association with many of Irvine's students and close teaching associates from those years, who included F.A. Bland, P.C. Spender, Persia Campbell and H.V. Evatt. In *New Outlook*, the magazine Irvine edited, he published work by a wide range of young people who later had great influence, like David Rivett, Flora Eldershaw and Jack Lindsay.[15]

---

12   Lucy Woodcock, interview with Bruce Mitchell. Cited in Mitchell, *Teachers, Education and Politics*, 37 note 26 (on p. 225). No notes have yet been found in Mitchell's papers, deposited in the University of New England archives.
13   Recognition in a federal award was only achieved in 1986, long after Lucy's death in 1968, Steve O'Neill, *Development of Federal Industrial Powers*, Background Paper no. 33 (Canberra: Commonwealth of Australia, Parliamentary Library Research Service, 1993).
14   B.J. McFarlane, 'Irvine, Robert Francis (1861–1941)', *Australian Dictionary of Biography*, National Centre of Biography, The Australian National University, adb.anu.edu.au/biography/irvine-robert-francis-6800/text11763, published first in hardcopy 1983, accessed online 14 May 2016.
15   Bruce Mitchell, 'Woodcock, Lucy Godiva (1889–1968)', *Australian Dictionary of Biography*, National Centre of Biography, The Australian National University, adb.anu.edu.au/biography/woodcock-lucy-godiva-9172/text16197, published first in hardcopy 1990, accessed online 12 November 2018; Michael Roe, *Nine Australian Progressives: Vitalism in Bourgeois Social Thought 1890–1960* (St Lucia: University of Queensland Press, 1984), 265–69.

In the early 1920s, Lucy had begun to organise the Sydney University night students to form a lobby group to represent their interests. All of them were people like herself, working long hours in paid jobs, as well as travelling to classes and the library to study at night. It was in organising these students that Lucy started to meet other activists, and one who became her lifelong friend and colleague was Sam Lewis, from an Eastern Suburbs activist Jewish background who was younger than her and already a teacher. Over the same time, Lucy drew closer to Robert Irvine and his daughter Ysobel. Both were artists and Robert Irvine was also an avid bibliophile, commissioning artists to create bookplates. During the 1920s, Robert Irvine lived first in Darlinghurst and then Paddington. His daughter Ysobel lived in a flat at 215A Lower George Street near Circular Quay in Sydney, which was also home to a number of innovative artists associated with bohemian Sydney. They included Grace Crowley and Margel and Frank Hinder, as well as Rah Fizelle, the painter with whom Lucy taught at Darlington from 1921.[16] Sometime in the 1920s or 1930s, Lucy rented another flat in that same block and used it frequently during her later life.[17] Lucy continued to follow Ysobel's career as she studied design at Julian Ashton's Sydney Art School and volunteered at the Children's Library in Surry Hills in the late 1920s. Lucy also remained interested in Robert Irvine's ideas, inviting him to lecture about contemporary economics and politics to Federation members in September 1939, on the eve of another war. Irvine discussed the importance of socialism – making it clear he was no friend of communism – and ended by endorsing H.G. Wells's statement that 'Education is the one hope of humanity'.[18] Eventually, Lucy cared for Irvine in his final years and became the custodian of his papers after his death in 1941.[19] Irvine's biographer, Bruce McFarlane, interviewed her in the 1960s. He found Lucy generous with her time and open to talking about Irvine but reticent about herself, saying only that she was involved with 'Bohemian friends'.

---

16 The Hinders pioneered abstract and kinetic art in Sydney in 1930s. See shared biography under Eileen Chanin, 'Hinder, Margel Ina (1906–1905)', *Australian Dictionary of Biography*, National Centre of Biography, The Australian National University, adb.anu.edu.au/biography/hinder-margel-ina-18079, published online 2016, accessed 3 January 2019. Lucy was transferred to Darlington in 1921.
17 Lucy's will indicates she never purchased this flat, and her only property on her death was her half share with her sister in the Enfield home.
18 Irene Leslie, summarising 'Dreams and Nightmares', Irvine's lecture, *Education: The Journal of the NSW Teachers' Federation*, 18 September 1939, 344, 369.
19 Ibid., 275.

The philosophy of bohemianism in Sydney in the 1920s had many attractions for Lucy.[20] Bohemianism seemed to possess an atmosphere of excitement. Its adherents had a lively enthusiasm for literary and artistic expression. These were the elements of the progressive educational philosophies that increasingly intrigued Lucy. She was interested too in the movement's critique of contemporary bourgeois culture, although, as Moore demonstrates, this body of artists still needed patronage from affluent mentors and engagement with a consumer market. Nevertheless, their assertion of independence from and contempt for capitalism was attractive for Lucy as a union activist. Perhaps, also, Lucy was drawn to the sexual freedom championed by bohemianism.

Bohemianism in Australia was distinctive, with more overtly political dimensions than Europe.[21] Although some of its Australian adherents were uninterested in actually opposing bourgeois capitalism, there were others, notably Jack Lindsay, who were active socialists for at least part of their careers. Moore points out that these politically activist bohemians in the 1920s included journalist and socialist Sam Rosa, the CPA co-founder Guido Baracchi (then a Melbourne University student and guild socialist), the poet Lesbia Harford (one of the few socialist women to acknowledge a relationship with another woman) and the writer and CPA member Katherine Susannah Prichard.[22] Betsy Matthias, the proprietor of the popular Café la Bohème, was associated with various socialist parties in Melbourne and Sydney and with the anarcho-syndicalist Industrial Workers of the World (known as the Wobblies or IWW) and eventually with the Labor Party. George Finey was another example of the active socialists at the centre of Sydney's 1920s Bohemia.[23] John Anderson, who became Professor of Philosophy at Sydney University in 1926,

---

20 Peter Kirkpatrick, *The Sea Coast of Bohemia: Literary Life in Sydney's Roaring Twenties* (St Lucia: University of Queensland Press, 1992); T. Moore, 'Australia's Bohemian Tradition' (PhD thesis, History, SOPHI, University of Sydney, 2007), whose *Bohemian Rhapsody* on the ABC was an important initiating point for the thesis.
21 Moore, 'Australia's Bohemian Tradition', 443–57, Conclusion: 'Bohemia Then and Now'.
22 The assumption of political inactivity is more evident in Kirkpatrick, *The Sea Coast of Bohemia*. Recognition of distinctive Australian dimensions to bohemianism is an argument developed by Moore, 'Australia's Bohemian Tradition', 443–57; Joy Damousi discusses the activist women, either in the socialist parties or in the Labor Party, who were also associated with bohemian networks in Sydney and Melbourne, Joy Damousi, *Women Come Rally* (Melbourne: Oxford University Press 1994), 13–56.
23 Damousi, *Women Come Rally*, 266.

was not himself part of the bohemian group. However, Andersonian libertarianism was an active political influence on the Left as well as others in the bohemian network.[24]

Moore may be less accurate in another point – he argues that an aggressive masculinism was a universal characteristic of Australian bohemianism, arising in part from the gendered (and racialised) segregation of Australian hotels. The exclusion of women from Australian pubs does appear to have encouraged many bohemians to exaggerate masculinism, celebrating not only the alleged benefits of the exclusion of women, but also excoriating those women opposing the abuse of alcohol in the Women's Temperance Union.[25]

Nevertheless, many women did participate in the bohemian movement, albeit with little criticism of its patriarchal values. A notable publicist was Dulcie Deamer, while women like Dora Birtles and Mary Martin were on the margins. Lucy knew a number of these women well, either through their social life, teaching or activism. They all participated in the celebration of drinking, imbibing in cafes, clubs and restaurants. Sam Rosa frequented some important venues in Sydney – cafes like the Roma in Pitt Street; Betsy Matthias's café, La Bohème, and Theo's Café, both in Campbell Street near Chinatown. In these places, alcohol was freely available as was news about unions,[26] and Rosa edited the union publications *Common Cause* and *Labor Daily* (from 1925 to 1934) before returning to *Truth*. As Betsy Matthias's life suggests, the influence of the IWW was strong among Sydney bohemians and unionists. The IWW had made a forceful critique of racism and sexism, which was sustained long after the Wobblies themselves had been forced off the industrial stage.

Some women challenged the segregation of hotels, not by drinking elsewhere nor by calls for temperance, but instead by demanding an end to segregation. Lucy Woodcock was one of those. She made scathing attacks on the Australian preference of spending money on alcohol rather than education. She did not demand abstinence; she insisted that

---

24   Ibid., 266–67; John Docker, *Australian Cultural Elites: Intellectual Traditions in Sydney and Melbourne* (Sydney: Angus and Robertson, 1974); See Anderson's letter co-signed with Lucy opposing censorship of literature on contraception, *SMH*, 25 March 1946, 2.
25   Moore, 'Australia's Bohemian Tradition', 443–57.
26   For example, the Australasian Coal and Shale Employees' Federation. Verity Burgmann, 'Rosa, Samuel Albert (Sam) (1866–1940)', *Australian Dictionary of Biography*, National Centre of Biography, The Australian National University, adb.anu.edu.au/biography/rosa-samuel-albert-sam-8264/text14475, published first in hardcopy 1988, accessed online 13 May 2016.

male-only bars humiliated women drinkers, creating a gender segregation that generated harm. She was quoted under the headline 'Women Seek Equal Rights in Drinking':

> Drinking conditions in Sydney hotels either denied women the right to have a drink or made it degrading for them to do so.[27]

The hotel under Lucy's home, 215A George St, was, for many years, the only one in Sydney that allowed women to drink in the main bar rather than a separate 'Ladies Bar'.[28]

As it was for many on the Left, Lucy's involvement with bohemians and bohemianism was complex. Bohemian society generated continuing tensions and conflicts as well as providing a supportive environment.

Her friendship with Robert Irvine is easier to understand. In 1920, 'liberal and radically minded students and staff' at Sydney University established a Public Questions Society and the League of Nations Union. Their goals were to debate contentious questions of national and international significance. The Public Questions Society set up five study circles, one of which, chaired by Robert Irvine, was on 'Women in Industry'. This topic must have been of immediate interest to Lucy Woodcock.[29] She would also have been sympathetic to Irvine's innovative and broadly political approach to economics. Lucy became one of Irvine's wide circle of staff and students, many of whom considered him the 'father of political economy', recalling affectionately not only his 'vivid lecture discussions' but his informal assistance outside the classroom. The Sydney University newspaper *Hermes* noted that his influence extended far beyond the university, encompassing art, literature and history as well as economics.[30]

Irvine consolidated much of his economic theory in *The Midas Delusion*, a book meant to be a weighty economic analysis. Yet its first chapter was a much more personal memoir about his time at Sydney University and the students with whom he formed such close bonds. Although he

---

27   *Tribune* (Sydney), 11 June 1946, 6.
28   Ken Muir, former teacher and a fellow active Federationist although much younger than Lucy, pers. comm. 2017.
29   Alan Barcan, *Radical Students: The Old Left at Sydney University* (Carlton, Vic.: Melbourne University Press, 1998), 23–27.
30   Peter Diderik Groenewegen, *Educating for Business, Public Service and the Social Sciences: A History of the Faculty of Economics at the University of Sydney, 1920–1999* (Sydney: Sydney University Press, 2009), 6–8.

chose not to name anyone in particular, he dedicated this first chapter to the 'good companions', and in it he gave a glimpse of the energy and excitement of the circle that Lucy joined in the 1920s:

> It was my good fortune, when the lecture halls knew me, to have a succession, year after year, of student comrades who were eager to join with me in exploring the dark and winding passages of the economic labyrinth. Exactly how this fellowship – for such it was – grew into so delightful a thing, I do not know. Perhaps it was the spirit of the times.
>
> … A new intellectual interest grew rapidly among us. We had encouraged each other to read books other than the textbooks and other than economic books: books that were alive and palpitant with the hopes and fears of men and women today. It did not matter particularly what – poetry, novels, belles-lettres, the more humanistic philosophy, the new psychology – anything that was vital, fearless and sincere in its interpretation of life.[31]

The warmth of this passage is striking and confirms the diversity of the discussions with students and colleagues, ranging across all genres, from fiction and poetry to emerging disciplines such as psychology. Just as compelling is Irvine's evident recognition and respect for the intellectual contribution of the women in the group. This was in marked contrast to Lucy's other world – that of teaching – at that same time. In the period 1890 to World War I, teaching was the only professional career available to the growing number of women emerging from the 'compulsory, free, public education' of the late nineteenth century in Australia. It enabled them to earn an independent living with community respect, without any need to be married to earn status. But single women became increasingly stigmatised and marginalised after World War I, as they came to be seen as deviant and threatening. The career structure for teachers from 1920 became more complex: the NSW Education Department constructed differences between primary and secondary education, which consolidated the gendered limits on certain roles. Such rules ensured that men always managed (as principals, masters or administrators) and that women taught always in subordinate positions, with lower income and less power.[32]

---

31   R.F. Irvine, *The Midas Delusion* (Adelaide: self-published, printed by Hassell Press, 1933), 1–11, and in particular pp. 3–4, 5.
32   Marjorie R. Theobald, *Knowing Women: Origins of Women's Education in Nineteenth-Century Australia* (Cambridge: Cambridge University Press, 1996), doi.org/10.2307/27516628; K. Whitehead, 'The Spinster Teacher in Australia from the 1870s to the 1960s', *History of Education Review* 36, no. 1 (2007): 1–17, doi.org/10.1108/08198691200700001.

In his introduction, Irvine emphasised the later careers – though not the names – of these young comrades, 'the men and women who have sought truth and understanding, above all things' and who 'stand high in their chosen professions or callings'. He noted with both irony and regret that some had gone into business but those emotions were absent in his commendation of those who had gone on to be the 'educators'. Irvine believed educators, regardless of gender, had an important and valuable role.

In 1922, when Irvine was 63, he was forced to resign from his role as Dean of the Faculty of Economics and from Sydney University. McFarlane believed that 'the post-war wave of anti-socialist hysteria that swept Australia probably contributed to his removal from the university'.[33] The immediate issue was an accusation of a long extramarital affair with an American woman who had assisted him in the faculty for some years.[34] This caused widespread dismay among fellow staff and students. Lucy organised a gift from students to mark their appreciation for Irvine's teaching and she was a prominent signatory of the student testimonial presented to him.[35]

Ten years after his forced resignation, Irvine reflected in the *Midas Delusion* on those warm friendships amongst the young economics students in the early 1920s. He finished that introductory chapter by admitting that, at the time, he had failed see the dynamics of the group. Only in retrospect did he comprehend that this fellowship relied on the insight and emotional work of a small number of these 'good companions':

> Looking back now, I can see, more clearly than I did then, how much our coterie owed to the devotion of a few of their number who gave themselves, heart and soul, to the better ordering of our activities. Theirs, in fact, was the 'invisible hand' that kept us together. They were very wise for their years …
>
> And so it dawned on us, borrowing thus widely and subject to such influences, that the 'dismal science' was, after all, the most human and perhaps the greatest of all studies. We saw that nothing

---

33 McFarlane, 'Irvine, Robert Francis (1861–1941)'.
34 *Daily Telegraph* (Sydney), 7 July 1916. It is important to note that McFarlane apparently interviewed Lucy Woodcock about Irvine's life and – given that she was still then in possession of his papers – she was able to facilitate McFarlane's full access. The high value of this interview to McFarlane is discussed by Roe, *Nine Australian Progressives*, 276, in a note to Roe's footnotes for his own chapter on David Irvine.
35 *Northern Star* (Lismore), 14 October 1922, 10; Roe, *Nine Australian Progressives*, 275.

human was fully foreign to it and, rightly or wrongly, we felt that
we were sharing in a reorientation of thought that seemed to make
it possible to frame a 'New Economics'….[36]

Although he did not name those 'wise young people', Irvine's description of their thoughtful nurturing of the group is similar to the descriptions written by women activists in a heartfelt obituary in the United Associations' newsletter after Lucy's death. Certainly, by 1933, Lucy had proven herself an excellent friend to Irvine, giving him the attention he needed to live independently in Ysobel's flat and eventually caring for him until his death in 1941.

***

Despite juggling work and study, Lucy, like many university students, took every opportunity to seek out like-minded new friends. Two teaching colleagues – from different sides of the political fence – remembered these early years vividly. At the Teachers Federation tribute to her on her retirement in 1953, during the intensifying Cold War, Sam Lewis, a left winger, one of Lucy's lifelong friends and a former president of the Federation, said:

> I remember Miss Woodcock in the 1920s when she was a fresh young woman in her early thirties. The first time I saw her was at the University where she was active in the Evening Students' Association …
>
> She was in at the birth of the Federation and has been a doughty champion of many causes of women teachers. But then she sees women's rights as Union rights. She has been a champion of assistants, but she saw the assistants as part of the whole teaching service and now that she has been a Mistress for many years, she has seen the Mistress's interests, but has never failed to see the interests of the assistants and of the Federation as a whole. She has seen the welfare of women teachers as part of the welfare of all who make a contribution to the life of our community

---

36   Irvine, *The Midas Delusion*, 7.

> As far as I can see, she is one of those people whose mental power has grown with the years. I want to say that she is one of the most respected persons on the Labour Council, and possibly about the only person on the Council who will be listened to by all sides with respect and in silence.[37]

At the same 1953 gathering, Harry Heath (a moderate who had just won Lewis's position as Federation president in 1951) explained that he had met Lucy later:

> My first recollection of Miss Woodcock goes back to the very earliest days of my teaching career in 1924. At the time I was a member of the Federation Council and Miss Woodcock was one of the leading members of the Council …
>
> She is the last pupil-teacher … Miss Woodcock is the last person in the service who did the whole five years of pupil-teaching.
>
> She was not trained in a college and, in the course of her career as a teacher, she has risen to the highest position a woman can occupy in our teaching service: that is, she has been the Mistress of an A. Department for a number of years. In addition to that, she has been a woman of immense energy and her interests have not been entirely confined to the Federation …[38]

Lucy's energy and wide interests ensured her continued involvement in the university evening students' organisation she had helped to found, still managing social events that developed the relationships that would allow this notoriously difficult-to-organise community to make itself both visible and audible. She became president of this organisation by the end of her enrolment.

Her 1921 transfer from Lidcombe Public School to Darlington came just as she was beginning her economics degree. This brought her into direct contact with inner-city communities, at a time when a boom in manufacturing led to increased employment in the surrounding factories and the Eveleigh Railway workshop. As a university student and a teacher in the local public school, Lucy became involved in the University Settlement,[39] a community social welfare organisation that, from its

---

37   Sam Lewis, 1953, UAW Files, AU NBAC Z236, Box 32, NBABL.
38   Harold Heath, retirement testimonial speech, December 1953, ibid.
39   Established 1891 by the Sydney University Women's Society, rebadging itself as the Sydney University Settlement in 1913, just before Lucy began her first degree.

inception in 1891, operated on the settlement principles of the nineteenth century, emphasising reciprocity, partnership and collaborative work to tackle entrenched social problems and provide social support. Here she met the people in the area with the lowest income and who were the most vulnerable. Among them were Aboriginal people, some of whom she knew from the South Coast. Lucy became increasingly aware of the challenges faced by working people, including Aboriginal families who had been living in Redfern for many years, as her analysis of the economics of urban Australia developed through her studies. She became well known in the Aboriginal community, as Jack Horner attested when he met her in 1956, because she was interested in adult education. Even though she could not provide it herself, she was able to direct local mature-aged Aboriginal people to attend the Cleveland Street Evening School.[40]

While studying and developing new relationships in her working environment, Lucy was also throwing herself into the work of the new Teachers Federation. She earned a reputation as 'a hard worker on the Council' and, in November 1924, was elected for the first time as a NSW Federation delegate to the next Interstate Teachers' Conference in Hobart in January 1925.[41] Her fellow delegates included three male teachers and one other woman, the veteran teacher – and fellow Granville local – Margaret Swann, the retiring headmistress of Parramatta Primary School. Swann was much older than Lucy and had been involved in more conservative organisations like the Country Women's Association and the Parramatta Historical Society, but had nevertheless asserted the activist role of women and teachers.[42]

Lucy remained deeply troubled by the gender discrimination in pay in the teaching profession. The Teachers' Association had been divided on the multifaceted issue of women's pay. In 1910, single women teachers, while supporting pay claims, had won a vote in the Teachers' Association to force women teachers to resign on marriage. The then Labor Government, perhaps influenced by women members who were also teachers, like Kate Dwyer, did not proceed with corresponding legislation. The Teachers' Association abandoned the 'resign on marriage' provision and instead put in place an 'Equal Pay for Equal Work' platform in 1913.[43]

---

40 Jack Horner, *Seeking Racial Justice: An Insider's Memoir of the Movement for Aboriginal Advancement, 1938–1978* (Canberra: Aboriginal Studies Press, 2004), 18–19.
41 *Northern Star* (Lismore), 15 November 1924, 14.
42 *West Australian* (Perth), 6 January 1928, 6.
43 Mitchell, *Teachers, Education and Politics*, 26.

When the new Teachers Federation was formed in September 1918, this Equal Pay policy was not included in its platform, indicating the ambivalence among teachers about these issues. The call for Equal Pay was, however, included in the Federation's first claim before the Arbitration Court, which ruled in 1920 that women teachers should receive not equal pay, but no less than 80 per cent of the male rate in any comparable job. The Teachers Federation responded by finally altering its formal policy to include 'Equal Pay for Equal Work', but, in practice, ignored it in the Federation's campaigns over the following years. In any event, the issue was massively complicated by the differential classifications and promotion rates of male and female teachers. There were some jobs in public schools that were not available to women, no matter how experienced or highly trained.[44]

Lucy had campaigned strongly on Equal Pay from the very beginning of the Federation's existence in 1918, assuming an increasingly vocal role in the intimidating and divided atmosphere of the Federation conference. In the final Federation meeting of 1924, supported by two other 'lady teachers', Miss Beatrice Taylor and Miss Ettie Cunningham, Lucy demanded that the union take a strong position on equality of pay and opportunity for its women as well as its male members by challenging this 80 per cent limit. The Labour press congratulated her on her criticism of the department that upheld this pay injustice, but her attack was directed as much against the men in the Teachers Federation who failed to carry through on their promises:

> Miss L. Woodcock got a good one home on the men. 'Women teachers,' she said, 'are fully alive to the dangers of men who only half carry out their platform. We women are fully organised, and will fight for the principle of equal pay. We are prepared to stand by and defend our position.'[45]

In the end, Lucy and her supporters lost their original motion but won a subcommittee to draw up a schedule of pay for women teachers.

Members viewed their Teachers Federation as being overly dominated by headmasters and headmistresses over its whole existence. This was one of the reasons Lucy had continued to be active in the Women Assistants' Association, becoming its vice president in 1924, the same year that she was elected as an interstate representative for the overall Federation.[46]

---

44 Ibid., 57; Lucy Woodcock, 'Brave Hearts Led Bid for Equality', *Our Women*, March–May 1964, 26.
45 *Australian Worker* (Sydney), 31 December 1924, 2.
46 *Evening News* (Sydney), 1 March 1924, 3.

Lucy's advocacy for Equal Pay and her concern over the domination of senior staff in the Federation in particular and in the teaching profession as a whole is obvious in her co-authored 1925 booklet *Justice vs Tradition*, published under the authorship of the Combined Women Teachers' Association of NSW.[47] Bruce Mitchell, Lucy's biographer and colleague, regarded her as the key author of *Justice vs Tradition*.[48] The book rebutted the 1924 argument for higher salaries for male teachers over women teachers made by the London School Masters' Association, a prestigious body of headmasters in highly regarded British secondary schools.[49]

In their challenge to the London headmasters, whose argument had received wide support among Australian male teachers, the Combined Women Teachers' Association attacked the injustice of unequal pay in the education sector particularly but more broadly across society. They drew on two arguments very strongly in *Justice vs Tradition*, which were in some contradiction to each other. One relied on an assumption of biologically determined aptitudes in women – in what today would be called an essentialist argument – in asserting that all women were innately – biologically and temperamentally – suited to the teaching of children, whether or not they had actually borne offspring. In contradiction to this was their other argument – an anti-essentialist argument – that women, as equal citizens, by virtue of their qualifications and citizenship, were as capable as men of teaching children.

Yet, while Lucy and the other authors of this booklet were attacking the gendered hierarchies of their own patriarchal society, they endorsed the racial hierarchies of the colonial world. Their book began with the statement that women are better off in the 'West', then went on to condemn discrimination against women in the teaching profession. The authors argued that the comparative disadvantage faced by women in India, Turkey and China demonstrated that these countries had attained a low 'stage in race evolution', thereby justifying continued colonial control by the West.[50]

---

47 Women's Propaganda Committee for Combined Women Teachers' Association of New South Wales, *Justice vs Tradition* (Sydney: Epworth Press, 1925).
48 Mitchell, *Teachers, Education and Politics*, 58. Mitchell strongly criticised *Justice vs Tradition* because it did not effectively challenge the status quo, meaning the details of the complex gendered 'glass ceiling' discrimination in the teaching service. It could be argued, however, that the whole premise of the book is a rebuttal of any type of gendered discrimination.
49 London School Masters' Association, *Equal Pay and the Teaching Profession* (London: The Association, c. 1924).
50 Women's Propaganda Committee, *Justice vs Tradition*, 8 for quotation and 7–10 for broader discussion. Lucy came to disagree strongly with this view.

Despite the entanglement of *Justice vs Tradition* in eugenics and in the politics of colonialism, it was an unprecedented and courageous step by women teachers to fight against the discrimination they faced. Its very production and wide circulation were a triumph for its authors. Yet it provides an uncomfortable window into the ways in which arguments for gender equality in the West could also contribute to the justification of colonial domination.

Equal Pay for Equal Work remained as Teachers Federation policy: it survived challenges in 1921, 1925 and 1927.[51] The Federation, however, repeatedly failed to back its own policy, shuffling what its male members found to be a difficult question into the 'too-hard' basket. There continued to be pay-offs and benefits for male teachers in the Education Department. To confuse the issue even further, some jobs were only offered to men and other, less well paid jobs offered to women. Reluctant to deal with the question, the Federation ignored its own policy, to the increasing frustration of its women members.

Figure 2.1: Lucy in her early days of teaching.
She enjoyed wearing fashionable and striking hats.
Source: *Warwick Daily News* (Qld), Wednesday 11 March 1942, p. 3. Trove, National Library of Australia.

---

51 Mitchell, *Teachers, Education and Politics*, 58.

Lucy was incredibly busy in the mid-1920s, becoming vice president in the Teachers Federation, graduating with two degrees, excited and stimulated by the learning at university and by her circle of friends there, teaching intensively at Darlington and volunteering at the University Settlement as well. In addition, she also took an office-bearing role in the Sydney University Women's Graduates Association and the Sydney University Economics Society. She spoke before the National Council of Women (NCW) on at least two occasions, once with fellow economist Persia Campbell. Both spoke about child endowment and contributed to a NCW submission to the sitting Royal Commission on Endowment.[52]

All this came crashing to a halt – quite literally – when Lucy was hit by a speeding ambulance as she tried to cross Liverpool Road in Enfield to catch a tram in August 1926. Badly injured, she spent a month in hospital and was off work for more than nine weeks. Characteristically, Lucy decided to fight a case in court for compensation. Lucy argued that the ambulance driver had been negligent because he had failed to sound the 'gong' or give any other warning, before speeding from behind the tram. She took the NSW Ambulance Board to the District Court where a jury awarded her compensation.[53] This was a salve to her pride but it did not repair the permanent damage to her right leg. Her limp forced her to use a walking stick from the late 1930s.[54]

Lucy may have considered international exchange teaching as an opportunity to have a break away from the pressures in NSW as well as to expand her horizons. She was concerned, however, that the NSW Education Department expected teachers to use their long service leave entitlements for the exchange. Lucy's opinion, expressed through the Teachers Federation, was that the experience of British culture would definitely benefit NSW teachers, but it was unfair to expect them to use their own leave. In fact, she said, the NSW Education Department should encourage teachers to gain this experience by funding it![55]

---

52 *Labor Daily* (Sydney), 19 November 1927, 7; *Daily Telegraph* (Sydney), 20 November 1927, 26; *Sunday Times* (Sydney), 20 November 1927, 16; *SMH*, 21 November 1927, 4.
53 Michelle Hoctor, 'Ambulance in the 1920s', NSW Ambulance Service Media documents, www.ambulance.nsw.gov.au/Media/docs/Ambulanceinthe1920-0b8abfe6-0c68-4538-9990-8828685a042a-0.pdf, accessed 18 October 2018; *SMH*, 17 September 1926, 18 November 1926.
54 Sam Lewis referred to her accident and the walking stick outcome in his 1953 testimonial speech.
55 *Maitland Weekly Mercury*, 24 July 1926, 13.

She herself was granted leave to spend all of 1927 in the United Kingdom. Exchange teachers in the UK were often given relief teaching – a punishing schedule in many different schools.[56] This was what Lucy did – teaching in over 20 inner-city schools – but it was an exciting time. These were underprivileged 'slum schools', managed by the London County Council, then at the cutting edge of innovation, drawing on creativity through theatre, for example, in the experiment of 'progressive' education.[57]

In the UK, she met Rosemary Benjamin, who was working with the London County Council to encourage theatre. Benjamin volunteered with the YWCA and Girl Guides and founded two theatre companies, 'The Lyndians' for adults and The Young People's Theatre for Children. These theatres had Australian connections: they were influenced by Australian actor Joan Luxton's previous work in London on similar projects.[58] Lucy also met another Australian exchange teacher in London at this time. Edna Nelson – later Edna Ryan – became a lifelong friend.[59]

Lucy learnt a great deal from the ferment of new ideas circulating in the UK about 'progressive' and 'child-centred' education. She did *not*, however, learn any reverence for English 'traditional' education. Instead, she was fascinated by the new strategies being developed there to address physical and psychiatric disabilities, as she reported to the Australian Teachers' Union on her return:

> She was particularly impressed with the educational work that was being done by the London County Council, and praised very highly the system of grading the children in Group schools. There adequate provision was made for the mentally defective child and for the physically defective child: while there were schools for the deaf and dumb and for the partially blind. These children were as well catered for as the normal child. In the cripple schools

---

56 K. Whitehead, 'Exchange Teachers as "Another Link in Binding the [British] Empire" in the Interwar Years', *Social and Education History* 3, no. 1 (2014): 1–24.
57 Lucy Woodcock, Report to UA on UK, Japan, and China. UA *Newsheet*, October 1955, 3–4; *Telegraph* (Brisbane), 22 January 1930, 14; Rosmarie Benjamin, 'The Story of the Theatre for Children', typescript play, c. 1949, held online by State Library of Victoria, digital.slv.vic.gov.au/dtl_publish/pdf/marc/3/2125895.html, accessed 17 November 2018.
58 Benjamin, 'The Story of the Theatre for Children'; John McIntyre, 'Rosemarie Benjamin and the Theatre for Children in Sydney, 1937–1957', 2013, www.artpages.com.au/Theatre_for_Children/McIntyre_Theatre%20for%20Children.pdf, accessed 17 November 2018.
59 Ruth Fink Latukefu, pers. comm., 3 September 2015.

particular attention was paid to fitting the child to earn a living. In fact the aim was to make these children as socially efficient as it was possible for them to be considering their physical condition.[60]

Lucy added that support was available to teachers as well as children:

> The London County Council, Miss Woodcock declares, was not only interested in the children attending the schools within its jurisdiction. But it paid special attention to the teachers in its employ, of whom there are more than 20,000. During the winter months each year a special course of lectures is given for the benefit of the teachers to help them in their work and to inform them as to the latest development in teaching practice.[61]

It was not surprising then that Lucy was offended by the suggestion, made by the Australian High Commissioner to the UK, that the benefits of exchange teaching would largely flow to Australians from British culture. Instead, in London in July 1928, in the middle of her exchange year, Lucy was adamant that the benefits were reciprocal. Under headlines like 'No Lopsided Gain', many Australian newspapers reported her words:

> Miss L. G. Woodcock, formerly vice-president of the New South Wales Teachers' Federation, declared that contact with English traditions and culture was most valuable to Australian teachers. On the other hand, English teachers would gain valuable instruction by watching a young country tackle educational and industrial problems.[62]

Characteristically, on her return to Australia, she threw herself into organising teachers who had been on exchange. By 1930, an Exchange Teachers' Club had been established, and Lucy became honorary treasurer, a position she held until 1934. The club enabled exchange teachers to keep in contact with each other and also welcomed and entertained international teachers coming to Australia. In 1937, Lucy was still hosting visiting teachers and taking them on trips around Sydney.[63] Most visitors in this period were from the UK, Canada or New Zealand and, from them, Lucy learnt more and more about women's lives and work outside Australia's shores.

---

60   *Telegraph* (Brisbane), 22 January 1930, 14.
61   Ibid.
62   *Daily News* (Perth), 20 July 1928, 7; *Register* (Adelaide), 21 July 1928, 12; *West Australian* (Perth), 21 July 1928, 19; *Mercury* (Hobart), 24 July 1928, 5.
63   *SMH*, 25 February 1932, 3; 5 January 1934, 8; 12 March 1934, 4; 3 June 1947, 7.

Scars: 1930s

3

Hunger

The Depression changed Lucy Woodcock. Until then, she had been an activist within her profession – helping to shape the NSW Teachers Federation and speaking out for women teachers and particularly women *assistant* teachers. Her university education had introduced her to wider circles of ideas and people – drawing her into Sydney's bohemian world and sharpening her critique of the economic processes shaping Australia. At Darlington, she had experienced the tough life of inner-city poverty but also, as she had done in London, had consolidated her commitment to new learning, with its encouragement of creativity and cultural expression, in working-class schools.

It was not till some tragic events at Cessnock that Lucy's activism moved outside the school boundaries into the wider community. She found that quality learning was impossible unless hunger among her students was addressed. For the rest of the decade, she battled with poverty, overcrowding as well as plain starvation. Lack of food was the urgent issue, but there was hunger for other things too – for safety, for space and for beauty. She campaigned passionately for these things and they became her focus in the later 1930s.

The coalfields city of Cessnock was already doing it tough before the Depression. Although rural employment in New South Wales had increased by 80 per cent between 1911 and 1929, the emergence of alternative sources of power cut the state's mining by 18 per cent.[1] These reductions had been bitterly fought at every step and, by 1929, the

---

1 Annette Salt, 'Women of the Northern Coalfields of NSW', *Labour History*, no. 48 (May 1985): 44.

mining unions, having faced decades of dangerous working conditions and poor pay, were militant and angry. The Teerman family came from Broken Hill. Jack Teerman had been a miner in the BHP lead, silver and zinc mines, and exposure to lead had severely damaged his health. Jack, accompanied by his family, and forced to leave mining in the west, came to the coal-mining districts of Elrington and Rothbury near Cessnock to work as a shaft sinker. Unfortunately, the coal dust exacerbated his already damaged lungs. Jack and his wife Ethel were vocal advocates for the miners as they had been at Broken Hill. Jack was the secretary of the Elrington Miners' Lodge from 1925 to 1930, leading three successful strikes. Ethel, like many miners' wives, was not literate but determined to oppose injustice. She joined the Militant Women's Group in Cessnock, which affiliated with the Communist Party in 1927. In August 1928, her description of the poverty faced by miners' families after a decade of mining cuts was reported in a *Labor Daily* article, headed 'Dire Poverty on the Coalfields: How it is affecting the children'.[2] The women's group went from 'house-to-house' to ask about nutrition status and found that many children suffered chronically from poor diets. They demanded that the authorities recognise that poverty affected whole families. They used World War I experiences to point out the damage done to the nation's health as a whole. The lengthy article focused on overcrowding for families in flimsy structures, poor nutrition and precarious, casualised work.

As the year wore on, the mining companies threatened further pay cuts, which unionists refused to accept. In March 1929, the mine owners locked the workers out to force them to accept lower pay and, to increase the pressure, the owners brought in 'scabs' – non-union strikebreakers whom the companies called 'free labourers'.[3] The coalminers refused to concede defeat, which meant they had no income for the impending winter. This coal dispute was symptomatic of company attempts to reduce costs at workers' expense. Waterside workers around the country were already in revolt: in September 1928, the federal government had imposed the 'Dog Collar' Act, intervening in waterside workers' shifts and conditions.[4] In Melbourne, in November 1928, a wharfie protesting at the use of scabs had been shot dead. In February 1929, in Glebe, timber workers were locked out for refusing a pay cut. The coalminers, embittered after years of struggle, now joined them in their symbolic repudiation of these

---

2   *Labor Daily* (Sydney), 18 August 1928, based on information from 'E. N. Teerman, organiser'.
3   *Workers Weekly*, 26 April 1929, 2.
4   The *Transport Workers Act 1928* (Cth), assented to 24 September, applied to all sea trade ports.

consequences of the Depression. The leadership of many Miners' Lodges was initially wary of outside assistance but it soon became essential to call on miners' families and wider community support. Ethel Teerman assured the unions that women's auxiliaries were useful while Jack Teerman, advocating a Citizen's Relief Committee, was at pains to explain that none of these tactics would undermine the Strike Committee's leadership.[5] Jack and Ethel's militancy was heroic – at one stage Ethel led 500 women in a deputation to local shopkeepers, threatening a consumer boycott if they served the police protecting strikebreakers.[6] In spite of this heroic resistance, the impoverished conditions of mining families made for a bitter winter.

Lucy Woodcock arrived in June 1929, in the middle of that tense winter, as the new assistant girls' teacher at Cessnock Public School. The impact of the lockout on schoolchildren was already visible and, before long, activist coalminers' wives like Ethel Teerman were organising daily soup kitchens to feed the children. All the teachers in Cessnock became heavily involved in the soup kitchen. It was quickly established that children would be fed at the schools and this service would continue in the holidays. The *Newcastle Sun* in August shows some of the schoolchildren being fed.[7]

The conservative NSW Government declared it would not support soup kitchens at schools, citing 'confidential reports that there was no necessity', purportedly from teachers, for additional nutrition. The Citizen's Relief Committee expressed surprise because 'all members of the [school] staff had shown themselves willing to assist the committee in every possible way'. The Cessnock branch of the Teachers Federation, with Lucy an active member, wrote formally to explain that, while financial support for the soup kitchens was a matter for individual teachers, the staff at Cessnock and their union fully supported the Citizen's Relief Committee and the distribution of food to schoolchildren. The Relief Committee emphasised that all teachers had been unstinting in their assistance and it was unlikely that they were the source of criticism. 'We have always felt', the committee continued, 'that we had the support of the teachers.'[8]

---

5   *Newcastle Sun*, 30 May 1929, 7; *Cessnock Eagle and South Maitland Recorder*, 10 September 1929, 19 March 1937, 9; *Workers Weekly*, 26 March 1937, 4.
6   Jean Lewis, 'For a Dancer', a memorial to her mother, Ethel Caroline Lewis. Ethel was the daughter of Jack and Ethel Teerman. Both the older and the younger Ethel at times used 'Nelson' as a middle name (Jack Teerman's brother was called Nelson and it seems to have been a Teerman family name).
7   *Newcastle Sun*, 15 August 1929, 1.
8   *Newcastle Morning Herald and Miners' Advocate*, 4 September 1929, 8.

Figure 3.1: This *Newcastle Sun* photo showed the soup kitchens for the children of locked-out and striking miners.

These soup kitchens were run by the Citizen's Relief Committee, led by Jack Teerman. Lucy and many of her fellow teachers contributed their time to these soup kitchens to feed their hungry students.

Source: *The Newcastle Sun*, 15 August 1929, p. 1. Trove, National Library of Australia.

Like her fellow teachers, Lucy daily faced the real life consequences of the Depression on the bodies of her students, this malnourishment exacerbated by conditions at home as had been described so powerfully by Ethel Teerman, Jack's wife.

The miners continued to refuse the pay cuts and the lockout continued. Despite the Women's Auxiliary and the Citizen's Relief Committee continuing their assistance, conditions worsened.[9] The miners attempted to organise peaceful demonstrations and established picket lines to deter scab labour at many mines, but the state government tried to intimidate the picketers with armed police. The inevitable happened: on 16 December, as picketers defended their line at Rothbury, the police fired into the crowd and killed a 19-year-old miner, Norman Brown.[10] Shock rippled through the mining community and their supporters in the Cessnock area and ultimately affected the whole country. Despite the mass protests by mining workers, the lockout continued.[11] Ultimately, the mine workers were starved into accepting the pay cut and forced back to work early in 1930. They face severely reduced working time and many lost their jobs.

---

9   *Newcastle Sun*, 2 December 1929, 5.
10   'The Tragic Story of Yesterday', *Newcastle Morning Herald and Miners' Advocate*, 17 December 1929, 7.
11   *Cessnock Eagle and South Maitland Recorder*, 22 December 1929, 1; *SMH*, 23 December 1929, 11; *Cessnock Eagle*, 24 December 1929, 1.

Lucy was transferred out of Cessnock in February 1930, but she remained in contact with her close friends there and, in particular, the Teermans. The Teermans' daughter, Ethel Caroline, had been studying teaching at Sydney University while Lucy was at Cessnock.[12] But the younger Ethel was as much of an activist as her parents. After she graduated as a teacher she worked in the area from 1930, first at Lithgow and then West Wyalong. She also became active in the Teachers Federation. There she met other young activists, becoming involved in a relationship with Lucy's friend from university Sam Lewis. Lucy was close to Ethel through their common work in raising awareness of the worsening conditions of workers' families and their children during the Depression.

Lucy's transfer in 1930 was also a promotion – she became Headmistress of Girls at Grafton. Lucy was uneasy about her promotion given her long commitment to junior 'assistant' teachers. But in Grafton she found a different type of Depression poverty to that she had seen in Cessnock. Rural agriculture in Grafton was not in as desperate a state as mining in Cessnock, but it was far from the images of idyllic rural prosperity imagined in urban centres. As early as 1928, a severe drought had begun to undermine the families of her students. Lucy's experience of this rural distress was clear during her 1932–33 national role as president of the Federated State School Teachers' Association, when she frequently raised the needs of rural schools for better funding and more appropriate training for teachers.[13] Lucy sustained this concern when she was transferred to urban schools, often speaking out during her long career to protest about the marginalisation of rural schools and the failure to admit girls to agricultural occupations.

After Grafton, Lucy spent a brief time at Abbotsford and, in August 1933, was transferred to be second-in-charge at Erskineville. A co-educational inner-city school, it catered to primary school students in classes segregated by gender. A headmaster had the final control over the school and Lucy's work. In general, however, as 'Mistress of Girls', Lucy had charge of girls in the infants' and primary schools (attended by both boys and girls), and the girls' high school, in what was sometimes referred to as the Home Science Department. The Erskineville boys generally went

---

12   Ethel graduated BA and Diploma of Education, majoring in, and later teaching, Latin.
13   *Education*, 11 March 1935, 161.

off to Newtown Technical College (Tech)[14] for their secondary education, but the girls (except for the few who went to the academically selective Sydney Girls' High) stayed on at Erskineville, learning 'Home Science', till they reached the school-leaving age of 14 or until they had completed three years of high school, when they could, if they chose, sit for their Intermediate examination.

Erskineville was a proud, industrial area, but it had been badly affected by the Depression when Lucy arrived. Popularly known as 'Erko', the suburb had, two years earlier, witnessed a bloody battle in Union Street when police tried to evict families who were behind with their rent. Thousands of militant unemployed workers massed in the streets to defend their homes against the police, leaving casualties on all sides. With her two university degrees and her long career in teaching, Lucy could have used this appointment to leverage a much more comfortable posting at an eminent selective high school, like Sydney Girls' High. Instead, Lucy declined a number of attractive promotion offers and stayed working with the community, close both to students and their parents, particularly their mothers. This community role was the one she had always liked best.

What struck her immediately was the condition of the children whose parents were unemployed. Her experience at Cessnock as well as her economics training under Irvine had shifted her to the Left.[15] Lucy believed that the Depression was caused by human financial mismanagement, and she supported expansionary fiscal measures to overcome its effects:

> It is no use offering the financial position as an excuse for unemployment and for a starved child endowment. The financial situation is man-made and can be overcome by man.[16]

By early 1934, Lucy had drawn other staff members at Erskineville into her concerns about the children. They observed that many children were listless and became increasingly sleepy in the afternoon. Lucy organised a house-by-house survey of the children's families, and realised that these problems related to poverty and poor nutrition. In her speeches at the Federated State Schools Conference in January 1935, Lucy said:

---

14 Newtown Technical High School – from which one could only go on to an apprenticeship, not to matriculation or to a university degree. This site is now Newtown Performing Arts High School.
15 Mitchell, 'Lucy Godiva Woodcock'.
16 *Australian Worker* (Sydney), 16 January 1935, 5.

> In my district, Erskineville, 60 per cent of the people knew no other income but the dole. They never saw butter on the tables, and the mothers were fortunate to have a new dress in six years.[17]

Her focal target was the fundamental inadequacy of the dole offered as relief to unemployed workers. With little food in the house, the children often came with very little money to purchase lunches. There was no cafeteria in the school grounds so pupils had to walk across surrounding roads to the nearby shops, where they invariably made poor nutritional choices such as sweets – which gave them a fast 'sugar hit', but did not sustain them for the afternoon's lessons. As Lucy explained, 'with virtually not enough food to keep their strength up for the afternoon, they soon became drowsy and listless'.[18]

Lucy and the Erskineville staff initiated a number of practical strategies. First, they developed a series of lessons to educate the children during schooltime about how to make better food choices at the shops. Lucy then negotiated with each of the shopkeepers where the children spent their lunch money. She persuaded them to provide nutritious foodstuffs and have them on display for the children who came into the shop. In later years, worried by the danger of crossing the busy roads, Lucy changed this approach. The children would order their lunches in the school from a list of healthy recommendations and then two lunch monitors would collect and bring back the lunches.[19] Later, the staff campaigned to have a cafeteria installed at the school, so that children did not have to cross the road at all. Overall, Lucy argued that the dole needed to be supplemented with an increased child endowment payment.[20]

Lucy took her demands to the federal and state education union conferences in the beginning of 1935, where she called for an increase of the mandatory minimum school-leaving age as well as the level of child endowment. She also wanted the latter to be continued till the minimum

---

17   *Daily Standard* (Brisbane), 10 January 1935, 5; *Mercury* (Hobart), 11 January 1935, 11; *Northern Miner* (Charters Towers, Qld), 11 January 1935, 4, all reporting the FSSTA Annual Conference Brisbane.
18   Lucy was interviewed at length in 1938, giving more details of the strategies used in 1934 at Erskineville. *SMH*, 12 December 1938, 12.
19   Beverley Bates, interview with Heather Goodall, Devleena Ghosh and Helen Randerson, 1 September 2016.
20   *SMH*, 12 December 1938, 12.

leaving age so that families would not be disadvantaged if children continued at school rather than being sent to work. As she explained, Erskineville was an area in which many casual labourers lived:

> Since the depression conditions had grown steadily worse. The older girls were kept from school, to look after the smaller ones while their mothers went to work ... Child endowment in NSW ceased when children reached 14, and before a child reached that age parents pleaded that it be allowed to leave school to 'earn the rent.' ... We go on muddling, and refusing to give the children the heritage which is their right.[21]

There was some ambivalence about this issue among unions with predominantly male members as well as in the Communist Party. These organisations considered child endowment as undermining the basic wage (set by the Harvester Judgement in 1907 as the fair and minimum male wage, on the assumption that it was only male breadwinners who provided for dependents).[22] Lucy stressed that the government's obligation was to the whole family and child endowment offered a way to target resources towards children. 'The children were the sufferers', she said, 'under conditions which were appalling in any country calling itself a democracy.'[23]

Lucy's call for improved nutrition for children of unemployed families was strongly supported by the NSW Teachers Federation and received wide publicity because it tapped into a general public concern about the ongoing effects of the Depression. The NSW Education Minister D.H. Drummond insisted there was no problem – he cited studies done in Cessnock in 1930 and, during 1935, in four unnamed urban areas, two industrial and two 'better off'. Drummond argued that in 1935 the Education Department doctors found that the 'better off' areas showed poorer nutrition than the industrial areas – although he did not produce the actual reports. The issue kept surfacing and the Sydney press was eager to quote doctors in inner-city hospitals, particularly Dr Harvey Sutton, of the newly established Sydney University School of Public Health. Professor Sutton drew on research into growth patterns in NSW and on a coming survey in Victoria to assert that a quarter of NSW schoolchildren suffered

---

21 *Daily Standard* (Brisbane), 10 January 1935, 5; *SMH*, 13 August 1936, 17.
22 Commonwealth Court of Arbitration and Conciliation, 8 November 1907, before Justice H.B. Higgins.
23 *SMH*, 20 July 1939, 11.

from growth retardation due to malnutrition. Neither minister nor professor were careful in their references but this dispute reflected a widespread public uneasiness reflected in repeated parliamentary questions. For example, the Sydney City Council made statements about international perceptions of Australia's reputation because of Sutton's assertions.[24]

Lucy had, by 1935, returned to the role of senior vice president in the NSW Teachers Federation, a role vacated when she was in the United Kingdom and when she had later been president of the Federated State School Teachers' Association. This gave her a highly visible presence so her determination to investigate and improve the conditions faced by the families of unemployed workers had wide repercussions.[25] Lucy shaped the work, for example, of the writer Dymphna Cusack, then at Sydney Girls' High, who had spent some time teaching at Broken Hill. Cusack's biographer explained:

> Dymphna soon entered Woodcock's sphere of influence. Following her appointment as SGHS School Counsellor in 1936 Dymphna became involved with Lucy Woodcock's social justice agenda, and in particular her field research study reporting on the welfare of children of the unemployed.[26]

In February 1937, a federal government survey in Melbourne identified malnutrition among schoolchildren, adding fuel to the concerns of the NSW public and teachers.[27] In March, a deputation of industrial unions and teachers, including Dymphna Cusack, met with the NSW education minister and argued that there needed to be a careful study of the nutrition levels among children of the unemployed. Disputing Drummond's statements that the Education Department doctors were best placed to survey children's health, Cusack pointed out that local doctors – as well as those like Professor Sutton – had repeatedly expressed concern that

---

24   *SMH*, 16 October 1935, 13; 17 October 1935, 12; *Labor Daily* (Sydney), 17 October 1935, 7; *Sun* (Sydney), 20 October 1935, 11; *Cessnock Eagle and South Maitland Recorder*, 22 October 1935, 6; 25 October 1935, 9; *Newcastle Morning Herald and Miners' Advocate*, 24 October 1935, 10; *Newcastle Sun*, 17 October 1935, 12; 21 November 1935, 13.
25   *SMH*, 13 August 1936, 17.
26   Marilla North, 'Dympha Cusack and the Hunter: A Reciprocal Impact', in *Radical Newcastle*, eds James Bennett, Nancy Cushing and Erik Eklund (Sydney: NewSouth Publishing, 2015), 144–51.
27   *Australian Worker* (Sydney), 17 February 1937, 8.

children of the unemployed were going hungry.²⁸ Drummond continued to deny the necessity but agreed to survey the children living in coalfields to assess nutrition levels.²⁹

The survey dragged on. Dymphna Cusack and Lucy Woodcock continued their campaign for careful investigation and fast, practical remedies. They found some important arenas for their concerns in the series of conferences held by the NSW Teachers Federation in June 1938, which held sessions in each of the major cities in coastal and inland NSW. The theme of the conferences was 'Education for a Progressive, Democratic Australia'. Outlining the goals of these conferences for the Newcastle press, Cusack argued that attention to health and nutrition were a crucial part of education reform for a stronger democracy:

> The present system of annual medical and dental examination (in country districts they are not even annual!) is wholly unsatisfactory and one of the most important demands of the conference is the establishment of efficient health services, and, where necessary, provision of meals and milk services.³⁰

Lucy's major contributions to the conferences were based on the conditions of the unemployed, in nutrition, housing and environmental health and overall amenity. In September 1938, in Wollongong, for example, Lucy argued for greater attention to these issues, insisting that there was:

> a lot of malnutrition in N.S. Wales. This was not due to ignorance, but to the low standard of living. Everyone was entitled to a decent standard and all should cooperate in seeing that slums and poverty were wiped out.³¹

Finally, in December 1938, the results of the survey of Cessnock schools were released. Drummond offered many media interviews, arguing that the average of nutrition status in the three schools in Cessnock was not below the state's average. However, the crucial figures compared the three schools – one of which, Cessnock West, was in a wealthy area, the second in a middle income area while the third, Cessnock East, drew its pupils primarily from the adjacent land where unemployed workers' had set up makeshift camps. The results showed that, though the average percentage

---

28 *Cessnock Eagle and South Maitland Recorder*, 9 March 1937, 2.
29 *Newcastle Morning Herald and Miners' Advocate*, 8 March 1937, 9.
30 Ibid., 8 June 1938, 4.
31 *South Coast Times and Wollongong Argus*, 30 September 1938, 17.

of malnutrition in all three schools was slightly higher than the state's average, individually, malnutrition was much higher in the school adjacent to the unemployed workers' camps – at 2.5 per cent.[32] The arguments made by the Cessnock teachers and the coal unions in 1929 and Lucy Woodcock's survey in Erskineville in 1934 were vindicated. The children of unemployed workers were indeed undernourished.

Drummond had by this time – perhaps partly to strengthen Australia's national reputation for fitness with the prospect of looming war – agreed to support better nutrition and physical fitness in schools.[33] The worst of the Depression had passed and, with more jobs available, there were more resources available for families. Nevertheless, the NSW Education Department only supported the provision of free milk to schools, benefiting NSW dairy producers, a law enacted in 1941.[34] Lucy Woodcock, however, had argued for the provision of lunches, not just milk, and, more fundamentally, for an increase in unemployment benefits and child endowment to improve overall nutrition for children and for their families. There is irony, therefore, in the enduring association of her name with the free school milk program. In fact, in 1942, Lucy protested about the inept and discriminatory way in which this poorly conceived policy was being implemented.[35]

Lucy never lost sight of that fundamental hunger – the very basic lack of food – which haunted her years at Erskineville and Cessnock. In this period, anxiety about war escalated. It was not only about the battle in distant Europe – news of which was brought to Australia in the 1930s by refugees. Anxiety was more acute about events closer to home: the Japanese invasion of Manchuria in 1931 and the continuous 'incidents' that followed led to the Australian Chinese community calling for support for mainland China. In August 1937, the Japanese invasion of northern and coastal China began with the terrible battle of Shanghai and by December they were at the gates of Nanking. The disturbing news about the bombing of Chinese communities in the port cities reached Australia. Australian racism meant, however, that condemnation of the Japanese was not usually

---

32 *Newcastle Morning Herald and Miners' Advocate*, 16 December 1936, 11; Drummond had used the statistic misleadingly (reported in *Newcastle Sun*, 16 December 1938, 7) when he stated that he was explicitly excluding the children of the unemployed when he asserted that the average level of malnutrition in Cessnock schools was the same as that for the whole state.
33 *Newcastle Sun*, 16 December 1938, 7.
34 *SMH*, 22 February 1941, 13.
35 *Sun* (Sydney), 11 April 1942, 2.

accompanied by compassion for the Chinese victims, nor for the continuing terrible casualties of the Depression. When a member introduced a motion at a meeting in August 1937 arguing that the Teachers Federation should express support for the Chinese victims of the Japanese bombing and protest to the Japanese Consul General, Lucy added:

> members must not forget, while expressing sympathy with the Chinese people, that thousands of children in New South Wales were suffering under a more refined cruelty than bombing … the children of the unemployed.[36]

***

Yet hunger for food had not been the only issue that made Lucy step outside the school fence at Erskineville. When she first arrived in 1933, she had realised that the severely crowded conditions endured by many unemployed families also took a toll on their lives and health.

One of her students in the 1930s was Betty Makin, who was born in 1926 and had always lived in the area around Erskineville. She had grown up in Waterloo, attended primary school at Redfern Public and high school at Erskineville under Lucy. Her adult life was spent in a Housing Commission house in Redfern.

This is how she described her 1930s childhood in the area:

> Most people that were born in Waterloo or Redfern usually married women within a mile around because they never went any further. They worked there because there were heaps of factories and you knew everyone as you were growing up. Both my mother and father were born and grew up in this area.
>
> I was born in 1926 and grew up in the Depression years. Mum was having babies and Dad wasn't getting any more money at work [but at least he always *had* work]. You didn't get any child endowment in those days if your husband was working. We always had Nanna living with us and lots of aunts and uncles who couldn't afford to live anywhere else. The kids were just piled into beds, on floors, anywhere we could put them. I was the second one out of nine children.

---

36 *Newcastle Morning Herald and Miners' Advocate*, 27 September 1937, 7.

> Without my Nanna, I don't know how we would have survived. Nanna was blind, but I'll never forget her sitting washing socks … I'd chop the wood and boil the copper. At that time, we had our gas cut off … When Nanna's little pension came in, we paid the gas bill. Everyone in the area helped each other and if your gas had been cut off, then someone would cook at their place, or they had that penny-in-the-slot gas then, and you'd run around there and say 'Could I just put a shilling in your slot?'
>
> … The boys never wore shoes and the girls had sandshoes. Mum had to buy them in turns and if it wasn't your turn, you had to put cardboard in the bottom. On hot, sunny days, when they had black tar footpaths, if it was bubbling, you'd have to walk along the kerb because your feet would be burning. But this happened to every family, not just ours.[37]

Betty Makin's description of the overcrowded home in which she grew up and lived for much of her early married life was not unusual. Lucy was acutely aware of the impact of housing on the children at her school and on their mothers. From 1937, Lucy was involved in the debate around the plans to build model housing in Erskineville, known as the 'Erskineville Housing Scheme'. This scheme produced 16 blocks of flats and the Lady Gowrie childcare centre on parkland at Erskineville, a housing scheme criticised in later years as isolating and constricting.[38] At that time, however, many of the old, rented Victorian workers' cottages and terraces in Erskineville were dilapidated, damp and in need of extensive repairs. Lucy considered that the new flats provided a healthier, more pleasant environment for families.

In 1939, at a meeting at Erskineville Town Hall, in a discussion on housing conditions and unemployment, Lucy described living conditions at Erskineville as 'appalling':

> Prize stock were housed better than the people of Erskineville …
> The houses had outlived their usefulness, and should be demolished.
> They were patched until they could be patched no longer.[39]

---

37   Betty Makin, quoted in Mitchell, *The Matriarchs*, 46–47.
38   *SMH*, 24 August 1937, 11; 27 August 1937, 12; City of Sydney, 'History of Erskineville Oval', 27 October 2016, www.cityofsydney.nsw.gov.au/learn/sydneys-history/people-and-places/park-histories/erskineville-oval, accessed 18 October 2018; Betty Makin, 'Betty Makin's Redfern', Documentary for CTV1, DarrenGrayManagement, uploaded to YouTube, 17 July 2011, in two parts, youtu.be/rY9PEHAqDGo and youtu.be/tYtTu2S9Auo, accessed 18 October 2018.
39   *SMH*, 20 July 1939, 11; *Barrier Miner* (Broken Hill), 20 July 1939, 5; *Wellington Times*, 20 July 1939, 1; *Dubbo Liberal and Macquarie Advocate*, 20 July 1939, 1.

Figure 3.2: Erskineville was a working-class industrial suburb that had been badly affected by the Depression.

This Fairfax photograph from 1939 gives a glimpse of the environments faced by many of Lucy's pupils. 'Backyards in Erskineville in Sydney's inner-west, 15 December 1939'.

Source: Metro Media, *Sydney Morning Herald* picture by Tom Fisher, FXB306610.

She pointed out that she had been witness to the conditions in Erskineville in the past seven years as headmistress of the Erskineville Public School, saying she was appalled that any children should have to live under these conditions of poverty in any country calling itself a democracy. Erskineville had the highest birth rate in New South Wales and, therefore, she claimed, its need for redress should be prioritised over other districts. Like Betty Makin, she used shoes as a symbol of distress to explain the corroding effects of poverty. The press reported:

> [Lucy] felt hurt when she offered a child in her school second-hand clothing, a child denied good boots and wool clothing. You could not get a first-class personality out of second-hand clothing and she felt that, while alleviating the child's distress, she was destroying its pride.[40]

---

40   *SMH*, 20 July 1939, 11.

Following this meeting, she spoke on national radio on 28 August 1939 in 'Slum Clearance and its Problems', the first of an Australian Broadcasting Commission (ABC) series called 'Burning Questions' in which speakers first spoke separately on opposing sides of various arguments and then in debate. The ABC hoped to make radio interactive by encouraging groups of listeners to take up contentious issues. Lucy's speech, 'Living in the Slums', drew directly on her knowledge of Erskineville. A week later, N.H. Dick spoke on 'Housing Reform – the problem surveyed'. The next week the two speakers met to discuss 'What should we do first?' and answer each other's questions.[41]

Lucy's concerns with the overcrowded and impoverished state of housing in Erskineville led to her determination that public education for working-class children should take place in surroundings that were both safe and beautiful, to stimulate a desire for learning. She wanted children to value their education and enjoy their time at school. She wanted above all 'to give the working man's child a chance to be educated'.[42]

Lucy's views on the importance of the physical environment had been shaped both by her teaching experience and also from the ideas she encountered from R.F. Irvine's work in urban design, the influence of the New Education Fellowship (NEF) and the Children's Library movement (see Chapter 4) and, perhaps, above all by her many close friendships with creative artists.[43] She wanted to improve urgently the physical environment of public schools not only so working-class children would value their education, but also so its value would be better recognised by outsiders.

---

41 *SMH*, 9 August 1939, 10; 23 August 1939, 9. The second and third 'Burning Questions' were to be 'Defence vs Social Services' and 'Australia and the Refugees'. This was clearly the forerunner of the ABC program of today known as *Q&A* that uses email and twitter as well as audiences to bring questions to the speakers as well as to make a running commentary on the points raised. The *Daily Mercury* in Mackay, Queensland, carried a report on 29 August 1939 (p. 9) but only repeated the earlier ABC press release about the overall series, making no comment on the first event, Lucy's talk, which had gone to air the night before.
42 *Education*, 28 January 1939, 76.
43 Rah Fizelle, Thea Proctor and George Lambert were close friends whom Lucy spoke of during her interview with Bruce McFarlane, the biographer of R.F. Irvine. McFarlane, pers. comm. to Heather Goodall, 8 August 2015.

As Lucy explained in a speech about 'Education for the Future' in Wollongong on August 1938, the consequences of failing to improve school environments were dire. The only way to ameliorate this was to improve the standard of living and eliminate poverty. Her warning was stark:

> War hangs over us – poverty breeds war.[44]

Earlier in 1938, the Department of Education had appointed Lucy and Rev. C.T. Parkinson, a fellow NEF member and former principal of the King's School Parramatta, to inspect NSW schools. She communicated her findings to a number of key meetings. In June, at a Sydney meeting of the NEF, Lucy described the positive effect that pieces of pottery, pictures, paintings of the school and strips of garden had on the children of Erskineville Public School. 'Sydney schools had not been planned as schools', she said. 'Winds swept through them, and sunshine never reached many classrooms. Their builders had looked for flat pieces of land, not sites for schools. If they had been planned there would have been no trouble about heating them in winter.'[45]

Lucy believed that children needed to respond emotionally to school buildings. Many playgrounds were small and made of asphalt without grassy spaces where children could play comfortably. Lucy's ideal school had unique characteristics as well as ample space for recreation and sport with trees and gardens. It would be the centre of its students' lives and have no more than 600 children. She considered the current classrooms too small and hoped that, in future, since children and teachers spent so much time in schoolrooms, that they would be planned by the best architects. Walls and floors should be painted in restful colours to give ease and comfort, not in the common, cold and uninviting grey prevalent in NSW classrooms. She thought that school desks were relics of the past and commented favourably on the Canadian movable desk, which she thought might well be copied in Australia. She wanted most of the heavy schoolroom furniture to be scrapped and schoolroom material stored in presses. She was certain that children, once introduced to beautiful rooms with curtains, bright pottery, surrounded by gardens, would react favourably to such an environment. According to her, every school should possess an adequate assembly hall, rooms for music, art, physical culture

---

44   *Illawarra Mercury*, 30 September 1938, 3.
45   *SMH*, 28 June 1938, 11.

and toilet requisites.⁴⁶ It was around this time that Lucy planted an oak tree in the otherwise barren playground of Erskineville Public School to provide the students with some shade.⁴⁷

At the August 1938 Wollongong session of the Teachers Federation Conference on Education for a Progressive, Democratic Australia, Lucy introduced a successful motion:

> That the conference is in favour of (1) provision of properly equipped playing fields with an appropriate area with the view to possible expansion; (2) provision of gymnasia in all schools for recreation and for general physical training; (3) provision of suitable public playing spaces, especially [in] congested areas; (4) provision of satisfactory sport equipment in all schools; (5) training of special teachers for physical training; (6) provision of adequate facilities for training of children in hygienic practices, provision of hygienic sanitary accommodation and disposal of garbage (school); (7) appointment of permanent regional medical staffs to include doctors, dentists, nurses and the necessary clerical assistance for them; (8) erection of buildings to accord with modern educational standards, on suitable sites, and the provision of up-to-date equipment, including text books, materials and libraries.⁴⁸

In speaking to this motion, she stressed that standards of living had to rise to ameliorate the malnutrition of children:

> **War hangs over us – poverty breeds war.** In an industrial community such as the one in which they were situated, they should conserve and preserve their rights to a decent standard of living. They should agitate for improved conditions at their schools. They should insist on 10 acres as a playing area, not the two acres as at present exists in the metropolitan area, where children cannot run – all they can do is stand and stare. Schools should be equipped with up-to-date furniture, with new type of classrooms.⁴⁹

---

46   *Newcastle Morning Herald and Miners' Advocate*, 9 August 1938, 5.
47   Gloria Phelan, *Women in Action in the Federation: A Series of Articles* (Sydney: NSW Teachers Federation, 1981), 8.
48   *Illawarra Mercury*, 30 September 1938, 3.
49   Ibid. (emphasis added).

Mr E.C. Barton, who seconded the motion, agreed: 'An education system should be devised which would train the child to live usefully and happily, and no child could so live without a strong body.'[50]

Some have argued that the attention paid by Lucy[51] and others to school conditions and equipment diverted the NSW Teachers Federation from its campaign for improved wages and broader social change.[52] Lucy's career, however, demonstrates that she was driven by her passion for equity for working-class schools and progressive education so as to shape active, independently minded citizens. Her campaign was not just to end hunger for food but to give working-class people – and children – access to safety, space and beauty, to the high-quality and inspirational learning environments available to the wealthy.

---

50   Ibid.
51   The editorial of *Education* in January 1938 was almost identical, word for word, to a number of her speeches, suggesting she had taken a major hand in its drafting.
52   John Michael O'Brien, 'The NSW Teachers Federation, 1957–1975' (PhD thesis, University of Wollongong, 1985), 121–22.

4
Love

Lucy's campaigns were never just about abstract principles. She seemed to others to be very single-minded: as Dymphna Cusack remembered her, Lucy was a tenacious battler for social justice. Faith Bandler laughed when she recalled Lucy in 1956, when Pearl Gibbs had asked her to chair the meeting that formed the Aboriginal-Australian Fellowship (AAF). Lucy, Faith said, 'was a woman who knew how to conduct a meeting. And how! She would rule with an iron rod'.[1]

Yet for all her toughness, Lucy was a warm and good-humoured friend to those who got to know her in the 1920s, like her activist fellow teacher Sam Lewis and her old Sydney University lecturer Robert Irvine.[2] Lucy had certainly grown more reserved over time – and perhaps became more cautious when she had to take on the role of headmistress. Certainly the elderly men who had been small boys at Erskineville in the 1930s still remember Lucy as a formidable, authoritarian figure.[3] But some students, particularly among the girls, became aware of Lucy's softer side. This chapter draws on their memories. Betty Makin was one student who got to know Lucy in the late 1930s, along with Ruth Fink about the same

---

1   Faith Bandler, interview with Carolyn Craig, 2016, Session 10, Transcript, State Library of NSW.
2   Sam Lewis, retirement testimonial speech, December 1953, UAW Files, AU NBAC Z236, Box 32, NBABL; Irvine in *The Midas Delusion* (Adelaide: self-published, printed by Hassell Press, 1933), 1–11; Michael Roe, *Nine Australian Progressives: Vitalism in Bourgeois Social Thought 1890–1960* (St Lucia: University of Queensland Press, 1984), 275.
3   *Back to Erskineville*, video recordings, 2007, Sean Macken; Ruth Fink Latukefu, interview with Heather Goodall, 3 September 2015.

time, while Beverley Langley (now Bates) came into the school during the war years of the early 1940s, which for many like her family, with her father serving overseas, were just as hard as the Depression had been in the 1930s. Judith Mitchell (now Emmett) was there only a little afterwards, attending the Opportunity Class.

So this chapter is about Erskineville Public School and Lucy's 20 years there from 1933. It is a history of the affection and emotions that Lucy felt towards her students and their families – but seldom showed. This chapter also offers a glimpse of Lucy's private life, the side of herself that she sheltered so carefully.

Erskineville on the line

Lucy, as we have seen in the previous chapter, refused to leave Erskineville once she arrived as headmistress mid-year in 1933. Her experiences at Erskineville infused every public intervention Lucy made for those 20 years – and beyond. It was how she measured all the calls she made for educational and social reform. How would these work – she would ask herself and her audiences – in Erskineville? In the 1940s, when Lucy was more often speaking at national meetings of teachers, rather than to those within the NSW Teachers Federation, her public statements became broader and more applicable to both rural and inner-city schools – and sometimes to those overseas. So she mentioned the name of Erskineville less often, but the themes and principles about which she talked were all drawn from her close experience of the tough life of Erko.

Erskineville was not only a working-class school, which is where Lucy's interest lay, but it also came to fill an emotional gap for her. It was on tram and train lines linking her mother's home at Enfield, where she lived for much of the 1930s, with the flat Lucy had rented in the artists' block at 215A George Street, the block where her friends like Rah Fizelle, Robert Irvine and his daughter also lived. As an old friend, Lucy kept an eye on Irvine in his later years, until his death in 1941. This George St block contained the flats of so many members of the bohemian network with whom Lucy had become involved over her time at university that she felt at home there.[4] The Enfield family home had become increasingly empty. Lucy's mother died in 1941 and then her sister Jane died soon after, at just 46, in 1942. So, at the same time as Erskineville School was absorbing more of her time, the George St flat became her main home. This was where she met friends in later years and held meetings for the organisations she championed like the New Education Fellowship.[5] It was here too, around Lucy's small kitchen table, that Pearl Gibbs gathered the activists like Faith Bandler to form the AAF in 1956.

While Lucy brought her experiences from London, Cessnock and Darlington, she learned much in Erskineville, particularly about the women in the working-class community who were struggling with severe overcrowding and poverty. She became aware of the exhaustion of many women – there seemed to be few reliable ways of controlling the arrival of babies. Making ends meet with large families was hard enough even when there was work – but in the Depression it was next to impossible. Poverty and its accompanying problems like illness, malnutrition and, in some cases, domestic violence stalked the families of Lucy's students as she was very aware. Teachers, if they are taking notice, have a bird's eye view not only of the young students in their classes but of the families in which they live. Lucy was taking notice.

Girls, pupils and mothers

There are few glimpses of any earlier interactions Lucy might have had with her pupils – just a fragment in a letter from a child at Lidcombe, another inner-Sydney suburb, where Lucy had taught in 1916. Ten-year-old Nora Dalton wrote her first letter to an editor, 'Uncle Jeff' of the children's page, in the *Albury Banner and Wodonga Express* to which her own uncle subscribed. Nora wrote:

---

4   In the 1930s, 215A George St was a centre for Sydney artists including Grace Crowley, Rah Fizelle and the Hinders. Both Robert Irvine and his daughter Ysobel Irvine were artists, and Ysobel was also a voluntary worker with the Children's Library movement, connecting her with Elsie Rivett. Will Ashton, another co-signatory on the Erskineville lease with Lucy and Elsie, was also an artist, a Director of the NSW Art Gallery, and in 1944–47 was Director of David Jones Art Gallery. When Will was Director of the NSW Art Gallery, Jessie Street became president of the NSW Art Gallery Women's Auxiliary Committee (1937). Will Ashton also organised children's art exhibitions. Mary Alice Evatt took art classes with Grace Crowley and Rah Fizelle, and in 1943 became the first woman to become a trustee of the NSW Art Gallery.
5   Obituary, *New Era: The World Education Fellowship Journal* 49, no. 8 (September/October 1968): 229.

> I go to school at Lidcombe and I am in the fourth-class. I like school very much and I will be ten in May. My teacher's name is Miss Woodcock and she is very nice.[6]

But for Betty Makin, who came to Erskineville in the girls' high school in the mid-1930s, Lucy offered constant support and encouragement. Betty remembered Lucy this way:

> My teacher, Miss Lucy Woodcock, had a great influence on my life. In my first year of High School (around 1935) she was the Head of the Teachers' Federation in New South Wales. She taught us girls we must always stand up for ourselves. The greatest thing I remember is her saying that men were no different. In fact, they weren't as clever as us! That we were the ones who have the babies and rear them with no training and we are the clever ones. She used to instill that. She was a gorgeous lady. I think she got the idea by seeing so many downtrodden women in our area. Every woman you saw had a baby on her hip.[7]

Betty described her memories as an older sister in a family with nine children:

> I loved where we lived … you could never be lonely. We were all allocated our own babies. My eldest sister had the first boy and I had the next, and so on. We adored them … When we played, we always had a baby on the hip, but it didn't matter because so did everyone else. That's how our mothers managed. They would never have been able to light their fuel stove or cook their tea with all those screaming kids around. When I was about thirteen or fourteen, Mum had the third youngest so I had to leave school and look after all the others …[8]

As an adult, however, Betty had reflected on all the families she knew there:

> When I was growing up, the average family was nine or ten. I don't know whether there was any contraception or not. People didn't talk about it. Even if they had known a doctor who would abort them, they didn't have the money. I'm not saying it wasn't going on but if they had it done, it would have been from a loan and by the time they'd paid it off, they'd be pregnant again.[9]

---

6   *Albury Banner and Wodonga Express*, 21 April 1916, 12.
7   Betty Makin, quoted in Susan Mitchell, ed., *The Matriarchs: Twelve Australian Women Talk about Their Lives* (Ringwood, Vic.: Penguin, 1987), 46.
8   Ibid., 47.
9   Ibid., 49.

Betty's experience reflected the lives of many of Lucy's students and the families she met as she got to know the area – and the need to put power over family planning into the hands of women became a continuing campaign for her. It was Lucy's immersion in the community life around Erskineville that lay behind many of her union speeches and media interviews over the next two decades. She tried to protect the education of older girls by calling for the state to raise the leaving age and increase child endowment so mothers could afford child care outside the family. Just as persistently, she demanded sex education for all children and especially for girls. As we shall see, this concern continued in very practical ways into the future.

Beverley Langley was born in 1942 and came to the school as a child much younger than Betty Makin had been. Beverley lived near the school in Lord Street and then in John Street, Erskineville. She was enrolled in the primary school in the mid-1940s and has warm memories of Lucy:

> She was one of the kindest, most beautiful women and I'm not just saying that! A lot of kids don't like their teacher but she was loved because of her attitude and the help she used to give people. It was hard times, it was through the war and she was nothing to give kids a bit of fruit or bring them a banana …[10]

Erskineville had residents of many different backgrounds with a number of Aboriginal families sending their children to the school, as can be seen from the year photos of the '30s and '40s.[11] One of Beverley's friends, for example, was Virginia Watton, photographed with Beverley in 1947. Beverley remembered Lucy's repeated teaching to all the children: 'Everyone's the same. You're born the same, you die the same and you don't have privileges of what colour your skin is.'[12] Beverley recalled that Lucy would encourage children to share lunches with any other child who needed extra at lunchtimes, including those from other cultures; where any child was in need, Lucy herself 'would slip a penny or a halfpenny for a piece of fruit'.[13]

---

10   Beverley Bates (née Langley), interview by the authors, 1 September 2016, Rathmines, NSW.
11   See Erskineville Public School Parents and Citizens's Association Facebook pages, especially the History of Erskineville Public School Facebook page, www.facebook.com/ErkoSchoolHistory/.
12   Beverley Bates, interview, 1 September 2016.
13   Beverley Bates, contribution to History of Erskineville Public School Facebook page, www.facebook.com/search/top/?q=History%20of%20Erskineville, accessed 11 August 2016.

Figure 4.1: Class 2C, 1947, in which Beverley Bates (née Langley) is front row (marked with cross) and Virginia Watton is in the second row, just behind and to Beverley's right.
Source: Erskineville Public School Parents and Citizens's Association and Beverley Bates's personal collection.

Lucy was involved with Aboriginal families as well as their children, as Jack Horner remembered. The relationships Lucy built up at Erskineville with Aboriginal adults were the foundation of her friendship with Pearl Gibbs, leading to Pearl's confidence in asking Lucy to chair the inaugural AAF meeting. Horner recalled that Lucy had assisted Aboriginal family members wanting to learn to read and other skills to go to the Cleveland Street school's adult education programs.[14] Such a relationship is suggested in one of the few items that Lucy kept throughout her life: it was a Christmas card from 'the Watton family' in 1955.[15]

Beverley also appreciated Lucy's attention to the girls' sense of dignity:

> As we got older and grew into young ladies she used to call us 'Miss' because by that time the boys were over in another part of the school. So I was 'Miss Langley' or the other one would be 'Miss Virginia Watton'. So it was really nice the things that she'd done for us.[16]

---

14 Jack Horner, *Seeking Racial Justice: An Insider's Memoir of the Movement for Aboriginal Advancement, 1938–1978* (Canberra: Aboriginal Studies Press, 2004), 18.
15 Held in Lucy Woodcock papers, courtesy of Kit Edwards, who was tutored for his matriculation by Lucy in the last years of her life.
16 Beverley Bates, interview, 1 September 2016.

Learning, class and curriculum

As headmistress, Lucy's role included oversight of the Opportunity Classes (OC) for gifted children in years 5 and 6 (senior primary), which had started at Erskineville in 1932 under Harold Wyndham, for children 'who are specially picked by psychologists' (that is, with IQ testing), but 'only after qualifying in scholastic tests'. Lucy described Erskineville as an experimental school and publicly promoted the OC classes there, believing that there was no sign of the children being pushed or crammed, and that their keenness was greater through being trained in a group in which no one lagged behind. She saw cooperation as the aim:

> With the abolition of competition as an important object, a new aim was a co-operation between the pupils for the betterment of the group, with each child striving for honours in subjects [for the whole group] instead of for top place.[17]

At the same time, Lucy was vehemently opposed to the tests known as the 'primary final', which all students had to take at the end of Year 6 before progressing to secondary school. These tests graded the children and determined which type of secondary school they could attend – an 'academic' school at which they could go on to matriculate for university or a 'technical' high school, from which graduates would go to apprenticeships (if they were boys) or vocational training. Optimistically, Lucy declared: 'We hope that 1936 will see the end of the primary final as we know it.'[18]

Throughout the 1930s, Lucy argued that changes needed to be made to the school curriculum to bring it more in line with modern educational theories and so better equip children for a changing world. She had developed her interests in emerging educational ideas in the 1910s as a new, young teacher. Her exchange teaching deepened her experience with progressive education – that is, 'child-centred' learning, led by the interests of the children who were pupils, rather than by a set curriculum. The London County Council, which managed the inner-city schools where she worked in 1927, had embraced progressive education and in their schools Lucy could explore how the methods worked. In London too she was able to see more of the New Education Fellowship (NEF),

---

17 'Women's World', *Courier Mail* (Brisbane), 9 January 1935, 19.
18 *Newcastle Sun*, 16 December 1935, 7.

about which there were regular reports in the Teachers Federation journal *Education*. The NEF had been founded in 1921 by Beatrice Ensor, a Theosophist and public school inspector, and the NEF exhibited the Theosophical interest in cultural openness as well as the student-centred and experiential learning advocated by Dewey and others. The NEF nurtured many of the innovative educational approaches influential in later decades, including A.S. Neill's *Summerhill*. Ensor's own and Theosophy's international interests ensured the organisation expanded; it later became known as the World Education Fellowship.[19] In the London working-class schools in which Lucy taught in 1927, it was the attention focused on the needs of each child – whether they were from impoverished families or were gifted or had disabilities or other special needs – which she had praised and hoped to replicate.

Lucy's interest in progressive education had motivated her on her return from the United Kingdom. For many in Australia, however, the expression of 'progressive education' was most evident in private schools, such as Frensham, an innovative but expensive school set up in the Southern Highlands of New South Wales. At Frensham, Winifred West and Phyllis Clubbe were able to explore ideas about creative, child-centred education that drew heavily from the NEF and other movements of progressive education in the UK. Winifred West was aware that one of the strong influences in the NEF was that of Theosophy, with its interest in Indian religion, and one of her closest lifelong friends was Pramila Chaudhuri (née Bannerjee), whom she had met at university, then visited in India in 1921 and 1931, travelling with her to Russia in 1935. Lucy, too, would have been aware of the strong links that the NEF had with Theosophy and with India. Throughout the 1920s, the NEF had had a regular column in *Education* in which Theosophists like George Arundale wrote frequently about India.

But unlike the private school site chosen by West and Clubbe for their exploration of progressive education, Lucy was primarily interested in how all of these ideas might be enacted in public schools, catering for children from all social sectors, but particularly for those from working-class communities.

---

19 Christopher Clews, 'The New Education Fellowship and the Reconstruction of Education: 1945 to 1966' (PhD thesis, Institute of Education, University of London, 2009).

Lucy felt that 'children were not being given their rights. Education had not made any great progress in the last 50 years, except in the case of a privileged few'.[20] She argued that curricula should be child-centred rather than subject-focused, providing continuous growth for children to develop. She also believed that there should be more art, music, handwork and literature in the public school curriculum.

At the same time, Lucy wanted schools to teach children to recognise and analyse the contemporary realities of their everyday world. So she argued that the school curriculum should set out key facts and interpret the chief features of Australian life, its resources and industries, but it also needed to provide opportunities for critical thinking. Politics, international history and elementary economics should be included. She believed that education should not stop once a student left school, therefore government commitment for training schemes for unemployed youths and the introduction of a scheme for adult education were essential.

What was so unusual about Lucy's position was that she insisted that such education initiatives should be applied to schools with working-class as well as more affluent populations. It was her trenchant defence of the right of working-class children to have access to the most advanced education that makes such a startling difference from the most usual application of 'Progressive' educational principles. She expressed her frustration to the students and their families, as Betty Makin has remembered:

> We knew that none of us could ever go to university – there was no subsidy then. Miss Lucy Woodcock said at a Mothers' Meeting one day that we were the brightest children and it was a tragedy that we wouldn't be able to advance ourselves through education. The brains were there but not the opportunities. I knew that you didn't have to just accept everything. You had to learn to ask the reason why.[21]

---

20   *Newcastle Morning Herald and Miners' Advocate,* 11 January 1935, 12.
21   Makin, in Mitchell, *The Matriarchs,* 50.

Progressive education in practice

Lucy was just as unusual in that she had a vision of how learning could take place in many venues and support many aspects of community life. She saw education in a holistic way, for the whole suburb, welcoming ventures that would offer support far beyond the school fence. In 1944, for example, an Erskineville YWCA Girls Club was established, the first decentralised YWCA club in Sydney, in the community hall of the Lady Gowrie Pre-school Child Centre. Lucy welcomed the club because it would 'provide a place where the girls could work together in a spirit of comradeship'. She was no doubt proud that many of the YWCA girls who organised the club had attended Erskineville Public School. Support came from the local mayor and council and the club organised physical culture classes and bushwalks.

She was still only new to the role as a headmistress when she arrived at Erskineville but it allowed her to consider how these ideas might be used to shape public education. At Erskineville Public School her determination to change educational practice could be united with her commitments to working-class education and to fostering girls' education and women's rights.

If children were to be encouraged to explore ideas and seek information by following their own interests it was necessary in the 1930s that they have access to books. The Children's Library and Craft Movement was the materialisation of this idea, first initiated in 1924 by Mary Matheson and her sister Elsie Rivett with a Children's Library in Surry Hills. Mary and Elsie were among the seven children of the Rev. Albert Rivett, a pacifist in World War I who had written often for the *Australian Worker*. All of the siblings were socially active, including the eminent scientist David and the teaching missionary Eleanor, whose work in India had moved her far closer to Indian nationalists and feminists than to her European missionary colleagues.[22] Elsie never married, remaining at Gordon in the family home, but spending much of her time in voluntary

---

22 Margaret Allen, 'Eleanor Rivett (1883–1972): Educationalist, Missionary and Internationalist', in *Women Leaders in Twentieth Century Australia*, eds Fiona Davis, Nell Musgrove and Judith Smart. Australian Women's Archives Project (Melbourne: eScholarship Research Centre, University of Melbourne, 2011), 45–63. Also at www.womenaustralia.info/leaders/fff/pdfs/rivett.pdf.

social work. While Mary was often a spokesperson for the Children's Library, their father regarded Elsie as the key mover in establishing the movement. In 1939, he wrote about Elsie as his 'talented daughter':

> whose activities on behalf of the mostly slum children of Surry Hills has been so fine that she is regarded as a fairy godmother. She is responsible for the establishment of the Children's Library, with its Art and Craft Club, at 119 Devonshire Street — a club that is unique because it is the first of its kind in Australia. In this club, week by week, hundreds of youngsters are creatively busy, and their work is both constructive and educative. In connection with this library there is a Children's Holiday Home, 'Popoorokh,' at Point Clare, in which many a Surry Hills boy and girl has spent a never-to-be-forgotten holiday-time.[23]

Despite their interest (and the family resources), the Surry Hills Library languished through the 1920s and all but disappeared as the Depression took hold.

When Lucy Woodcock arrived at Erskineville in 1933, she surveyed the school's resources. There was little enough at the school and, in the poverty of the Depression, the surrounding community would struggle to nurture the imagination of the area's many children. Lucy saw the potential of the Surry Hills Library to offer the resources her Erskineville pupils – and indeed all working-class children – needed. The library would be separate from the NSW Government school system, but available to the whole community. With a vision very close to Lucy's own, Mary Matheson and Elsie Rivett had written about their hopes for the Children's Library in 1926:

> We are of no sect or creed, or perhaps, of all sects and creeds. Protestants, Catholics, Jews, children of any or no persuasion, and of as varying race, meet on the common basis of childhood's need. And that need is surely for conditions in which the inner promise of each may be so nurtured as to unfold most perfectly.[24]

---

23   'Rev. A. Rivett: 75th Birthday', *Australian Worker* (Sydney), 21 May 1930, 7, Point Clare was on Brisbane Waters, near Woy Woy.
24   Elsie Rivett and Mary Rivett, 'The Children's Library, Surry Hills', signed and handwritten summary, 1 March 1925, in Ida Brown's compilation of Rivett Family papers, SLNSW.

Figure 4.2: Elsie Rivett c. 1926, co-founder of the Erskineville Children's Club and Library and long-time Peace activist.
Source: Mitchell Library, SLNSW, Creative Leisure Movement papers, VII: History Files 1920–1991, MLMSS 7550/18/4, Photo album, File 3.

So Lucy made contact with the Rivetts, seeking not only for a new library to emerge at Erskineville, but also to strengthen the existing but moribund Children's Library organisation as a whole. In December 1934, the Children's Library movement was restructured to set it up more formally as the Creative Leisure Movement and to register it as a charity. Lucy became a Trustee, with Elsie Rivett and Charles Bertie, the Librarian of the Sydney Municipal Public Library.[25] In reaching out to the Rivetts, Lucy made another discovery. She met Elsie.

---

25   *SMH*, 12 October 1936, 8; 12 November 1936, 22. Bertie was appointed in 1909 as the Librarian of the Sydney Municipal Library, establishing there the first public lending library for children as well as his support as Trustee for the Children's Library service. He retired in 1939 and died in 1952.

Her posting to Erskineville had given Lucy a role not only in the school but also among the wider Depression-hit families of the suburb. And in Elsie, Lucy had found a partner for all her later work. Over many years, Elsie shared Lucy's passion for child-centred learning, for working people's rights and for the Peace movement. They worked together, first to find the location for what they called the 'Children's Library and Club', in a disused factory building at 16–20 Rochford St, Erskineville, which had a large area around it that could be turned into a playground. Lucy and Elsie leased the building together, with Charles Bertie formally involved although he was seldom there in person. The library was just a few blocks away from the public school – close enough to be handy for after-school activities, but deliberately very separate from the school environment. The library opening in October 1936 and its rapidly expanding membership of children over the next few months were featured in a number of newspaper articles with photos not only of its children but also of the murals donated to the new library by design diploma students from East Sydney Technical Colege, who painted in modernist style – and often with Australian Aboriginal themes.[26] When the third and fourth children's libraries were established in Phillip Street in the city and then in Woolloomooloo, the photographs were often still taken at Erskineville Library. A spread in the 29 November 1947 issue of *Pix* featured a marvellous photograph of Beverley Langley reading a Girls' Annual, with other photographs of her friends including Virginia Watton.[27] Beverley remembered the library as a place to which the children would enjoy going after school and at which many of the activities she loved at school, like making up and performing plays, were continued, with puppets and lots of dressing up as well as making and decorating boxes for the puppet shows:

> That was one of our favourite things, the paper mash puppets, to paint them and then they'd let you take them home when they were all dry, you know … [We did] plays and they had boxes with clothes or curtains draped over them and that, you know, whatever they could, and decorate it and you got behind and you made up your little things. Oh yes, my word![28]

---

26   *SMH*, 9 October 1936, 12 October 1936, 12 November 1936, 13 February 1937, 16 June 1937, 2 November 1937, 1 June 1944, 20 December 1951; *Telegraph* (Brisbane), 30 December 1936.
27   *Pix* (Sydney), 29 November 1947, 3–5; Photo of Beverley reprinted, with slightly wider crop, in the *Sun* (Sydney), 13 March 1950, 10.
28   Beverley Bates, interview, 1 September 2016.

CHILDREN roll up to centre the moment it opens. Erskineville gets no financial support towards rental and salaries from local authorities, badly needs funds.

Figure 4.3: The Children's Club and Library on Rochford St, Erskineville, which Lucy helped to establish and of which she was a co-director.
Source: *Pix*, 19(48), 29 November 1947, p. 4. Trove, National Library of Australia.

4. LOVE

NEW MEMBER Dick Innes seems doubtful about something as Mrs. P. L. Renton "signs him up" at Erskineville centre, where these pictures were taken. Children attend library in age groups — boys 6-14; girls 6-14; boys and girls 12-15.

Figure 4.4: Children at the Children's Library, including Beverley's friend Virginia Watton in the middle.

The Watton family sent Lucy a Christmas card in 1955.

Source: *Pix*, 19(48), 29 November 1947, p. 4. Trove, National Library of Australia.

Figure 4.5: Beverley Bates from the *Pix* story about the Children's Library.
Source: *Pix*, 19(48), 29 November 1947, p. 3. Trove, National Library of Australia.

Mary Matheson explained to the *Sydney Morning Herald* in November 1937 that:

> The club is in no sense a school. Children go there with a sense of freedom and as individuals. They go into an atmosphere of freedom and mutual consideration in which the heavy hand of the school has no part. They read the books which would never have found a way into their homes, play games, listen to stories being read and gather in small circles to learn useful crafts … some of the older children who have been attracted to the clubs by the arts and crafts activities, and would ordinarily never read, have developed a genuine taste for reading.[29]

Drawing a very direct link with the NEF, which had brought a number of overseas speakers to contribute to a major conference in Australia earlier in the year (see Chapter 6), Matheson said:

> The Clubs supply the things which are so much a part of their [the children's] need. We are providing an essential service – not a charity. We are giving the children of poorer people the things which are theirs by right, but which are denied them by circumstances. Mrs Beatrice Ensor, when she was here for the Education Conference, declared that the movement provided exactly the type of new education in which she believed.[30]

Lucy and Elsie went on to share many interests over the years, including in particular the Peace movement's organisations. The series of meetings held to prepare an Australian Convention on Peace and War in 1953 was one example, where Elsie was a convenor and where Lucy took a key speaking role.[31] The NSW Peace Council, in which they were both involved, presented Lucy with an award at the end of that year for her tireless Peace work.[32] Although Lucy saw Elsie less often after her retirement in December 1953, they continued to work together in organisations such as the Australia–New Zealand Congress for International Cooperation

---

29   *SMH*, 2 November 1937, Women's Supplement 13.
30   Ibid.
31   *SMH*, 28 September 1953, 4; *Cessnock Eagle and South Maitland Recorder*, 17 November 1953, 3; Convention Flyer, for Elsie's and Lucy's roles. Reproduced at 'Australian Convention of Peace and War (1953)', *Reason in Revolt*, last modified 12 February 2007, www.reasoninrevolt.net.au/biogs/E000493b.htm, accessed 18 November 2018.
32   Unidentified and undated newspaper clipping (probably *Tribune* late 1953 or early 1954 as it refers to Lucy's retirement), Lucy Godiva Woodcock ASIO file, Vol. 1, f 120, A6119, 2030, NAA.

and Disarmament, where in 1959 Lucy was on the Education Committee and Elsie was on the Women's Committee.[33] Until her death in 1964, Elsie continued to be closely involved with Lucy in the activities that were central to Lucy's life, including those of International Women's Day.[34]

***

Lucy took the children on excursions to museums and art galleries, but she was particularly eager to encourage drama, despite the limited resources of the school. When Beverley remembered the children writing and performing their own plays, she pointed out that Lucy would often be directly involved:

> When we put on plays, there was one room up near the front of the school and all the old boards you'd get splinters off! It did have desks and that in there but that's where we went, sometimes all the desks would be put around in a circle at the end and you did your plays beside it, dress up in old clothes and whatever they could find in the toy box … We were taught to make up if we could but sometimes they'd be written down and you took from there but you were allowed to express yourself with it within a certain limit of course, but yeah she used to really like that. We used to do a lot of plays in one of the rooms there and she'd often come in and sit there and watch while we're practising or doing things. She loved seeing our school plays.[35]

Discipline and beyond

Erskineville Public School, like any public buildings, had no luxuries in the 1940s. It was heated by coal fires and Beverley remembered the daily routine of trying to make the rooms warm:

---

33   See letter from Elsie to Lucy, 8 February 1954, one of the few papers that Lucy kept until her death, Lucy Woodcock papers, courtesy Kit Edwards; Press Statement by Rev. A.M. Dickie, 4 June 1959, Victorian Peace Council Collection, Box 6, Folder 3, UMA/SC.
34   Joyce Stevens, 'The Nineteen Fifties and Sixties', in *A History of International Women's Day in Words and Images* ([Pennington, SA]: IWD Press, 1985), 15–26, and for Elsie's role as Guest of Honour at the 1957 IWD meeting, 20; *Tribune* (Sydney), 13 March 1957, 9.
35   Beverley Bates, interview, 1 September 2016.

> The old coal bins were under the school down where the infant school used to be, underneath the floorboards. You'd crawl in there and you fill up the little buckets. It took two to carry them and you'd take them up to the classroom so they could get the fires going. They had a chimney and like a grate-thing, some of the classrooms had the old fireplaces.[36]

It was not just the conditions that were hard. Lucy was strict – Beverley remembers that she would tell people 'quick smart' if they were doing what they shouldn't be doing, 'but she was still good. She wouldn't blame someone without getting to the bottom of the situation and she would look into it'.[37]

Teachers, however, regularly used the cane, which was then an expected form of discipline. Some were worse than others – one teacher who always had a reputation for painful canings eventually became severely disturbed. It was Beverley who caught the worst of it. She suffered a terrible beating from this woman who smashed her head against the blackboard. Beverley did not report the incident immediately, she was so injured she just tried to get home. She collapsed, however, on the way and had to be taken to hospital, where she was ordered to have complete bedrest for three months but then to return only to part-time schooling.

Beverley remembers that when Lucy had been informed, she had ensured the teacher was dismissed:

> She got expelled, when Miss Woodcock found out, I think it was only a few days and she got the education department and they'd come and expelled her for doing it. So I never, ever seen her again, that teacher.

> And after that, Miss Woodcock gave up her time of a day to come around home – she'd walk up despite her bad feet and her walking stick! – and sit on the side of my bed for a little while on the lunch hour.[38]

---

36 Ibid.
37 Ibid.
38 Ibid.

Beverley remembers Lucy to have visited frequently, indeed 'every couple of days', and then, when the child could return to school, Lucy had her sit in the head's office rather than in a classroom:

> When I went back to school she used to let me go up to the office and do my work up there. She caught me up for what I had missed while I was off. And she used to let me answer the phone, and that was a big privilege, you know! Or 'Go and make a cup of tea for the teacher', that was lovely! And she had a good sense of humour – sometimes she'd get really cross and in the middle of it she'd look over to me and give a little smile![39]

Jobs

From the time of her appointment at Erskineville, Lucy foregrounded local interests in her public statements. Employment was the most urgent of these issues for her students and their families in Erskineville so that Lucy raised it repeatedly. The survey Lucy and the Erskineville staff had done in 1934 had demonstrated that 60 per cent of the parents were dependent on the dole and that many of the children at the school were malnourished and without adequate clothing.[40] As she described it, Erskineville was an area 'in which casual labourers lived, and since the Depression, conditions had grown steadily worse. The older girls were kept from school, to look after the smaller ones while their mothers went to work'.[41]

In 1934, in protesting against the Public Service Salaries Reduction Act,[42] she reported to the national teachers' union, the Federated State School Teachers' Association (FSSTA) that schoolteachers at Erskineville Public School were already on miserable wages: 'I have girls on my staff living away from home who draw £3/18/ a fortnight! A waitress gets more.'[43]

---

39 Ibid.; Beverley Bates, contribution to History of Erskineville Public School Facebook page, www.facebook.com/search/top/?q=History%20of%20Erskineville, accessed 11 August 2016.
40 *Mercury* (Hobart), 11 January 1935, 11; *Northern Miner* (Charters Towers, Qld), 11 January 1935, 4. Both were quoting Lucy's speech at the FSSTA Annual Conference Brisbane.
41 'Peace Depends Upon Children', *SMH*, 13 August 1936, 17.
42 *Public Service (Salaries Reduction) Act 1930* (NSW).
43 *Glen Innes Examiner*, 16 August 1934, 10; *Daily Advertiser* (Wagga Wagga), 27 March 1936, 5.

She argued too that the government's economy measures were so severe that teachers were forced to buy materials for schools out of their own pockets.[44]

She saw the question of raising the school-leaving age again in terms of the local conditions, which were those faced not only in Erskineville in the 1930s but across Sydney. With a low school-leaving age, children were leaving school with little hope of finding long-term employment. If they got a job at all, they found they were badly paid as 'juniors' and then sacked as they grew just a few years older. Lucy argued that the goal of educational policy was the future well-being of the individuals and society, so that the cost of long schooling was not a problem if the outcome was a better-trained population. 'Cost alone', she told the FSSTA Conference in Brisbane, 'should not be considered so much as the right of the child'.[45]

Beverley Langley was one of the girls who saw Lucy put this concern into practice:

> Now when she got me my first job, I'll never forget it! I was at school and a lot of the children were leaving at 15, unless you were really clever and you wanted to go to another school. But otherwise you stayed there 'til, you know, 'til you finished. A couple of them were leaving and then also now I've got this idea. But she said, 'No, not unless you do something.' So she spoke to my mum and she said, 'Well leave it with me'. Then she came back one day and she said, 'I want you to come tomorrow for an interview to a shop in Newtown.' And Mum got ready and Miss Woodcock was there and we went up to this place, and I got a start within a few days. She gave me a lovely reference and I think Mum still had my reference. Yeah, even in that she put Miss Langley in the reference and, yeah, so it was lovely. And then after that I made quite a career in shopping. I worked at all those shops down there and I did a junior buyer's course, in those days you just didn't go and get behind a counter, you had to treat the people right, you know? So she gave me my first start as that.[46]

---

44   *SMH*, 2 April 1935, 11.
45   Ibid.
46   Beverley Bates, interview, 1 September 2016.

Figure 4.6: Beverley Bates (centre) shared her memories of Lucy and Erskineville in an interview for this project.
She is shown here with co-authors Helen Randerson and Devleena Ghosh.
Source: Heather Goodall.

Lucy had influenced the way young women saw themselves in the workplace, as Betty Makin remembered. As Lucy had said to the Mother's Club meeting mentioned by Betty Makin, there were few possibilities for young people in Erskineville or the suburbs around it. Betty remembered her first job, in a local factory, which was not so different to many other people's experiences:

> When I first went to work we weren't allowed to talk. And you weren't allowed to go to the toilet unless you asked the forelady who sat up in a box that was like a stage in the middle of the floor, looking over all of us all day. You had to ask her if it was all right to turn the machine off if you needed to go to the toilet. And on Friday, we had to scrub around the wooden floor where our machine was in our lunchtime which was half an hour.
>
> … My Dad was a real conservative. The boss could have stood on his neck and he would have said 'That was very nice of you to do that'. He called me a communist when I was thirteen because my ideas were different to his.
>
> … If the Union people came around they were told to get out. If anyone spoke to them, they'd be sacked. There would be three or four waiting to step into your job. I used to say to the other girls, 'We shouldn't have to do this'. I wanted to join the Union but if I'd been sacked, then Mum would have suffered. Miss Woodcock told me that Russia was a beautiful country and not to believe what I read in the papers. She said things weren't as bad in Russia as they wanted to you to believe. I knew things weren't too good where we were![47]

From Betty's retelling of this story in the 1980s, it may have been that she had consulted Lucy after she left school when she was on her first job. Or perhaps this was something Lucy had said while Betty was still enrolled. But in any case, Betty had embedded Lucy's words within her memories of the job. What had shaped Betty's working life had been Lucy's attitude to asserting workers' rights and to unions, in Australia as well as to Russia.

Lucy's interest extended even further. She was determined that girls get proper training and she had been concerned since her time at Grafton that girls did not receive the vocational training that boys received. Lucy's

---

47   Makin, in Mitchell, *The Matriarchs*, 49–50.

awareness of the very high rate of youth unemployment in Erskineville led to her increasing her efforts through the NSW Teachers Federation to lobby for more flexibility in available apprenticeship training. In the late 1930s, Lucy's efforts, together with Federation colleague Zillah Bocking, meant that the NSW Government finally introduced the Subsidised Apprenticeship Scheme for Unemployed Youths (19–25 Years) in February 1938. The government agreed to extend the age limit so as to allow young people in their 20s to gain an apprenticeship.[48]

Lucy was particularly concerned about young women's training in vocational and industrial skills. She spoke at the FSSTA conference in Melbourne in January 1934 of the importance of girls being able to access the equivalent of boys' training. Her comment that young girls were hired as waitresses without being able to balance a tray or remember two orders – since they were chosen, she said sarcastically, because of their 'physical qualifications' (that is, whether they were attractive) – caught the eye of journalists and so that became the headline. In fact, however, her main demand was for thoroughgoing training for girls in all trades, including those involved with waitressing like the sciences of hygiene and the crafts of cooking in restaurants:

> nothing had been done to train girls on a skilled basis for industrial and process work in factories. A man, she added, had five years' apprenticeship as a hairdresser, but for a girl only six months' training was necessary. Pre-vocational training at present was inadequate.[49]

Her role went further still. Lucy had first known Judith Mitchell, who grew up in Erskineville, when she became an OC student at Lucy's school in 1950. Judith had gone on to a selective secondary school in 1952, the same year the family moved from Chippendale to Belfield. At the end of her secondary schooling, Judith had won a highly competitive Teachers' College scholarship, which would have allowed her to attend Teachers' College, although the attached bond would be a formidable repayment if the student did not go on to teach. At the same time, Judith was offered an office job, an option that Judith's parents preferred, so she was not able to take up the scholarship.

---

48   *Catholic Press* (Sydney), 3 February 1938, 26; *Lithgow Mercury*, 21 February 1938, 2; *Singleton Argus*, 19 June 1939, 2.
49   *Kalgoorlie Miner*, 8 January 1934, 4; Melbourne Annual Conference of FSSTA.

At Belfield, Judith had met Isobel and Richard Woodcock, Lucy's brother. They invited Judith to visit their home during one of Lucy's visits because Lucy wanted to meet her again. Judith approached this meeting with uneasiness – long before, as a pupil at Erskineville, she had found Lucy an intimidating figure. During the visit, Lucy quizzed Judith about what she was doing now she had completed her Leaving Certificate. When Judith told her she was working in a shop, having not been able to take up the teaching training scholarship, Lucy snapped: 'That's nonsense!'

Judith wryly observed that Lucy 'had not lost any of her zing!'

Distressed to hear that Judith's opportunity would be lost, Lucy stepped in. Judith recalled her saying, 'Bring me the papers and I'll sign them and I'll pay the bond!' It was Lucy's sponsorship, along with the support of the Althorps, a couple whom Judith recalls had 'adopted' and mentored her over many years, that allowed Judith to study and work as a teacher. She went first to teach in the country, then later enrolled in university studies, by correspondence, and then graduated to a further long teaching career in adult education. Judith remembers Lucy – and the Althorps – to have been communists because of their strongly held left-wing views. Judith sums up Lucy overall as having 'always had a willingness to stand up for things that were not popular!'[50]

Lucy kept touch with many of her former students, not only Beverley and Judith. As late as 1959, she was writing to Rewi Alley asking him to look out for – and hopefully to employ – a young woman called Bonnie McDougall:

> She was at Erskineville and did very well in her Primary School and then obtained an excellent leaving certificate. She decided to go to Peking and I understand from folks that she is studying Chinese and hoping to attend University. She is really a fine lass and should be able to help you Rewi for she writes splendid English and has some imagination that should be a help.[51]

---

50 Judith Mitchell, now Judith Emmett, phone interview, 31 July 2017. Judith was – and remains – a very active Christian and she met Isobel and Richard Woodcock, and their son Barry, in the Belfield church after the family had moved from Chippendale to Belfield in 1952.
51 Lucy Woodcock to Rewi Alley, 3 April 1959, Rewi Alley Papers, MS-Papers-6533–307, NLNZ.

Erskineville after the war

In keeping with the high local birthrate, the numbers of children attending Erskineville Public School continued to grow during Lucy's time there. When she arrived in 1933, Lucy had been in charge of 400 girls – but by the late 1940s, she was supervising around 750 girls in her capacity as headmistress.

In an interview with a journalist from the *Tribune* in 1946, Lucy described her ideal school. This was 'a community centre type of school which would include a recreation hall, theatre, gymnasium, swimming baths, library and facilities for arts and crafts. Trained after-school staff would be needed to lead the children in their activities'. She added that:

> Child endowment stopped at 16, just when it was most needed by parents who wished to give their children added years at school. Organised nursing help for mothers was absolutely necessary if older children in large families were to be given a fair chance of extra schooling. Nursery schools for all children between two and five would also assist to free the older child, as well as benefiting the small children themselves.

Lucy noted that there were five hotels within a mile of Erskineville School, 'but in all Erskineville there is not a single building to provide club facilities for adolescents'.

The *Tribune* journalist observed that:

> A morning spent in Erskineville School was enough to show that in spite of its manifest handicaps of space and equipment and the usual dreariness of a school, it was already a worthwhile force in the community. The children were well and quietly spoken. During play-time there was noise, of course, but none of the yelling and bawling which could often be heard in the streets and in some homes. The school has its own library, which the parents have helped to build, and its own puppet theatre, for which the children write plays.[52]

Although Lucy contrasted the vast amount spent on alcohol with the inadequate amount spent on the education budget, she was broad-minded on a range of social issues, consistent with her continuing bohemian

---

52 *Tribune* (Sydney), 1 November 1946, 6.

interests. She had no objection to drinking in itself and she herself both drank alcohol and smoked. In 1946, long before the 1965 protest where women chained themselves to a bar to demand access to public bars in hotels, Lucy had demanded equality of opportunity in drinking for women. She had argued that women were either denied a drink or segregated in pokey and degrading 'Ladies Lounges'.[53]

In the 1940s, Lucy continued to promote progressive education reforms and the importance of education as a key to encouraging personal development, international cooperation and avoidance of war. In 1949 she commented:

> 'If civilisation is to be preserved and the present chaotic situation solved, education must play the leading role in society … In the past education has been allowed to take an insignificant part in human affairs. Education must take its part as the most powerful weapon man can devise to grapple with the situation. … The magnitude of the task should not daunt a society which could provide funds for the most deadly weapon ever invented – the atom bomb. The present age demanded that education must be provided, and that it be geared to meet modern requirements.'

> 'The school began its life cheaply, and unfortunately we have not yet emancipated ourselves from the tradition of educating "children on the cheap",' she continued. 'From an economic point of view this is short-sighted; for education, properly financed, is one of the most productive of all human activities and one which repays handsomely in dividends.'[54]

Throughout her time as headmistress at Erskineville, Lucy continued to advocate publicly for her local community and for a greater government commitment to education, while at school she tried to put into practice many of her strongly held ideas. She paid individual attention to students' needs and encouraged them according to their abilities, whether they were primary students, OC students or home science secondary students. If a child was not a native English speaker, Lucy provided additional assistance to help prepare them for high school.[55] When a child needed

---

53 *Tribune* (Sydney), 11 June 1946, 6.
54 Quoted in *Advocate* (Tasmania), 12 May 1949, 5.
55 Dr Ruth A. Fink Latukefu, pers. comm. to Heather Goodall, 1 September 2015. Dr Latukefu was the child of German Jewish refugees and her story will be told in more detail in the following chapter.

a reference to help find employment in a local factory, Lucy hand wrote a reference for them.[56] Where a child's handwriting was illegible and the child had a talent for writing, Lucy recommended the use of a typewriter.

One of the children for whom she did this was the brilliant investigative journalist Murray Sayle (1926–2010) – Lucy may have kick-started his career! Sayle's report 'Did Hiroshima End the War?' in the *New Yorker* magazine in 1995 on the 50th anniversary of the decision to drop atomic bombs onto Hiroshima and Nagasaki would have made Lucy very proud.[57] Gloria Phelan recorded in 1981 that local Erskineville residents who remembered Lucy characterised her as 'a fund of humanity but no nonsense'.[58]

In 1953, at Lucy's retirement, the Minister for Education Mr R.J. Heffron paid tribute to her work at Erskineville:

> The other night I was invited to go to Erskineville to a send-off Miss Woodcock was being given by the school in which she had laboured for 22 years. The greatest tribute of all was the large number of people assembled there. Miss Woodcock was not only an outstanding teacher, and outstanding headmistress; but her work did not end when the classes ended. During the dark days of the depression she built up a great reputation as a humanitarian, because many of the children living in that under-privileged area were very poorly fed and scantily clothed, and the local residents will tell you what she did by way of the provision of meals at the school, the provision of clothes to give some of the children something in addition to the education they were getting at school. No one will ever know how much came out of Lucy's own pocket to help the children of Erskineville at the time. Indeed her self-sacrifices did not stop here. Never a person to speak about her own troubles she was always ready to give of her time and experience to help others in their difficulties.[59]

---

56   Lucy G. Woodcock, reference written for Donna Hayward, 8 August 1952, reproduced for Erskineville School Parents and Citizens Association, at History of Erskineville Public School Facebook page, www.facebook.com/ErkoSchoolHistory, accessed 10 May 2016.
57   Ruth Fink Latukefu, pers. corr. to Heather Goodall, 1 September 2015. 'I know that Lucy rescued other young people, one of them a brilliant journalist Murray Sayle, who was allowed to use a typewriter because his handwriting was illegible.' Sayle, 'Did Hiroshima End the War?', *New Yorker*, August 1995; Hendrik Hertzberg, 'Remembering Murray Sayle', *New Yorker*, 23 September 2010.
58   Gloria Phelan, *Women in Action in the Federation: A Series of Articles* (Sydney: NSW Teachers' Federation, 1981), 8.
59   R.J. Heffron, retirement testimonial speech, December 1953, UAW Files, AU NBAC Z236, Box 32, NBABL.

When Sam Lewis spoke at Lucy's Teachers Federation testimonial, he also recounted the poignancy of that farewell at Erskineville School. Over 200 ex-students had attended but he had been most moved by seeing the students' mothers. Despite their severely limited financial means, the women of Erskineville had collected enough to give Lucy a beautiful pair of suitcases and a travel rug – symbolic both of their affection for her and of their insight into her intentions for her active future life. Sam continued:

> these things came from the people of Erskineville and this is because in her teaching career in Erskineville, and elsewhere, she has never been neutral. She has always been positive in her approach to education and other questions … She has always held up the lamp of education to the people of Erskineville and to the children wherever she has been. She has worked to raise the material and cultural standards of the people of Australia, including in the first place its children. She has striven for the organised action of teachers and people right to the end of her teaching career. She has been true to herself, her profession, her professional organisation, the Trades Union movement, the people of her district and to humanity itself![60]

---

60   Ibid.

5

Unity and Betrayal

This chapter turns from the close focus on Lucy's relationships to people and community at Erskineville to consider Lucy on what became the very public stage of state and national politics. The shift in Lucy's awareness to the importance of public campaigning, beyond the school grounds, which had begun in Cessnock in 1929, can be seen too in the way she responded to the political challenges of the Depression.

By the late 1920s, the NSW Teachers Federation was rising in influence and – at least for a time – in membership. Lucy had worked hard throughout the 1920s, advancing the cause of women teachers in public schooling, working closely with allies like Jess Rose, Hettie Ross and Beatrice Taylor while always considering the union as a whole. But as the Depression loomed, Lucy was working in the bush. She had felt the Depression earlier than her colleagues in the city, first in the grim conditions of Cessnock and then at Grafton Public School. She had developed a concern about the marginalisation of rural schools and the failure to admit girls to agricultural training that lasted throughout her later city postings. In her national role as president of the Federated State School Teachers' Association, she frequently raised the needs of rural schools for more attention, better funding and more appropriate training for teachers.[1]

---

1   *Education*, 8 December 1932, 50.

Pay cuts

From 1929, the city too began to feel the impact of the global financial collapse. As economic pain spread, the old antagonism towards married women teachers began to resurface. Lucy's commitment to the recognition of women teachers had been unswerving. In 1920 the NSW Arbitration Courts had set the pay of women teachers at 80 per cent of that of a male teacher for the same work. Nevertheless, the Teachers Federation policy of Equal Pay for Equal Work – agreed in 1920 (after a major struggle by women teachers) – was held intact. Lucy had continued to support this Equal Pay policy within the Federation, demanding not only equal pay but better training and real career paths for women as assistants and as senior teachers. This tenacity of hers had been a key factor in fighting off the challenges to the Federation's policy of Equal Pay in 1921 and 1925.[2] Not only had she led the mobilisation on the floor of the Federation's Annual Conference, but she had been a key element in the resistance on the Federation Executive to the headmasters' attempt to undermine the pay claims by headmistresses (of infants' schools) in 1927.[3] Lucy's strong commitment to this issue was shared by a number of women teachers, some in the Communist Party of Australia like Hettie Ross and many others outside it, including Margaret Kent-Hughes, Beatrice Taylor, Rose Symonds, Ruth Lucas, Jess Rose, Margaret Swann, Clarice McNamara and Elizabeth Fordyce. All of them had acted many times through the 1920s to defend the hard-won Federation policy calling for Equal Pay.

As the Bavin-led conservative NSW Government struggled through the first months of the Depression, pay cuts for everyone became a reality. The NSW *Public Service (Salaries Reduction) Act 1930* cut all public service wages and brought the wages of teachers into line with those of the rest of the public sector, which meant in effect that the earlier guarantee that the pay level of women teachers would be 80 per cent of that of a male teacher, which had been won in 1920, was overridden. From June 1930, women teachers were only guaranteed 54 per cent of the wages of male teachers for the same work.[4]

---

2   Bruce Mitchell, *Teachers, Education and Politics: A History of Organisations of Public School Teachers in New South Wales* (St Lucia: University of Queensland Press, 1975), 57–59.
3   Mitchell, *Teachers, Education and Politics*, 59. Lucy as vice president had been on the Executive 1924–27.
4   *Education*, 8 December 1932, 50; *SMH*, 20 December 1932, 9; *Maitland Daily Mercury*, 10 January 1933, 8.

Unionists' betrayal

To make matters worse, talk of forcing married women teachers out of the NSW service re-emerged. Teachers were seen as receiving a relatively high salary and there were certainly many others who were far worse off. But the rising anxiety among teachers that they too would face further cuts in pay and dismissal had a number of contradictory effects.

The Educational Workers' League (EWL) – associated with Communist Party members like Sam Lewis, Hettie Ross, Ethel C. Teerman and (later) Harry Norington but also with labour activists like Beatrice Taylor – initially took an uncompromising stand against all pay cuts. Consisting of only a few members, the EWL was a minority group, but it worked effectively through the Men's Assistants' Association to put its views forcefully before Federation Council and campaigned strongly against the Bavin Government. Two of its number – Sam Bendeich and Alf Paddison, both Federation members – had stood for parliamentary election in November 1930, and the Teachers Federation campaigned for them.[5] The Women Assistant Teachers' Association, the body with which Lucy, Beatrice Taylor and, in later years, Hettie Ross were associated, took a more cautious stand at this stage, criticising the Federation for circulating 'political propaganda' in the election campaign.[6] Nevertheless, they campaigned strongly against the pay cuts. Taylor had been increasingly recognised in the Federation, serving as one of four vice presidents from 1921 to 1933 but elected as senior vice president for a year in 1929. Lucy adhered to R.F. Irvine's economic arguments at this time, which opposed the austerity measures of Bavin and the banks and, instead, supported the expansionary strategies advanced by Keynes and others. This view was seen as being close to the policies of Lang's state Labor opposition to Bavin's government.

The election of November 1930 had resulted in a landslide victory for Lang, who argued against austerity cuts and was for a time strongly supported across the political spectrum. His government went on famously to challenge the demands of English banks (and the Commonwealth Government) by defaulting on the interest on loans owed by the state. In a tone more aligned to an austerity agenda, however, Lang's Education

---

5   Mitchell, *Teachers, Education and Politics*, 94–95.
6   Ibid., 95.

Minister William Davies had barely assumed office before he announced in December 1930 that he would take up the suggestion put to him by senior public servants that the government should dismiss women teachers if they married employed husbands, so as not to unfairly increase the income of their families. This echoed the call made in 1911 by another Labor minister, G.S. Beeby, that his new government would dismiss married women teachers.[7] Just as in the 1910s, there were immediate responses, from both male and single women teachers within the Teachers Federation, who agreed with the minister. Beatrice Taylor, Ettie Cunningham (soon to marry Sam Bendeich) and Lucy Woodcock (who was still at Grafton) argued at the annual Federation Conference in December 1931 that it was unfair for married women teachers to be dismissed, but a series of male Federation members contended that such a policy would 'solve the problem of employment for many young Australians'.[8]

Lang later suggested this policy had never been considered seriously by his government, but Davies's statement had drawn so much support within the Teachers Federation itself that it was regarded as a real threat by many. Just like the earlier challenges to the NSW Teachers Federation's Equal Pay platform, in 1921, 1925 and 1927, this reactivation of the threat to married women teachers' work demonstrated that many men – and some women – within the Federation were broadly opposed to the rights of women.

Lucy was to demonstrate in later years how deeply she understood the labour movement – she could brief Rewi Alley in the 1950s on the ALP and trade union delegations to China by giving him the most minute details of labour leaders' voting histories, their loyalties and alliances. She knew where all the skeletons were hidden.[9] She had been in the innermost circles of union decision-making, not only in her own union but in the NSW Labor Council and the Australian Council of Trade Unions. She remained loyal to the labour movement all her life. Yet this conflict in the NSW Teachers Federation over married women teachers' jobs forced Lucy to face the reality that within the organisation she had helped to build, which she saw as offering the collective unity that teachers needed

---

7   Ibid., 26.
8   Ibid., 57–59; *SMH*, 23 December 1931, 9. Hettie Ross had married a fellow CPA member in 1928 but divorced in 1931 after a childless marriage. She drew closer to Lucy Woodcock in later years and was, like Lucy, a close friend of Rewi Alley.
9   LGW to RA, 1955–1965, Rewi Alley Papers, MS-Papers-6533-307, NLNZ.

to advance their conditions and interests, there were nevertheless deep divisions. She began to look around outside the union, among middle-class feminist organisations, for allies.

The struggle to defend the jobs of married women was not, however, the only pay battle. In August 1931, the Lang Labor Government enacted its *Public Service (Salaries Reduction) Amendment Act 1931* to cut wages still further, although not by the same rate as the previous Bavin Government's initial Salaries Reduction Act of June 1930. Nevertheless, Lang continued the situation of enforcing a higher proportional reduction in the salaries of women teachers.[10] Opposing this was a difficult case to argue – it meant demanding the restoration of wages to all teachers, male and female (despite teachers being seen as privileged compared to industrial workers because teachers had some sort of job security), and then arguing for a further increase to those of female teachers to bring them back up to the 80 per cent level. Lucy made the case frequently but she was aware of the challenges it posed.[11]

Lucy was in an even more difficult position than other activist teachers. As a single woman, she had been confident that she had the backing of all women teachers, single or married, when she had argued in the 1920s for Equal Pay. But in defending the rights of married women to retain their jobs, she was taking a stand against the views of many single women teachers, who believed that their own jobs were threatened by women continuing to teach after they had married. This insecurity on the part of single women teachers was even more acute in the uncertainty of the early 1930s. Education historian Marjorie Theobald has named the very few single women teachers, other than Lucy and Beatrice Taylor, who took prominent roles in defence of married teachers' jobs: of those Theobald identified, only Lucy and Beatrice were in NSW – the others were Phoebe Watson in South Australia and Florence Johnson in Victoria.[12] Most of the activist women in NSW had married, like Clarice McNamara, Hettie Ross (although briefly) and, from late 1931, Ettie Cunningham, so even those who were CPA members were firmly located within the mainstream

---

10   *Education*, September 1932, 363–64, 368, 378; October 1932, 394–96; November 1932, 8, 10, 12; and December 1932, 50.
11   See her speech as FSSTA President: *SMH*, 10 January 1933, 12; *Education*, 15 February 1933, 138–40.
12   Marjorie R. Theobald, 'And Gladly Teach? The Making of a Woman's Profession', in *Women Teaching Women Learning: Historical Perspectives*, eds Elizabeth Smyth and Paula Bourne (Toronto: Innana Publications, 2006), 76.

of conventional gender roles.[13] Lucy was the most prominent and the most senior of the single women who insisted that there was only one issue, the rights of all women teachers, so that married women's jobs and Equal Pay for all women teachers were the same struggle.[14] Lucy made her decision to stand on principle, to defend the right of all women to have security of tenure based on competence not on gender. In doing so, she risked alienating precisely the women in her union who were most like herself, women who had chosen, for whatever reason, not to marry.[15] There may have been very few married women teachers who recognised the enormous risk those like Lucy and Beatrice were taking on their behalf.

Building alliances

Predictably, it was the threat to married women's employment, rather than the question of all women teachers' wages, which raised concern outside the Federation. Among those alarmed were the numerous feminist organisations then in existence. Most were middle class but had a broad interest in women's legal rights, so although they may not have sympathised with unions, they were nevertheless disturbed by threats of discrimination against married women. Lucy Woodcock had previously had little contact with these feminist bodies, having instead focused her attention on teachers' organisations like the Women Assistant Teachers' Association and the Federation. Nevertheless, the rising interest of the feminist organisations offered activists like Lucy a strategy to put pressure not only on the government but on the NSW Federation itself, which as Lucy knew only too well was still dominated by senior male teachers who were openly sympathetic to the idea of the dismissal of women teachers.

In February 1931, soon after the Federation Annual Conference where the activist women called for the defence of married women teachers' jobs, Lucy addressed the United Associations of Women (UA), led by Jessie Street, which had set up a subcommittee to work with teachers.

---

13 Marjorie R. Theobald and Donna Dwyer, 'An Episode in Feminist Politics: The Married Women (Lecturers and Teachers) Act, 1932–47', *Labour History*, no. 76 (1999): 63.
14 Another was Beatrice Taylor, although the memory of her activism has been more closely associated with her membership of the CPA, her membership of the Educational Workers' League and her trip to the Soviet Union in March 1932.
15 See Theobald and Dwyer, 'An Episode in Feminist Politics', 65–66, for the strong undertow of opposition to married women working as teachers, among single women as well as from a majority of men.

An umbrella organisation linking feminist groups from across the political spectrum, the UA had been active since 1929 on issues like suffrage, prostitution and temperance – as well as the need for more and better trained domestic servants. It had been influenced by a number of movements, including Theosophy and the New Education Fellowship, which was another of Lucy's affiliations.[16] Jessie Street had drawn a wide range of women's organisations together and continued to exercise strong leadership: her fearlessness and fluency on public platforms being as much a factor as her social and political position, coming as she did from an affluent landowning family and married to the Supreme Court judge Sir Kenneth Street.

At that time, however, the UA seldom took the same position as a union like the Teachers Federation, despite the Federation's white-collar membership. While Jessie Street's energy and practical approach was essential to many feminist campaigns, her class position was evident in, for example, her approach to the shortage of domestic servants. Jessie had set up an employment agency for domestic servants, the Home Service Company, in 1923, although the conditions she hoped to assure for the servants, with some time off guaranteed, seldom materialised. Jessie nevertheless was to oppose an award for domestic servants in April 1937, on the basis that public opinion was not yet ready to accept it, despite the UA supporting the newly formed Domestic Workers' Association in November 1937 when it made an unsuccessful attempt to obtain an award.[17]

When Lucy Woodcock spoke to the UA in February 1931, it had already expressed concern about the threatened dismissal of married women teachers. Lucy saw the opportunity to build an alliance between the activist women teachers and the UA on the issue.[18] Jessie Street, as UA President, wrote to the Lang Government, cautioning against the move Davies had flagged. This intervention assisted the Teachers Federation to force the government to retreat.[19] No further moves were made against married women teachers by Lang's government, but after its dismissal in

---

16 Marilyn Lake, *Getting Equal: The History of Australian Feminism* (St Leonards: Allen and Unwin, 1999).
17 Pat Ranald, 'Feminism and Class: The United Associations of Women and the Council of Action on Equal Pay in the Depression', in *Worth Her Salt: Women at Work in Australia*, eds Margaret Bevege, Margaret James and Carmel Shute (Sydney: Hale and Iremonger, 1982), 280–81.
18 *SMH*, 5 February 1931, 3.
19 Theobald and Dwyer, 'An Episode in Feminist Politics', 61–62.

May 1932 the incoming conservatives, under Premier Bertram Stevens with Education Minister D.H. Drummond, immediately revived the plan to dismiss married women teachers, bringing a Bill before parliament within months. This time Jessie Street made a more public protest through the *Sydney Morning Herald* in August 1932, signalling the growing support of the UA and other feminist organisations.[20]

The Federation held its position to protect married women teachers' jobs, but there had been rising support for Drummond from many of the male Federation members and certainly amongst its then all-male executive group. Some male teachers, however, demonstrated sustained opposition to any discrimination against married women teachers. The most consistent and vocal of them was Sam Lewis, who moved that the Federation Council call a 'mass meeting of married women teachers and student teachers' to protest against the new government's austerity measures. His motion was rejected by the August council meeting.[21]

The Senior Executive at that stage was entirely male – President Alfred McGuinness, Deputy President C.H. Currey and Senior Vice President E.J. Rourke[22] – and this group met with Minister Drummond in September 1932 to discuss the sacking of married women teachers. President McGuinness later told Federation Council that he, with this all-male Senior Executive group, had done 'all he could' to have the minister reconsider. Theobald and Dwyer have pointed out how little public outcry the NSW Teachers Federation had made when they had the chance.[23] Council meekly accepted the president's account, confirming for Lucy that her senior male colleagues could not be relied upon to defend the interests of women teachers.

Despite her determination to work through the Federation to achieve a unified strategy on all problems, the ambivalence of the leadership of her own union on this issue must have given Lucy cause to stiffen her position

---

20 Ibid., 59.
21 *Education*, 15 September 1932, 264.
22 *Education*, February 1932 for all three names. In Mitchell, *Teachers, Education and Politics*, this deputation is mentioned but only the office titles are given, with no names attached. This is then quoted directly in Theodore and Dwyer, 'An Episode in Feminist Politics', but they assume the senior vice president to have been Lucy. In fact, Lucy had no office in the NSW Federation in 1932, because she was holding the arduous post of president of the Federated State School Teachers' Association (FSSTA). She returned to the NSW Federation as one of four vice presidents in 1933 and was then finally re-elected to the senior vice president role only for 1934, a post she held till her retirement in 1953.
23 Theobald and Dwyer, 'An Episode in Feminist Politics', 67–68.

and consolidate her new relationship with the UA. Lucy had always been good at building alliances: into this one, she brought the name of the powerful NSW Teachers Federation, in which there was a large majority of female members, many of whom had been campaigning for Equal Pay, like her, for decades.

Lucy and Jessie Street in the UA found common ground in their concerns about discrimination against and between women, although they came to it from very different positions. Jessie was the elite and affluent mother of four, who had often in the past been the respectable face of women's activism. Lucy was a single woman from a lower middle-class family of limited means. Her personal life was ambiguous; she was unmarried and childless. She had worked to pay her own way through two university degrees to rise as far as possible for a woman within her profession, to be then obstructed by the entrenched prejudice against all women in the Education Department. Despite such differences, the two women were of a similar age, and may have shared many common values.

Although Lucy was such a staunch unionist, overall the status of teachers was understood to be intermediate, at least in the eyes of many teachers. Like other professional women, such as nurses, who were struggling for recognition, teachers often regarded themselves as a cut above industrial workers in class terms. Lucy had certainly always stressed the professional nature of the teaching service. Many teachers held an aspirational belief in their higher status, which had been one of the great difficulties in forming the teachers' unions. Politically, Lucy and Jessie were both moving further to the left in their alliances over the 1930s and so may also have found common ideological interests as well as developing a warm personal relationship. In any event, Lucy joined the UA at some time in 1931 or 1932, although her major commitments at this time were to teachers' unions rather than to any of the women's organisations.

The UA events were widely attended during the Depression by women from all political affiliations. The CPA activist Phyllis Johnson, for example, remembered attending a UA seminar in which Lucy spoke about Equal Pay at some time in the 1930s, indicating the widespread interest in the UA despite the CPA leadership criticising it as 'bourgeois feminism'.[24]

---

24   Phyllis Johnson, interview with Heather Goodall, 10 May 2007; Joy Damousi, *Women Come Rally* (Melbourne: Oxford University Press, 1994); P. Griffiths, 'Women and the Communist Party of Australia, 1920–1945' (Honours thesis, Macquarie University, 1998).

Creating a federal union

As well as dealing with the rapidly developing problems at state level, Lucy was taking a major role in creating a federal teachers' union. As the Depression bit deeper, it became increasingly urgent to try to bring all teachers' unions into the ambit of the federal Arbitration system, to allow a more consistent approach, which teachers like Lucy hoped would counter the divergent policies of state governments. Lucy had been actively involved with the national teachers' organisations – first the Australian Teachers' Federation (ATF, formed in 1921), which merged with the Federated State School Teachers' Association (FSSTA) in 1928.[25] She was elected to the presidency of the FSSTA in January 1932, the first woman ever to have been in this role. So during the year of Lang's dismissal, Lucy's attention was taken up with the interstate organising demands of the FSSTA.

From this national perspective, although Lucy was deeply disappointed by the betrayal of senior male teachers in the NSW Federation, she was forced to recognise the widespread divisions among women teachers themselves over the issue in many states outside NSW. NSW was not alone in having a high proportion of single women teachers who opposed the employment of women teachers who married.[26] Ambivalence was widespread in other states and became even more evident in South Australia when the Women Teachers Guild refused a request from the UA to support the NSW Federation call for the reinstatement of married women teachers.[27]

After struggling on a national level throughout 1932 with the deepening economic crisis and the rising tide of antagonism to women both inside and outside the profession, Lucy used her final speech as FSSTA President in January 1933 to lay out her strongest criticisms and her vision for the future. First, as an economist, she condemned the austerity measures now being imposed by conservative federal and state governments:

---

25 Mitchell, *Teachers, Education and Politics*, 26.
26 Ibid.
27 K. Whitehead, 'The Spinster Teacher in Australia from the 1870s to the 1960s', *History of Education Review* 36, no. 1 (2007): 14. The Women Teachers' Association was in existence in South Australia from 1936 to 1951. It refused the UA request in 1941.

> Our troubles are entirely man-made, arising out of pure mismanagement … If a household were conducted upon the same principles as nations had recently been conducting their affairs, we should have the spectacle of some of its members being gorged to excess, and others dying from hunger, although all the pantries were bulging with food. Clearly, our problem to-day is not deficiency but our failure to make sane use of the actual abundance which surrounds us on every side. The world is richer than ever – its people infinitely poorer.[28]

She reserved her most stinging attack, however, for what she called the 'Sex Distinction' against women in the teaching profession in all states. She outlined the many different ways in which all women were disadvantaged as teachers in each state, ranging from salary discrimination to blockages to promotion through to outright dismissal:

> While the salaries of teachers remained at the mercy of politicians, there would always be cause for unrest. An overhaul of the national educational policy was long delayed. The woman was debarred from advancement in the teaching profession because of sex distinction. The higher positions in the service were closed to her, for it was the administrative policy to give men preference. Women plead that capacity to hold down a job, and not sex, should be the determining factor in remuneration.
>
> The assault upon the married women teachers in New South Wales showed how deeply implanted were the prejudices that governed the position of women. Women did not ask for privileges, but they asked that prejudice should give way to reasoned judgment.[29]

In the midst of this attack on industrial discrimination, Lucy gave a glimpse of herself:

> The real trouble is that nobody really believes (except herself) that a grown-up woman should be allowed freedom to live her own life. Her personal freedom must be always controlled. Not only is she expected to live more timidly, but half of the population feel it is their bounden duty to compel her to do so. It was in obedience to the dictates of people who hold these views that the Married Women's Bill was introduced.[30]

---

28 *Education*, 15 February 1933, 138.
29 *SMH*, 10 January 1933, 12; *Education*, 15 February 1933, 138–40.
30 *Education*, 15 February 1933, 139. Lucy included the parenthetic phrase '(except herself)'.

It is not hard to hear the personal anger – and the pain – within her words.

Lucy remained determined that women should be properly recognised and respected in the teaching profession. Her outspoken challenges to her fellow Council members at the Federation and her sustained demands for women teachers across the nation were recognised among women unionists. The Windsor–Richmond branch of the Federation for example, in September 1934, forwarded 'a letter of thanks and appreciation to Miss L. Woodcock for her determined stand in the interests of women teachers'.[31]

Figure 5.1: Lucy c. 1930s, at the height of her union organising.

Detail from undated photograph of Teachers Federation executive, late 1930s or early 1940s.

Source: NSW Teachers Federation archives, undated photograph P10168.

Yet despite her frustration over the mismanagement of the economy and her intense anger at the discrimination against women, Lucy ended her FSSTA Presidential Address in January 1933 with hope. She outlined a vision of lifelong learning, the expression of progressive education aimed at nurturing independent inquiry, democratic debate and principled decision-making:

> We still, in practice retain an out-of-date conception of education as the mere imparting of knowledge. Our examination system is largely responsible for the maintenance of this conception … It is necessary to remind ourselves that the real value of education is not measured by the amount and variety of knowledge we can force into the minds of the young …
>
> The aim, I take it, is to train the mind to observe accurately, to think clearly, to discard prejudices, to weigh evidence, to make judgements on the weight of evidence … We should aim to create

---

31 *Windsor and Richmond Gazette*, 21 September 1934, 6.

a living intellectual interest in minds … The curricula of the schools should be based on the conception of man as a citizen of the world instead of a citizen of a small State …

Our schools may be said to have succeeded if we can arouse a deep and abiding interest in the search for knowledge in all who pass through their portals. Our pupils should not be a standardized product, when they leave us, knowing so much of this and that, but young people equipped with well-balanced minds; young citizens who will go further along the pathway of life unprejudiced and untrammelled in quest of knowledge and pursuit of it until life's journey ends.[32]

Lucy remained active in the FSSTA but, late in 1935, the organisation dissolved itself. Its sole goal had been to achieve 'a real Australian Union', in the words of NSW President A. McGuinness, for teachers across all states through recognition in the federal Arbitration Court.[33] A High Court decision in 1929 ruling that education was not an 'industry' had made that impossible, but the FSSTA had battled on for some years, hoping to achieve a referendum that would change the law on which the High Court decision had been based. Lucy believed that access to the federal Arbitration Court would at least achieve 'stabilization of the rates paid to the Assistant Teachers in every state'.[34] Eventually, late in 1935, the state unions from Queensland and South Australia decided they would withdraw from the federated union forcing the FSSTA to dissolve itself in January 1936.[35] Lucy said of the FSSTA: 'If the Association had done nothing else, it had brought about an improvement in the morale of teachers, who, prior to 1922, had been content to accept what was given.'[36] The Australian Teachers' Federation then immediately reconstituted itself, without expectations of access to a federal industrial award, and Lucy continued to take a high-profile role in its attempts to draw teachers together across state borders.

32   *Education*, 15 February 1933, 137–40.
33   This principled goal was more in keeping with the non-industrial organisation the Australian Teachers' Federation, formed in 1921. The FSSTA had formed in 1922 to attempt to gain a federal Industrial Court award when the NSW Government removed the NSW Teachers Federation (along with the Public Service Union) from Industrial courts. The ATF merged with FSSTA in 1928 and their goals *were* then the same for some years.
34   *SMH*, 10 January 1933, 12.
35   The 1929 High Court decision was that education was not an industry. Ann R. Shorten, 'The Legal Context of Australian Education: An Historical Exploration', *Australia New Zealand Journal of Law Education* 1, no. 1 (1996): 20–21. It left no avenue for further activism. The Australian Teachers' Federation eventually won recognition in the federal Arbitration System in 1986.
36   *Advocate* (Tasmania), 6 January 1936, 9. Report of the Hobart Conference of the FSSTA in which it made the decision to dissolve itself.

Defending Beatrice Taylor (1932–33)

While Lucy was throwing all her energy into her Australia-wide work as FSSTA President, from January 1932 to February 1933, her long-time colleague and ally Beatrice Taylor had become the focus of controversy and departmental discipline. Taylor had been a founding member, with Sam Lewis and others, of the Education Workers League, a small activist group in the NSW Teachers Federation. Many members, like Lewis, were associated with the Communist Party and all its members were committed to challenging the attacks on education funding being blamed on the Depression. Beatrice Taylor, then teaching at a primary school, was sponsored by the EWL in March 1932 to travel to Europe where she visited the Soviet Union. She gave a lecture in November 1932 about the condition of education there and the NSW Education Department demanded she explain her views. Taylor refused, arguing it impinged on her civil rights as a private citizen. In response, the department suspended her for misconduct and wilful disobedience.[37]

There was widespread public reaction through December and January. The UA – in which Lucy was an increasingly active member – was one of the 278 organisations that supported Taylor, demanding that she be reinstated. The Paddington Town Hall was packed for a meeting just before school was due to start on 31 January 1933. Supporters then held a widely attended Sydney Town Hall meeting. Jessie Street's friend Clive Evatt took Taylor's case before the Public Service Board that early in February 1933 found in Taylor's favour, leading to her reinstatement and later promotion.[38] While this case turned out well for Taylor, it was a troubling indication of the power of the Public Service Board to sit in judgement over teachers. With Lucy so occupied in the FSSTA, she was not prominent in this case, but the problem rankled. Her concerns resurfaced in later years when Sam Lewis was himself disciplined in 1955. Lucy's defence of Lewis, published in 1956, was aimed directly at the powers held over teachers by the Public Service Board.[39]

---

37 Martin Sullivan, 'Taylor, Beatrice Mary (1893–1982)', *Australian Dictionary of Biography*, National Centre of Biography, The Australian National University, adb.anu.edu.au/biography/taylor-beatrice-mary-15677/text26875, published first in hardcopy 2012, accessed online 17 November 2018.
38 'Defence Committee Will Continue to Function', *Newcastle Morning Herald and Miners' Advocate*, 10 February 1933, 9.
39 Lucy Godiva Woodcock, *The Lewis Case and You* (Sydney: self-published with donations, 1956).

5. UNITY AND BETRAYAL

Equal Pay and Equal Status: 1937

The Public Service Salaries Reduction Act of 1930 and the associated Amendment Act of 1931 were finally done away with in 1937, but this did not restore the 1920 guarantee that women would be paid 80 per cent of male salaries for equal work. But this 80 per cent figure had never been Lucy Woodcock's goal – instead she had always insisted that the goal was full equality of salaries for women and men.

Figure 5.2: Lucy Woodcock as caricatured (affectionately) in the Teachers Federation journal *Education* in January 1939.

The cartoon reflects her courage and tenacity in the face of the failure of many male colleagues to support her long campaign for equal pay.

Source: *Education: Journal of the NSW Teachers Federation*, 28 January 1939, p. 110. Courtesy, State Library of New South Wales.

Her alliance with the UA contributed to the establishment of the Council for Action on Equal Pay (CAEP) in May 1937, initiated from the Federated Clerks' Union by John Hughes and Muriel Heagney. This alliance between activist unionised women and the elite middle-class feminist organisations held until at least the war years. There were disagreements in the CAEP between the unionists (notably Muriel Heagney, who became honorary secretary) and the UA about whether there should be a demand for immediate full pay equality (Heagney's position) or an incremental rise. But the UA remained within the CAEP until 1939, when it suspended its membership for six months, before finally withdrawing in August 1940. Even then, it continued to be in communication with the CAEP throughout the war, because Lucy Woodcock, by then Senior vice president of the Teachers Federation but also a UA member, moved into the position of co-chair of the CAEP with her fellow Federationist Robert L. Day in 1942.[40]

The overall position of the CAEP did not, however, meet all the concerns of the NSW Teachers Federation, where women still faced the glaring problems that had preceded the sacking of married women. First, as discussed earlier, their campaigns for Equal Pay for women teachers appeared to be going backwards as Depression measures took effect – the 80 per cent of male teachers' salaries, won by women teachers in 1920, had been reduced still further due to the cuts to NSW Public Service salaries.[41] Even more fundamentally, as Lucy's FSSTA speech had pointed out, all women continued to be blocked from significant leadership positions. So at the same time as the CAEP was formed, Lucy and other Federation activists like Una F. Ellison established an Equal Pay and Equal Status Committee within the Federation. As Lucy said at the birth of the CAEP:

> We do not admit that all the grey matter and wisdom is in the head of a man. Equal opportunity must be demanded in addition to equal pay.[42]

The new Federation Equal Pay and Equal Status Committee worked closely with the CAEP, and drew support from CAEP co-founder, John Hughes from the Federated Clerks. Lucy invited him to speak to the Teachers Federation members on 4 June 1937, soon after the CAEP was formed.[43] Hughes paid deference to the Teachers Federation – and to Lucy:

> The principle of sex-equality is one that has been heard much of in the last decade. The Clerks' Union is not the pioneer mover. The Teachers' Federation has already been partially successful and Madam Chair (Miss Woodcock) has played an important part.[44]

---

40   Beverley Symons, 'Muriel Heagney and the Fight for Equal Pay During World War II', *The Hummer* 3, no. 1 (Summer 1998–99): 1–13.
41   *Public Service Salaries Act (No. 2) 1931* (NSW). See *Education*, 8 December 1932 (W.J. Hendry, NSW TF Sec to Ed. Min D. H. Drummond, 14 November 1932); *Education*, 15 November 1932, 12–14; 15 April 1933, 189; *SMH*, 20 December 1932, 9.
42   *Truth*, 23 May 1937, 18.
43   'Equal Pay for the Sexes', *Education*, 21 August 1937, 311.
44   Ibid.

As always, it was a struggle to mobilise male members of the Federation, as male staff benefited very directly from the glass ceiling confronting women in the teaching service. Nevertheless, the Equal Pay and Equal Status Committee struggled on, supported by leading male activists like Sam Lewis and drawing others in wherever possible.

There was to be a major change, however, with the coming of World War II, which dramatically escalated interest in the CAEP among mainstream unions. The war brought more and more women into employment, often into jobs men had vacated to go into the armed forces. These big unions, with majority male memberships, suddenly saw themselves threatened by low-paid women workers, still usually forced to work for 54 per cent of the male rate, which made the issue of Equal Pay into a serious industrial campaign for a few years. At the same time, women saw opportunities to demand a role in planning for a new society after the war was over.

6

Refugees and Hope

Over that grim decade of the Depression, Lucy had anchored herself in the community of Erskineville; at the same time, she had taken major roles in the campaigns to defend teacher's salaries. In the struggle to defend women's jobs, however, Lucy had been disappointed by the men in her own union who had failed to stand behind her, so she had turned instead to an alliance with the women's movement. This allowed her to access a different group of people – many of whom had little understanding of the industrial conditions of either professional or working-class employees. Nevertheless, they had responded against the injustice of defining women by familial relations. Lucy, as a trade union leader, was able to bring access to a wider range of women activists than the middle-class feminist movements had been able to reach, and so, while their interests were not identical, Lucy was able to show the common ground. Lucy's work in these campaigns was well known to both groups – the feminists valued her role in bringing the strength of trade union activists, and the women in the trade union movement welcomed her facilitation of the support of feminist organisations.

Yet at the same time there was another arena in which Lucy was working of which little was known then nor has it been recorded later – and yet it reflected the fundamentals of all of the rest of her passionate commitments. At Erskineville, despite focusing on the children and their families, Lucy had still seen them in relation to the wider world. This sense of the world beyond the school walls was glimpsed in the children's library – deliberately located outside and unconnected with the school.

This was the vision that had motivated her throughout her career and, at the same time as she was finding her feet at Erskineville, she was reaching out to that wider world.

Lucy had never forgotten the Robinovitz family, who had offered her such kindness but had also shown her the cost of European racism and persecution. Her response to their story was inextricably linked with Lucy's commitment to progressive education, an interest that had been sharpened in her 1927 exchange experience with inner-city schools run by the London County Council. One of the programs the County Council had supported in its schools was the extensive use of theatre to foster children's psychological and social development and it drew on Rosemary Benjamin, who came to live in Sydney in 1936.

Her time working in London County Council schools had strengthened Lucy's skills in delivering creative progressive education in working-class schools. It was clear from Beverley Langley's memories of her early schooling at Erskineville that Lucy had fostered creative drama for all the children in her school.

Yet Lucy's time in these London schools had also made the experiences of the East End Jewish community very visible to her. Many among the East End community had faced persecution in Europe, just as the Robinovitz family had done, and the pressures on them were increasing as the Depression worsened.

Once she had returned to Sydney, Lucy retained her connections to exchange teachers, taking an active role in welcoming visiting teachers and maintaining contact with the schools and teachers who had already been part of the program. While the New South Wales teaching exchange program sent teachers mainly to the United Kingdom and Canada, it was the connections Lucy had made in her own exchange experiences in London, and the arrival of migrants from just those settings like Rosemary Benjamin, that maintained contacts that went far beyond Britain. This internationalism was strong among the small network of progressive educators with whom Lucy was mixing after her return, including the founder of Frensham, Winifred West, with her London and Indian contacts.

The Depression had challenged Australian teachers and their unions, as we have seen in the previous chapters. But there was far worse emerging for Jews in Europe, for whom the 1930s saw rising dangers. Australian teachers with Jewish family backgrounds, like Sam Lewis, were becoming aware of these growing pressures, but otherwise it was mainly teachers like Lucy who had worked overseas, or those who kept abreast of the news, who were learning about the emergence of fascism across western Europe. Some, like the Newcastle teacher and writer Dora Birtles, travelled to Europe. Lucy had known Dora since university days when, as passionate writers of poetry, Dora and her lover Bert Birtles had caused an uproar in 1923, making the front page on the *Sun* and leading to the university expelling Bert altogether and forcing Dora out for two years with a suspension. This was just after Robert Irvine had been forced to resign as an outcome both of his left-wing politics and his long-running affair with his American assistant. Lucy had taken a major role in defending him.[1] Dora argued too that the expulsions she and Bert faced were political – imposed by a conservative university in the politically and sexually repressive climate of the early 1920s.[2] Dora returned – not to her BA but to Teachers' College – but she did not stay silent. Instead, she become the editor of the Teachers' College newsletter and, after qualifying as a teacher in the mid-1920s, went on to teach at Newcastle schools, at the same time as Lucy was teaching in the area, along the Hunter Valley at Cessnock and then, not far to the north, at Grafton.

Dora travelled through Europe in 1933, observing the rise of fascism there before settling in London where she campaigned for feminist causes and supported the Republican Government in Spain when the Spanish Civil War broke out. Dora sent back regular reports to the Sydney press, like that about Germany in September 1933, where Dora described how everyone she met was anxious and fearful about politics. She reported that the Nazi organisation was 'devastatingly thorough', with all the children in Boy Scout or Girl Guide movements wearing miniature uniforms and saluting 'in the approved style'. Very few people wanted to criticise the new Nazi government – and those who did were silenced by the anxiety of those around them. In the port city of Hamburg, the dock workers 'gave the Bolshevist greeting of the clenched fist', but elsewhere there were only 'Heil Hitler' salutes, while the streets bristled with 'the black swastika' and Nazi uniforms were everywhere.[3]

---

1   See Chapter 2, this volume.
2   Deirdre Moore, *Survivors of 'Beauty': Memoirs of Dora and Bert Birtles* (Sydney: Book Collectors Society of Australia, 1996).
3   Dora Birtles, 'A Newcastle Woman among the Nazis', *Newcastle Sun*, 21 September 1933, 4.

Among the people Dora met in Germany were Siegfried (known as Friedel) and Lotte Fink, both medical doctors – a psychoanalyst and a gynaecologist – practising in Frankfurt. Soon after Dora met them, they were both denied the right to practise because they were Jewish. The tempo of discrimination increased. Their older child, Thomas, won a competition for designing an aeroplane but was not allowed to take up his prize, a flight in a real plane, because he was Jewish. Then, in 1935, Thomas was prevented from attending his German school in Frankfurt, so the Finks took the advice of Thomas's headmaster and sent him to England as the foster child to a Quaker family, Nan and H.G. Newth, a biologist, in Birmingham.[4] Conditions deteriorated still further and the Finks decided they must emigrate. They first had to obtain exit visas so they and their young daughter, Ruth, could get out of the country. Friedel had wanted to go to the United States where many of his psychoanalytic colleagues had settled, but he had been born in Posen, which had become Polish after World War I, and the US quota for Polish immigrants was already full. They decided to try to get help from their Australian friend Dora Birtles, who had returned to Australia in 1937. She was able to sponsor the Fink family's entry into Australia, and so Lucy met the family soon after, beginning a long friendship.

Another activist who had begun her working life as a teacher was Fanny Reading, who came to Sydney in 1922. Fanny had been born in 1884 in Russia, from where her family had been forced out, in conditions similar to those of the Robinovitzes. Reading's family migrated eventually to Melbourne, where Fanny became a language teacher. She decided to pursue medical studies and after graduating she moved to Sydney, to set up in private practice in Kings Cross with her brother in 1922. An advocate for women's rights within Judaism, Reading established the National Council of Jewish Women (NCJW) in 1929, by which time Lucy had already become a close friend. Lucy went on to host the first annual meeting of the Western Suburbs committee of the NCJW at her home in September 1942. When Dr Reading introduced Lucy at a number of meetings held by the National Council, she sketched out Lucy's work from 1935 to assist Jewish migrants escaping European persecution. This organisation was, in the later 1940s and '50s, associated with the Women's International Zionist Organisation in which Australian Jewish women like Ruby

---

4   Thomas came to Australia in the 1940s, studying Aeronautical Engineering at Sydney University, before travelling to the UK with his wife in 1947. He returned with his family in 1956 to take up a Chair of Mechanical Engineering at the University of NSW.

Rich participated. Rich usually took conservative positions in the many women's organisations she was involved in, yet she became very active in this body representing the goal of establishing a Jewish homeland.[5] The threats to Jews in Europe were horrifyingly real, even in 1942 before the worst was known outside Germany. An affiliation to Zionism was at that time unquestioned by many, although not all, of those who were facing the terrors of fascist Europe.

By the time she helped found the Erksineville Children's Library in 1936, Lucy was already in touch with other Australians who had similar concerns and she had begun to assist Jews escaping European persecution. It was difficult to gain entry to Australia – many British Dominions did not welcome Jewish refugees and some, like New Zealand, had refused to allow almost all Jewish migration. Even if they were able to gain entry, many new arrivals, like the Fink family who arrived early in 1939, struggled to re-establish themselves in their chosen careers in a new country in which they often felt uneasy and challenged. Medical doctors, for example, had to undertake a complicated course of re-examination to become registered to practise. Friedel Fink did undertake this process but his wife Lotte, overtaken by childcare and homemaking duties, only ever practised informally after her migration, advising women about contraception and reproductive health.[6] Just as disturbing was the anti-Semitism that was widespread in Australia at the time, making resettlement even harder. Lucy found a role in supporting both the employment of Jewish migrants as teachers and their attempts to enter training in order to qualify as teachers – or have their previous qualifications recognised. For some people, like the Goldschmidt family, Lucy was able to offer accommodation in her home and a continuing role as sponsor.[7] As Fanny Reading was to introduce her in 1942:

> Dr Reading … spoke of the wonderful work Miss Woodcock had done for Refugees during the past seven years. She had herself assisted in bringing more than 160 people out and placed them in positions as teachers and also helped some of them to continue their studies at the University.[8]

---

5   *Hebrew Standard of Australasia*, 8 June 1951, 8.
6   Friedel Fink was naturalised in 1945 but was not able to register under the NSW *Medical Practitioners' Act 1938* until 1947. He served as an 'Alien Doctor' in NSW Mental Hospitals.
7   The account of assistance to Stephanie Goldschmidt and her family has been gathered from registers of naturalisation, indicating residence at the Beaumaris St, Enfield, home until the late 1950s and Stephanie's role hosting the 1942 NCJW meeting there, where Lucy was guest speaker.
8   *Hebrew Standard of Australasia*, 1 January 1942, 6.

In the uncertain conditions they faced in their new country, many Jewish migrants to Australia looked for organisations that reflected the ideas and interests in which they had been involved in Europe. Innovative education and child development were closely related fields in which many Jewish refugees were interested, including those like the Finks who had been part of an intellectual and highly educated class of professionals in Europe. (As in all warfare, working-class and impoverished Jews seldom had the means or opportunity to escape.) So for those who did come to Australia, the organisations that reflected innovative and cutting-edge progressive ideas were attractive. The New Education Fellowship (NEF) was important in this regard: it was familiar to the European emigrés because it had been most active in Europe in engaging with innovative theories of education, and it took a broad view of learning, fostering a recognition that education took place widely across society, not just in schools or universities. Just as important were its origins in Beatrice Ensor's commitment to Theosophy during the 1920s. Although Theosophy was politically ambivalent in aligning itself with both right- and left-wing movements in different places, it sustained an involvement with non-Western cultures, through 'Eastern' philosophies like Buddhism and Hinduism. This meant that the NEF offered a cultural receptiveness and cosmopolitanism that was very unlike the narrowing Christian Eurocentrism of the US progressive education bodies.

Yet the Depression had challenged many of the NEF ideas, reflecting an upheaval in the theories surrounding progressive education in Europe and the UK. These changes were to have a significant impact on educators like Lucy in Australia. The European shifts can be charted through a series of NEF conferences held from 1921 to 1936 in the UK, Switzerland, France and Denmark, which showed a number of emerging – and often contradictory – trends.[9] The strongest source of ideas remained the old NEF focus on child-centred education in which attention was paid to the best methods of meeting the needs of each child, and an underlying interest in cultural diversity, arising from Theosophy.

---

9   Kevin J. Brehony, 'A New Education for a New Era: The Contribution of the Conferences of the New Education Fellowship to the Disciplinary Field of Education, 1921–1938', *Paedagogica Historica* 40, nos 5 & 6 (2004): 733–55, doi.org/10.1080/0030923042000293742.

One shift, however, was that the NEF call for better training for teachers in order to equip them with better methods had heightened the involvement of university academics and added to calls for stronger research into education. In these European conferences over the 1930s, academics increased in number, although never becoming the majority of attendees.

Another major shift was a rising interest in the collective or social setting of children, rather than attention only to individual needs, demonstrated clearly in the 1932 conference at Nice in France.[10] This shift was interpreted through the lens of the political alignments of the time. As a network, the NEF had been strained badly because its conferences were attended by small numbers of representatives from fascist states, although Ensor felt it was important that there should be no censorship even of difficult ideas. However, the anxieties expressed more often were about left-wing influences, with only thinly disguised anti-communism emanating from the Americans at what they termed a 'retreat from freedom'.[11] It was, possibly, related concerns that led to a shift in the funding for the NEF conferences, which were so important to nurturing its stimulating impact on teachers. Much of this funding had been provided by US philanthropic organisations but, in the early 1930s, the Rockefeller Foundation withdrew its support. The shortfall was met, however, by the Carnegie Corporation of New York, which rose in significance as a funder not only in Europe but in Australia through the Australian Council for Educational Research and in the Pacific through the Institute of Pacific Relations.[12]

The final trend visible in the European conferences to 1936 may also have been related to the political climate or to the funding sources. The rising influence of psychology as a discipline was an important source of ideas about research in education to determine what the 'real' needs of children might be. The trends in the United States in the 1930s, however, were strongly towards the quantification involved in testing of the 'intelligence

---

10 Brehony, 'A New Education for a New Era', 749–51.
11 Ray Hemmings, *Children's Freedom* (New York: Schocken Books, 1973), who has associated it first with A.S. Neill then, in 1932, with Fred Clarke, who was the newly appointed Director of the Institute of Education in London.
12 Fiona Paisley, 'The Spoils of Opportunity: Janet Mitchell and "Idealistic Realism" in the Interwar Asia-Pacific', *History Australia* 13, no. 4 (2016): 575–91, doi.org/10.1080/14490854.2016.1249273; Julie McLeod, 'Educating for "World-Mindedness": Cosmopolitanism, Localism and Schooling the Adolescent Citizen in Interwar Australia', *Journal of Educational Administration and History* 44, no. 4 (2012): 339–59; Julie McLeod and Katie Wright, 'Education for Citizenship: Transnational Expertise, Curriculum Reform and Psychological Knowledge in 1930s Australia', *History of Education Review* 42, no. 2 (2013): 170–84.

quotient' or IQ, of individual children, as a means of identifying not only needs and interests but the class and racial potential for 'educability'. This was an interest also strongly demonstrated in South Africa, and written on by E.G. Malherbe, who was in 1937 to organise the South African NEF Conference and then come to Australia, and whose work included producing standard IQ tests to compare 'the intelligence of the African native and the white people'.[13] This class basis or racialisation of IQ testing was of great interest to social planners drawing on eugenics to address issues like the class-based analysis of 'juvenile delinquency' and the tensions of interracial conflict, both being social conflict issues evident in South Africa, the US and in the Pacific. Such interests in 'scientific' testing to identify class and racial 'educability' became evident also – although not dominant – in the European arena of the NEF conferences.[14]

Such issues were of importance in the areas where the NEF held greatest sway, which as well as Europe had continued to be the British Empire. This was of course a period when the League of Nations had made both development and colonial power into very hot topics. On the one hand, European states like the UK and France sought increasingly to justify their continued control, often disguised as League protectorates, over old colonies. On the other hand, and at the same time, the United States and many British Empire Dominions were debating strategies to control immigration and to plan 'racial hygiene' measures like IQ testing to justify eugenicist measures like sterilisation. So, in different ways, both were using the IQ testing as ways to justify continued control and discrimination. Yet the emerging discipline of psychology argued that it was justified in using the term 'child-centred' because IQ testing would free children from the tyranny of uniform examinations and allow curricula to be designed to meet the specific needs of each child (as determined by the IQ metrics).[15]

Lucy was torn by the debates around IQ testing. The children in the Opportunity Classes (OC) in which she had taught at Erskineville were selected through IQ testing, which was being used in experimental

---

13 E.G. Malherbe, ed., *Educational Adaptations in a Changing Society: Report of the South African Education Conference held in Capetown and Johannesburg in July, 1934, Under the Auspices of the New Education Fellowship* (Capetown-Johannesburg: New Education Fellowship, 1937); K.S. Cunningham, ed., *Education for Complete Living, the Challenge of Today: The Proceedings of the New Education Fellowship Conference Held in Australia, August 1 to September 20, 1937* (Melbourne, London, Edinburgh: Melbourne University Press with Oxford University Press, 1938), 298–310.
14 Brehony, 'A New Education for a New Era', 752.
15 McLeod, 'Educating for "World-Mindedness"', 339–59; McLeod and Wright, 'Education for Citizenship:', 170–84.

situations in NSW and with a degree of caution.[16] Lucy had argued that at Erskineville school, the OC children had thrived on a learning environment where they were encouraged to learn together, in cooperation, rather than to compete.[17] There were clearly a number of different things at play here – and, as became clear in the South African and US situations, the testing could be used to very different effects. Moreover, Lucy continued to campaign bitterly against the tests for high schools imposed on all NSW children at the end of primary school, which sorted them into 'academic' and 'technical' high schools, denying most the opportunity ever to go onto further post-secondary study. 'The NSW child', she observed in 1935, 'is being reared in a system of tests like cheese and butter.'[18] In 1959, Lucy was to reconsider her views on IQ testing. When the tests began to be used to rank students for entry into high schools, Lucy became much more critical, arguing that the test could not predict the future performance of a child.[19]

In 1937, for the first time, the NEF conferences moved outside the geographic area of Europe. The conferences were held in British Commonwealth dominions or colonies – first in South Africa, where Ensor had worked, then to New Zealand and then Australia. The NSW Teachers Federation was active in organising the NEF Conference from the Australian side, and Lucy was on the organising committee. A cavalcade of British and European educators associated with the NEF, led by Ensor herself, spoke at the conferences. Only a few speakers in the lengthy program were from non-European countries, and most of those were from the US, Canada or the white population of South Africa. Three were not – Dr Hu Shih from the University of Peiping in China and the Institute of Pacific Relations; V.S. Srinivasa Sastri, Vice-Chancellor of Annamalai University in the southern Indian state of Tamil Nadu and Indian delegate to the League of Nations; and Yusuke Tsurumi, an author from Japan and also associated with the Institute of Pacific Relations. Dr Sastri may not in fact have arrived, and neither of the other two were reported widely in Australia nor were there any non-Europeans mentioned at all in the NSW Teachers Federation journal *Education*.[20]

---

16   *Education*, 10 December 1936, 13–14.
17   See Chapter 4, this volume, for Lucy's comments on Erskineville Public School Opportunity Classes.
18   *Newcastle Sun*, 16 December 1935, 7.
19   September–November 1959, cited in Lucy Godiva Woodcock ASIO file, Vol. 2, f 137, A6119, 2031, NAA.
20   *Education*, August 1937; P. E. Hornibrook *Education*, October 1937, 379–80; McLeod, 'Educating for "World-Mindedness"', 341.

The dominance of European and North American speakers in 1937 contrasted with the cultural interests of Theosophy, which had so influenced Ensor, and had by 1900 established strong bases in India and Ceylon. The 1937 dominance of the NEF by European and British/Anglo speakers also contrasts with the NEF conference held in Australia in 1946, after the globalising impact of World War II, and which will be discussed later in Chapter 9. The 1937 conference reflected the height of Eurocentrism in the NEF – by 1946, the organisation had shifted focus dramatically to orient itself to the decolonising world, taking on the South and South-East Asian networks of its parent Theosophy and expanding rapidly beyond it to include Latin America and Africa until in 1966 it finally renamed itself the World Education Fellowship.

Nevertheless, despite its shortcomings and tensions, there was an exciting array of people and ideas on show at the 1937 NEF conferences in Australia. The list of those who did speak reflected the cutting edge of thinking, research and practice in progressive education. Among them were two women of great significance to many in Australia. One was the NEF founder, Beatrice Ensor, whose continued interest in Theosophy had sustained a cultural openness in the NEF that allowed the organisation to extend its membership far beyond Ensor's own work, which was limited to Europe and South Africa. The second was Susan Isaacs, the leading Freudian in child development, who had greatly influenced not only educators but workers in creative fields like Rosemary Benjamin through her work in theatre. So even though the 1937 conference demonstrated the tensions between the conflicting trends in 'progressive' education outlined earlier, and which would all continue to be in conflict in the future, it was still true that overall the Australian conference was a powerful statement of the core focus of the NEF on 'child-centred' education. It was this progressive message that was reflected in the NSW Teachers Federation report.[21]

An Australian NEF had existed for some time in Melbourne, but Lucy took the lead in setting up a NSW branch as a direct result of the 1937 NEF Conference in Sydney. Lucy became its first president and its committee included many passionately involved people, reflecting the diversity of people interested in the broadest sense of learning and education, rather than its narrow expression in formal education. Despite its members' enthusiasm, the organisation was short of money, and for the first few

---

21 See *Education*, August 1937, 301–3 for conference report, 303–10 for summaries of a number of key papers.

years of its existence all the planning work of the NEF went on in Lucy's George Street flat.[22] Clarice McNamara took on the role of honorary secretary and sustained her contribution over many years, a committed life that was reviewed by her daughter, Margaret Henry, in 2007.[23]

A newcomer to Sydney who became involved was the Londoner Rosemary Benjamin, just then establishing The Theatre for Children in Reiby Place. When Benjamin first arrived late in 1936, she had not intended to settle in Sydney, but she found a great interest in her children's theatre and a congenial community in the émigré Jewish networks developing in Australia. Among the growing community of refugees with whom she was able to work in Sydney were the Viennese choreographer of modern expressionist dance Gertrud Bodenweiser as well as the musician and composer Kurt Kaiser (a German-born Jewish-Peruvian, known in Sydney as John Kay), both of whom worked collaboratively with Benjamin's children's theatre. This allowed her to offer children in Sydney an extraordinarily rich resource. Lucy would have known Benjamin in 1927 in London when she was working closely with the London Country Council on children's theatre projects. Benjamin had been heavily influenced in London by Susan Isaacs, who had been a leading speaker at the 1937 NEF Conference.

Lucy Woodcock, who by this time knew both the broader educational community and the network of Jewish émigrés very well, used her NSW NEF presidency to circulate an impassioned message of progressive education, an end to examinations and strong support for young working-class people. She drew on her long-established links with the writers and artists of bohemian Sydney when she spoke to the Australian Fellowship of Writers in May 1940 on 'Education and Creative Expression'.[24] For her, the NEF stood for:

> educational improvement throughout the world, so that every individual shall be educated under conditions which allow of the full and harmonious development of his whole personality and lead to his realising and fulfilling his responsibilities to the community.[25]

---

22 World Education Fellowship, NSW Section, *News Bulletin*, April 1968, 2.
23 Margaret Henry, 2007, 'Flowering, Fading and Facing the Facts: World Education Fellowship in Queensland – 1970 to 2005', *New Horizons*, 114: 2–6.
24 *SMH*, 11 May 1940, 9.
25 Ibid., 20 July 1940, 10.

It was on this basis that she wrote as NEF President, for example, in 1940 to call for community support rather than criticism for the Boys' Town initiative at Engadine because it was aimed at:

> directing the energies of underprivileged boys into socially useful channels by methods of gentleness, love, and interesting activity instead of by force and fear and hatred.[26]

But the broader Australian reaction in 1937 to the international NEF conference was outrage in the popular press at what was perceived to be criticism of Australia by outsiders. P.E. Hornibrook, writing in the Teachers Federation journal *Education* in October 1937, satirised this popular press response as a belief that:

> a nefarious band of ignorant foreigners, led by a boorish Scot, abusively and discourteously insulted the educational system of NSW, which, as all know, is perfect.[27]

Hornibrook argued that there had been very little criticism from the speakers, whose exciting ideas were being ignored simply because they were from overseas. This was ingenuous – there was, in fact, significant criticism. Craig Campbell, for example, was one later analyst who pointed out that 'many of the visiting educational experts had been shocked by the centralisation and bureaucratic control over public education which occurred in the Australian States'.[28] The NSW Teachers Federation, planning a series of major conferences in the following year, was determined not to appear as limited in its audience and as elitist as the NEF conference had done.[29]

It was clear to everyone that war was looming and Lucy was drawn into debates about the conflict itself. In the meetings at which she spoke over these early war years, Lucy was on the same platform as activists well known to be in the CPA, bringing her increasingly under the notice of Australian security organisations like ASIO. In April 1938, she took part in a Peace conference titled 'Victims of Aggression' in which she defended teachers as the real educators for Peace, pointing out that teachers 'daily' had to correct the influence of children's home environments, including their

---

26   Ibid.
27   *Education*, October 1937, 379–80, article by P.E. Hornibrook.
28   Craig Campbell, '*Education for Complete Living* (1938)', *Dictionary of Educational History in Australia and New Zealand*, 18 March 2014, dehanz.net.au/entries/education-complete-living-1938/, accessed 17 November 2018.
29   See Chapter 7, this volume.

mothers' views, which were what shaped in children the 'spirit of national (i.e. racial) superiority and hate that brought men to the battlefields'.[30] Then in November 1939, at the Left Book Club, Lucy was one of the featured speakers in a public meeting called 'What are we fighting for?' where she appears to have spoken in a similar vein to her words about war and education on other occasions. In Newcastle in October 1938, for example, she had called for a complete revision of the school syllabus:

> Civilisation had reached the crossroads. Man was facing two crises: the threat of war, which would destroy all they had built, and the dread of poverty, of which Newcastle had its share. Man had failed to adopt conditions which would ensure the abolition of poverty and to make the world secure from the ravages of war …
>
> Children were being crammed with prescribed does of information. The democratic citizen in his childhood must be taught certain fundamental principles so that he could learn to know the truth and search for it. He must be taught to analyse and judge free from the prejudices and superstitions of the past. They should argue as free people not as shackled citizens.
>
> Although a child was bound by environment, he should not be given second hand thought that would prevent free thinking after school life. He should be critical and tolerant …[31]

A decade later, in 1950, at a NSW Peace Council conference on Education for Peace, Lucy argued that:

> Education is the number one defence of civilization, yet it is the greatest casualty when war is declared. Education pays no dividends, except in happiness and security. If the money expended on war had been spent on education there might not have been a Second World War.[32]

And in 1952, speaking before the Teachers Federation during a vote to adopt a Charter of Education based on the UN Declaration of Human Rights, she called for the 'defence of the child, the teacher and the school' against the 'inroads into educational budgets due to the expenditure on armaments and as a result of high prices and profits'.[33]

---

30 *SMH*, 8 April 1938, 4.
31 *Education*, October 1938, 803, Newcastle Conference for a Progressive, Democratic Australia.
32 *Tribune* (Sydney), 14 June 1950.
33 *Biz* (Fairfield), 17 January 1952, 5.

Education was invariably her chosen field of activism. In the late 1930s, Lucy held at least some power to support refugees in her position as a headmistress and as a senior and active unionist. One long-term strategy was to educate young Australians about international history and politics. Lucy and Jess Rose (Lucy's ally in the Equal Pay campaign) moved at the national FSSTA Conference in Hobart in January 1936 that 'international history be a feature of all school syllabuses with the object of fostering world peace'.[34] Fanny Reading had pointed out two other – more immediate – ways that Lucy had been using her power. One was to bring people into the teaching profession. Hilde Byk was one of this first group, a young woman who arrived in Australia in January 1939 as a 25-year-old dressmaker, hoping to find a stable career for herself. By 1941, Lucy had assisted her to enter Sydney University's teaching course, which allowed Hilde to take up a position teaching at Winifred West's school, Frensham, at Bowral.

The other way that Lucy used her power was to help younger people through the secondary school system as students.

Ruth Fink was one of this second group.[35] Lucy was becoming aware that it was not only the adults with whom she was becoming friends who had been scarred by their persecution. The children also carried scars. The medical doctors, Lotte and Friedel Fink, for example, had tried to hide the worsening situation in Germany from their young daughter Ruth, but after she arrived in Sydney, at only seven years of age, Ruth wrote a story about a tyrant called 'Hitilar' who forced everyone to do his bidding on pain of death. Lotte and Friedel were shocked at how unsuccessful their attempts to shield their daughter had been, despite their care and concern to do so.

Ruth Fink spoke no English when she arrived in 1939.[36] Her parents found a flat in Kings Cross and enrolled Ruth in the nearby school, a very small private school named St John's, where, without English, she struggled to learn. The one place where she felt comfortable was in Rosemary Benjamin's Theatre for Children, where Ruth was able not only

---

34 *Mercury* (Hobart), 9 January 1936, 10.
35 We have some other names from this second group, including Hans and Stefanie Goldschmidt (although, see earlier, Lucy also assisted this family with formal sponsorship and accommodation) but many have either already passed away or are no longer able to be interviewed. As Ruth pointed out, Lucy was never one to promote her own activities and so it is difficult to trace much of what she did.
36 Born in 1931. Information drawn from Ruth Fink Latukefu, interview with April Garner, 29 April 2010, held in NLA; and Ruth Fink Latukefu, interview with Heather Goodall, 3 September 2015, Newport.

to act in plays but to write them. Ruth remembers it as 'an outlet, not in the school itself, for things to be more creative'.[37] In 1941, the play she wrote and acted in was 'Tramps become Gentlemen'. Without the Theatre for Children, Ruth reflected, 'it would've been terrible'.[38]

The importance of creative expression was exactly what Lucy was stressing at this time in her role as headmistress at Erskineville.[39] But it was not going to be enough to get Ruth into a high school. The teachers at St John's were pointing to her poor examination and IQ test results – all based on English language and idioms like proverbs – to prove she had no future in secondary education.[40] Lucy had become close friends with Lotte Fink, who was an active member of the NEF, and Lucy became aware of Ruth's unhappiness at school and her parents' rising anxiety about her secondary schooling.

Ruth explains it in this way:

> Lucy didn't know me then, but I imagine my mother telling Lucy that she had been told I might not be capable of further education, and perhaps I should leave school at about 15. And it was Lucy who felt that this was quite wrong, she must have felt, 'No, there's something wrong here.' I think she was already on the lookout for children who fell through that system, because there were others … I was clearly one of those. And similarly there were Australian children who didn't quite fit into the mould of the system, and so they got lost in it. She was there trying to rescue such children.[41]

So Lucy organised for Ruth to be admitted to classes in Erskineville, where direct attention could be focused on her language skills, in order allow her entry into an academic high school. Ruth began Year 6 at Erskineville at the beginning of 1943. She didn't go into the OC and there was no special remedial teaching, so it was just the ordinary class, where Ruth remembers 'trying to catch up what I'd missed at St. John's'. The time was lonely – there was only one other 'foreign' student and Ruth has few memories of Lucy from this time – Miss Woodcock was only the distant school headmistress who happened to be a friend of her mother's. But the

---

37   Ruth Fink Latukefu, interview, 29 April 2010, NLA interview with April Garner.
38   Ruth Fink Latukefu, interview, 3 September 2015.
39   See *Hebrew Standard of Australasia*, 3 September 1942, 10; Beverley Bates (née Langley), interview with Heather Goodall, Devleena Ghosh and Helen Randerson, 1 September 2016.
40   At that time, the NSW Education Department's secondary schools were divided into 'academic' and 'technical' categories. If one failed to qualify for an 'academic' high school, there would be no access to university or any other further education.
41   Ruth Fink Latukefu, interview, 3 September 2015.

Erskineville teaching worked: Ruth was able to pass well enough for entry to the William Street High School, which, while not a highly ranked school, was at least an 'academic' school. At her Intermediate examination, Ruth's pass was even stronger and she was able to transfer to Sydney Girls' High, one of Sydney's elite, academically selective high schools. Both high schools were a struggle for Ruth, but she was determined to master the syllabus. In the end, she passed her Leaving Certificate with very high grades, and headed off to university, against all the predictions from 'IQ' testing and her teachers at St John's and William Street.

It was only when Ruth went to Sydney University, studying anthropology and psychology, that she became much closer to Lucy, who took a keen interest in her university courses and was eager to talk with her about her plans for research in north-western NSW. Lucy remained close friends with Ruth's mother, Lotte, until Lotte's death in 1960. Ruth's own friendship with Lucy continued, finding common ground in Lucy's interest in Aboriginal issues such as the assimilation policies of the time. Lucy remained in touch with Aboriginal friends from Erskineville, like the Watton family, and in 1960 invited Ruth to speak to the United Associations of Women about her north-western fieldwork.[42] Later, Ruth met her future husband, Sione Latukefu, a Tongan Methodist minister and the first Tongan professional historian. In June 1966, just 18 months before her death, Lucy was among the many guests who celebrated Ruth and Sione's wedding at the Wesley Chapel. Sione's parents had made their first overseas visit to share the event. At the reception organised by Ruth's brother Thomas, Lucy was among a diverse gathering of academics, former missionaries from Tonga and refugee families who had been close to Ruth's parents, to hear young Tongans from Sydney singing beautiful Tongan hymns.

* * *

Although Lucy had seemed distant to a child, as Ruth was during the war, Lucy was in fact close friends with émigrés like the Finks as well as to the broader network of those opposing fascism. Her networks were connected – many of the émigrés were interested in the innovative, progressive education in which Lucy was so passionately involved. So there were a number of members of this community who joined the NEF. Ruth remembers her mother in particular to have been an active member

---

42   The Watton family to Lucy, Christmas card, 1955, in Kit Edwards's collection; Lucy to Ruth, 26 August 1960, letter held by Ruth Fink Latukefu.

of the NEF, but she did not join the organisation to meet other émigrés, although a number, like Rose and Max Seidler, the parents of architect Harry Seidler, joined as well. Instead, as Ruth remembers, Lotte was interested in the NEF as a way to meet and interact with the progressive and active intellectual elites of her new country.

The NEF attracted those who believed in a progressive view of the future. With the continuing openness to diverse cultures, inherited from Ensor's Theosophy, the NEF uniquely brought together innovative educators, left-wing activists (including communists), anti-racism and anti-fascism activists like the Christian Socialists and, as well, some individuals among the émigré groups. Lucy herself acted as a meeting point for a number of different movements. Lucy was close, on the one hand, to the members of the NEF and its various activist members. On the other hand, she was linked to the many teachers who, like Dora Birtles, were active in the anti-fascist movements. Dora, as a novelist, poet and journalist, was close friends with Vance and Nettie Palmer, whose elder daughter, Aileen, was in the Ambulance Corps supporting the Republicans in Spain in 1936. Lucy was close also to the Palmer's younger daughter, Helen, who was to step in to take Lucy's place at an international Peace conference in China in 1952 to which Lucy was denied a passport because the federal government feared communist influence. Helen, in turn, was close not only to members of the émigré group, like Emil and Hannah Witton, but to Elsie Rivett, about whom she wrote a moving tribute sent to the Rivett family on Elsie's death in 1964.[43] This was a set of networks in which membership of the Communist Party was common but by no means universal. Most of the people in these extended networks would have seen themselves to be on the Left politically but many would not have been in the CPA. The NEF and its related activist network was one of the few meeting places for 'progressives' whether they were inside or outside 'the Party'.

During 1942, Lucy accepted a number of invitations from the NCJW – introduced by her friend Fanny Reading – to speak about her views on education. The accounts of her talks to the NCJW give important insights into her whole approach to education and to teaching at Erskineville,

---

43 Ron Witton, email pers. comm., 9 October 2015; Helen Palmer on Elsie Rivett, cited in Gwyn Long (Elsie's nephew) to Ida Brown for Judith Godden in 8 January 1987, in Papers of Elizabeth Long (Gwyn Long's mother) re Rivett family, Mitchell Library, SLNSW, Reference code: 4922528. See also Creative Leisure Movement papers, VII: History Files 1920–1991, MLMSS 7550/18/4, for letters from Gwyn Long to Judith Godden.

insights that are seldom available from her political speeches to and on behalf of the Teachers Federation, which were usually focused on single issues. These articles in the *Hebrew Standard of Australasia*, although brief summaries, cover much wider ground, pointing to Lucy's goals of fostering independence of thought among young students so they could grow up to exercise their rights in active democratic debates and decisions.

She explained first that she had worked for the Jewish people:

> in recognition of the kindness she had received as a young teacher at a country place where a Jewish family (Robinovitz) had been so kind to her. Now she felt that she wanted to repay that family by helping their unhappy fellow Jews.[44]

In a later talk, Lucy described her approach to learning:

> The old system of memorizing subjects was giving way to learning by practical experience. All facilities were now given children so that their creative abilities could be awakened. The child was learning how to govern himself, how to control meetings. Reason was given place over parrot fashion learning. Visits to museums, art galleries and factories gave children practical lifelong illustrations. It was important nowadays to know what the child is thinking and therefore group discussions were encouraged. This method was the only way to make the children stand on their own feet and not be imitators, not a machine-made individual but one who would build on its own foundation.[45]

Over this time, in the years just before and then during the war, Lucy was able to draw the many threads of her life together: her long commitment to women's rights, her sustained internationalism and opposition to racism, her passion for teaching in child-centred learning environments, her unionism and her desire for a peaceful future. Each of these were to be sustained, although often woven together in very different ways, through the rest of Lucy's long and active life.

---

44 *Hebrew Standard of Australasia*, 1 January 1942, 6. This was the friendship described so movingly by Queenie Symonds in later years and referred to in Chapter 2. Queenie Symonds, interviewed by Brenda Factor, NSW Bicentennial oral history collection [sound recording], 1987. Held in National Library of Australia (Session 1 of 2, 42:47–43:45), nla.gov.au/nla.obj-216364926/listen?searchTerm= Woodcock%20jewish%20refugees, accessed 15 October 2017.
45 *Hebrew Standard of Australasia*, 3 September 1942, 10.

Figure 6.1: Photograph of Lotte Fink (on left) and Lucy, talking and smoking, in Lotte's back yard in Sydney in the 1930s.

Source: Courtesy Ruth Fink Latukefu, from her personal collection.

7

What Sort of Australia? 1938

In 1938, many currents came together for Lucy and the organisations in which she was so active. It was the Sesquicentenary Year – marking 150 years since the British had claimed sovereignty over the continent. It was well known that state and federal governments would make the Sesquicentenary an occasion to celebrate British settler society and there were many people who either wanted their voices heard in the events or wanted to challenge them altogether. Yet the threat of war was also growing – so while some citizens were raising jingoistic national pride, there were many others who were trying to defend the peace.

The NSW Teachers Federation had been planning since 1935 to hold a major conference in the sesquicentenary year to foreground the importance of education for building a new nation in Australia.[1] But Aboriginal people, too, had been planning for some time to hold a counter demonstration – asserting their opposition to the official 'celebrations' and to the British occupation. The plans for the Day of Mourning were underway well before 1938, led by Aboriginal activists Bill Ferguson (who brought the Australian Workers' Union and other unions), Jack Patten (who brought the nationalist Australia First movement as well as his friend, the unionist, sometime socialist and Theosophist Michael Sawtell) and Pearl Gibbs (from Brewarrina, who brought alliances with the women's movement organisations including the United Associations of Women).[2]

---
1 *Education*, 15 June 1935, 239, FSSTA plan for linked 1938 World Education Conference.
2 *The Abo Call*, 1938, Issues 1–6, edited by Jack Patten for the Aborigines Progressive Association.

Yet from 1935 also, as war fears grew, some teachers tried to address the increasing tensions by teaching children about maintaining the peace. One way to do that was through the League of Nations, established in the wake of World War I with the express hope of fostering increased international communication to avert future hostilities. Teachers were finding that it was difficult to obtain League publications to include in their course materials, so in August 1937 they turned to the NSW Teachers Federation for assistance through its Peace Committee, then chaired by Ethel Teerman, who had become a high school teacher and Federation member. As much an activist as her parents had been in Cessnock, the younger Ethel had been busy in the Peace Committee, building links with the International Peace Campaign (IPC) with which the Federation had affiliated. The IPC had been founded in Britain as a reaction to fascist Italy's invasion of Abyssinia in October 1935.[3] It aimed to influence public opinion internationally and to organise popular support for the peacekeeping tasks of the League of Nations by coordinating groups across the whole political range, from communist to conservative, from atheists to the religious. Its leadership demonstrated this broad base: it was led by the British conservative Robert Cecil, Viscount of Chelwood, and the French radical socialist, deputy and later minister of the Popular Front Government Pierre Cot. Ethel followed up the concerns teachers raised with her and, by early 1938, she had secured permission for the NSW Education Department to publish League of Nations publications as teaching resources.

The Day of Mourning was planned for Australia Day, 26 January 1938, as an Aboriginal-only gathering at the Australian Hall in Elizabeth St, Sydney. The Communist Party of Australia criticised it as separatism but it was strongly supported by the nationalist Australia First movement.[4] The Aboriginal campaign had pushed the state government into acting too. During 1937 there were two inquiries in process. One was a State Parliament Select Committee inquiring into the conditions of Aborigines, to which Ferguson had given evidence, basing much of his information on the community research of Pearl Gibbs at Brewarrina Station in the previous months. Other witnesses included Caroline Tennant Kelly, an anthropologist working at Kempsey under the direction of Professor

---

3   'International Peace Campaign: History', SNAC [Social Networks and Archival Context], snaccooperative.org/ark:/99166/w62n95mj, accessed 17 November 2018.
4   Heather Goodall, *Invasion to Embassy: Land in Aboriginal Politics, 1770–1970* (St Leonards: Allen and Unwin, 1996), 202, 230–46.

A.P. Elkin, who was seeking recognition for a formal role for anthropologists in the state's administration. There was also, however, a Public Service Board inquiry into the Aborigines Protection Board itself, and Elkin, well connected in political circles, concentrated on this inquiry as he saw it as a stronger possibility for assisting anthropological involvement in future administration.

The Day of Mourning was held as planned, with some publicity and photographs published in *Pix*,[5] but political interest in the Select Committee hearings waned. In February it finally collapsed for want of a quorum. The Aboriginal campaigners used this collapse to gain further publicity for the problems with the state government's apparatus. Pearl Gibbs and Caroline Kelly both rallied the women they knew in the feminist groups – both right and left wing – who demonstrated en masse at the final hearing of the Select Committee, gaining a striking photograph and headline in the *Truth*: 'We Are Absolutely Disgusted'.[6] The United Associations of Women (UA) was there, among a range of women's organisations from across the political spectrum. There is no roll of the 'fifty prominent women' who attended this protest, but if Lucy was not there, she certainly knew about it.

This was only the beginning of a tumultuous year for Lucy as an activist. As we have seen, Lucy was already immersed in the campaigns to improve nutrition and housing for the families of Erskineville and in the development of policy to improve the physical environment of schools. But by 1938, many among teachers and the public knew of the growing power of fascism in Europe. Lucy had already been assisting Jewish refugees bringing news from Europe since at least 1935, and she was well aware too that the presence of representatives from fascist Italy and Nazi Germany in the NEF conferences was troubling many who had embraced its progressive education and internationalist messages. As the senior vice president of the NSW Teachers Federation, Lucy knew Ethel Teerman's work on the Peace Committee and the two worked closely together in the events around the Peace movement and women in the early months of 1938.

The first was the National Women's Peace Conference, closely aligned with the IPC and held in two synchronised sessions – one in Sydney and one in Perth on 10 and 11 April 1938. The Sydney session brought

---

5   *The Abo Call*, April 1938, Issue 1, 1.
6   *Truth*, 20 February 1938, 35.

together women interested in Peace from across the political spectrum, from the UA to more conservative bodies like the National Council of Women. The synchronised Perth conference was convened by the influential conservative feminist Bessie Rischbieth and attended by a range of women including the CPA member Katherine Susannah Prichard.[7] The program for both conferences addressed five key themes: treaty obligations, armaments reduction, strengthening the League of Nations, establishing international conflict resolution mechanisms and the child and peace. Ethel Teerman was a part of the Sydney organising group for the conference and coordinated the NSW Teachers Federation involvement, which focused on the sessions on 'The School Child and Peace' and 'The Pre-School Child and Peace'.

Lucy chaired the session on the 'School Child' and gave an important keynote address to it, titled 'Prejudices'. Her activism at this time was in just this area, and her speech must have addressed prejudice against women but also racial prejudice against both Jews – in Europe and Australia – and against Aboriginal people. Lucy offered no simplistic 'maternalist' line but instead pointed out that it was mothers who fostered much of the prejudice that was exhibited in schools. She closed by arguing that 'A school for mothers is long overdue … Teachers are daily correcting misconceptions passed on by the mothers to the children'.[8]

Ethel herself spoke in this session, discussing the need to teach children in both primary and secondary schooling about the possibilities for peace and about the League of Nations. Then the anthropologist Caroline Tennant Kelly spoke, describing the prejudice against 'pommies' that she had felt as a child of English immigrants when she attended school in Australia, and then pointed to the prejudice she had observed as a researcher against Aboriginal children in public schooling. Finally, Marie Gollan spoke in the later session on the Pre-School Child and Peace, supporting Lucy's arguments by pointing out that 'it was the mothers of bygone years, as well as the schools, who fostered the spirit of national superiority and hate that brought men to the battlefields', continuing: '[i]f we wish to bring about permanent friendship and peace among nations we must begin with the child of today'.[9]

---

7   *West Australian* (Perth), 2 April 1938, 8.
8   *Education*, 24 May 1938, 636.
9   *SMH*, 8 April 1938, 4.

Soon after, a 'Mother's Day Peace Conference' was held in Sydney in May but it had a very different tone, essentialising women as maternal peacekeepers. While Spanish and Chinese women drew on the brutal invasions of their own countries to make their passionate demands for peace, the tone was set by the overall conference leadership, which was by Christian organisations, although they ranged from the more conservative through to more militant bodies. Lucy spoke prominently here too, continuing her emphasis on the child and education but with a softened line towards mothers:

> The weakness lies in the way we educate children ... The present system of education bred the competitive spirit and love of power that would destroy all that women's organisations stood for.[10]

Perhaps unsurprisingly, given the involvement of groups like the Salvation Army, the headline read: 'Mother's Army: Women to work for peace'. The frequent portrayal of women by speakers in such militaristic language contributed to the distinctive message of this conference compared to the April one, despite the involvement of similar people – including Caroline Tennant Kelly and Ethel Teerman and the Teachers Federation Peace group she led. Caroline Tennant Kelly (called Mrs Timothy Kelly!) said: 'I do blame the mothers who took their children to the military tattoo ... I think there is something wrong in the dramatic presentation of war.'[11]

These were the major Peace gatherings in 1938 specifically aimed at women, but the Peace movement itself became increasingly active over the year, as war became ever more likely. Within the Federation, Ethel Teerman's Peace Committee published curricula such as that for 'International Peace', amplifying the call made by Lucy Woodcock and Jess Rose in 1936. The Peace Committee now encouraged the Teachers Federation Council to go further by establishing a Peace Society in which all teachers could take part. It called on the IPC and the League of Nations to pressure the Australian Government to honour its treaty obligations.[12] In October, British Prime Minister Neville Chamberlain made his 'Peace in Our Time' announcement of the Munich Agreement between Britain, Germany, France and Italy, allowing Germany to annex parts of Czechoslovakia. The agreement did little to allay grave fears about

---

10 *SMH*, 9 May 1938, 13.
11 Ibid.
12 *Education*, September 1938, 790; November 1938, 24.

coming warfare. The price paid during World War I – which had been paid in blood by so many families in Europe and Australia, including Lucy's own – was never far from public memory.

Since 1936, after the invasion of Abyssinia, the Teachers Federation had organised a major rally on Armistice Day, 11 November, the anniversary of the end of World War I. In 1938, the third of these rallies occurred, with leading speakers from the IPC, the Public Service Association, the League of Nations Union and the Federation itself. Ethel Teerman delivered the Federation message, echoing those of the other keynote speakers: 'the greatest enemy to peace was the inactivity of the people'. She sketched out the difference between 'those who say smilingly "It can't happen here" and those who say with determination, "It won't happen here"'.[13]

It was this belief in the need for widespread, citizen responsibility that underlay the major activity of the Teachers Federation over the sesquicentenary year: its call for 'Education for a Progressive, Democratic Australia'.

Lucy worked closely with the overall coordinator, Sam Lewis, to plan this broad campaign, which organised a series of conferences in major cities across the state, sent deputations to government and initiated strategies to intervene in the wider structures of education, such as the university examinations, against which Lucy had campaigned for years because they shaped all earlier schooling. Whereas the NEF conference in 1937 had concentrated on the educational profession, the Teachers Federation was determined to include the Australian public in the debates during these conferences. The Federation announced 'We Go To The People' and argued 'we must become evangelists in the cause of educational reform. We must convince hundreds of thousands of people of the need for educational reform, for educational expenditure'.[14] To each event, the Federation invited the peak organisations of farmers, unions, doctors, dentists, journalists, public servants, parents' and citizens' organisations, women's organisations, surrounding shires and municipal bodies. After an initial, large four-day conference in Sydney in early June, there were gatherings in Cessnock in July, Tumut and Bankstown in August, then major conferences at Wollongong late in September, then in Newcastle and later still in Goulburn.

13 *Education*, December 1938, 54.
14 *Education*, April 1938, 591.

Figure 7.1: Lucy Woodcock on the executive of the Teachers Federation with her allies in the campaign for the role of education in a vision of Australia's democratic future.
Source: NSW Teachers Federation archives, undated photograph P2255.

As the senior vice president of the Federation and a school headmistress, Lucy was a headline speaker in the conferences. Her speeches repeated her view that the goal of public education was to nurture a child to become an independent-minded, thoughtful, questioning and creative person, who could take their place as a well-informed and independently minded democratic citizen. This view of the school as the centre of a democratic society was one she was to repeat on other occasions, like that in Melbourne in January 1940 when she addressed the Australian Teachers' Federation (successor to the Federated State School Teachers' Association). 'The school', she said, 'should be a centre in the life of the district, fitting the child for life in a democratic community.' She cited Erskineville Public School as one example, explaining how it was associated with a branch of the Sydney Day Nurseries Association and a Children's Library managed by voluntary workers under the Creative Leisure Movement, as well as having informal parents' groups.

Fundamentally, all her speeches showed her deep conviction that education could achieve social justice and peace.

The main conference in 1938 was held over four days from 8 to 11 June. Lucy was the central speaker in the session on 'Curriculum, Extension of School Leaving Age and Country Education' where she spoke on the need for a complete revision of the existing curriculum. The theme of her talk, according to the program (which she had had a role in formulating), was to be:

> the fitting of the syllabus to the child and his [sic] present and future needs – greater freedom to be allowed to both teacher and child. The curriculum to be linked up with the child's real world and the world with which he will come in contact when he leaves school … Greater attention to be paid to technical education and to real commercial and rural education … Increased attention to be paid to the conditions and institutions of people in other countries and to the effect of the interaction of people of different countries on each other.[15]

The key elements of Lucy's speech were reported in *Education*.[16] As well as pointing to the importance of educational opportunities for country children and the need for a new course of training for teachers, she focused on the urgency of curriculum change to create 'well-balanced, tolerant, critical young people'. In a period when eugenic interest in biological explanations for abilities and attitudes was widespread, among the Left as well as the Right, Lucy insisted that it was instead social forces that determined the capacity of people to be informed and active democratic citizens. Education, she argued in this speech, must be about more than 'reading, writing and arithmetic'. It must support individual creativity, respond to the challenges children faced in the real world and nurture inquiry and independent thinking.

In the conference at Newcastle, Lucy expanded on these themes, arguing that human society faced two threats: that of war, which would destroy all they had built, and that of the dread of poverty, of which Newcastle had its share. She warned that:

> Man had failed to adopt conditions which would ensure the abolition of poverty and to make the world secure from the ravages of war. They had been told that democracy had failed, but had they ever given it a fair chance?[17]

---

15 *Education*, June 1938, Insert: Conference program, p. 6.
16 *Education*, July 1938, 705.
17 *Education*, October 1938, 803.

Education must respond to these threats, she insisted, by teaching children 'to analyse and judge free from prejudices and superstitions of the past. They should argue as free people, not as shackled citizens'. Lucy continued:

> Although a child was bound by environment, he should not be given secondhand thought that would prevent free thinking after school life. He should be critical and tolerant. He should be given a curriculum which he would love and respond to … Here could be suggested a basic principle on which a real and lasting democracy could be built.
>
> Competition was not cooperation; and if [we] shared and thought together [we] would eliminate arming against each other … With a new curriculum, [we] could remould and rebuild society so that war and poverty would be abolished.[18]

Lucy Woodcock was no friend of tradition. She had titled her 1925 book *Justice vs Tradition*, and throughout her life she clearly believed that tradition made justice impossible. On the contrary, tradition was the source of prejudice and discrimination. In Newcastle she continued:

> With a new curriculum, we could remould and rebuild society so that war and poverty would be abolished. If we had made them in the past, we could unmake them in the future. In this regard, we owed a great debt to Russia where tradition did not exist. If we were free from tradition, we could build anew.[19]

Her interest in Russia was to be sustained over many years, although there continued to be no evidence that she was ever a member of the Communist Party, despite frequently expressing support for Russian innovations in education and social relations. The NEF, too, expressed these views – which Clews argues was one reason for its falling financial support after 1945 from the US.[20] Lucy's position in 1938 was, however, similar to many of the people she was by then associating with, including Jessie Street who campaigned strongly for support for the Soviet Union over the 1930s and '40s. Lucy was certainly close friends with

---
18 Ibid.
19 Ibid. The journal reported this in the third person – for clarity here, the word 'they' has been transposed into 'we'. Lucy probably also delivered this speech in the present and future tenses, rather than in the past tense as the journal rephrased her words.
20 Christopher Clews, 'The New Education Fellowship and the Reconstruction of Education: 1945 to 1966' (PhD thesis, Institute of Education, University of London, 2009), 107–22.

colleagues in the Federation who were in the CPA, like Sam Lewis and Ethel Teerman. Lucy's own position, however, as we have seen in earlier chapters, was strongly socialist but had been formed during the 1920s in her years among bohemian friends and unconventional lifestyles as well as the influences she drew on from Irvine and others during her economics studies. At Erskineville, those who were her students in the 1930s believed Lucy to be a communist and ASIO kept trying to find evidence of her membership in the party but failed completely. It seems most likely that, like Jessie Street, Rev. Alf Clint, Bishop Ernest Henry Burgmann and others of the time, Lucy greatly admired Russia but did not ever join the Communist Party – or indeed any others.[21]

The leading role Lucy took in this campaign was not only as the senior vice president of the Federation but as the new president of the NSW Branch of the NEF. In doing so, she located herself strongly with those advocating the significance of the social interactions of the child. Lucy believed that the development of the human mind was a social as well as an individual process. Therefore the curriculum should be 'planned on broad lines … social studies, conditions of the world, general science, creative projects, music, art, literature, the living environments'.[22] The curriculum should, therefore, provide for each child both as an individual and social being.

The campaign overall did not end with conferences and meetings. A permanent committee was established in September 1938 to continue the campaign and to raise funds for ongoing local communication so that the broader public would have a role in and awareness of educational innovations.[23] There were then a series of deputations to the Minister for Education, putting forward the goals arising from the conference resolutions. In one deputation on 26 October, the Federation also put strongly the case for the repeal of the 1932 legislation that forced the dismissal of married women teachers.[24] Minister Drummond conceded that the Act had been introduced as an emergency financial measure

---

21   Ernest Henry Burgmann, High Anglican Bishop of Canberra and Goulburn, was called by newspapers of the day 'The Red Bishop', Anne Sanders, 'Burgmann, Ernest Henry (1885–1967)', *Obituaries Australia*, National Centre of Biography, The Australian National University, oa.anu.edu.au/obituary/burgmann-ernest-henry-9626/text24834, accessed 10 July 2018, e.g. *Argus* (Melbourne), 25 September 1948, 5. When Lucy's passport was obstructed by the federal government in 1954, the representations made on her behalf by Rev. Alf Dickie stressed that she had never been a member of any political party. Lucy Godiva Woodcock ASIO file, Vol. 1, f 138, A6119, 2030, NAA, 11 June 1954.
22   *Education*, 15 July 1938, 705, report of conference.
23   *Education*, October 1938, 807.
24   *Married Women (Teachers and Lecturers) Act 1932* (NSW).

during the worst years of the Depression, but argued that it had now been demonstrated to reduce sick leave among remaining women and make administration smoother, despite causing some problems in the supply of trained teachers.[25] As well as the deputations to the state minister, the NSW Teachers Federation organised a deputation to the federal government facilitated by Billy Hughes and including the Australian Teachers' Federation, arguing that educational reform was a national responsibility not only a state one.[26]

In one of the first results from the Federation's 1938 conferences, the NSW Minister for Education D.H. Drummond began the process of surveying and improving the physical environment of schools. The Teachers Federation embraced this, as it was in accord with the goal Lucy had long argued: the need to have environments that would evoke positive emotional responses from students, where they would want to engage and learn.[27] Federation President Malcolm Mackinnon and Lucy, as senior vice president, were relieved of other duties to carry out an inspection of schools across the state, an experience that Lucy brought to her later conference speeches and which she wove into her campaigns for better housing for working-class communities.[28] The Federation participation in arguing for improvements in the space, buildings, infrastructure and equipment – the hardware – of education has been criticised by some commentators as being a retreat from the intellectual content of education, but it arose from the complex of concerns about progressive education and working-class environments.[29] It may have been easier for governments and parents' organisations to contribute money to infrastructure rather than tackle the more complex intellectual challenges of education. But it should also be seen in the context of its time, when eugenicist biological causes were being increasingly propounded to explain educational disadvantage. In this setting, a focus on the environment of schools was a significant challenge to eugenic 'solutions'. In any case, the school infrastructure was certainly not the only concern of either the Federation or of Lucy herself. In February 1937, Lucy Woodcock and Zillah Bocking had called on the Australian Teachers' Federation meeting for parents' and citizens'

---

25 *Education*, November 1938, 46–48.
26 *Education*, February 1939, 118.
27 *Newcastle Morning Herald and Miners' Advocate*, 9 August 1938, 5.
28 *Education*, July 1938, 696.
29 John Michael O'Brien, 'The NSW Teachers Federation, 1957–1975' (PhD thesis, University of Wollongong, 1985), 121–22.

bodies nationally to pay more attention to research into education than to equipment.[30] The government concern with building was nevertheless an immediate and visible recognition of the Federation's calls for reform.

In what was a parallel process, rather than a direct result, the primary final examination was abolished. This had been a major demand that Lucy had made on many occasions, although in practice it did not meet her concern – or that of the progressive educationists – that education would be shaped by the needs of the child rather than by the needs of the education system and its secondary and, ultimately, tertiary structures. In mid-1938, in regional areas, the primary final examination was replaced by a combination of intelligence testing, a new and problematic tool of the emerging field of educational psychology as discussed earlier, and an unreliable assessment of work in sixth class. In Sydney, Parramatta and Newcastle, the high school entrance component of the primary final examination was retained for those seeking admission to high, intermediate high and junior high schools. This was because positions remained competitive for schools in these areas, and among students seeking bursaries.[31] It had been this high school entrance component that had stopped so many children from working-class families going from primary school to the type of secondary school that would allow them entrance to a university. It was not till 1943 that the high school entrance component of the primary final examination, even in the cities, was replaced by the combination of intelligence testing and assessment of work in sixth class. While this was seen as less draconian than the original primary final, the process of sorting children into different types of high school – and ultimately into career options – was continued.

One major direction, however, which arose from both the 1937 NEF Conference and the Teachers Federation campaign in 1938 was the rising emphasis in the NEF on discussion and free exchange of views as an educational methodology.[32] Lucy referred to this as a key element in her approaches to developing learning environments to foster democracy in her Erskineville classes where:

---

30 *Education*, 17 February 1937, 76.
31 *Education*, July 1938, 696; 'Facts and Figures: Examinations', NSW Department of Education, education.nsw.gov.au/about-us/our-people-and-structure/history-of-government-schools/facts-and-figures/examinations, accessed 6 August 2017.
32 Margaret White, 'Traversing Personal and Public Boundaries: Discourses of Engagement in New Education, 1930s to 1980s', *Paedogogica Historica* 43, no. 1 (2007): 156–57, doi.org/10.1080/00309230601080634.

group discussions were encouraged. This was the only way to make the children stand on their own feet and not be imitators, not a machine made individual, but one that would build on its own foundation.[33]

This approach shaped the way the NEF developed in Australia. It initiated a program of summer schools, such as the one at Newport in January 1940, aimed at bringing together educators and students from many different environments and expanding its focus from education within schools to lifelong 'leisure' education, that is to learning in the community. It emerged to be a powerful learning situation – highly valued by participants like Clarice McNamara, Lucy's long-time colleague in the NSW NEF. In the words of one analyst, discussion became 'a significant technology in education'.[34]

A specific strategy emerged as well from the Teachers Federation campaign. In August 1938, the Federation Council decided that despite the partial removal of the primary final examinations, the university entrance requirements still exercised iron control over all secondary and primary public schooling. The Federation decided that it should attempt to intervene at the university level itself, nominating for graduate seats on the University of Sydney Senate in order to raise a voice for public schooling.[35] Lucy evaluated the plan and reported back to the council in October, leading to the nomination of two teacher graduates for Senate positions, one man and one woman. Lucy was the woman, nominated by fellow Federationists R.B. Noble, Ethel Teerman, L.A. Walsh and L.A. Gordon. These nominations both failed, but the Federation had not given up. Lucy was again nominated in 1942 by the same colleagues, except for Ethel, who had married Sam Lewis in 1940 and so had been forced to retire from teaching.

---

33 National Council of Jewish Women (NCJW), first annual meeting of Western Suburbs Committee, in the Enfield home of Miss Lucy Woodcock, *Hebrew Standard of Australasia*, 3 September 1942, 10. Lucy may have let out some or all of this house to Jewish refugee friends, the Goldschmidt family, whose entry to Australia she had sponsored. Stephanie Goldschmidt called and hosted this meeting, and the family had given the 7 Beaumaris St, Enfield, address of Lucy's home as their residence on their naturalisation applications in 1949 and 1950.
34 Clarice McNamara, 'Summer School of Leadership, Newport, NSW', *New Horizons*, Autumn 1940, 15; White, 'Traversing Personal and Public Boundaries', 156; Martin Lawn, 'Reflecting the Passion: Mid-century Projects for Education', *History of Education* 33, no. 5 (2004): 506.
35 *Education*, September 1938, 795.

This time, Lucy was elected, becoming the first woman graduate to be elected by her fellows to serve on the university's Senate. *Smith's Weekly* ran a half-page spread on Lucy in April 1942, titled 'Sees New Vistas for Education', choosing to focus (ironically given her internationalist outlook) on her 'settler' family origins and her commitment to Australia, with 'Love of Australia' written above her portrait.[36] She was described as a woman from a working-class area who had risen to the heights of service in the public education system, highly regarded by her peers and students alike as well as attaining distinction in her hard-won, evening-course university degrees. Her decade of country teaching explained her wide understanding of the whole country. The warmth of her relationships with those rural communities was demonstrated by the note of congratulations she had received on her Senate election from the community at Eden, where she had known the Robinovitz family.

Figure 7.2: 'Sees New Vistas for Education'. Sketch of Lucy for article in *Smith's Weekly* about her election to the University of Sydney Senate.

Source: *Smith's Weekly*, 4 April 1942. Trove, National Library of Australia. No attribution for artist.

---

36 'Sees New Vistas for Education', *Smith's Weekly*, 4 April 1942, 14.

Just as Lucy and the Federation had hoped, the election allowed her to explain her philosophy and call for reform. In her school at Erskineville, the *Smith's Weekly* reporter explained, in some surprise:

> modern methods and progressive ideas are encouraged, with the basic idea that that a child should be a personality to be developed rather than a phonograph disc to be impressed with a hieroglyphic jumble of facts. Miss Woodcock aims to develop the creative faculties of the mind, to make children aware of their own power in original effort. Startling though it may seem, she even encourages them to write poetry, frequently with interesting results.[37]

Lucy's role as NSW NEF President over the previous two years was called on to demonstrate the credibility of her ideas and her international connections, all brought into the service of her Australian vision. To confirm this, her deep commitment to the Erskineville community was stressed:

> Miss Woodcock has also taken a deep interest in sociology and is particularly concerned with the question of housing, especially of poor people. Since her school is in an industrial area where over-crowding exists, its incidence is inescapably and more or less continuously before her, so that, on this subject, she can speak with particular knowledge.

The reporter summed her up:

> Miss Lucy Woodcock is a fine public speaker, an impressive personality, capable, humane, kindly and confidence-inspiring.

This description would have been recognised by Beverley Langley, Betty Makin and others of her students, even if not by all – given that a few remember her as distant and 'terrifying'. The sketch published with the article accords with this glimpse of her softer side. Certainly distinguished and imposing, it is nevertheless a poignant image of a woman with a sadness about her eyes.

---

37   Ibid.

Expanding Visions:
1939–1946

8
Women and War

The outbreak of war in September 1939 was a bitter disappointment to Lucy as it was to many who had campaigned for Peace. Lucy's pacifism had been deepened with her brother's death in World War I, both the sadness and the conviction staying with her throughout her life.[1] As World War II approached, Lucy had been a staunch advocate of the need to build international understanding by negotiation and interaction, not by armaments.

But the immediate issue for her in confronting a new war was that it greatly worsened the problems she had been campaigning to solve. One was the problem of older sisters being kept out of school to look after younger children in the family. The other was the government's decision in 1932 to sack married women teachers and refuse to employ any woman who had married. Both problems were intensified by the war, and Lucy tried to mobilise the organisations in which she was heavily involved – the NSW Teachers Federation and the United Associations of Women (UA) – to campaign for justice on them. In the process, however, Lucy's calls for action were to be redirected in unexpected ways.

This chapter offers a very different view of the 'home front' – this is not an account of how home resources and labour were mobilised to win a war, nor is it about the glamorous and fragile world of troop romances and tragic disappearances. Instead, it is about the grim struggle many working-class families had just to stay afloat as conditions worsened.

---

1   Kit Edwards, interview with Heather Goodall, 30 November 2017, Hardy's Bay.

***

Lucy had become increasingly associated with socialists and communists among her Federation colleagues during the 1930s as she found, for example, that it was Ethel Teerman and Sam Lewis who most consistently supported the campaign to restore jobs for married women. After a period as a rank-and-file member of Federation Council (1930–33), Lucy had been re-elected as senior vice president from 1934 onwards. While maintaining her alliances with the core group of women activists within the Federation, like Beatrice Taylor, Lucy became more involved in many campaigns with Sam Lewis, Hettie Ross and other teachers who were Communist Party of Australia (CPA) members. Others to whom Lucy became close, like Clarice McNamara, secretary of the New Education Fellowship (NEF), had been associated with the CPA when younger. The Australian Security Service, ASIO, believed for a time that Lucy had been a member of the CPA herself, but never found any evidence. Despite her increasingly close alliances, Lucy seems to have distanced herself from the awkward twists and turns imposed on CPA members by the Comintern policy about the war. Rather than the shift to the 'United Front' approach imposed on CPA members after June 1941, Lucy held a consistent opposition to war and its diversion of funds from what she saw as the more urgent tasks of building up independence and critical thinking and 'cooperative spirit' among young people to ensure an educated public in the democracy of the future.[2] Lucy's statements throughout the war all condemned the way that Australian expenditure of public funds on warfare and 'destruction' diverted those funds from the more urgent tasks of reconstruction, which in her view were primarily about education. She continued to take this view to the end of her life, writing to Rewi Alley in 1956 about the coming atomic testing at Maralinga: 'Huge preparation and much money going up in smoke that could help ordinary people to get many things they can't get now.'[3]

***

In order to try to keep girls in schools, Lucy had argued in 1938 for three things that would address this in her working-class area: raising the school-leaving age, increasing child endowment payments to mothers and

---

2   *Mercury* (Hobart), 19 January 1936, 10; *SMH*, 8 April 1938, 4; *Argus* (Melbourne), 8 January 1948, 5; *Mercury* (Hobart), 12 May 1949, 8.
3   Lucy G. Woodcock to Rewi Alley, 14 March 1956.

creating better and more accessible childcare. All of this was aimed at practical support for the employed women of Erskineville and their older daughters. Lucy had made the case for these three linked measures in each of her speeches at the Federation's 1938 conferences for a progressive, democratic Australia. But the whole problem was made far more urgent with the war because many adult women, who had previously been at home, were drawn into war jobs – either those jobs vacated by men who enlisted or the new jobs created to build munitions and other war supplies. It was the older girls in working-class families who paid the price of war work through their lost schooling and lost opportunities to gain job skills.

The Federation strongly supported the goal of training more childcare staff and equipping them to be educators rather than only carers. Linking early childhood training to that of primary and secondary teachers had been a key demand from left-wing teachers like Marie Gollan during 1938 and 1939. As pressure increased on all women to take up war work, the need for more childcare, better trained staff and better facilities all escalated. The UA initiated a body to address these issues in April 1941, known as the Women's Forum for Social and Economic Reconstruction, which was jointly run by the UA and the Teachers Federation.[4] Jessie Street chaired this but it seems that Lucy was actively involved, along with Clarice McNamara (as the NEF representative), and Mona Ravenscroft as secretary. Certainly the committee's interests in improving economic conditions and accessing credit for women's needs were in line with Lucy's goals. The major outcome from this Women's Forum was the discussion on the theme of childcare at the UA conference in August 1942. Lucy spoke there to call for the immediate construction of additional childcare centres – saying that the heaviest cost of the war effort had fallen on the group of women who 'in normal times would be looking after their young families'. Strategically, she evoked alarmist images: 'Many cases of delinquency were found among children whose parents were away from home working during the day or night'. She was supported by unionist Flo Davis from the Hotel, Club and Restaurant Employees' Union, who detailed how her members were making do with poor food – if any at all – to ensure there was support for their families.[5]

---

4   *SMH*, 4 April 1941.
5   Women's Forum (with Flo Davis) *SMH*, 9 May 1941, 4; *Land* (Sydney), 20 June 1941, 13; *SMH*, 7 July 1941, 7.

The Teachers Federation in turn generated a new body, the Committee for the Care of the Child in War Time, which brought unionists together with 'suburban groups of women working for childcare'. This body organised a conference, held on 12 December 1942, chaired by Lucy and attended (on the model of the 1938 Federation conferences) by a range of community organisations, including the Kindergarten Union and the Sydney Day Nurseries Association, as well as academics and professionals in child health and development.[6] This December conference generated many views – some openly denigrating young working-class women and leading to headlines like 'Girls Deceive Homes: "Wages" from Soldiers'.[7] Others, however, were far more supportive of women, including those expressing concern that 'the health of the child was suffering, and of the mother, too, who is carrying a double burden of worry and work'.[8]

The headlines arising from this committee were nevertheless sensational. The *Sydney Morning Herald* screamed '"Worst Wartime Social Problem": Children Running Wild', while the Perth *South Western Advertiser* added figures: 'Twelve Thousand Children Running Wild: "Worst War Time Social Problem"'.[9]

Lucy's concerns, however, were firmly rooted in the conditions of the working-class communities around her at Erskineville. She was horrified at the appalling conditions into which the children of working-class families were forced when their mothers were doing war work. As she spoke to the NSW Teachers Federation soon after:

> Pigs were better treated than many children left in some privately owned 'minding' schools ... Several such schools were run for profit in slum conditions, in single rooms and back yards. Ordinary standards of decency and cleanliness were often not observed and no attempt was made to isolate sick from healthy children.[10]

As chairperson, Lucy wrote up the report of the December 1942 conference, which the Federation printed and circulated widely.[11] Some at this conference spoke about a rising and uncontrolled epidemic

---

6   *Hebrew Standard of Australasia*, 26 November 1942, 6–7.
7   *Sun* (Sydney), 31 January 1943, 7.
8   *Murrumbidgee Irrigator* (Leeton), 25 June 1943, 3, quoting Lucy's report of this December 1942 conference; *SMH*, 2 December 1943, 4, briefly reporting the conference.
9   *Sun* (Sydney), 3 October 1943, 7; *South Western Advertiser* (Perth), 11 November 1943, 4.
10 *News* (Adelaide), 21 November 1944, 4.
11 *Murrumbidgee Irrigator* (Leeton), 25 June 1943, 3, citing Lucy's report, the 'Emergency Plan of the Joint Committee'.

of delinquency, runaways and truancy, notably the state government representatives and A.P. Elkin, representing the academic voice. The report, however, was less alarmist and far more constructive. In it, Lucy stressed the importance of the Commonwealth assuming control for a well-planned and well-resourced strategy across the country to increase childcare facilities and improve care worker training in childcare and early childhood education. This would ensure places for the many thousands of children of war workers who needed assistance to care for their families while they were engaged in essential national services.

This reflected a narrowing of the goals that Lucy had advocated before the war. No longer were the educational needs of older sisters a priority, but rather the health and well-being of babies – the citizens of the future nation – and to a lesser extent that of their mothers as breeders, rather than as citizens. And, after all this, there is little evidence that this hysteria led to any support for childcare from the state or federal governments during the war or in its aftermath.[12]

Lucy did, however, continue her calls for family planning and contraception advice, responding in part to the attacks made on young women's sexual activity. Instead of bemoaning promiscuity, Lucy insisted that sex education should be an essential part of all education for children – and should be extended to parents as well. In agreeing with a proposal from the Director of Education to initiate sex education classes for parents as well as children, Lucy's statement reflected her focus on equipping children for real life and independently minded democratic citizenship:

> 'The education of a child is incomplete without sex education,' Miss L. Woodcock, vice-president of the Teachers' Federation said recently. 'Child education on sex should begin with elementary biology when the pupil enters school and should continue until the pupil leaves with a fair knowledge of sex and sex hygiene.' ... Such education would produce frank and ethical citizens.[13]

Lucy's assertiveness on this probably reflected her friendship with Lotte Fink. Prevented from gaining an Australian practising certificate by her family responsibilities, Lotte had turned her medical training to assisting women with contraception and family planning advice.[14]

---

12 Stuart Macintyre, 'Women's Leadership in War and Reconstruction', *Labour History*, no. 104 (2013): 65–80, doi.org/10.5263/labourhistory.104.0065; *SMH*, 25 February 1944, 4; *Sun* (Sydney), 21 May 1944, 5.
13 *Cairns Post*, 14 December 1942, 3.
14 Ruth Fink Latukefu, interview with Heather Goodall, 3 September 2015.

***

Lucy was more frustrated by the wartime impact on the campaign to restore the jobs of married women teachers. Pressures had led to the policy being amended in 1935, but these changes simply disadvantaged most women teachers still further. Although first enacted in the emergency of the Depression, this policy had proved very convenient for the government, giving it a flexibility it had not had previously to respond to changing student numbers. Theobald and Dwyer put it succinctly:

> the Dismissal Act augmented the pool of cheap and malleable labour available to the Education Department. Those responsible for staffing the schools soon became addicted.[15]

At least the Federation's policy had continued to demand the repeal of this Act, even though many male teachers – and some single women – had supported the dismissals. In the Federation Annual Conference immediately after the war broke out, in October 1939, a motion was passed calling on the Minister for Education yet again to repeal the law. Ethel Teerman spoke on behalf of the Federation, arguing that 'the war is just another sane reason for the repeal of this Act'.[16] The government refused the demand – yet again.

Things got much worse as the war developed. As more and more male teachers left to enlist, the department needed to make up their numbers and did so by re-employing married women who had formerly been teachers. But it would not take them back into continuing full-time employment. Instead, it would employ them only on casual contracts at a far lower rate of pay than they would have been entitled to as full-time staff. Lucy spoke passionately on this issue to an audience of North Coast teachers, both men and women, in 1940. She pointed out that many of the wives of male teachers were also there. She explained how important it was to 'win the peace as well as the war' by ensuring that education was at the highest quality for all children, with a higher leaving age, better adult education for parents and better training for teachers. Then she continued:

---

15   Marjorie Theobald and Donna Dwyer, 'An Episode in Feminist Politics: The Married Women (Lecturers and Teachers) Act, 1932–47', *Labour History*, no. 76 (1999): 59–77, doi.org/10.2307/27516628; Judy Mackinolty, 'To Stay or To Go: Sacking Married Teachers', in *In Pursuit of Justice*, eds Judy Mackinolty and Heather Radi (Sydney: Hale and Iremonger, 1979), 71–72, 140–47.

16   Theobald and Dwyer, 'An Episode in Feminist Politics', 72; the restoration of married women's positions was a sustained presence in Teachers Federation demands, e.g. *Education*, 20 November 1943, 1.

> As a keen woman member and a foundation member of the Federation, I feel strongly on the matter of equality of sexes in the teaching profession. We are all on one footing, except that when a woman teacher gets married, she has to give up her job. This is a shocking inequality and in no other profession does it apply, and this is the weakest link in our Union organisation.[17]

It was hard to argue for the repeal of this discrimination in the middle of the war, which appeared to demand sacrifices. Indeed, Lucy signed a Teachers Federation advertisement in August 1943 – endorsed not only by all the office bearers of the Federation but by 'Peter Finch (Gunner)' – which called on all 'professional men and women of every political belief' to unite behind Prime Minister Curtin and ensure the war effort through national unity.[18] In this climate, it was unlikely that the burden on married women would be lifted. Nevertheless, it was the efforts of married women, badly paid and employed only on casual contracts, which kept the teaching service afloat through the war. Even in 1947, two years after the war ended, there were 1,200 married women teachers employed on temporary contracts – one-twelfth of the teaching service.[19]

Along with common ground in her alliance with the UA on the question of married teachers' employment, Lucy also found similar views in opposition to racism. Yet while there had been a strong interest in Aboriginal people in the UA, most of the women who had focused on this question had very different perspectives than those to which Lucy had become educated in Erskineville. Led by Mary Bennett and other women involved in northern and central Australia, such as Phyllis Duguid, the UA had shown a dominant concern with the intrusion of settlers and settler society into the lives of 'Full Blood' and 'Tribal' peoples, along with a construction of Aboriginal women as victims and in need of 'protection'.[20] There had also, however, been some protests about the White Australia policy. Vida Goldstein in 1930, for example, and Eleanor Hinder, with experience in China in the mid-1930s, had criticised the short-sightedness of Australia's discriminatory immigration laws. At the same time, as Lake has pointed out, Linda Littlejohn and Jessie Street had

---

17 *Macleay Chronicle*, 16 October 1940, 2.
18 *SMH*, 19 August 1943, 3.
19 Theobald and Dwyer, 'An Episode in Feminist Politics', 72.
20 This is a simplification of the tensions within the feminist organisations and personalities, but in general, even the most liberal like Mary Bennett was criticised by the emerging Aboriginal spokespeople in the eastern states, like Ferguson, Patten and Gibbs, as seeking control over Aboriginal people by 'protection' rather than supporting Aboriginal people in the decisions they took themselves.

moved the UA into an alliance in the mid-1930s with the US group Equal Rights International, thereby raising the prominence of arguments for equal rights within the UA at the expense of arguments about the special needs of women.[21]

**

Attention during the war, however, was focused outside Australia. Lucy was very aware that whatever the injustices faced by women teachers or working-class mothers in Australia, the gravest dangers were being faced by European Jews. The incoming refugees with whom Lucy had become involved before the war were carrying deeply disturbing news of murderous violence.

Dr Fanny Reading, then president of the National Council of Jewish Women (NCJW) in New South Wales, with whom Lucy had become close friends, was calling by 1943 for the creation of an Anglo-American agency with immediate authority to facilitate the large-scale immigration and rehabilitation of refugee Jews from Europe to Australia. Fanning argued:

> Our minds were too blunt to realise that 4,000,000 Jews in Europe had been cruelly done to death in most fiendish ways. That was a world catastrophe unprecedented in history. We have been asked to wait for impending victory, but unless something is done speedily, there may not be a single Jew left in Europe to enjoy the benefits of victory.

Lucy had already begun to work with the various defence organisations to help people get out of danger and bring them to Australia, after which, as we have seen in Chapter 6, she was able to assist refugees to find employment in education or, like Ruth, ensure they had access to language training so they could climb the education ladder. Fanny Reading said that, by January 1942, Lucy had already assisted 160 people coming into Australia. Lucy spoke at a number of meetings of the NCJW during 1942, each chaired by Reading. In September, Lucy's Enfield home was the venue for the first annual meeting of the Western Suburbs branch of the NCJW, which had been meeting regularly at Bankstown. In November, both Lucy and her friend Lotte Fink spoke at the meeting held in Bondi.

---

21   Marilyn Lake, *Getting Equal: The History of Australian Feminism* (St Leonards: Allen and Unwin, 1999), 163, 168.

The topics on which Lucy chose – and was invited – to speak, allow us to see her two major preoccupations: progressive education and Equal Pay for women. But these issues also show the causes to which she thought the Jewish community – both long established and newly arrived – could contribute. Many of the recently incoming Europeans were, as we have seen, interested in the New Education Fellowship, both because it reflected their own home experience but also because they hoped to meet progressive Australians in an area in which they could take part. Lucy gave two talks about education – one in January 1942 about the changes that had already taken place in Australian schools (a rather optimistic talk it must be said!) and then another in September about what progressive educationists hoped to achieve, such as an end to university-dominated examinations. In both she stressed the importance of discussion and creative expression, as both would teach a child 'how to stand on their own feet and not be imitators'.[22] Her talk on Equal Pay was framed very explicitly in the international experience of her audience. Speaking not only in her Federation role but as joint president of the Council for Action on Equal Pay (CAEP), Lucy outlined the history of women's employment in Australia and then explained the international significance of the call for Equal Pay:

> In the USSR and Chile women received the same pay as men. In Holland, Norway, Denmark and Switzerland, women teachers receive the same pay as men.[23]

On each of these issues, Lucy was calling on her audience to locate Australian conditions in comparison to those existing internationally, appealing to their broader European experience as well as to their commitment to progressive social justice. She hoped that refugees as well as the established Jewish community would be contributors to the climate of justice and innovation that she wanted to create in the Australian future in which they would all now share.

***

The UA had been expecting that women would be recognised as having a key role in the postwar reconstruction process. The women's movement was bitterly disappointed when Curtin offered no seat at all to any women's organisation in the 1942 Constitutional Convention

---

22   *Hebrew Standard of Australasia*, 3 September 1942, 10.
23   Ibid., 26 November 1942, 6–7.

that considered reconstruction.²⁴ It was from this point that the UA and the broader women's movement turned to alternative strategies to have women's voices heard.²⁵

An immediate model was the Atlantic Charter, 14 August 1941, which, as many analysts have pointed out, meant little to the US and UK leaders who drafted it, but was understood widely by the Left and particularly by colonised peoples around the world to embody a promise by colonisers to withdraw from colonial power.

More broadly, the concept of a charter was of course a very old one in British law – not just as a granting of rights and powers but as a claim for justice, as was the Magna Carta. In the twentieth century, the League of Nations from 1918 had used the term 'covenant' but the concept was a continuity of the inspirational 'charter of rights', which continued to be important and was used frequently in the formation of the United Nations from 1945. The term was used more widely around the globe than in Britain itself and its echoes in the Anglophone colonial world were ones that Australians heard.

The charters or statements of rights that offered more immediate models for Australians were those of the anti-colonial movements, in which many Australians saw themselves to have a role.

They were particularly aware of political upheavals in the UK – the Easter Rebellion in Ireland, for example, had resonated throughout Australia where a high proportion of the population shared an Irish background. Stories about the Irish anti-colonial movement were carried widely in the Australian press. The Irish independence campaign was not seen in Australia as a phenomenon of Europe but as one of the British Empire. The British army's attacks on the Irish nationalists, for example, were compared in Australian newspapers with the Amritsar massacre in India.²⁶ One way that anti-colonial nationalist movements were underpinning their demands for independence was by using a statement of rights as the basis of their campaigns. As early as 1927, the Women's Indian Association (WIA), associated with the Theosophical Society in India (and with Margaret Cousins, herself from Ireland), was an example of this

---

24   Convention ran from 24 November to 2 December 1942, cited in Macintyre, 'Women's Leadership in War and Reconstruction', 73 note 38.
25   Ibid., 73–74.
26   *Catholic Press* (Sydney), 15 July 1920, 27; 17 March 1921, 13.

approach with its 'Charter of Womanhood's Vision of a Reformed India', which had circulated widely in India and internationally.[27] It went on to become embedded in India's most significant documents.

While it is not clear whether women in the Australian women's movement knew about this 1927 WIA Charter, the issue of equality of the sexes became more prominent as it was embraced by the nationalist movement. By 1930, Gandhian nationalists had shifted their position on women's rights significantly during the Salt March demonstrations, with women invited into the movement in a new way. Participation was still dominated by elite and middle-class women who were concerned about 'respectability' and being mistaken for prostitutes.[28] Nevertheless, the shift towards recognition of women's activism had become clear in the Karachi session of the Indian National Congress in 1931, when Gandhi supported the Fundamental Rights Resolution, 'which assured complete equality between men and women as a basic principle for free India'.[29] This declaration echoed the WIA Charter in stating explicitly that women were to have equal civic rights with men in the new India. It was later quoted and fully endorsed as the first recommendation of the Sub-committee of the National Planning Committee on Woman's Role in a Planned Economy, reporting 1938, under the heading 'Chapter 1: Civic Rights':

1. All citizens are equal before the law, irrespective of religion, caste, creed or sex.
2. No disability attaches to any citizen by reason of his or her religion, caste, creed, or sex, in regard to public employment, office of power or honour, and in the exercise of any trade or calling.
3. The franchise shall be on the basis of universal adult suffrage.[30]

---

27 WIA Charter and references to it in Theosophical Society Archives.
28 Geraldine Forbes, 'The Politics of Respectability: Indian Women and the Indian National Congress', in *The Indian National Congress: Centenary Highlights*, ed. D.A. Low (Bombay: Oxford University Press, 1988), 54–97.
29 Vina Mazumdar, 'Women's Participation in Political Life in India', Report for UNESCO Meeting of Experts on Participation of Women, SS–83/CONF.620/8 (Paris: UNESCO, 1983), 2.
30 Quoted in National Planning Committee (India), *Woman's Role in a Planned Economy*, Report of the Sub-Committee (on women) (Bombay: Vora, 1948), 37–38, 225. Such ideas circulated widely among other independence movements, which developed similar statements in later years. For many, like the African National Congress in South Africa, its statement of women's rights in 1955 was the precursor and model for its later (and far better known) 'Freedom Charter' on the rights of the imagined new nation and its citizens. Helen Hill, *Canberra Times*, 9 August 1986, 7B for the tenth anniversary of the Soweto uprising.

Such ideas may have been discussed in London when Lucy was there in 1927, when her hectic year exchange teaching had located her in the inner city where populations had been racially and culturally mixed and highly politicised. But they had been much more evident to the younger students there in the 1930s. One such person was Rachel Makinson, whom Lucy met in Sydney during the war and who had been actively involved in the circulation of new ideas in UK universities just before she had migrated to Sydney in 1939. Makinson was a young physicist who had married an Australian scientist, Richard Makinson, arriving with him just months before the war. Rachel and Richard were both Peace advocates and socialists, which drew them into Lucy's circle. While Rachel is best remembered today as a wool scientist who broke the glass ceiling to become first female Chief Research Scientist at the CSIRO, she had brought much with her beside her scientific talent.

At Cambridge in the 1930s, Rachel Makinson had been close to many of the young Indian women who had come to the UK as students, like Renu Chakravartty, Vidya Kanuga (later Munsi) and Kitty Boomla, some of whom later came to Australia and all of whom were anti-colonial nationalist activists. Rachel recalled the political activity in Cambridge during the 1930s:

> I belonged to Cambridge University Socialist Club and I still remember attending my first torchlight procession. And I was fairly active. And also there were a great many Indians in Cambridge at the time. I think they were about one sixth of the total, and, well, if they weren't all nationalists, they were at least leaning towards it, under those conditions. And I used to attend their meeting, at the Majilis [Hotel] fairly frequently ... Oh, there was all sorts of stuff going on. I went to most of it. The peace movement was very strong, too.[31]

The universities in London, like Cambridge, were sites of active interchange of ideas and movements not only from Europe but across the British Empire.

---

31 Kathleen Rachel Makinson, interview by Dr Ragbir Bhathal, 1 March 1997, Australian Women Scientists – Oral History Project, NLA. Rajani Dutt (1896–1974), former Marxist theoretician and Communist leader, recalled beginning to study Marxism during the 1930s with other Indian students at these meetings at the Majalis in London, with him becoming the first secretary of the 'London Majalis', in Panchanan Saha, *Rajani Palme Dutt: A Biography* (Kolkata: Biswabiksha, 2004), 58.

Australian women had been organising around women's rights issues, both at home and in the British Empire, for many years, but they had made little impression at the upper levels of government or legislation. This contrasted with the emerging independence movements – in India, China and other non-Western places – which had been able to take such questions into what they planned to be the fundamental documents for their future nations.

India was known to have a large proportion of its population living in poverty and illiteracy, so there could have been few illusions among Australian feminists about how far the goals of elite women's organisations like the WIA and the All India Women's Conference (AIWC) might actually go.[32] Nevertheless, India continued to be an important source of ideas for Australians because there were continuities with earlier links, including the small number of Christian missionaries who had become interested in the independence movement, like Elsie Rivett's sister Eleanor and the continuing connections through Theosophy and education, not only in the NEF but among Australians who had gone to India to teach in Theosophical schools.[33]

Perhaps even more significant for Lucy's awareness, the Peace movement had turned its attention to 'Oriental philosophies' – and more particularly to Gandhi's non-violent strategies, in the 1930s. Although it had arisen in the West particularly after World War I, the Peace movement had become aware of Gandhian philosophies about non-violent non-cooperation during the Salt Marches in 1930. War Resisters International (WRI) in the US was, for example, seeking Indian speakers in 1932 to discuss 'Oriental philosophies' (a reference to Gandhian strategies) that contributed to peace.[34] During the 1930s, this interest in Gandhian strategies brought some Western women associated with the Women's International League for Peace and Freedom (WILPF) to India where they made connections

---

32   *Stri Dharma*, WIA Journal, 1920, 1921, 1928, Theosophical Society Archives, Adyar; Women's Indian Association, *Annual Report* 1929–30, Theosophical Society Archives, Adyar; *Roshni*, AIWC Journal, 1927–47, AIWC Archives, New Delhi.
33   Margaret Allen, 'Eleanor Rivett (1883–1972): Educationalist, missionary and internationalist', in *Founders, Firsts and Feminists: Women Leaders in Twentieth-Century Australia*, eds Fiona Davis, Nell Musgrove and Judith Smart, Australian Women's Archives Project ([Melbourne]: eScholarship Research Centre, University of Melbourne, 2011), 45–63; also at www.womenaustralia.info/leaders/fff/pdfs/rivett.pdf.
34   Kapila Khandvala, speaking in a session titled 'Lessons from the Far East', Program, Third Annual Conference on Militant Pacifism, War Resisters League, NY, 6–8 May 1932. Peace Palace Library: www.peacepalacelibrary.nl/.

with women's organisations, even though WILPF as a body had no meetings outside Europe until 1970.[35] The World Fellowship of Faiths (WFF), associated with WILPF, was similarly drawn to India on the basis of its understanding of Indian philosophy. In 1938, a Mrs Lankaster, who had been in India as a colonial wife 20 years before and was now visiting Madras from the UK as a WILPF and WFF representative, told the WIA that she had come to India 'in quest of peace' and that the organisers of WILPF and WFF 'all remember that the fundamental teaching of this country [India] is "non-killing"'. As a result of such interest and occasional contacts, themselves built on past colonial connections, the WILPF journal published a quarterly report from its Indian Committee. This echoed the 'maternalist' concerns of much middle-class feminism aiming to 'protect' colonised women, rather than to acknowledge their agency or empower them.[36] Nevertheless, this quarterly WILPF report also carried updates on various Indian women's campaigns, which allowed news to circulate around the WILPF network.[37]

Lucy's awareness of India may have been sharpened by her knowledge of Winifred West's long-established connections with Bengali families (friendships forged in the UK initially and later by West's visit to India),[38] and it was certainly raised by her increasing contacts with Jessie Street as Lucy became more involved with the UA. Jessie had been born in India and, although she did not return until late in 1945, she had an interest in developments there.[39] Although Jessie's autobiography and other published material focused on the roles she played and her own speeches, rather than on what anyone said to her, we can see from later reports by Lucy and others who travelled with her that her experiences must have been of great interest to those in Australia.

---

35 WIA, *20th and 21st Annual Reports*, 1936–1938, 34–37. Theosophical Society Archives, Adyar.
36 Lake, *Getting Equal*, 72–86; Fiona Paisley, *Glamour in the Pacific: Cultural Internationalism and Race Politics in the Women's Pan-Pacific* (Honolulu: Hawai'i University Press, 2009), doi.org/10.21313/hawaii/9780824833428.001.0001; Margaret D. Jacobs, *White Mother to a Dark Race: Settler Colonialism, Maternalism and the Removal of Indigenous Children in the American West and Australia 1880–1940* (Lincoln: University of Nebraska Press, 2009).
37 Margaret Jacobs, *White Mother to a Dark Race*, 34 (Lincoln: Nebraska, 2009), referring to the activities of Mrs Lankaster, Secretary of the India Committee of WILPF, London, reported in her speech to WIA group, 10 January 1938, Madras.
38 West (1881–1971), founder of the progressive girls' school Frensham (1913) in the NSW Southern Highlands. Priscilla Kennedy, *Portrait of Winifred West* (Sydney: The Fine Arts Press, 1976), 15–16, 87–91.
39 Lenore Coltheart, ed., *Jessie Street: A Revised Autobiography* (Sydney: Federation Press, 2004).

Equal Rights for Women and the Charter of 1943

So, when the government failed to include women at all in the new Department for Post-War Reconstruction in late 1942, women turned to considering an Australian Woman's Charter, on the models of the League of Nations and particularly the Atlantic Charter.[40] Jessie Street, through the UA, called a conference for November 1943, titled the 'Australian Women's Conference for Victory in War and Victory in Peace'. This was the largest-ever gathering of women's organisations to have occurred in Australia – 90 organisations came together to contribute to a conference that, at first sight, was dominated by the war, as was the whole of Australia. In November 1943, the Japanese held what seemed an unbreakable hold over much of South-East Asia and threatened Australia and the whole region with further advances. But the speeches of the conference – and certainly its resolutions – were aimed squarely at a future beyond the war.

The conference had few international speakers – wartime travel, as the government pointed out when asked for funds, was limited – but in any event, the conference was aimed at the Australian federal government. To do so, the conference addressed many themes, and a key one was education. Lucy delivered a major speech called 'Planning Education for the Future' and, although the full text has not survived, it was quoted and summarised prominently in a number of newspapers.[41] From these fragments, we can see that her speech drew directly from her active work over the previous decade.

Lucy called firstly for a need to plan for diverse students, referring to her experiences in East End London in 1927 and then in inner-city Erskineville from 1933 to 1943. She insisted in this speech that education should not be 'in a vacuum' but should reflect 'the real world' and 'the community as it is', including by recognising the diversity among students. She argued that such diversity arose from many sources. She pointed out firstly that there were varying intellectual or physical capacities among children. One source for her information was her experience in London with

---

40 Macintyre, 'Women's Leadership in War and Reconstruction', 72–73.
41 'Plea for Aid to Jews', *SMH*, 22 November 1943, 7; 'Educational System: Need for Free and Full Facilities', *Age* (Melbourne), 22 November 1943, 2; 'Woman Author Condemns Trashy Novels', *Newcastle Morning Herald and Miners' Advocate*, 22 November 1943, 3; 'Child Welfare: Women in Conference', *West Australian* (Perth), 22 November 1943, 4.

education for the physically and mentally handicapped children, while another source was her work in Erskineville, establishing and teaching in one of the state's first Opportunity Classes for gifted children. But she also talked about diversity arising from inequality in access to education and cultural resources. Her examples, drawn from Erskineville, were the crushing economic handicaps faced by working-class children and the frustration they faced as bright children in being unable to pursue higher studies because of their families' poverty.

Lucy used this speech to call for the need for education for the future to stress creativity and exploration – to allow this diverse student body to develop in ways which suited each child. She was drawing clearly here on the themes of progressive education. She rejected the sorting of children through testing: not only the gatekeeping examinations in academic institutions but presumably also the new IQ testing.

Her call was not, however, to plan education for students just as individuals, but to build in them 'a spirit of cooperation'. Lucy wanted social responsibility to be part of the outcomes of education, which engaged with her interest in education linking students with the community 'as it is'. This was accompanied by the goal of encouraging each child to take responsibility for their own decision-making, which was aimed at fostering active participation in the democracy of the future.

This shift to a child-centred and creativity-focused real-world education must involve the training of teachers, Lucy argued, and this was a cost the government must recognise as socially important. She pointed out that:

> It took four years to train a veterinary scientist but only two to train a teacher of children.[42]

Finally, Lucy stressed that she wanted reforms to begin immediately – not to wait till some hoped for peacetime changes. She demanded a recognition of the enormous cost of war – to which she referred uncompromisingly as 'destruction'. Furthermore, she demanded that it be recognised who it was who was paying the price for the massive expenditure on destruction – it was not taxpayers, she insisted, but the children whose future education was being damaged and delayed.

---

42   *West Australian* (Perth), 22 November 1943, 4 (similarly, *Kalgoorlie Miner*, 24 November 1943, 4).

While Lucy's paper did not comment on issues other than education, it is clear that her experience in Erskineville with its racially diverse population would have been very different from that of remote-area feminists, including the radical and innovative Mary Bennett. Coming from an inner-city suburb where Aboriginal people were struggling with Depression-ridden contemporary urban economies, Lucy would have found little of relevance in the call for inviolate reserves for 'tribal' Aborigines. It would be reasonable to assume that Lucy would have supported motions – had there been any – that demanded equal access for Aboriginal people to primary and secondary education as well as adult education, rather than the calls for isolation and protection.

Perhaps the major demonstration, however, of Lucy's interest in a new agenda on racial discrimination was the high-profile speech of her long-time friend Fanny Reading, president of the NCJW. Its outcome was the 'special resolution' on 'Racial Persecution' that called for Australian Government and women's movement action 'in the name of justice and mercy' to assist Jews to escape from the barbarism of Europe and to resettle 'in Palestine or elsewhere'.[43]

This urgency was not only felt in Fanny's speech – and in the special resolution of the conference. It was also a key issue for Lucy, who spoke directly to the federal Minister for Education Clive Evatt, who attended the conference. Lucy insisted that reforms to education could not wait till the war was won, they had to be started immediately and be a part of fundamental planning for the war and for the peace.

For Lucy, the urgency applied right here in Australia, not just in far away Europe. Just as with education, Lucy was compelled by the urgency of acting in relation to Jewish people but she wanted to stem the expression of discrimination in Australia as well as trying to protect those escaping from Europe. Lucy was by this time taking an active role in the organisation of International Women's Day (IWD). In March 1944, she invited her close friend Lotte Fink to speak at the IWD conference. Lotte, representing the Association of Refugees of NSW, protested at the treatment of all 'refugee aliens' by the Allied Works Council, which was making them work 'under humiliating circumstances' alongside interned 'enemy aliens', for low rates of pay. As she explained:

---

43 Fanny Reading, 'Plea for Aid to Jews', *SMH*, 22 November 1943, 7.

> Most refugees have a high opinion of Australian working conditions … and we protest at having to work for less than Australian rates of pay and at being used as scabs against our will. We want equal duties but we also want equal rights.[44]

Woman's Charter resolutions: A 'living document'

The Charter conference's 28 resolutions were published as a booklet early in 1944, just a few months after the conference. It was intended that these resolutions would be discussed and modified as they circulated widely around women's organisations in all states. The Charter was to be a living document, reflecting the up-to-date concerns of Australian women.

The original 28 resolutions covered all of the concerns of the women's organisations present, including not only health and women in public life but also moral standards and alcohol. The themes did not, however, cover the concerns of all Australian women – and must have been a deep disappointment to women like Lucy who had been campaigning for sex education and family planning. In the 'Health' theme there were no resolutions at all on birth control or on abortion. While Lake has pointed out that the views of younger women on birth control may have been marginalised because these organisations were largely composed of middle-aged women,[45] it was also older women like Lucy, closely involved with working-class communities, who were angered and frustrated by this lack of recognition. The eugenic theme was strongly evident, in the resolution on 'Birthrate' in which the Charter stressed the importance of raising the birth rate and of protecting the maternal health of women by training more gynaecologists. It called for any obstacles to the marriageable age to be removed where necessary. In other words, the Charter called for the age of marriage to be *lowered* where requested.

Nevertheless, the conference did demonstrate a strong emphasis on equal economic rights for women. This reflected the alliance built during the Depression between feminist organisations and the women unionists like Lucy Woodcock in the Teachers Federation who had been campaigning for Equal Pay as well as the restoration of jobs for married women.

---

44 *West Australian* (Perth), 14 March 1944, 2.
45 Lake, *Getting Equal*, 197–202.

In the Charter publication, the conference sessions were presented as key themes with subthemes reflecting the specific resolutions moved and accepted. The first theme, 'Women in War and Peace', contained much about the duties of women as citizens during the war. It included many obligations to contribute to total mobilisation for the war effort, including enlistment in defence forces (although without specific mention of the armed services, but did specify nursing in the services or work in the land army), as well as volunteering in various ways to assist the home front.

Theme 15 on 'Education' called for all of the things for which Lucy had been arguing, including childcare for the benefit of children. It was a blueprint for progressive educational goals, which did not include the emerging psychological testing of intelligence quotients that had been in evidence in the 1937 NEF Conference.[46] Rather, this Charter was for the more humanitarian orientation within progressive education. Specifically, it called for nationwide free primary, secondary and tertiary education, and for academic and technical training to be designed to fit the students to meet the expanding needs of modern community life. It addressed specific subjects for study, in a call for the syllabus to be shaped to meet the diverse needs of each child as well as to contribute to future world peace. In particular, all students would be required to study the Atlantic Charter as the basis for future societies, to learn about science and the study of nature, and to learn about public health. The Australian women's resolutions called for more generous federal funding directly to education, given its key importance for the future of the nation. They also argued for the development of a national arts and cultural fund in order to enable these creative areas to contribute to education. Despite avoiding the 'modern' educational theories grounded in psychology, the Australian Woman's Charter argued strongly for greater training for teachers and for a research body into education to be established. In a final recognition of the importance of class and rural limits on children's leisure and experiences, the Charter called for more holiday homes, a program nurtured by the NSW Teachers Federation, which contributed heavily to Stewart House.

---

46   Julie McLeod and Katie Wright, 'Education for Citizenship: Transnational Expertise, Curriculum Reform and Psychological Knowledge in 1930s Australia', *History of Education Review* 42, no. 2 (2013): 170–84.

While the Charter theme on 'Education' was expansive and drew on many recent developments, the theme on Aborigines was notably limited in geography and in politics. It focused on 'full-blood' and 'tribal' Aboriginal people, arguing for inviolate reserves and coercive 'protection' for women. The section on education for these Aboriginal people spoke only of 'potential equality' rather than any current condition. This theme reflected in many ways the strongest assertions of the importance of supporting Aboriginal women, drawing much of its energy from Mary Bennett in Western Australia, who was regarded as far more radical than the conservative women who were seeking largely to have white women employed as 'Protectors'. Yet, in November 1943, there had already been over five years of very active and assertive Aboriginal political spokespeople in south-eastern Australia demanding full citizen's rights and an end to the interventions of 'protectors' altogether.[47] This 1943 Woman's Charter theme on Aborigines not only looks limited in retrospect, but even in 1943 it must have been an unwelcome shock to many activist Aboriginal women like Pearl Gibbs and Margaret Tucker. It must also have been hard for Lucy – with her contacts with local inner-city Aboriginal people through Erskineville Public School – to see the irrelevance of these Charter demands on Aborigines for any of the Aboriginal people she knew.

The 1943 Woman's Charter conference may have had shortcomings for Lucy, but it had been largely outside her control to meet them. However, she was on the committee for organising ongoing consultation and amendments of the resolutions of 1943 and on the committee to organise the next conference.

Some follow-up meetings did occur, but the campaigns by women for Equal Pay and for a place in the planning for reconstruction suffered further major setbacks. By October 1943, partial demobilisation was occurring, bringing men back into the workplace. The largest union, the Federated Ironworkers' and Sheet Metal Workers' Union, withdrew from the CAEP late in 1943 and, over the following year, the other big unions with predominantly male membership began to withdraw effective

---

47 And this is only the most recent of the Aboriginal advocates for the abolition of 'protectors', see John Maynard, *Fight for Liberty and Freedom* (Canberra: Aboriginal Studies Press, 2007). For 1930s political activity, see Jack Horner, *Vote Ferguson for Freedom* (Sydney: Australian and NZ Book Company, 1974); Heather Goodall, *Invasion to Embassy: Land in Aboriginal Politics, 1770–1970* (St Leonards: Allen and Unwin, 1996).

support.[48] Leadership passed to the unions like the Teachers Federation that had substantial female membership and Lucy became CAEP Joint President with fellow Federation member Robert L. Day.[49]

Over the same months, with the war far from won, Prime Minister Curtin's health began to fail and he devolved a number of pressing social issues to his ministers in order to concentrate on the prosecution of the war. Curtin had attempted to have a large number of powers transferred from the states' control to the federal government, including postwar reconstruction as well as control over employment, profiteering and prices and, at the last minute, powers over Aboriginal people. While all states seemed to have agreed at a Constitutional Convention convened in December 1942, by February 1943 it became clear that a number of states were actually reluctant to undertake the transfer. This made a referendum necessary, with all the powers bundled together to be accepted or rejected together. Curtin argued that the powers were all related and the minister with carriage of the referendum, Jessie Street's friend H.V. Evatt, agreed. This made an unwieldy 14-point bundle. The UA members, including Lucy, campaigned actively on behalf of the 'Yes' vote for the referendum, focusing particularly on the transfer of both the postwar reconstruction powers and the Aboriginal powers. But the complex question appears to have confused electors and, despite a significant 'Yes' vote, the referendum failed to win a majority in all states, and was therefore rejected in total.[50]

---

48 Penelope Johnson, 'Gender, Class and Work: The Council of Action for Equal Pay and the Equal Pay Campaign in Australia During World War II', *Labour History*, no. 50 (1986): 145, doi.org/10.2307/27508787.
49 Beverley Symons, 'Muriel Heagney and the Fight for Equal Pay During World War Two', *The Hummer* 3, no. 1 (Summer 1998–99): 1–13.
50 Macintyre, 'Women's Leadership in War and Reconstruction', 65–80.

9

Recognising Race: Decolonisation

When World War II ended, there was a major shift in the political environment in which Lucy was working. The war had been for Lucy a period when pressures on working-class women intensified. She had focused on two issues – the lack of childcare for war-working mothers and the injustices of women's economic rights, shown most clearly in the refusal to employ married women teachers as permanent staff but visible across the board. Lucy's role in the Council for Action on Equal Pay (CAEP) had intensified and many of her concerns had been addressed in the 1943 Australian Woman's Charter. There were, however, other issues she championed like family planning and the demands of urban Aboriginal activists, which were not well addressed. Lucy had been acutely aware of the impacts of racism against Aboriginal and Jewish communities and so her activism already targeted discrimination on the grounds of race as well as sex. The entangling of race and gender came into sharper focus immediately after the war. This chapter will compare the 1943 Charter with the new environment shown in both the Indian Women's Charter of 1946 and the revised Australian Charter of the same year, and then in the Teachers' Charter adopted and circulated by United Nations Educational, Scientific and Cultural Organization (UNESCO) from 1947 to 1954 and beyond.

Figure 9.1: The shops in front of Lucy's flat in upper 215A George Street where she spent most of her time and where all her political activities were carried out – the NEF met there, the NSW Peace Council met there and the Aboriginal-Australian Fellowship was created there.

Looking north along George St from between Grosvenor St and Essex St, 2 October 1963.

Source: City of Sydney Archive, City Engineers Photographic Negatives, 1953–1973, SRC6089 Originally CRS 268/3687.

***

Within months of the end of the conflict, there was a rush of activity to create the new world that had been glimpsed and imagined while the war was on. But there was a sense of urgency because tensions had already begun to rise as the tide turned in the war. Both the hopes and the fears about communism had re-emerged and polarisations began that would shape the coming Cold War. At the same time, the war had shaken European imperial holds over colonies and, in many cases, nationalist movements were rising in prominence and public awareness, including some with apparently feminist agendas. As Sluga, Zachariah and others have argued, 1945 was a brief time poised between a world war and an even more all-encompassing Cold War, a time when new worlds really could be imagined despite the looming conflicts.[1] In this time of both internationalism and nationalism, the United Nations (UN) was envisaged, drawing much from the old League of Nations but built on the new principles of human rights, theoretically beyond the nation state. In its fundamental paradox, however, the whole UN edifice depended on the endorsement of nation-states to come into reality.

In the scramble to fulfil the hopes that were already under threat, many organisations were created in the months after the conflict ended. The British trade union movement initiated the World Federation of Trade Unions (WFTU) in London on 3 October 1945, then the United Nations itself, long planned, came into being on 24 October after the San Francisco conference. Lucy was particularly interested in UNESCO, inaugurated in Paris on 16 November 1945, the United Nations body that was to focus efforts in education, science and cultural expression. The United Associations of Women had been represented through Jessie Street at the San Francisco conference, where she attended as a non-voting member of the Australian delegation. After this, Jessie travelled to Paris for the first meeting of the Women's International Democratic Federation (WIDF) in December, then on to India where she attended the All India Women's Conference (AIWC) in Hyderabad (later in Pakistan), in January 1946.

The concept of a Charter of Rights was circulating actively. The United Nations itself was founded on a Charter, a treaty between the victorious Allied nations. Jessie Street took the 1943 Australian Woman's Charter with her to San Francisco where she used it to support the argument to have women specifically mentioned in the UN Charter and to support the planning for a Commission on the Status of Women. This was eventually created in mid-1946, with Jessie being later sent as a delegate. The Indian Women's Charter was already in draft form late in 1945, drawing substantially from the 1931 Karachi Resolution of the Indian National Congress, which had in turn drawn on the 1927 Women's Indian Association Charter. The 1946 Indian Women's Charter of Rights

---

1   Glenda Sluga *Internationalism in the Age of Nationalism* (Philadelphia: University of Pennsylvania Press. 2013); Ali Raza, Roy Franziska, and Benjamin Zachariah, eds, *The Internationalist Moment: South Asia, Worlds, and World Views, 1917–39* (New Delhi, Thousand Oaks, London, Singapore: Sage. 2015), doi.org/10.4135/9789351507994.

and Duties was presented, moved and adopted at the AIWC congress in Hyderabad in January 1946, which Jessie attended. Her speech notes show that she spoke very briefly, presenting an overly positive view of the situation of gender equality in Australia and then summarising the goals of the 1943 Charter as:

> We are fighting for the elimination of sex discrimination and the realization of the principle of equal status, rights and opportunities for men and women.[2]

After its adoption at Hyderabad, the Indian Women's Charter of Rights and Duties was taken by Hansa Mehta to the UN in April 1946 and circulated there, as the 1943 Australian Women's Charter had been circulated in San Francisco. This Indian Women's Charter was next brought to Australia in August 1946 by Kapila Khandvala and Mithan Lam, who came as delegates from the AIWC. They may have met Jessie Street at the Hyderabad conference, or even at the initial WIDF meeting in Paris, but they represented the earliest international guests for whom the Australian Charter Committee could organise passports. Some others, notably the Soviet and Chinese delegations, were not able to get into the country while the Americans were not able to get out of their own. But the Indian women, then British subjects, were able to obtain visas and brought their Charter to be discussed among the women attending the conference to consider the second Australian Woman's Charter, which was adopted in August 1946 and was in existence till the 1960s.

At this second Australian Woman's Charter Conference, Lucy chaired the session on education and was closely involved with day-to-day conference management as the sessions occurred. The analyses of the 1946 Australian Woman's Charter to date have centred on the widely reported Cold War debates that blew up on the conference floor, splitting the women's movement into opponents and supporters of communism. Less attention has been given to comparing the contents of the charters in 1943 and 1946, and even less attention to comparing the Indian Charter with those of Australia. No attention at all has been directed to what was said on the floor of the conference but which might not have been reported.

---

2   Speech Notes by Jessie Street, Hyderabad, 28 December 1945, Scanned, AIWC Archives.

Figure 9.2: Kapila Khandvala and Mithan Lam at the 1946 Australian Woman's Charter meeting.

The meeting participants were gathered for this photograph on the rooftop of the city building where the conference was held, which overlooked Hyde Park with glimpses of Sydney Harbour in the distance. Mithan Lam and Kapila Khandvala, in saris, were in centre of the participants' group. Jessie and Lucy can be seen with others in a small organising huddle on left.

Source: Jessie Street papers, MS 2683, NLA.

The changes in the Australian charters' contents suggest that the 1946 shift arose firstly because of pressure from Indigenous Australian activists but also from the same sources that had shaped the Indian Charter: the international campaign for decolonisation. These 1946 changes broadened the Australian Charter into a movement calling for equality between racial as well as gender groups, which was quite a different goal than that in 1943. The new focus of the 1946 Charter was exactly the focus of the concurrent 1946 NEF Conference, which was focused on the theme of 'Education for International Understanding'. Lucy was an organiser for both.[3] The NEF held sessions in all major cities and Lucy

---

3   See photo of Kapila Khandvala and Mithan Lam with participants of 1946 Charter conference overlooking Hyde Park. Jessie Street and Lucy Woodcock visible among planning group in lower left-hand corner. Jessie Street papers, MS 2683, NLA.

had ensured that Kapila, as a senior educator, would speak at each, often accompanied by Mithan. Both spoke also in each city to the peak union bodies, organisations to which Lucy's leadership role in the Australian and NSW Teachers Federations, as well as the overall labour movement, allowed them introductions.

The concept of a 'charter' continued to hold evocative power throughout the decade. In another charter in which Lucy was directly involved, UNESCO began, after its 1947 Mexico conference, to work through teachers' unions among all its member states to draft, circulate and eventually endorse an International Teacher's Charter in 1950, later called, from 1954, a Charter on Education.[4] This final UNESCO Charter was based on the fundamental principle that the questions of racial and gender discrimination were linked, and, like discrimination against religions, were obstacles both to fair working conditions and universal access to education. In all these conferences – for the Australian Woman's Charter, the New Education Fellowship and the Teachers' Charter discussions at UNESCO – an end to discrimination on the basis of race, sex and religion was at the core of any new world.

Although the women's movement had become more fragmented with the early impact of the Cold War, this engagement of gender with racial and religious equality was to mark the later careers of many of the women activists involved. It was also a characteristic of the UNESCO work on the Charter for Teachers and Education. The NEF also offered many opportunities to take this path, and as a member of the NEF Federal Council, hosting the NSW NEF meetings in her flat, Lucy was well informed and supported its recommendations on child migrants in 1947. These aimed to address children's educational needs in order to avoid what was even then the well-known abuse that had occurred in earlier decades when English child migrants to Western Australia had been given no training and instead used as cheap labour.[5]

---

4   The UNESCO-commissioned summary of the 1954 Charter was summarised by Christiane Dazaud, and published in Australia in various newspapers, discussed at end of this chapter.
5   *Advertiser* (Adelaide), 3 June 1947, 6.

Recognising decolonisation

The Indian Women's Charter of Rights and Duties, 1946

We know from the Australian Woman's Charter agenda and Kapila's report to the AIWC that the two Indian delegates spoke in detail about the Indian Women's Charter on a number of occasions during their Australian visit. Yet there is a silence in the accounts we have of the conference proceedings, probably arising from the tensions between the anti-communist and the left-wing groups among the women's organisations attending. Whatever its cause, this absence in the Australian documents of the time makes it easier to understand why later Australian historians have failed to notice whatever contribution these Indian visitors may have made to the 1946 outcomes.

This Indian Women's Charter used similar language to that used in the 1943 Australian Woman's Charter, and had much common ground, but it also contained some significant differences. It had nine key principles, but, like the Australian charters, each principle contained a number of subpoints. In the areas of common ground, the first principle, civic rights, called for full adult franchise but then included the complete topic of education as it was regarded as a civic right of all. Many principles of the Indian Charter, for example, 'Marriage' (VII), contained all the material that in the Australian Woman's Charter was addressed under a number of different principles. In the Australian Charter, headings covering marriage included: 'Women as mothers', 'Childcare', 'Moral Standards' (which called for equal moral standard for men and women and continued penalties for prostitution but *both* parties to be guilty of offence), 'Legal Reforms', 'Divorce', 'Widows' Pensions' and others. The difference between the two in this area of marriage was that the Indian Women's Charter contained no reference to prostitution at all. The fundamental common ground was that women were not to be regarded as property but to have full equal rights of decision-making with their husbands over children throughout their lives, both inside the marriage and in any divorce. Similarly, there should be no gender difference in property law.

There was similar common ground in the area of civic and legal rights, with both charters asserting that full adult franchise should be the rule regardless of sex and also of family status, and that women should be eligible to stand for all public offices. Women similarly should receive pay equal to men and have equal access to jobs, regardless of marital status. But at the same time there should be provision made for breastfeeding mothers, for crèches and for maternity benefits to ensure that equal access to work was a reality.

The Indian Charter was called 'The Indian Women's Charter of Rights and Duties'; this suggests a stronger pressure to define women's responsibilities than in the Australian Charter, which was entitled simply 'The Australian Woman's Charter'. Yet when comparing the documents, three of the six clauses in the final Indian principle 'the Duties of Women' (IX) are very similar to those in the Australian Charter's article one: 'Women in War and Peace'. Both charters argue for the accessibility of war work for women – although neither charter mentions armed services – and make it clear that women carry equal responsibility with men to serve their country in times of crisis.

The clauses that differ are, firstly, one in the Indian Charter that defines the responsibility of women to be of 'high moral standards'. This was not like any included in the Australian Charter – although it was certainly part of the unspoken assumptions among Australian feminist organisations. The second of the divergent clauses called on Indian women to take responsibility for modernising Indian culture – for condemning purdah, for example, and caste. The third different clause calls for Indian women to commit themselves to work for world peace. These 'duties' of Indian women are not then about submission to men, but rather about service to a vision of a modernised state and an internationally peaceful world.

There were two further points of difference. The Australian Woman's Charter argues for the right to have the age of marriage lowered, while the Indian Charter calls for raising the age of marriage. Such differences are well explained by the different cultural histories of marriage in each country but they make a striking contrast. The other difference is less easily explained – in the 'Women's Place in the Family' clause (VIII), the Indian Charter states unequivocally that a woman has a right to limit her family and the state has the responsibility to provide her with the necessary knowledge and facilities to do so. Given there is no mention of contraception at all in the Australian Woman's Charter of 1943, this is an important difference, and it is a significant clause in placing control for family limitation into women's hands, with no requirement for consultation with husbands or family, unlike the other clauses contained in this principle.

The overarching context, however, of the whole Indian Women's Charter of Rights and Duties is that it is directed at a future, independent and democratic, India. It begins with the words 'We believe that freedom and equality are essential to human development' in what was a direct call for the end of colonialism. The duties and responsibilities of Indian women were therefore directed to this independent India, not towards the Raj of the day, under British control. The strongest message of the Indian Women's Charter to Australian women was perhaps that these women wanted the same as they did – and were arguing even more strongly to get it – which brought home the injustice of colonial control.

The Australian Women's Charter Conference, 1946

The major changes in the 1946 Australian Woman's Charter from the 1943 Charter were in the clauses about Aboriginal people and about the world outside Australia. Two influences that must have contributed had been occurring before 1943 but had had no expression in the Charter that emerged. With a new committee, however, including Lucy, these influences did find expression. One was the ongoing activism of Aboriginal Australians, like Bill Ferguson, Jack Patten and Pearl Gibbs, who had made a direct linkage with feminist movements through the anthropologist Carolyn Tennant Kelly in 1937; this led to Kelly mobilising a large group of women from the Feminist Club, the United Associations of Women and other women's organisations to witness the collapse of the hearings of the NSW Select Committee into the Protection Board in February 1938.[6] The collapse of the Select Committee, publicised widely by women's organisations, contributed support to the Aboriginal campaign for full citizens' rights, adding to the impact of its best publicised event, the Day of Mourning in January 1938. The organisers of the 1943 Charter conference had been advised by women with remote-area interests, but the committee for the 1946 Charter had much more experience in south-eastern Australia, which brought very different concerns into the foreground.[7]

---

6   *Truth*, 20 February 1938, 35.
7   *The Abo Call*, 1937–38, throughout each of the six issues; Heather Goodall, *Invasion to Embassy: Land in Aboriginal Politics, 1770–1970* (St Leonards: Allen and Unwin, 1996), 178–206, 274–93; Victoria Haskins, *One Bright Spot* (London: Palgrave Macmillan, 2005).

The second influence was the impact on Australians of Jewish experiences of racism, retold by refugees from Nazism like Hilda Byk and the Fink family, with whom Lucy was able to use her standing in public and progressive education to facilitate supportive networks.[8] After Fanny Reading's impassioned speech at the 1943 Charter conference, the issue of racial persecution was far more prominently on the agenda in 1946.

The third was not evident in 1943 and created the most urgent impact on the Charter conference of 1946. This was the globalising effect of the war itself. It had made Australians vividly aware of Asia in an unprecedented way: bringing Indonesians into Australian political and social networks, creating widespread sympathy in Australia for the Chinese in their struggle against the Japanese invasion, making Australians aware of Indians in shared combat zones in all theatres of war, eliciting deep fear and anger against the invading Japanese in the Pacific theatre but then rising horror as the effects of the 1945 atomic blasts were brought home. The war and its immediate aftermath brought the anti-colonial nationalist movements of decolonisation, including the non-violent strategies of Gandhi, into direct contact with activists within the 'dominions' like Australia.

All of these influences shaped the 1946 Australian Woman's Charter, as did the very changed circumstances of the times. In 1943, the Charter conference had marked the high point of the Australian women's movement, with its active alliance between unionised working women and feminist groups. In 1946, however, the Charter conference saw a deeply divided Australian women's movement. The weakening of union support for equal pay for women from 1944 has been discussed above, with the strongest unions withdrawing from the CAEP as demobilisation began to reduce the number of women in the workforce. Cold War tensions had invaded the UA just as they had the union movement. Jessie Street's strong support for Russia during the war and her outspoken appreciation of the gains made by women under socialism had frightened both anti-communist feminist bodies and the anti-communist unions. Some feminist organisations refused to take part in the 1946 Charter conference at all, others came but argued strongly against Street's leadership. Although some international delegations were unable to come due to the rising Cold War tensions, the Indians were there, along with the Sri Lankans, New Zealanders, Yugoslavs and French.

---

8   See Chapter 5, this volume; Lucy Godiva Woodcock ASIO file, Vol. 1, f 156, A6119, 2030, NAA.

The two Indian women who came were extraordinarily impressive. Both senior women in their professions, each experienced, well-travelled and articulate, they were able to make repeated contributions to the conference discussion and to the many public meetings that occurred around the Charter conference. Mithan Lam (1898–1981) was the acknowledged leader of the two and the first Indian woman to become a barrister, being admitted to the Bar in London. Beautiful and elegant, she was a member of the Tata family, a family more powerful and far more wealthy even than Jessie's family, but she was nevertheless an activist and a nationalist. Mithan was to go on to become the president of the AIWC during the later 1950s and '60s. Kapila Khandvala was a leading educationalist from Bombay who had trained in India and gained a higher degree in the United States. She had travelled widely in Europe as well as Asia, taught in a rural social development organisation and, by the early 1940s, had risen to become the first woman to take control of primary education for the City of Bombay. Kapila's father, T.C. Khandvala, a successful Gujarati eye doctor in Bombay, was a member of the Brahmo Samaj, which meant he was committed to a reforming and modernising Hindu practice. He ensured education for his four daughters and encouraged marriage outside religious and caste restrictions. Kapila, however, had been determined to make her own decisions, and did not marry at all. Instead, she chose to live with her partner, C.M. Trivedi, for her whole life. Trivedi was already committed in an earlier marriage and had left his wife and children to live with Kapila. They lived together for the rest of their lives, clearly devoted to each other, but the relationship deeply disturbed her family as well as his. So, although she came from a privileged background, Kapila was negotiating social disapproval for living an unconventional life, which in some ways put her into a similar situation to Lucy.

Mithan and Kapila were significant in Lucy's story because she went to visit them both, in Nagpur and then Bombay respectively, along with Jessie Street early in 1955, after attending a Peace conference in Madras. It appears that Lucy kept in touch with them, although we cannot be sure because she left few letters or papers – all we have from this period are Jessie's breezy communications addressed to them all. We do know, however, that Lucy reported speaking to women in trade unions and in agricultural areas during her visit to India, meetings that are likely to have been organised by Kapila, who made these types of arrangements for other visitors like Lotte Fink in 1952 and Lee Brown (now Rhiannon) in the 1970s.

Kapila Khandvala and Mithan Lam are even more significant overall because their extensive reports to the AIWC about their Australian observations give us a very different perspective on the events of the Charter conference and their other Australian travels. As well as her 20-page report, Kapila submitted an itinerary of their whole trip that documented a gruelling program of meetings, speeches and travelling, from Brisbane to Perth, from their first press interview on 3 August to Kapila's final speech at the NEF conference on 12 October. Kapila recorded the topics of their speeches, as well as the dates and locations, and listed the speakers and sessions in the conferences they attended, so we know that, once again, Lucy had organised for Fanny Reading to chair a Charter session.[9]

We know from Kapila's records that both Mithan and Kapila talked about the Indian Women's Charter in detail at the Australian Woman's Charter sessions and at a public meeting under the auspices of the Charter, where Kapila noted that she had spoken on:

> The Charter framed by the AIWC, about the trade union movement in India and the food crisis facing India.[10]

We also glimpse the events around the main Australian Charter conference. As was to become her usual practice, Lucy Woodcock was actively involved with the organising during each day of the conference but did not give a paper. Kapila noted that Lucy had chaired the session on education, which was for her one of the most interesting, and at which Kapila herself spoke about the role of education in fostering peace. Beyond the formal conference sessions, however, Lucy had brought Kapila to speak at a meeting of the Assistant Teachers' Union and later at another meeting of the Teachers Federation, at which Kapila had been made an honorary member.[11] Kapila spoke about trade unions in India at a NSW Trades and Labour Council meeting and on similar themes at various other union meetings. On her return to India she gave the AIWC a list of all the trade unions who had been responsive to her accounts of industrial and women's issues in India, with advice to develop the relationship with follow-up contact.

---

9   Kapila Khandvala, 'A Detailed List and Itinerary of the Conference at Australia', 10 December 1946, 1–5; 'Report on the Australian Conferences to A.I.W.C.', 10 December 1946 (unabridged, 20 pages). Both in AIWC Archives, New Delhi.
10 Khandvala, Report, 12.
11 Meetings held 1–2 October 1946. Khandvala, Itinerary, 5; Report, 17.

Perhaps the most powerful and memorable event of the conference had been the closing Peace march, during which floats decorated in the national costumes and colours of the conference guests and up to 2,000 women, including women from the various war service bodies, marched through the Sydney city streets. All traffic was stopped for them to pass. They marched to the Cenotaph, where a Brigadier from the Salvation Army read a prayer for peace and Jessie Street laid a wreath to those who had died in the war. Then the procession marched to the Domain, where the speakers included both Mithan and Kapila as well as the visitors from Yugoslavia and France. Kapila met Rachel Makinson, who had spoken a number of times at the conference about the danger of atomic weapons and the importance of Peace, which was again her theme at the Peace rally. Kapila reported to the AIWC that all the speeches stressed that there could be no peace without unity and freedom.[12]

In her report, Kapila made special mention of the conditions faced by Aboriginal Australians, expressing grave concerns about their welfare and independence. While she repeated the fears held for the disruption of traditional culture, she was most concerned to point out that all Aboriginal people should have the right of equal wages and of full payment in cash, just like fellow non-Aboriginal workers. She argued also for the importance of Aboriginal people being free to vote for their own representatives.[13] She linked their well-being with the suggestions, which were just beginning to be made at that time, that there should be a range for testing rockets across the Western Desert lands, necessitating major incursions into the homelands of Pitjantjatjara and other Western Desert peoples. Although in 1946 there had been no hint of testing atomic weaponry, the idea of military rocket testing was enough to raise alarm bells not only for those opposed to incursions into Aboriginal lands but to those campaigning for an end to military spending.[14]

In her own speeches to the Charter conference, Kapila reported that she had continually stressed the importance of freedom and independence, a theme she repeated at trade union meetings and in her speeches at the New Education Fellowship conference sessions, on 'Education for International Understanding'. Kapila's NEF speech read in part:

---

12   Khandvala, Report, 14–15.
13   Khandvala, Report, 7–8.
14   Khandvala, Report, 4.

> Equality, justice and freedom are the three fundamental principles essential for peace. These very ideas must also form the basis of education, the world over, if humanity is to have peace. It is because these ideas are sadly neglected in education that problems of the coloured and colonial peoples, arising out of racial discrimination and hatred, still exist as the most disturbing factors to world peace. So called peace conferences, and high-sounding talk of international goodwill and peace, are not likely to achieve anything, unless a world organisation like the New Education Fellowship takes upon itself the task of bringing about a radical and fundamental change in the ideals of education all over the world. It is possible for education to mould the new generation with the ideal of furthering the democratic and peaceful way of life. The aim of education should therefore be not only to stop all wars, but to build up and maintain peace.[15]

Mithan Lam's keynote speech to the Woman's Charter meeting in Sydney was published in the AIWC journal *Roshni*, in February 1947. Titled 'Freedom and Equality', her address covered many aspects of AIWC work, but it made her position on independence very clear:

> Our object should be not merely to nail down the world order, so that the bomb cannot fall again, but we must remember that security is obtained by eliminating the grievances which … have to be removed before the body politic can become healthy. Social inequalities are at the base of many upheavals while the racial arrogance, the exploitation of the weaker and less advanced peoples, the trade rivalries caused thereby provide fertile soil for internal as well as international bickering and war.
>
> If we want real peace in the world, there will have to be no room for narrow sectarianism. Therefore I appeal to you to study dispassionately the other side of the question, from the coloured people's point of view, and use your undoubted influence to guide – and if need be to curb – your statesmen.[16]

---

15   Kapila Khandvala, 'Education, International Understanding and Peace', in *Education for International Understanding: Selected Addresses to the International Education Conference Held in Australia from 31st August to 12th October, 1946*, ed. Rupert Best (Adelaide: New Education Fellowship, 1948), 113.
16   *Roshni*, February 1947, 49–50.

These speeches were not recorded in the final Australian published version of the Charter, and they are certainly not visible in Jessie Street's autobiography or in the later histories of the Australian women's movement. But the text of the 1946 Australian Woman's Charter suggests the extent to which the presence of Kapila Khandvala and Mithan Lam may have enhanced the directions that were already shaping the women's movement emerging into the Cold War.

What was *in* the 1946 Australian Woman's Charter?

The 1946 Australian Woman's Charter was comprised of 35 clauses, presented in five sections, and was followed by a series of 16 resolutions moved from the floor, most amplifying the content of the basic clauses. The overall tone of the Charter document in 1946 was very different from the confidence and optimism of 1943. In general, the 1946 Charter was responding to the worsening situation for women at the end of the war as well as to the bitter experience of having been ignored and bypassed by the Labor Government in the postwar reconstruction.

In the Charter's fourth clause, 'Unity and Cooperation', as just one example, fell just before 'Woman in Public Life' (clause 5). Instead of speaking about commitment to the war effort as the 1943 Charter had done, the 1946 Charter stated that it 'views with alarm the tendency to force women back to be exploited as cheap labour', to obstruct the work of women's organisations and to restrict women's access to childcare.

Similarly, the sixth clause 'Equal Status, Opportunity, Responsibility and Reward' stated that: 'The indispensable contribution that women make to all phases of human life is at present inadequately recognized'. The Charter conference therefore demanded amendment to the constitution, changes in laws and full access to employment at equal pay. The Charter expressed regret that the Women's Employment Board was now in demise. While some, including Lucy, felt it had only been of benefit to a few,[17] it had nevertheless recognised the presence of women in the workforce, a recognition the Charter conference felt was a fast disappearing.

---

17   Lucy Woodcock's 1963–64 assessment of the long campaign for Equal Pay found in *The WA Teachers' Bulletin*, May 1963, 106; and *Our Women*, March–May 1964, 26.

In amplification of clause 6, the third of the 16 Conference Resolutions on 'Dismissal of Women' stated:

> We deplore the dismissal of women after efficient and faithful service from the many positions of responsibility attained by them during the war; and declare that ample opportunities for the employment of women could be created by the adequate development of the resources of the country and other construction work.

And furthermore:

> This Conference deplores the fact that all countries have again denied women a voice in the shaping of the peace treaties ...[18]

Apart from this overall tone of disappointment and frustration, there was much that was similar in the 1946 Charter when compared to its predecessor in 1943. For example, the clause on 'Birthrate' (clause 25) still concentrated on the need to increase births. So the conference called for better community facilities for care of children and for the 'removal of obstacles to early marriage'. It did, however, add a call for the removal of the causes of war.

But there was still no mention at all of contraception or abortion. So, once again, women wishing to limit their families and control their own fertility were ignored. In 'Social Hygiene–Equal Moral Standards' (clause 30) the Charter still regarded prostitution as an offence, but it now criticised the injustice of directing punishment for prostitution only at women. Its recommendation was to remove the specific offence of prostitution, keep only the general nuisance laws and make men equally punishable. Even with such minor tweaking, much of the substance remains the same as in 1943.

The dramatic differences lie instead in the clauses of the Woman's Charter on Aborigines (34) and on 'World Peace' (clause 1 and resolution 16). In relation to Aboriginal people, the whole clause was named differently, having become '(Clause 34) Aboriginal and Coloured People'. Then the following recommendations on Aboriginal people were a competing tangle of contradictory directions, revealing the conflicts between

---

18 Australian Women's Charter Conference, *Australian Woman's Charter, 1946–1949: Which Comprises the Resolutions Adopted by the Australian Women's Charter Conference* (Sydney: Australian Women's Digest, n.d., c. 1949), 28.

women's organisations. The subsections included a substantial number of the original 1943 recommendations, aimed at keeping 'tribal' people and their land inviolate and protectable, but the rest were totally different.[19]

Firstly, there was the right to full and equal pay, equivalent to fellow white workers, to be paid in cash each payday to the workers who were 'Aboriginal and colored people' (recommendation e). This call for equal pay was a major challenge to the existing labour hierarchies. Furthermore, the clause was not based on any guess about the possible 'admixture' of Aboriginal 'blood' and instead insisted on equal pay as a right.

Next there was the recommendation (g) calling for the right for Aboriginal people to organise and elect their representatives in any way they chose and without interference. This may have arisen directly from contact with the Aboriginal communities most affected, either through Caroline Tennant Kelly over the NSW Select Committee or Lucy Woodcock in Erskineville. But it arose, too, from contacts in other states with militant, organising Aboriginal activists. In Western Australia, for example, while older feminists like Mary Bennett were still influential, there were newer voices like that of the author Katherine Susannah Prichard, in touch with the Pilbara strikers who had walked off their pastoral worksites at the end of the war to begin a three-year strike. Most notable of the differences on Aboriginal people was recommendation (c), which called for 'the extension of national independence to the colonial and semi-colonial peoples'. While this did not explicitly mention Aboriginal people, there must have been some who saw parallels. And clearly this completely new clause must have been influenced by the presence of Kapila Khanvala, Mithan Lam and presumably Mrs Opie, who was the delegate from Ceylon (Sri Lanka), whose voice is absent even from the reports of Khandvala and Lam.

In relation to world peace, the Charter clauses were unremarkable, with Clause 1 calling for a world free from war, the following clauses 2 and 3 calling for support for the United Nations and for its Committee on the Status of Women. Then, however, the conference resolutions went far beyond amplification. Instead, Resolutions 15, in relation to atomic energy, and 16, on world peace, were completely new and had clearly been shaped by the tumultuous events of the war and its aftermath. Resolution 15 welcomed the discoveries of atomic energy but declared that the knowledge associated with its peaceful use should be disseminated to all.

---

19   Ibid., 25–26.

Furthermore, the resolution called for the complete outlawing of atomic weapons and any form of atomic energy that could be used for warfare. Resolution 16 on world peace argued that the defeat of the fascist forces was not enough to ensure peace, and that instead close relationships must be developed between the world powers, explicitly mentioning the Soviet Union and 'all other democratic countries' through the United Nations, with the goal of fostering unity and ensuring the effectiveness of bans on all uses of atomic energy that could be used for war. The resolution then drew on the principles of the 1941 Atlantic Charter to ensure all nations recognised 'the principles of equality of nations and the rights of the people of each nation to choose freely, without foreign interference, their form of government'. Even more unequivocal was the next segment, calling on all nations 'to recognize the need for the extension of national independence to the colonial and semi-colonial people'.[20]

Both the resolution on 'Atomic Energy' (15) and the resolution on 'World Peace' (16) discussed the use of atomic power and weapons. This of course was also all new in comparison to 1943, arising from the horror at the dropping of the atomic bombs on Hiroshima and Nagasaki at the end of the war with Japan. This was the area to which Rachel Makinson had made a strong contribution during the conference, impressing Kapila Khandvala with her knowledge and thoughtful approach, in which she called for recognition of the potential positive uses of atomic power as long as its technology was open and shared and as long as all weapons were banned.

As well as the clauses on national independence on which Kapila and Mithan probably had an influence, there was at least one other in which they were certainly involved. There was a formal resolution on an 'Appeal for India' (13) for food and medical supplies that resulted directly from their explanations of the grave fears held across India that a repetition of the food shortages of 1943, best known in the West for their catastrophic effect on Bengal, were again looming.[21]

---

20 Ibid., 31–32.
21 Ibid., 30.

Indian disappointment

The Australian Woman's Charter Committee published a brief outline of the events of the 1946 conference as an introduction to their booklet containing the full resolutions of the Charter. This account presented the Indians bringing greetings and news, and indeed as excelling with their 'colourful float' in the Peace procession.

> Mrs Mithan Lam, LLB and Miss Kapila Khandvala, MA, BT, Director of Primary Education Bombay, brought greetings from the All India Women's Conference and the Bombay Presidency Women's Council. Audiences listened with deep interest to vivid descriptions of women's progress, of conditions of work, and the Trades Union movement in India. A final appeal was made for food to help the famine stricken people of that Country.[22]

The newspapers were full of the visit by the two Indians, but mainly in order to comment on their exotic saris.[23] Neither the newspapers nor the Charter booklet contained any account of assessments these two highly accomplished women may have made, but the Indian sources allow us to see at least some. While Kapila Khandvala was diplomatic in her report, Mithan Lam was more straightforward in her 'Impressions of the Women's Charter Conference in Sydney', published in a special edition of *Roshni* in November 1946, in terms that must have resonated strongly with Lucy Woodcock.[24] Mithan discussed the impending loss of Australian women's employment with the war's end and continued with a broad description of the conditions they had observed:

> Women do not generally hold important top posts: for instance the highest post that a woman can aspire to in the educational service would be that of inspectress of girls' schools. They [Australian women] were surprised to find in India, which they had been led to believe was very backward, Miss Khandwala holds such an important post. Even the magistrates presiding over juvenile courts are men (not necessarily trained welfare workers) who were assisted by women J.P.s. In that field we do better here, at least in Bombay. Married women are not encouraged to carry on their work however brilliant they may be; even in the

---

22　Australian Women's Charter Conference, *Australian Woman's Charter*, 6.
23　*SMH*, 24 July 1946, 6; 3 August 1946, 3; *Argus* (Melbourne), 27 July 1946, 10; 20 August 1946, 10; *Barrier Miner* (Broken Hill), 6 August 1946, 1; *Townsville Daily Bulletin*, 12 August 1946, 6; *Courier-Mail* (Brisbane), 2 September 1946, 3.
24　*Roshni*, Special Issue, November 1946, 42–48.

> universities they are generally given positions on a temporary basis and thus have no security of tenure. The things grieved us greatly, for we were under the impression that women in Australia were very advanced.

Mithan continued:

> The clauses of the Charter which interested us particularly and were of international importance were those which dealt with peace and the affirmation of the belief of the conference that 'to win a lasting peace oppression must be eradicated, true democracy established throughout the world and justice, liberty and equality enjoyed by all peoples in all countries without distinction as to colour, race, creed or sex.' An affirmation of these important principles is good these days, when the coloured people are fighting for their just rights … In my speech, I spoke on that part of the clause quoted above, telling them that the white people must face the problem of colour squarely if they wished to have a lasting peace.[25]

We catch a glimpse of the day-to-day arrangements over their whole visit from Kapila Khandvala's report to the AIWC, and it is clear that Lucy Woodcock played the major role in organising this visit by Kapila and Mithan. Lucy chaired the education session of the Charter conference in August, after which Kapila and Mithan spoke to a number of organisations associated with the UA. From then on, Lucy appears to have been even more closely involved with the visit. As an office holder in the NSW NEF, Lucy managed Kapila's speeches to the NEF seminars in Brisbane (2 September) and Sydney (7 September) then Melbourne (12 September), Perth (16 September) and Adelaide (26–27 September). Along the way, Lucy organised dinners at the University of Sydney and at the Fellowship of Writers, and she had set up a speech by Kapila to the Victorian Parents' and Teachers' conference (23 September). In October, at the end of this Australia-wide trip, Lucy hosted Kapila in speaking to the Assistant Teachers' Union (1 October), organised for her to speak at various school assemblies and then to speak alongside Mithan Lam to members of the Teachers Federation (2 October), where she had organised for Kapila to be made an Honorary Federation member. As a Teachers Federation delegate to the NSW Trades and Labor Council (TLC), Lucy had invited Kapila, Mithan and Jessie to speak there, also on 2 October, introducing them to the assembled TLC delegates, after which she organised a time spot for Kapila to speak on the Labor Party radio station, 2KY.

---

25   *Roshni*, November 1946, 44–45.

Figure 9.3: Lucy on the Teachers' Certification Committee 1943 – this shows both how she was often the only woman and how diminutive she was.

The amazing hat here must have been chosen to assist her to assert her presence.

Source: *Education: Journal of the NSW Teachers Federation*, 29 January 1943, p. 64. Courtesy of State Library of New South Wales.

While Lucy had had an exhausting role during 1946 – criss-crossing the nation as she travelled with her Indian visitors as well as organising with the UA and the NEF – she had not lost touch with her Teachers Federation colleagues. Women teacher friends had offered her the most sustained support for her campaign for equal pay and economic rights for all women, married or unmarried, but she had also had unfailing backing from Sam Lewis and a handful of male teachers, like Hal Norington, the Federation organiser. While they had taken no role in either of Lucy's major events in 1946, one of the principles Lewis shared with Lucy was his commitment to progressive education. He planned to attend the November 1947 conference of the new UN body, UNESCO, to be held in Mexico, in order to take part in the discussions around new models for education. Lewis, then secretary of the Teachers Federation, was elected as a delegate from the union, along with Frank Medworth, an art teacher from Sydney Technical High.

Although they were paying their own fares, they were given leave by the department for the duration of the conference. Because Lewis was a member of the Communist Party, there was an immediate outcry from conservative politicians, particularly from the anti-communist right-wing of the Labor movement, like former premier Jack Lang. All the press coverage prior to the conference was taken up with the controversy over whether CPA members should represent Australian organisations, even at their own expense. Tragically, Medworth took his own life after he arrived in Mexico City, and the press coverage switched immediately to cover his death, often luridly and with continuing anti-communist innuendo.

It is difficult then, amidst all these controversies, to find information about the outcomes of the conference, yet these were to be of importance to Australian teachers. The UNESCO resolutions from Mexico called for a Teachers' Charter and a Youth Charter, which would state the rights and goals of both teachers and students in all forms of education. The resolutions of the Mexico City conference and the next, in Beirut, set out the fundamental principles of these charters, as well as calling for further survey work from each of the member states.[26] These principles were that neither in the employment or work of teachers nor in the learning and teaching process was there to be any discrimination on the basis of 'race, colour, sex or religion'. Nor was any person, youth or adult, to be denied access to education because of their income.[27] This resonated immediately with the campaigns not only for gender equality but also for racial equality that had become Lucy's passionate commitment. Moreover, the rejection of any obstruction to education due to income – in other words, denial because of class – was just as important to her in her commitment to working-class education. Lucy had paid less attention to religion but most of these UNESCO principles were precisely in line with her own established positions.

---

26   United Nations Educational Scientific and Cultural Organization (UNESCO), *Resolutions Adopted by the General Conference During Its Second Session: Mexico, November–December 1947* (Paris: UNESCO, 1948), Resolution 3.11 and 3.12, p. 21, www.unesco.org/ulis/body/dec_res.html. Fundamental to both was that 'no bar founded on distinctions of race, colour, sex or creed should operate in any way in any branch of the teaching profession' or 'against any group of young people'. Furthermore social status and income was to be no barrier to either teaching or gaining access to education or certification.
27   Ibid.

UNESCO initially identified its work as being in 'Fundamental Education', by which it meant all forms of education, from early childhood learning through formal public schooling and technical training, as well as literacy, community and adult education. While UNESCO eventually restructured its organisation to reflect the more conventional segmentation of learning, this holistic approach reflected the vision of educators like Lucy, committed to progressive educational approaches. So furthermore, this resonated with her conviction that learning should be student-centred and engaged with 'real-life communities'. There were differences between the approaches of UK educators, often associated with the New Education Fellowship, to which Lucy subscribed, and those from the United States, but there was nevertheless a common interest in considering education widely across many forms and stages of life, rather than being limited to the conventional sequences, regulated and disciplined by universities.[28]

So there were many in the NSW Teachers Federation who, like Lucy, were eager to respond to the UNESCO call for draft charters to come from the teachers' unions of member states. Within a few months, the NSW Federation had formulated a draft that it was ready to share with international organisations. The NSW body was affiliated with the International Federation of Teachers' Associations (IFTA), one of three organisations of teachers that existed to bring teachers together across borders. One of Lucy's good friends in teaching, Ellen Grace Reeve, was in the UK on exchange teaching and attended the IFTA meeting held at Interlaken in Switzerland, in mid-1948. She carried the draft Charter proposed by the NSW Teachers Federation to the IFTA conference and was back in Sydney in time to report to the Federation's Annual Conference in December 1948. She was critical of the Eurocentrism of all three international teachers' organisations, pointing out that none of them had any significant representation from teachers from India, Africa or China.[29] Nevertheless, Reeve found the IFTA meeting valuable and reported to the Annual Conference of the NSW Federation that their draft had been discussed extensively and then endorsed with little amendment:

---

28 Joseph Watras, 'The New Education Fellowship and UNESCO's Program of Fundamental Education', *Paedagogica Historica: International Journal of the History of Education* 47, no. 1–2 (2011): 191–205.
29 Ellen Grace Reeve ASIO file, Vol. 1, N49946, f 9, 8 June 1949, A6119, 1500, NAA. Reeve's report to NSW Teachers' Federation dated December 1948.

> Members of this Council will remember that this Federation submitted to I.F.T.A the draft of a Teachers' Charter. This draft formed the basis for discussion for one session of conference and after certain amplification was adopted unanimously. I was asked by members of the conference to convey to the NSW Teachers' Federation, their thanks for preparing and submitting the Teachers' Charter.[30]

Lucy was then able to take this International Teachers' Charter to the Australian Teachers' Federation Annual Conference in Melbourne in January 1949 where, as past president and a continuing active member, she commanded significant respect. The Charter she proposed was accepted in full.[31] While no text of the Charter has been found to date, it seems that the NSW Federation – and therefore the International Teachers' Federation and then the Australian Teachers' Federation – had brought the two elements of the original UNESCO proposal together, so that the one Charter addressed the interests of both teachers and learners. The document was circulated and discussed at a number of levels and was accepted by UNESCO by 1950.[32] Lucy was heavily involved in gaining further endorsement from the Australian Teachers' Federation in 1951 and 1952. She argued (although losing these two points on amendment) that the continued purchase of armaments was directly undermining children's education and that individual teachers should become signatories to the Charter.[33] What is clear, however, is that the fundamental principle of both original charters was incorporated by the NSW Teachers Federation: 'no distinctions of race, colour, sex or creed' were to operate in any way, either for teachers or for students. Nor should any financial handicap act as an obstruction to free and full access to all educational opportunities for all.[34]

UNESCO itself was grappling with the challenges of decolonisation – it was forced in the most public of ways to revise its Eurocentric orientation to the central question of race. After undertaking in 1948 to provide a definitive statement of current knowledge on race, it did so in 1949, asserting that there were three human races, the Caucasian, Mongoloid

---

30   Ibid., f 6.
31   *Argus* (Melbourne), 4 January 1949, 5.
32   Ibid., 8 June 1950, 4.
33   *Tribune* (Sydney), 19 April 1951, 3; *Barrier Daily Truth* (Broken Hill), 12 January 1952, 3; *Biz* (Fairfield), 17 January 1952, 5.
34   UNESCO, *Resolutions Adopted by the General Conference During Its Second Session*, Resolutions 3.11.1 and 3.12, p. 21.

and Negroid races. But it was forced to issue a revised statement in 1951, retracting its first statement completely and explaining its erroneous conclusion as having been based on sociological opinion. Its revised 1951 statement corrected this with the conclusions of biological scientists, which were that there was in fact only one 'race' of human beings, *Homo sapiens sapiens*.[35] The implications of decolonisation and its challenges to European cultural dominance were clearly not a simple matter.

So it was not until after a meeting of non–state controlled teachers' unions in Moscow, in August 1954, that Christiane Dazaud was commissioned by UNESCO to summarise the Teachers' Charter. This text, published in a number of Australian newspapers in December 1954, included the following:

> Teachers and professors … who took part in the 19th session of the Joint Committee of International Teachers' Federations, unanimously adopted a series of resolutions – collectively entitled the Teachers' Charter – which, while claiming certain rights, sets forth many duties and obligations.
>
> The charter underlines the essential duties of the teacher, which are 'to respect the individuality of the child, to discover and develop his abilities, to care for his education and training, to aim constantly at shaping the moral consciousness of the future man and citizen, to educate him in a spirit of democracy, peace, and friendship between peoples.'
>
> The responsibilities of the teacher – not his rights – take first place in the preamble of the charter. 'The education of children is vital, not only for the development of the individuals, but also for the progress of Society.'
>
> It is obvious that certain rights correspond to those obligations but these are only safeguards which any citizen could legitimately claim for himself regarding appointments, professional liberty, freedom of association, decent salaries, paid holidays, &c. There is no question of privileges. Certain rights seem to be set forth in the charter merely to underline more clearly the obligations to which

---

35 Michael Banton, 'UNESCO Statements on Race', in *Encyclopedia of Race, Ethnicity and Society*, ed. Richard T. Schaefer (Los Angeles, London: Sage, 2008), 1096, 1098, doi.org/10.4135/ 9781412963879.n450.

the teachers pledge themselves … The authors of the Charter were more concerned with education than they were with the private interests of the educator.

In the same spirit, they underlined the essential mission of the school which 'should contribute to the development of character … A humane discipline in keeping with the self respect of both pupil and teacher, should exclude coercion and violence.'

It should not be assumed that the provisions of the charter are completely new. On the contrary, these resolutions, for the most part, reproduce in a more condensed and striking form those which the 16th and 17th International Conferences on Public Education had already drafted in detail at Geneva. What is new is the fact that teachers themselves, through their own international non-governmental organisations, have proclaimed them.[36]

***

These events reflected a time of significant decision-making for Lucy herself. As she approached retirement age, she was charting out a new and challenging pathway for herself. Her earlier work in education and women's rights was broadened during the 1940s to include racial as well as gender equality, along with an expansion of her internationalism as she engaged with Indians and the wider world through UNESCO. It was to expand further to include Asia as she pursued her commitment to the Peace movement as we see in the next chapter. Lucy worked – as always in very practical ways – to contribute to the broadened vision she drew from the processes of achieving the Australian Woman's Charter of 1946 and the Teachers' Charter of 1950.

---

36   *Queensland Times* (Ipswich), 9 December 1954, 3; *Morning Bulletin* (Rockhampton), 23 December 1954, 7.

Crossing Borders:
1945–1960s

10
Red Scare

> … the best means to understand people is to get to know them.[1]

Lucy had been a committed pacifist since her brother's death in World War I, but during the Depression she had focused her formidable campaigning on the issues of women's and working-class education and then, during the war, on gaining well-resourced childcare for working mothers. The end of World War II and the flurry of activity in 1946 were just the beginning for Lucy in her campaign for international peace. She had undergone an operation to restore movement in her damaged leg and, no longer needing to use a walking stick, she expected to be able to contribute even more. But her intentions to work for Peace met a series of unexpected obstructions, requiring all her negotiating skills to overcome.

***

One of the many things on which Lucy and Elsie Rivett had found common ground in 1936 was on the fundamental importance of Peace. The Rivett family had a long background in the religious world, but many were activists. Elsie's father, the Reverend Albert Rivett, was an unconventional Protestant pastor, born in 1855 in England and the son of a bricklayer. He had a Quaker training but took up a role as a cleric in the Congregational church, coming to Australia with the Colonial Missionary Society. He was a pacifist, who spoke out against the Boer

---

1 Lucy Woodcock, Foreword to Helen Palmer, *An Australian Teacher in China* (Teachers' Sponsoring Committee, NSW Peace Council, 1953).

War and opposed conscription.² Elsie's older sister, Eleanor (1883–1972), became a missionary teacher in Calcutta and later Madras, India, where she became an advocate of women's education and Indian independence.³ Elsie's brother David Rivett, a renowned scientist, was more circumspect than his father but was committed to internationalist principles.⁴ In his later years, Albert Rivett himself became a regular contributor to the *Australian Worker*, an outspoken advocate of international justice, strongly supporting C.F. Andrews's campaign against the indenture of Indians in Fiji.⁵ So Elsie's dedication to working-class children, to international justice for working people and to Peace were all well grounded in her family's interests, and she and Lucy had much in common besides the Children's Library in Erskineville. They would work together in the Australian Peace organisations for the rest of their lives.⁶

Lucy had always been a strong exponent of the New Education Fellowship argument that education was a powerful strategy for nurturing peace through understanding. As early as 1936, Lucy and Jess Rose had argued for 'international history to be a feature of all school syllabuses with the object of fostering world peace'.⁷ Lucy put this approach into practice in her teaching at Erskineville. Beverley Langley remembers Lucy to have fostered understanding across cultural barriers at Erskineville Public School by teaching children that skin colour was irrelevant and encouraging them to share lunches and to learn and play together at the school and the Rochford St Children's Library.

---

2   C.B. Schedvin, 'Rivett, Sir Albert Cherbury David (1885–1961)', *Australian Dictionary of Biography*, National Centre of Biography, The Australian National University, adb.anu.edu.au/biography/rivett-sir-albert-cherbury-david-8512/text14381, published first in hardcopy 1988, accessed online 31 January 2013.
3   Margaret Allen, 'Eleanor Rivett (1883–1972): Educationalist, Missionary and Internationalist', in *Founders, Firsts and Feminists: Women Leaders in Twentieth-Century Australia*, eds Fiona Davis, Nell Musgrove and Judith Smart, Australian Women's Archives Project ([Melbourne]: eScholarship Research Centre, University of Melbourne, 2011), 45–63; also at www.womenaustralia.info/leaders/fff/pdfs/rivett.pdf.
4   Judith Godden, 'Rivett, Elsie Grace (1887–1964)', *Australian Dictionary of Biography*, National Centre of Biography, The Australian National University, published first in hardcopy 1988, adb.anu.edu.au/biography/rivett-elsie-grace-8514/text14385, accessed 31 January 2013.
5   For example, 'Cheap Labour and Fiji', *Australian Worker*, 16 October 1919, 7; 'The Case for Indian Self-Government', *Australian Worker*, 2 April 1930, 14.
6   Campaign for International Cooperation and Disarmament (CICD) Papers, Box 52, 3/88, UMA/SC.
7   FSSTA meeting, Hobart, *Mercury* (Hobart), 9 January 1936, 10.

During the Sesquicentennial Year of 1938, Ethel Teerman had led a group of supportive teachers, including Lucy, in the NSW Teachers Federation Peace Group, which had affiliated with the International Peace Campaign. As a senior educator, Lucy led the discussions at the National Women's Peace Conference in April on the 'School Child and Peace'.[8] She expressed her concern at what teachers faced trying to counter the attitudes of 'jingoism' that children were learning from their families or the 'love of power' and 'competitive spirit' they were taught in the current school curriculum.[9] Knowing how damaging Nazi anti-semitism was for European Jews, Lucy nevertheless did not see war as a solution to racism – instead she was consistent in naming the war as 'destruction'.

Angered by the way the war effort was diverting funds from education in working-class areas by 1941, she was arguing 'that teachers would be failing in their job if, even in the midst of war, they did not attempt to awaken public responsibility to the fact that education was as necessary as guns'.[10] As an economist, Lucy pointed to the real financial burden. Rebuilding of the whole infrastructure of public schooling was going to be costly, as was better training of new teachers. The demands of war – not only for armaments and war machinery but for the training of soldiers – had all placed a grave strain on the national budgetary resources. Lucy made the point again and again that this cost had actually already been paid – by the children whose education had been undermined by the diversion of funds to war:

> Never again should cost be cited as a cause for the non-introduction of reforms, for we are spending more in one month of destruction than would finance the Federation's demand for an additional 25,000,000 for education.[11]

It was education that was in real need of expenditure, but as long as war seemed to be the more urgent demand, schools – and children – would suffer, just like it was the big sisters in families who were paying the real costs for poor childcare.

---

8   Held in Sydney and Perth, see Chapter 7, this volume.
9   'Train Children in Ways of Peace', *SMH*, 8 April 1938, 4; '"Mothers' Army": Women to Work for Peace', *SMH*, 9 May 1938, 13.
10 *Argus* (Melbourne), 8 January 1941, 2.
11 *SMH*, 22 November 1943, 7.

The terrible lessons of the war's end – the dropping of the first nuclear weapons on Japan – had shown Lucy how important education was. When giving a major lecture to the Tasmanian State Schools Teachers Federation, she insisted that ignorance was 'more dangerous than the atom bomb'.[12] In 1946, in the immediate aftermath of the war, Lucy had been an organiser for both the Australian Woman's Charter and the New Education Fellowship conferences – titled 'Education for International Understanding' – that had called for education reform to focus on strategies for peace. She had learned even more about decolonisation and the importance of freedom in the region from her time with Kapila Khandvala and Mithan Lam during their 1946 visit. This strengthened her motivation in becoming involved with the NSW Teachers Federation engagement with UNESCO, supporting Sam Lewis's role there in 1947 and working with Ellen Reeve to take the Teachers' Charter, based on the UNESCO principle of 'no discrimination on the basis of race, colour, sex or religion', to the Australian Teachers' Federation (ATF) meeting in January 1949. Ethel Teerman could no longer be directly involved in the NSW Federation's Peace work as she had married Sam Lewis in 1940 and so was forced to resign as a teacher, but the momentum of the Teachers' Peace Group was kept up by Ellen Reeve, who took over the role of secretary, while Thistle Harris and Lucy remained vice presidents.

By mid-1949, the various bodies working on Peace began to coalesce at a national level with the formation of the Peace Council, initiated with involvement of the Communist Party and clergymen in Melbourne. For some years, state-based branches operated largely independently. Much of the analytical focus has been on the extensive Melbourne archive, into which the records of the NSW organisations were eventually deposited but seldom noticed.[13] Organising had continued, however, after 1949 among Sydney activists in the NSW Peace Council, of which Lucy was an Executive member, hosting its meetings frequently in her George Street

---

12   *Mercury* (Hobart), 12 May 1949, 8.
13   Barbara Carter, 'The Peace Movement of the 1950s', 58–73; Ralph Summy and Malcolm Saunders, 'The 1959 Melbourne Peace Congress: Culmination of Anti-Communism in Australia in the 1950s', 74–98. Both in *Better Dead than Red: Australia's First Cold War: 1945–1959*, eds Ann Curthoys and John Merritt (Sydney: Allen and Unwin, 1986); Les Dalton, 'Politics of the Australian Peace Movement, 1930s to 1960s', *Centre for Dialogue Working Paper Series*, no. 2011/1 (Melbourne: La Trobe University, 2011).

flat.¹⁴ This group saw itself as part of the wider international movement, and it was understood by security observers to be the 'Asian and Pacific Peace movement'.¹⁵ For Lucy, achieving Peace necessitated influencing the federal government, so she challenged it at the ATF annual meeting in January 1950 to ensure that 'the States were defended educationally on the same basis as preparation for armed defence'.¹⁶

A few months later, in March 1950, Lucy chaired the meeting to affiliate the NSW Teachers Federation with the Australian Peace Council. Then in April, she chaired the Sydney meeting of the Peace Council itself, which was organised to hear the key speakers from a major Peace conference in Melbourne, notably the Dean of Canterbury.¹⁷ Soon after, the UNESCO journal *Courier* carried the front page headline 'All Wars Are Fought Against Children'.¹⁸ The Teachers' Peace Group had at the same time published its own first newsletter, headlined 'Education for Peace'.¹⁹

For Lucy, the Teacher's Charter initiated by UNESCO had a central Peace dimension as well as its value in securing fair conditions, status and respect for teachers. The NEF had been influential among the people and organisations who had initiated UNESCO, which in its 1947 Mexico meeting had echoed the theme of the 1946 NEF conferences in Australia: 'Education for International Understanding'. The core UNESCO principle, that there should be no discrimination on the basis of race, colour, sex or religion, was aimed at nurturing an orientation towards cultural openness and interaction among both learners and teachers. To this, UNESCO had added an activist dimension, which was the approach Lucy favoured – it was not enough to foster culturally open and non-discriminatory education, but it was necessary to campaign to ensure the prioritisation of expenditure to achieve high-quality education rather than divisive and militaristic policies, attitudes and expenditures.

---

14 Lucy Godiva Woodcock ASIO file, Vol. 1, ff 86, 90 and 104, A6119, 2030, NAA. Some of the papers of this NSW Peace Council, including the minutes of the planning meetings for the 1953 Convention on Peace and War, are now held by Melbourne University Archives in its Special Collections, in CICD Papers, Boxes 49 and 52, 3/88, and Records of the Victorian Peace Council (VPC), Box 6, Folder 3, UMA/SC. Deery has explored the material on the 1953 Sydney Convention in Phillip Deery, 'Menzies, the Cold War and the 1953 Convention on Peace and War', *Australian Historical Studies* 34 (2003): 248–69, doi.org/10.1080/10314610308596254, reviewing the perspective of Melbourne-based SRC observer, Geoff Chapman.
15 Lucy Godiva Woodcock ASIO file, Vol. 1, ff 86, 90 and 104, A6119, 2030, NAA.
16 *Mercury* (Hobart), 13 January 1950, 22.
17 Ellen Grace Reeve ASIO file, Vol. 1, ff 6–10, A6119, 1500, NAA.
18 UNESCO *Courier* 3, no. 4 (1 May 1950): 1, en.unesco.org/courier.
19 Ellen Grace Reeve ASIO file, Vol. 1, f 18, A6119, 1500, NAA.

Sam Lewis, who had attended the Mexico conference despite the outcry in Australia, made this point forcefully in his presidential report in December 1951 at the NSW Teachers Federation Annual Conference:

> the greatest single factor on the world scale causing inflation and leading to the undermining of the living and cultural standards of the people is enormous expenditure on production of armaments. Teachers are concerned very deeply with conservation: conservation of natural resources, conservation of human resources. They are the agents in the battle against material and moral erosion, against the scorching of human flesh and the searing of the human spirit.[20]

Lucy continued the theme at the next ATF annual meeting in January 1952, when she formally moved that it accept the Education Charter that was the outcome of UNESCO work on the Teachers' and Youth Charters. Her 1949 motion to the ATF to accept the draft Teachers' Charter had been passed unanimously and without amendment but, by January 1952, tensions around anti-communism had risen. There was an active Teachers' Anti-Communist League, formed inside the NSW Federation in 1946, and the campaign for Peace was regarded as a communist-controlled attempt to weaken the West.[21] So there was dissention over Lucy's wording of the 1952 motion because it called for the defence of the child and education against 'inroads into educational budgets due to the expenditure on armaments and as a result of high profits and prices'. Furthermore, she had called for teachers to sign the Charter to indicate their commitment. Both of these elements of her motion were removed by amendments, although the Education Charter itself was then endorsed completely by the ATF.[22]

Lucy did not retreat from her commitment to the Peace movement despite the atmosphere of rising hostility. As Judith Emmett had said of her, Lucy 'always had a willingness to stand up for things that were not popular.'[23]

---

20   *Tribune* (Sydney), 2 January 1952, 8.
21   *The Sun* (Sydney) 15 October 1948, 7; *Canberra Times*, 16 October 1948, 3; *Daily Telegraph* (Sydney) 22 December 1948, 14; *SMH*, 3 November 1949, 1.
22   *Biz* (Fairfield), 17 January 1952, 5.
23   Judith Mitchell, now Judith Emmett, phone interview, 31 July 2017. Judith was – and remains – a very active Christian and she met Isobel and Richard, and their son Barry, in the Belfield church.

So when she was elected as the NSW Teachers Federation delegate to attend the Asia-Pacific Peace Conference to be held in Peking in late September 1952, Lucy grabbed the opportunity and began organising her trip.[24] She applied to the Australian Government for travel documents and to the NSW Education Department for her well overdue long service leave to cover her absence. The coming trip was widely advertised and the invitations had been issued for friends to come to see the delegates off at the airport on 16 September. Lucy explained that her special reason for wishing to go was to 'study the development of education and the position of women in China and other Asian countries'.[25]

But, at the very last minute, the conservative federal government and NSW state Labor Government acted together. Lucy was told that her passport would be recalled and that she would be prevented from taking her long service leave. She was shocked – as were many sympathisers. Mrs Margaret Parker, from Erskineville, a mother whose four sons had all fought in World War II, where one was killed, had attended what she expected to be a rousing farewell for the delegates at Trades Hall on 10 September. Instead, as Mrs Parker wrote to the NSW Education Minister Mr Heffron:

> I was astounded when Miss Lucy Woodcock, Headmistress of Erskineville Public School, announced that she had received a letter from you refusing to grant her long service leave after 46 years of service … Up to date, war has never solved anything and, in my opinion, never will. I ask you to start thinking and working for peace and to assist all you can those who want to work for peace and seek the truth for themselves.[26]

With such short notice, it was difficult to organise a replacement who would be able to take leave, be able to speak for the Teachers Federation and bring home information about education both at the conference and more broadly in China. Hurriedly, a young teacher named Helen Palmer agreed to fill Lucy's place. One of the daughters of the authors Vance and Nettie Palmer, Helen had herself begun to write, but was a shy and retiring person, who had previously been reluctant to take

---

24   *Tribune* (Sydney), 3 September 1952, 4. See for comparison, John Burton's similar experience in Phillip Deery and Craig McLean, '"Behind Enemy Lines": Menzies, Evatt and Passports for Peking', *The Round Table. The Commonwealth Journal of International Affairs* 92, no. 370 (2003): 407–22, doi.org/10.1080/0035853032000111125.
25   *Tribune* (Sydney), 10 September 1952, 2.
26   *Tribune* (Sydney), 17 September 1952, 2; *Scone Advocate*, 17 September 1952, 4.

high-profile roles. Yet she wrote a thoughtful account of her time in China, titled *An Australian Teacher in China*, for which Lucy wrote the Foreword. In it, Lucy gave an insight into her own motivations as well as those of Helen Palmer:

> Miss Palmer went to China because like so many of us, she felt that the best means of understanding people is to get to know them ... I commend this small book to you in the hope that her courage will inspire others to seek the truth and serve the cause of peace.[27]

This was not the only foray outside the national borders in 1952. Late in the year, Lucy's good friend Lotte Fink made the long sea voyage to Bombay to attend a conference on family planning. Lotte made good use of her time on the ship and in India, not only meeting many people in the family planning field but also catching up with those people with whom she had shared common ground. One of those was Kapila Khandvala, who Lucy had introduced to Lotte at the 1946 Australian Woman's Charter Conference in Sydney. Lotte wrote back to her family in Sydney about her frequent contacts with Kapila, who had in turn introduced Lotte to women involved in the education structure that Kapila had been managing in Bombay. Through Kapila's introductions – and the use of Kapila's car – Lotte was able to visit a number of schools in and around Bombay to see for herself how they were operating in independent India. She compiled her thoughts into a talk she gave to the Sydney NEF some weeks after her return. So Lucy was able to keep in touch with the developments taking place as colonial rule was shaken off, as well as to have a taste of what she could see for herself if only she could get out of the country.[28]

***

Lucy had remained furious at the 1952 denial of her long service leave and her plans to get to China. Yet she held her frustration in check and simply redoubled her efforts in 1953 to contribute to the Peace campaign as best she could within Australia. At a meeting at Federation House on 10 April 1953, for example, Lucy spoke in defence of Julius and Ethel

---

27 Lucy Woodcock, Foreword to Helen G. Palmer, *Australian Teacher in China* (Sydney: Teachers' Sponsoring Committee, Australian Peace Council, 1953).
28 Lotte's letters have been transcribed by her daughter Ruth Latukefu and are cited here courtesy of Ruth. Letters, each written in Bombay, and dated 26 November 1952, 5 December 1952 and 11 December 1952.

Rosenberg, who had been condemned to death in the United States for allegedly passing secrets about nuclear weapons on to the Soviet Union. Lucy argued that the Rosenberg verdict had set a troubling precedent for Australian freedom of speech. Like the American laws, the Australian Atomic Energy Bill, then before parliament, would similarly categorise people who spoke out against nuclear weapons as traitors.[29]

Later in April, a group of 10 clergymen in Sydney developed a proposal for a conference that would bring together:

> a broad, representative section of the people in every city, town and country centre, to meet and discuss ways and means of winning the peace and saving humanity. Peace cannot wait – it must be won ...[30]

This initial gathering on 27 April was confirmed in a formal meeting on 18 May that set up the convening committee, drawn largely from Sydney activists, for what the group termed 'The Australian Convention on Peace and War', to be held in Sydney in September 1953. The minutes of this Convening Committee give an insight into how Lucy worked in the Peace movement, which had a different composition to either the trade unions or the women's organisations in which Lucy continued to take active roles.[31]

The clergymen's initial statement was endorsed by the 18 May meeting not only by those among them who went on to be listed as convenors like the Reverend N. St Clair Anderson, but also other clergymen who were to take a high-profile role including the Anglican priest Alf Clint, an activist in cooperative organisations in Papua New Guinea and among Aboriginal people in Queensland and New South Wales. Lucy Woodcock was present, as was Elsie Rivett and her sister Eleanor, along with Lucy's friends in the artistic world, like the children's illustrator Pixie O'Harris and the painter Rah Fizelle, who had taught at Darlington Public School with Lucy, had worked in London in 1927 when Lucy was there and

---

29 Executive Meeting notes 27 April and Minutes: 18 May, 25 June, 29 June and 22 July, 1953, CICD Papers, Box 52, 3/88, UMA/SC. Despite such meetings in support of the Rosenbergs, they were executed by the United States on 19 June 1953.
30 Extract from 'Roneo-ed leaflet issued by the Asian And Pacific Peace Movement', dated 29 May 1953 and held in Lucy Godiva Woodcock ASIO file, Vol. 1, f 90, A6119, 2030, NAA.
31 These minutes are some of the very few records of peace activism in Sydney that have survived the amalgamation of the NSW Peace Council with those of other states, eventually to be consolidated into a national organisation, CICD, based in Melbourne. CICD Papers, Box 52, UMA/SC.

lived in a flat near hers in the 215A George St block. There were, as well, long-time supporters of the Peace movement like the pharmacologist S.E. Wright and his university colleague Miss D. Lange and the architect and Lane Cove councillor Maurice Edwards, who all became involved in the Convention organising.[32]

Lucy and Elsie took joint responsibility for the mobilisation of women to take part, convening a women's planning meeting in August focused specifically on increasing the numbers of women as participants and speakers. They aimed for between 5 and 10 per cent of delegates to the Convention to be women. Lucy, long familiar with the practicalities of organising, undertook many of the tasks. She approached the mainstream and women's press, to try to gain publicity aimed more specifically at women; called meetings in Newtown and Erskineville, to build support and gather ideas to bring to the Convention floor; and finally wrote to the National Council of Women with the aim of contacting each of its affiliated women's organisations. This Convention Women's Committee advised the convenors to develop publicity aimed specifically at women. The committee's suggestions make uneasy reading today, as it argued that material aimed at women should be simpler and less wordy than that previously published. The committee proposed that women should be able to send in written responses to a simply worded question about the meaning of Peace, allowing them to avoid the discomfort – or the domestic conflict – of attending. Finally, the committee suggested that the Convention program be altered to include a session specifically for women participants, although it pointed out, emphatically, that this advice did *not* mean that women delegates were not to attend or speak at other sessions:

> We consider that women's point of view can be expressed at both sorts of session [with women-only or open attendance], but some women are so used to leaving all discussion publicly to men, that [an] attempt should be made to overcome this.[33]

One result of their work was a leaflet, one of the six produced by the Convention planning group, in which much of the Women's Committee advice was incorporated.

---

32 CICD Papers, Box 52, 3/88, UMA/SC.
33 Women's meeting, 11 August 1953, CICD Papers, Box 52, 3/88, UMA/SC. Some of the other women involved in this Women's Planning Committee were named in various sets of minutes as Mrs Kempster, Mrs E. Parsons and Mrs L. Barnes (a member of the Union of Australian Women).

Figure 10.1: The women on the organising committee for this 1953 conference, including Lucy and Elsie Rivett, attempted to address women's interests and tailor communication strategies towards women who were not in unions or existing peace organisations.

Source: Courtesy of University of Melbourne, Campaign for International Co-operation and Disarmament (CICD), Melbourne University Archives, Series 3, Box 52, 3/88: Australian Convention on Peace and War. 3 CICD (1979.0152 consolidated).

The title 'Peace and Women: We were drinking tea and talking' was followed by a line drawing that could have been straight out of a women's magazine of the time, depicting women sharing tea around a radio cabinet, from which they heard the news that a Peace conference was to be called in Korea. An older woman among the group is said to comment bitterly: 'A Conference will be arranged! They should have talked it over before a shot was fired!' The leaflet style was direct and accessible, putting peace into very personal terms, converting the statistics of the dead, of widows and orphans, into individual stories of death and loss. At the end of the four-page flyer, there was a tear-off section to allow women to write into the Convention, answering the simple question: 'What does peace mean to me and my family?'

Another result of their work – not only in this pamphlet but, perhaps more importantly, in their many formal and informal meetings with women activists – was the overall representation of women at the conference. Women made up 31 per cent of the delegates, an increase on expectations.[34]

To consolidate representation at the Convention, Lucy not only worked in convening the women's committee but continued working in the other arena she knew well, the trade unions. As Teachers Federation delegate to the NSW Trades and Labor Council (TLC), she moved in August 1953 that the TLC invite a speaker from the Convention to address members on the coming meeting, arguing that 'peace was the most important ingredient in the happiness of men, women and children'.[35] This view was being put within the Communist Party as well. In the same issue of *Tribune*, J.D. Blake argued that it was essential to consider peace and war as integral to any solution to problems about either industrial conditions or the problems of education, hospitals or housing, 'otherwise no real perspective for a practical solution of these problems was possible'. Yet at the same time, although less publicly, conflict among communists was building. Blake's article betrayed some of it when he insisted that:

> Communists must attentively heed the views of non-Communist people who desire peace ... We are opposed to any attempt to 'use' the movement for peace for any ulterior motive.[36]

---

34 *Convention Record*, 2.
35 *Tribune* (Sydney), 26 August 1953, 3.
36 Ibid.

While this was certainly a rebuttal of the anti-communist assertion that the peace movement was a 'communist front', it was also a reflection of the pressure against Blake's more liberal position, which was not held by party leaders like L.L. (Lance) Sharkey and others who sought more direct intervention in the broader movement.

Yet the grassroots work of the planning committees could not overcome the reality that Cold War tensions had escalated. The Peace Convention was being denounced as communist-inspired by the conservative Menzies Government and the strongly anti-communist Labor Party of the time. This was a continuation – and in fact an escalation – of the hostility that had blocked Lucy's attempt to attend the 1952 Peace conference in Peking. It resulted in 1953 in an effective blackout of news about the Convention – few articles and no advertising appeared in any of the mainstream newspapers.

At the same time, while there were effective collaborative relationships between the so-called 'peace parsons' on the Peace Council and the Communist Party of Australia (CPA),[37] there were also tensions. Those in the CPA who argued for engagement and dialogue with Christian pacifists, socialists, feminists and the many others associated with the peace movement were regarded with suspicion by the hardliners in the party. An example of the more inclusive approach was that of J.D. Blake, whose intellectual and political standing in the CPA seemed secure in 1952. He was, however, becoming marginalised over this time in an internal conflict with Lance Sharkey and Ted Hill that eventually confined him, in what he remembered bitterly as a humiliating defeat, to working only with the Peace movement.[38]

Yet, as the Cold War polarisation deepened, the CPA was losing the allies it had gained during the Depression and this led the party to increase its involvement with the Peace movement.[39] Early in 1953, the party executive had itself planned to initiate a conference on peace to take place late in the year. But once the Peace Council's Convention was announced

---

37 Ian Turner, 'My Long March', *Overland* 59 (1974): 36–38; Phillip Deery, 'Shunted: Ian Turner's "Industrial Experience", 1952–53', *The Hummer* 4, no. 2 (2004): 18–29.
38 Phillip Deery, 'The Sickle and the Scythe: Jack Blake and the Communist Party "Consolidation", 1949–56', *Labour History*, no. 80 (May 2001): 215–23, doi.org/10.2307/27516780.
39 Douglas Jordan, *Conflict in the Unions: The Communist Party of Australia, Politics and the Trade Union Movement, 1945–60* (Sydney: Resistance Books), Chapter 3; P. Deery and D. Jordan, 'Fellow-travelling in the Cold War: the Australian Peace Movement', in *The Past is Before Us. Refereed Proceedings of the Ninth National Labour History Conference*, eds Greg Patmore, John Shields and Nikola Balnave (Sydney: Australian Society for the Study of Labour History and University of Sydney, 2005), 115–23.

for September, the CPA shelved its own plans and decided to participate in the Convention on Peace and War. Seized documents showing that the CPA had planned to hold a Peace conference during 1953 were used by the federal Menzies Government to campaign relentlessly against the Sydney Convention, with the resulting refusal by the mainstream press to cover the preparations for the Convention. The Reverend J.E. Owen, a Presbyterian minister from Melbourne and a major figure in the Convention planning, protested in person to Menzies and was shown the security documentation that had exposed the CPA planning. This allowed Owen to point out that there was a confusion between the two conferences.[40] His insistence that the CPA was not in control of the September Convention was ignored not only by Menzies but also by the broader anti-communist lobby, including the mainstream press and most Christian churches. Only after the Convention were there some apologetic Church admissions that there should have been more support.[41]

Lucy was at the centre of this tension because she worked very closely with both Communist Party members and Christian peace advocates. Her commitment was personal and professional rather than religious: it was well known that she had been a consistent advocate of learner-centred education as a powerful tool in fostering intercultural communication. She had been involved in the Peace Convention planning with the Sydney clergy from the very beginning. Her close friendship with Elsie Rivett, who was embedded in a radical pacifist but Christian family, had consistently been expressed through shared work in the Peace movement. Through this relationship, Lucy was close to many of the activist clergy, particularly those who had strong socialist affiliations, like the Reverend Alf Clint, who was prominent as an advocate of decolonisation as well as being prominent in the Peace Council. At the same time, in the Federation and through her teaching in working-class schools like Cessnock and Erskineville, Lucy had become close friends and allies with teachers like Ellen Reeve, Ethel Teerman and Sam Lewis, all either members or associated with the CPA and actively involved in the party's activities. Lucy had been drawn to them not only because she supported their causes but also because of their sustained support for her own – in the Federation there were few men other than Sam Lewis who so consistently supported Lucy and the tight group of women who were advocates of Equal Pay. So Lucy embodied the reality of shared goals across widely diverse ideological positions within the Peace movement.

---

40 Deery, 'Menzies, the Cold War and the 1953 Convention on Peace and War', 248–69.
41 CICD Papers, Box 52, 3/88, UMA/SC.

Figure 10.2: A photograph of the only known remaining poster for the NSW Convention on Peace and War in November 1953.

This poster is now held in the Peace Archives of Melbourne University.

Source: Courtesy of the University of Melbourne, CICD papers, Box 49, 3/52, UMA/SC.

Her strength then, as it had always been in the Federation, was to make ideological space for all sides. She undertook this role during the five-day Convention.

The overall goal of the conference was to gather 'citizens together to discuss and promote international goodwill and peace', with representation of 'every constructive viewpoint'. There were to be three commissions inquiring into central questions of Australian responsibility to foster international peace, each with three subcommissions that were to undertake their discussions on the second and third day (Sunday and Monday) of the Convention, drawing their conclusions into consolidated 'Findings' over the fourth and fifth days (Tuesday and Wednesday). Lucy had a major role in Commission C, which was to inquire into 'how the best achievements and the promise of Australian life could be preserved and extended'. She chaired one of its subcommissions, which asked 'do war preparations affect Australian standards today?', while she also took a role in some of the 'special commissions', notably those focusing on women, youth and that on 'education and culture' chaired by C.B. Christesen.[42]

On the floor of the Convention, the conflicts were visible. Geoff Chapman, a Melbourne student who attended as a Students' Representative Council (SRC) delegate, kept notes of the proceedings, although he took part only in Commission A. He expressed frustration at a doctrinaire 'party line', which he and other participants felt had shaped all speakers on the joint first day of the Convention, but when the Convention broke into the commission and subcommission sessions, the dogmatic tone of the first day broke down. On the second and third days of the Convention, according to Chapman in Commission A, the tone had noticeably changed. Instead of dogma, there was very active debate between all sides, with the views of non-communists not only more evident but eventually dominant in the findings. There appears to have been active and broad-ranging interchanges in the other two commissions, although C.B. Christesen, the *Meanjin* editor who chaired the 'special commission' on 'Education and Culture', felt there were too many major themes to be discussed together. He felt, however, that there had been vigorous free discussion that had led to three major outcomes – the most urgent of which expressed:

---

42   *SMH*, 28 September 1953, 4; Convention Flyer, CICD Papers, Box 52, 3/88, UMA/SC; *Convention Record*, p. 3, VPC, Box 6, Folder 3, UMA/SC.

Profound dissatisfaction with the inadequacy of our present educational system and the gravest alarm for the future welfare of children. Delegate after delegate emphasized that conditions of peace were essential to permit the adequate education of children and adults and that, in turn, an enlightened educational system would play a highly important role in achieving world harmony and understanding among the peoples …[43]

Nevertheless, despite Christesen's reservations, there seemed to most participants to have been lively discussion and wide debate, rather than the imposition of any one party line. The CPA made the best of what appeared to Chapman and others as the failure of its intervention. *Tribune*, the party newspaper, published CPA member Bill Wood's full-page review of the Convention under a heading that reflected his theme: 'Came as Strangers, Parted as Friends'. He gave an account of his personal highlight:

This writer's big moment came when he heard a viewpoint violently opposed to his own being expressed at one of the Commissions. You don't usually like to hear your views trampled on, but this particular speech, like many others, showed that every viewpoint was genuinely represented at the Convention. The speechmaker was elected to a committee which drafted the Commissions finding. He wholeheartedly accepted the general findings of the Convention.[44]

Chapman was less sanguine – he felt that those with more right-wing views had not been welcomed. Nevertheless, the diversity of views was unusual and certainly far wider than any one position might advocate.[45]

What was particularly significant, too, about the proceedings of the Convention was the presence of two Aboriginal delegates, one of whom was Shadrack James, a staunch unionist who had defended Aboriginal workers in the harvesting industries along the Murray River. He was a Yorta Yorta man from Cummeragunja, the son of Ada Cooper, nephew of William Cooper and an articulate spokesperson for south-eastern Aboriginal people's identity and land interests, as all his family had been. His father, Ada's husband, was Thomas James, the Mauritian Indian who had turned his strong educational background and awareness of colonialism

---

43   *Convention Record*, p. 9, VPC, Box 6, Folder 3, UMA/SC; C.B. Christesen, Report, *Meanjin* Files, Box 274, UMA/SC.
44   *Tribune* (Sydney), 7 October 1953, 7.
45   SRC Report, VPC, Box 6, Folder 3, UMA/SC.

across the Indian Ocean to the service of education and campaigns of protest in Australia.[46] Shadrack James's speech to the Convention drew on this background to ensure that this Convention was not thinking only of remote and 'traditional' Aborigines, but instead was calling for justice for all Aboriginal people, including those of mixed descent who were working in the cash economy and living in south-eastern Australia.

This shift to a recognition of immediate Aboriginal demands as well as their colonial context was evident in the events of the time. The close of the Convention on 30 September occurred before the first detonations of British nuclear weapons on the Australian mainland, the Totem tests at Emu Junction in South Australia, on 15 October. It is notable that the front page of the *Tribune* issue that covered the Convention was dominated by news of the coming detonations, referring to the danger to the Aboriginal population of the area.[47] Unlike the earlier, widely circulated concerns expressed about the intrusion of the rocket and bomb testing grounds onto 'primitive' Aboriginal communities, which had been a hallmark of the previous campaigns, this 7 October 1953 coverage foregrounded practical, concrete dangers to living Aboriginal people rather than threats to their 'traditional' culture or inviolate reserve space. Its headline read: 'Aborigines in Danger. A-Bomb on Reserve?'

Sadly, such fears of irradiation to nearby Aboriginal people turned out to be accurate, although the decision to fire the tests against meteorological advice and in disregard of a known Aboriginal presence was not revealed till many years later.[48]

Much of the published findings of the Convention echoed Lucy's views. The findings of Commission C, on the 'Future life of Australia', began with a statement that she would have fully endorsed:

> There can be no true development of the Australian nation without the fullest participation of the people in all its problems. The full flowering of our nation requires an atmosphere freed from prejudice and intolerance, and implies love in its widest sense, and courage in the search for self-determination.[49]

---

46 George Nelson and Robynne Nelson, *Dharmalan Dana: An Australian Aboriginal Man's 73-Year Search for the Story of His Aboriginal and Indian Ancestors* (Canberra: ANU Press, 2014), doi.org/10.22459/DD.04.2014.
47 *Tribune* (Sydney), 30 September 1953, 1; 7 October 1953, 9.
48 Australia. Royal Commission into British Nuclear Tests in Australia, *Report of the Royal Commission into British Nuclear Testing in Australia* (Canberra: Australian Government Publishing Service, 1985).
49 *Convention Record*, pp. 7, 9, VPC, Box 6, Folder 3, UMA/SC.

Figure 10.3: Front page of *Tribune*, 7 October 1953, shows one of the earliest recognitions by Australia's Communist Party that living Aboriginal people were threatened by atomic testing, rather than an isolated culture.
Source: *Tribune*, 7 October 1953, 1. Trove, National Library of Australia.

In its specific statements on education, the Convention called for the recognition of the potential value of all forms of media to serve the best interests of Peace, rather than fostering militarism and conditioning children to war as contemporary media were doing. Then it called for prioritising of resources for education at all levels – in schools, in technical education and in lifelong learning – in order to made better democratic citizens, capable of independent thinking but also of cross-cultural awareness:

> In helping to make better citizens in a more peaceful world, ample opportunities for a broader development of our cultural heritage are desirable.
>
> In the field of Education, the guiding principle should be to promote to the full the capacities of all, so that each may faithfully play his part in the nation's development and in the determining of the people's destiny.
>
> … self-education would continue through life, and assist in achieving the elementary democratic principle of the participation of the people in Government at all levels, including their intelligent participation in the activities of the United Nations organization on a world level … We feel that only the allocation of adequate resources for the extension of educational facilities, including staff, broad cultural activities and freer provision of texbooks and also a better cultural content in technical education can resolve the crisis in education today.[50]

The Commission's findings were published partially in the mainstream press and then in full in the communist press, contributing to the conversations circulating at the time although doing little to alter the prevailing fears of communist control over the Peace movement. The Convention itself published its findings in full in the *Record*, with many resonating with the concerns Lucy had expressed over many years. In particular, those concerning 'Prejudices' accorded with the approach she had taken in 1938 in the public conferences hosted by the Teachers Federation when she spoke out against discrimination towards women and against racism both in Australia and in Europe. Her emphasis on continuing colonial inequalities had strengthened after her time with Kapila Khandvala and Mithan Lam in 1946, a theme that Shadrack James would have reinforced, which led to its prominence in the findings:

---

50   *Convention Record*, p. 7, VPC, Box 6, Folder 3, UMA/SC; *Tribune* (Sydney), 7 October 1953, 9.

Prejudices

> Cultural exchange must be facilitated. Obstacles such as restrictions on travel, the banning of books and films, and the censoring of news must be removed.
>
> Racial prejudices and hatred foster war and should be vigorously opposed. Basic education in racial understanding should be encouraged.
>
> Our national policy on the restriction of Asian immigration was established in our Australian way of life, but it could justifiably be revised in the future.
>
> We should use our natural resources and our technical knowledge to improve living standards of our Asian neighbours in the spirit of active goodwill, and not from motives of political expediency. The Colombo Plan should be continued and extended.[51]

Lucy wrote an article that was published in the back page of the *Convention Record*, with her words as its heading: 'Weight of military burdens falls on children'.

She was described at the Convention as 'a Sydney headmistress', although when she repeated much of this talk as the main speaker at a follow-up meeting held at Cessnock in November, it was her executive position as Federation Senior Vice President that was stressed:

> Since 1913, war has taken toll of the heritage of Australian children, has destroyed their chances of a good education. The Australian child of today is the citizen of tomorrow, but during war preparations he is practically forgotten. Our schools and national education have been malnourished and in some cases almost brought to a bankrupt state. At present, Australia faces a crisis in education which is unparalleled – for we cannot supply schools, teachers, or equipment necessary.
>
> If we have the time and we have the right setting for children, their minds can be set in the moulds of peace, but unfortunately these things cannot be done without money. Money is being found in ever-increasing amounts for war, but it is sadly lacking for children …

---

51   Embodied particularly in the findings of Commission B ('How Can Australia's Relations with Other Nations Be Improved?'), *Convention Record*, p. 11, and Commission C, *Convention Record*, p. 10, VPC, Box 6, Folder 3, UMA/SC; *SMH*, 1 October 1953, 2; *Tribune* (Sydney), 7 October 1953.

War preparation means malnutrition.

Peace is born in happiness. Peace does not thrive in fear and suspicion. Therefore it is on man the living being that the emphasis must be placed. We spend a lot of thought and preparation on atom bomb tests – I think it is ill-spent because the emphasis has been on the machine, not on the common man. It is on the common man that we must poise and rivet the attention. He must come into his own.[52]

The NSW Peace Council – including its Christian members – recognised Lucy's commitment. At its annual Christmas party in December, Lucy was the guest of honour, where she was presented with an award by the Reverend E.E.V. Collocott, a Methodist minister long associated with the Peace movement, 'in recognition of her sterling work for peace'.[53]

***

In December, too, Lucy's long career as a teacher reached an end. She retired, with first a farewell from Erskineville Public School itself and then a formal presentation evening at the Teachers Federation. Each in its own way offered a glimpse into Lucy's work and into her world. We have discussed some of the speeches at the Federation farewell in earlier chapters and we will return to it for its unique insights. With particular relevance to this chapter's focus on the Peace campaigns in Australia, some issues raised in speeches at Lucy's retirement give an insight into her political role. The Minister for Education in the state Labor Government – R.J. Heffron – praised Lucy for her courage and intelligence in the hard industrial negotiations in which she had been involved:

> I have come to know you by sitting on the opposite side of the table as a strong unionist insisting on things being better for teachers and better for the youngsters being taught. So I have learned to know you and to respect you.[54]

The then president of the Teachers Federation, Harry Heath, had just won the position in election by Federation members from Sam Lewis after a heated campaign. Heath was a right-wing candidate but, despite

---

52 *Convention Record*, p. 16, VPC, Box 6, Folder 3, UMA/SC; *Cessnock Eagle and South Maitland Recorder*, 17 November 1953, 3.
53 *Tribune* (Sydney), 6 January 1954, 7.
54 Transcript of speeches from Lucy Woodcock's Teachers Federation Farewell, on her Retirement in December 1953. UAW Files, Extracts from *Education*, 3 February 1954, 2, AU NBAC Z236, NBABL.

its efforts, the anti-communist case waged against all three Executive members had unseated only the incumbent president. The membership had re-elected Lucy as senior vice president, although her margin was reduced, along with Don Taylor as vice president. Nevertheless, Heath, like Heffron, was fulsome in his detailed praise of Lucy, 'an outstanding headmistress … of immense energy' who 'has given to teachers loyal and unstinting service'.[55]

Lucy's capacity to elicit such appreciation even from her adversaries was explained by the third speaker, Sam Lewis, who praised her tenacious advocacy for women teachers and her long-time service to the Federation itself. So all three of them had pointed to Lucy's skills and courage – but Lewis then explained that even though Lucy held strong and committed positions, she was nevertheless an excellent negotiator, who could bring together people from all sides. Lewis continued of Lucy's role as Federation delegate to the NSW Trades and Labor Council:

> She is one of the most respected persons on the Labor Council, and possibly about the only person on the Council who will be listened to by all sides with respect and in silence.[56]

***

The farewell from the Erskineville School community had been even warmer. Hundreds of former students and their families had come to say goodbye to Lucy and thank her for her role at the school. At the Federation farewell, Heffron, Heath and Lewis all pointed to this community affection as the greatest testament to Lucy's commitment and tireless advocacy on behalf of her working-class students and their families. Yet it was the mothers of Erskineville who gave Lucy the gifts that recognised her real intentions. Despite having few funds to spare, they had purchased a beautiful set of travelling luggage and a rug to keep her knees warm on her journeys.[57] They knew – better than the minister or even the union leadership – that Lucy did not plan any quiet retirement, but instead had bigger plans for an international, activist future.

***

---

55   Ibid.
56   Ibid.
57   Ibid.

For some, retirement from the profession to which they had devoted their lives might seem to mark the end of their active life. For Lucy, retirement was just the beginning! It released her from the chains of control by the NSW Department of Education so that she no longer had to keep her political campaigns so tightly under wraps. She had never been one to shirk a fight and so this release from constraints made her all the more visible.

Lucy was acclaimed late in 1953 as a hero of the campaign for women's rights, when the United Associations of Women (UA) honoured her alongside Dame Mary Gilmore and Henrietta Greville at a dinner to celebrate the 50th anniversary of Women's Franchise in Australia.[58] Lucy was very visible, too, at meetings of the Union of Australian Women (UAW), which aimed to address the goals of working-class women and had substantial communist as well as non-communist membership. Lucy attended their monthly lunch in February 1954, when she spoke about Equal Pay, and then was guest of honour in March, speaking about education.[59]

Over the same period, Lucy maintained her work in the Peace movement, contributing particularly to the emerging campaign against atomic weapons, which had been expanding since British testing on mainland Australia had begun the year before. On 8 April 1954, Lucy chaired a meeting at the Sydney Town Hall, attended by Chinese and Indonesian activists as well as Australians, condemning the first test of a hydrogen bomb on 1 March by the United States in the Marshall Islands.[60] In its May *Newsheet*, the UA announced a message from Vijaya Lakshmi Pandit, the president of the UN General Assembly, calling on all member nations – and particularly all women – to condemn the H-bomb.[61] This campaign was to become even more significant to Lucy when she later visited Japan.[62]

Her goal in 1954 was to make very direct and personal contact with the international Peace movement. Lucy had sustained her anger over the refusal of her long service leave and the withdrawal of her passport in

---

58 *Tribune* (Sydney), 27 January 1954, 9. UA event took place 16 December 1953.
59 Re November 1953 UAW meeting and coming February meeting, 26 January 1954, Lucy Godiva Woodcock ASIO file, Vol. 1, f 108, A6119, 2030, NAA; Re UAW meeting March 8 at International Women's Day, 3 March 1954, ibid., ff 112–13, NAA.
60 Re H Bomb Symposium, 13 April 1954, Lucy Godiva Woodcock ASIO file, Vol. 1, f 116, A6119, 2030, NAA; *Daily Telegraph*, 9 April 1954; *SMH*, 9 April 1954.
61 UA *Newsheet*, May 1954, 1.
62 See Chapter 12, this volume.

1952 when she had wanted to attend a Peace conference in Peking. It was, however, in recognition of her continuing high role in women's civil rights that the UA and the Australian Federation of Women Voters (AFWV) elected Lucy as their representative at the summer school to be held in Copenhagen from 28 July to 24 August on 'Women and their Status in the Community'.[63] Lucy planned to visit her friends in UNESCO in Paris as well as visiting Denmark, Sweden and other places in her study of education methods abroad.[64] At the same time as Lucy was seeking to travel, Bill Gollan and Freda Brown, both members of the CPA, were also making travel plans, which included some of the same events to which Lucy was going. The government was intensely suspicious of them all.

Lucy at first expected she would have no difficulty as she was a delegate from the UA and AFWV. So she booked her plane ticket for 10 June. In its classified files, however, it is clear that ASIO regarded her as a 'suspected communist' and viewed her with deepest suspicion. It knew that Bill Gollan had a current passport but withdrew it, while it began making inquiries about the validity of Lucy's,[65] including gathering further information from R.J. Heffron, who only months before had been so glowing in his praise of Lucy.[66] In an attempt to stop the delegation leaving at all, the federal government withdrew the passports of the former ALP senator Bill Morrow as well as CPA member Bill Gollan, and refused to issue new ones to two clergymen, the Reverend Neil Glover and Father A. Haley, Rector of Darwin, all due to attend the Peace conference in Sweden, the 'Stockholm Gathering on International Understanding'.[67] Lucy chaired the protest meeting held in the Teachers Federation Hall, attended by Alf Clint, Clarice McNamara (NEF) and many others, in which she said:

> I believe we have the right to our own opinions and the right to travel freely to other countries.[68]

---

63   Evaluation, 7 July 1954, Lucy Godiva Woodcock ASIO file, Vol. 1, f 144, A6119, 2030, NAA; *Tribune* (Sydney), 27 January 1954, 9; UA *Newsletter*, September 1954.
64   Memorandum, 25 June 1954, Lucy Godiva Woodcock ASIO file, Vol. 1, f 142, A6119, 2030, NAA.
65   Memorandum, 6 May 1954, Lucy Godiva Woodcock ASIO file, Vol. 1, ff 123–24, A6119, 2030, NAA.
66   Ibid., f 123, where she is referred to with Bill Gollan as 'the above named communists'. It is not clear if this was Heffron's terminology or that of the ASIO agent.
67   See St Clair Anderson's report in *Tribune* (Sydney), 24 November 1954, 10. Anderson attended the Stockholm 'Gathering'.
68   *Tribune*, 2 June 1954. Held in Lucy Godiva Woodcock ASIO file, Vol. 1, f 134, A6119, 2030, NAA.

Then Lucy learnt that her passport, too, was in doubt, forcing her to cancel her ticket, explaining to the travel agent that she was having trouble gaining access to a passport. In protest, she appealed to the clergymen in the Peace Council to mobilise support for her. The Reverend Alf Dickie pursued a number of options through the Victorian Peace Council, recorded in an ASIO report, which quoted Dickie describing Lucy as 'former leading member Teachers Federation, now retired, never belonged to any Party, life-long service to children's education'.[69]

After a flurry of such activity, Lucy was granted a new passport on 15 June 1954, with a visa allowing her to enter France. She left on 17 June with a one-way ticket to London via Amsterdam.[70] Sam and Ethel Lewis were there to farewell her, along with others, and so Lucy finally made it out of Australia. One of the first things she did once in Europe was to make arrangements to acquire a British passport so that the Australian Government could never detain her again.

But the Australian controversies did not end even though Lucy had finally left to go overseas!

As Lucy was leaving, she had mentioned to a friend that she was considering going to the last part of the Peace conference in Sweden as an observer if she were able to arrive in time. This 'friend' had passed the news on to ASIO and it had then inexplicably been given to Jack Lang, formerly ALP premier of NSW but, by 1954, a vitriolic anti-communist crusader, for whom any Peace-related activity was a sign of communism. Lang regarded Lucy's travel as suspicious, raising the earlier refusal of her passport to attend the Peace Council conference in Peking, and publishing his accusations in his *Century* newspaper. On this pretext, the AFWV on 20 July, just days after Lucy had finally left the country, telegrammed her and the various women's organisations associated with the Denmark workshop, cancelling its endorsement of Lucy 'because of the Press controversy'.[71]

The UA described the incident with deep regret, expressing 'great indignation ... that a woman of Miss Woodcock's distinction and integrity should have been subjected to such a humiliating experience on the word of a paper of the nature of *The Century*'. The *Newsheet* continued that

---

69 Report, 18 June 1954, Lucy Godiva Woodcock ASIO file, Vol. 1, f 138, A6119, 2030, NAA.
70 'Teacher Pierces Holt's Curtain', *Tribune*, 23 June 1954. Held in Lucy Godiva Woodcock ASIO file, Vol. 1, f 141, A6119, 2030, NAA.
71 UA *Newsheet*, September 1954, 2.

there had been no reason for the AFWV to act in the way it had, despite the 'scurrilous attack' by Lang's *Century*. After pointing out the lifetime of service Lucy had given to the cause of women as well as to education, the UA described Lucy's reaction to the AFWV cable as 'mystified' but reported that her reply had been 'characteristic of the writer – expressive of a spirit of the utmost generosity, dignity and poise'.[72]

Lucy had gone to Sweden but she cancelled her visit to Denmark after her disendorsement. She remained committed to working with the UA, which supported her strongly and encouraged her to continue to represent it in the Peace campaign and all other events. Lucy had in fact already delivered a UA report to the Open Door International Conference on the Economic Emancipation of the Woman Worker, held at Oxford from 26 to 30 July. This UA report was a concise and realistic outline of conditions in Australia. It recognised the divisions among women themselves and was honest about the setbacks faced as the war ended. Nevertheless, this was a constructive report, with a clear-eyed focus on the tasks to be accomplished to make improvements. This was the approach that Lucy's work in the Teachers Federation had always taken – realistic but constructive and strategic – so it must have confirmed her confidence in the organisation. It allowed her to begin her busy journey with a sense of purpose, which was ultimately demonstrated in the report on her travels that she delivered to the UA on her return in 1955.

For its part, the organisation wasted no time in making the decision to disaffiliate from the AFWV. As reported in its November *Newsheet*, the UA had decided 'after earnest consideration' that it should withdraw affiliation. The UA argued tactfully that financial difficulties had led to its decision, and pointed out that its own goals were more limited than those of the AFWV. The timing of the decision made clear, however, that the AFWV repudiation of Lucy Woodcock was the key issue. After assuring the AFWV that continuing opportunities for cooperation would be welcomed, the UA affirmed that its priority would be 'improving the status of women'. The UA pointedly explained that by this it meant focusing primarily on the issue of Equal Pay, which it felt would be best pursued by working on a national campaign with bodies as focused on Equal Pay as the Council for Action on Equal Pay had been earlier.[73]

---

72 Ibid.
73 UA *Newsheet*, November 1954, 1.

11
Into Asia

Lucy had been crossing borders for a long time. Since her 1911 meeting with the Robinovitz family to her 1946 work with the Woman's Charter, the New Education Fellowship and UNESCO, she had come to imagine a new world without discrimination against women. Her focus was no longer on the old world, where discrimination persisted, but on the new world of socialist revolutions and emerging nations. This was where sudden and complete ruptures after World War II had ushered in a new order where discrimination against women was outlawed.

Lucy crossed many more borders in the first few years after her retirement. Some of them were international borders and others were cultural borders inside Australia. Many were political borders, impossible to traverse while she was employed. This chapter tells the story of Lucy's first visit to Asia – travelling to China, Japan and India. This journey had a major impact on her work once she returned to Australia, an impact that is traced in the following chapter, 'Peace and Prejudice'.

***

Lucy's involvement in the Peace movement had intensified her desire to travel the routes of emerging equality for women. The long and terrible years of World War II had culminated with the horror of the atomic bombs in Japan, bringing home the vulnerability of people all over the world to the effects of warfare. For Lucy, the issue of discrimination was directly linked to warfare – ending inequality was an inextricable part of the commitment to peace. Her failed attempt to travel to Peking for a Peace conference in 1952 only sharpened her determination to explore this emerging world. When she finally managed to leave the country on 15 June 1954, she planned to go to very different places than her first trip in 1927.

In 1954, the atomic threat was uncomfortably close to home for an Australian like Lucy. Not only had the first hydrogen bomb test just been carried out in March 1954 by the United States at Bikini Atoll in the South Pacific, but, not long before that, in 1953, Australia had experienced the first British nuclear blasts on the mainland at Emu Junction in South Australia. In this trip, Lucy was a delegate for the NSW Peace Council and reported regularly to them while she was away.[1]

Yet, despite this focus on the Peace movement, her commitments to women's rights and to union organising were never far from her thoughts. Lucy had already told the United Associations of Women (UA) in March 1954 that she would be able to spend more time working in the organisation now that she had retired. She gave an insight into her vision of emerging nations leading the way forward:

> In this year of 1954, Australian women face an interesting challenge. Women in other parts of the world, during a few short years, have achieved an equality far greater than we have. We owe these women a debt. It is for us to make our women conscious of what can be done when women band together. We are inspired when we consider how the women of some countries have progressed. Who would have dreamed that a woman would have aspired to the greatest international position in the world today – Presidency of UN?[2]

Lucy went straight to the Stockholm Gathering on International Understanding as an observer, alongside the Australian delegate, the Reverend Norman St Clair Anderson, whose passport to travel to Sweden had been only grudgingly approved. *Peace News* had commented: 'Far from menacing Australia's security, peace conferences help relax tension and build up international friendship.'[3] Such cross-cultural interactions were

---

1   The *Peace News*, NSW Peace Council newsletter, for 1954 and early 1955, which was publishing Lucy's reports, was apparently only a typed and roneod document. Copies have not survived, unlike the later and more professionally printed NSW Peace Council newsletter, *Peace* (now held in the SLNSW), which was launched in April 1955. The Sydney *Tribune* scoured the 1954 issues of *Peace News*, however, reporting on and quoting many of its articles.
2   UA *Newsheet*, March 1954, 2.
3   *Tribune*, 23 June 1954, 10.

Lucy's goal as she pointed out in her introduction to Helen Palmer's report on the visit to the Peace conference in China to which Lucy had hoped to travel.

After Sweden, and despite the Australian Federation of Women Voters (AFWV) disendorsement (discussed in Chapter 10), Lucy spent time in London at the Open Door International Conference, delivering a UA report. The Open Door International was closely associated with the 'Six Point Group', with which the UA was affiliated, and focused on equality for women on six basic grounds: political, occupational, moral, social, economic and legal. Jessie Street had been an active participant in the Six Point Group during her time Britain.[4] The report was realistic, acknowledging successes in Australia but also the many problems women continued to face.

Lucy then travelled to the Soviet Union and Asia, first to China then Japan and India. She travelled with Jessie Street, with whom Lucy had formed a close friendship since first approaching the UA in an alliance in 1932 to restore the right of married women teachers to work. Despite their very wide differences in class and status, Lucy and Jessie found they shared a sense of humour, an interest in working-class and socialist politics and a deep commitment to the full equality of women as citizens.

Whereas Jessie was most active on the diplomatic level, influencing politicians and diplomats, Lucy was focused on educational strategies and industrial activism. Jessie's autobiography covers the many high-level diplomatic meetings she attended during the time they travelled together. Lucy's reports to the NSW Peace Council and her later speeches about the same trip are brief and concentrate on the person-to-person conversations with working women, trade unionists and, in Japan, the victims of radiation exposure. Both of their perspectives are needed for an appreciation of their journey.

---

4   Chloe Ward, 'Activism without Discrimination', in *The Transnational Activist: Transformations and Comparisons from the Anglo-World since the Nineteenth Century*, eds Stefan Berger and Sean Scalmer, Palgrave Studies in the History of Social Movements (New York: Springer, 2017), 227–56.

Figure 11.1: Jessie and Lucy sharing a drink and a laugh during this 1954–55 trip.

This uncharacteristic photograph of Lucy reflected the warm bond she shared with Jessie as well as her relaxed attitude to alcohol.

Source: Courtesy of National Library of Australia, Jessie Street papers, Box 30, Series 11, folder 4.

The China leg of this trip was the start of Lucy's exploration of Asia. She had been actively involved in the Australia–China Friendship Society from 1952 and, as she later said:

> In China, women are fully conscious of the part they are playing in the shaping of their country's future; there is a complete acceptance of women's right to do the job and a calm confidence that they can do it. And so you find the engineer in charge of the great dam construction works is a woman, the superintendent of one of the biggest State factories – a woman – and the head of the Teachers' Training College at Nanking, with its 12,000 students, is Mdme Wu Liu Feng.[5]

---

5   UA *Newsheet*, October 1955, 4.

Lucy commented frequently on the approach to education and the training of teachers in China, as an ASIO officer noted in a report on her speech to a 1956 Union of Australian Women (UAW) meeting:

> She described her visit to China where she said women were taking a very prominent part in the re-building of their country. Education in China, she stated, was playing a greater part than in any other country in the world. Teachers in China, notwithstanding their University degrees, undergo a special 2 or 3 year course to fit them for their role in education.

The ASIO operative added derisively that 'Miss Woodcock stated that the special course undertaken by teachers fitted them for education "on the right lines"', implying that this phrase could have only one meaning. In this and other speeches, however, Lucy suggested that 'the right lines' involved fostering friendships and tolerance across races and cultures. Lucy had gone on to contrast education in China with the very different situations she observed in Hong Kong and Japan, differences she felt were caused by the presence of large numbers of Allied troops and business people with the result that 'education is neglected and child immorality is rife'.[6] The more high-profile element of this visit was the meeting Jessie Street held with the Chinese Minister for Public Health, also a woman, shown in a photo published in the *Tribune* on 27 October 1954.[7]

Figure 11.2: The focus of Jessie's reports: the high-level diplomatic meetings during the trip.

Here are Jessie and Lucy with the Chinese Minister for Public Health.

Source: *Tribune*, 27 October 1954, 11. Trove, National Library of Australia.

---

6   Ibid.
7   *Tribune* (Sydney), 27 October 1954, 12.

More important for Lucy than the publicised meetings, however, was meeting women activists as well as getting to know Rewi Alley, the New Zealander who had come to China in 1927. Alley had assisted in setting up industrial cooperatives in Shanghai's factories (involved in forming the Chinese Industrial Co-operative Movement, known as CIC) and from 1945 to 1952 was headmaster at the Shandan Bailie School, set up to train workers for the cooperative movement.[8] In his socialism, his educational role and his involvement in the Peace movement, Alley was very like Lucy. In another way, too, his life resonated with hers. Rewi Alley was a homosexual man who found an acceptance of his lifestyle in pre-1949 China that had not been available to him in New Zealand. Yet he was always extremely reticent about his personal life, and left most observers, even those who were more openly homosexual, with only glimpses of the relationships that sustained him. The coming to power of the Communist Government in 1945 marked a significant step towards modernisation as well as its other impacts. Brady argues that such modernisation in the People's Republic after 1949, just as it did in Taiwan or Japan, led to a rejection of traditional Chinese acceptance of ambiguous and homosexual relationships and instead an embrace of Western puritanism about sexuality and an intolerance of homosexuality. Alley had to make choices in order to stay in China. He took up the role offered to him as an official 'Friend of China' and an NZ representative based in Peking of the China Peace Committee, the same group who had invited Jessie and Lucy to China. His reticence about his sexuality deepened and Brady argues he probably chose celibacy rather than risk being ejected in the way his former CIC colleague, Max Bickerton, had been. His commitment to China and its working people led Alley to stay there throughout his life, despite his frustrations with many aspects of the new People's Republic after 1949 and the severe difficulties he later faced during the Cultural Revolution.[9]

When Lucy met him in 1954, Alley remained optimistic that labour cooperatives and education could improve the lives of Chinese people, as well as being committed to promoting peaceful international relationships.

---

8   Anne-Marie Brady, 'West Meets East: Rewi Alley and Changing Attitudes towards Homosexuality in China', *East Asian History*, 9(June 1995): 98, 111. In his letters to Lucy, Rewi Alley spelled 'Shandan' as 'Sandan' and so this was how Lucy spelled it in her letters. The Bailie Schools, run under the CIC, were named after Joseph Bailie, and American missionary friend of Alley's with progressive ideas on the education of Chinese youth.
9   Ibid., 97–120; Anne-Marie Brady, *Friend of China: The Myth of Rewi Alley* (London and New York: Routledge Curzon, 2003).

He asked her – as he probably did with many who visited China – to write to him to keep him updated with their local and international politics as well as on the progress of the Peace movement. Lucy was one who did not disappoint him – she wrote to him twice or three times a year over the next decade, in letters just as reserved about her private life as he was about his. Yet her letters were full – she crowded into aerograms as much detail as she could about Australian politics and world affairs, not only in relation to the Peace movement but in terms of how China was seen in the world. In return, Alley wrote to her with his latest diary entries and poems, much of which was later published, giving her a vivid – if too optimistic – account of the course of life in China. Although they shared so little overtly about their personal lives, Alley valued Lucy's letters, as shown in the letters from Alley, which were among the very few items that Lucy kept.[10] Rewi wrote to her late in 1955 that 'your letters are grand to have' and 'I look forward very much to your accounts of how you find things', finishing another letter to her with:

> Do tell us what you are all doing. Australian mail quite weak these days. Despite the many promises of people when they are here. I have no complaint about you though. You have been most kind.[11]

After leaving Peking, Lucy travelled with Jessie and an interpreter, Ms Chou Ien Fong, (known to Rewi) seeing 'much of the new China and its developments'. But Lucy had other priorities. 'I was most interested', she wrote, 'in the progress being made in China so far as education is concerned.'[12] Lucy sought out a number of educators, including the Reverend Ting, Head of the Theological College in Nanking, and Miss Wu, head of a middle school in Shanghai, who spoke to her largely about the horrors of the old regime.[13] But it was when they left China to spend three weeks in Japan that Lucy had the experiences that left her most shaken.

She had already made inquiries in Europe about the effects of atomic weapons. She wrote to the NSW Peace Council, for example, that she had met Professor Nishiwaki from Japan, who believed the abnormally rainy weather in Europe had been caused by the US H-bomb and feared that

---

10   Lucy's few papers and books were conserved after her death by Kit Edwards and are now held in his personal collection.
11   Rewi Alley to Lucy, 17 October 1955; 6 November 1955. Kit Edwards collection.
12   Lucy Woodcock to Rewi Alley, 3 December 1954, Rewi Alley Papers, MS-Papers-6533–307, NLNZ.
13   Ibid.

it might be followed by a dry spell that would ruin the world's harvest. He explained that the blast had thrown 100 million tons of pulverised coral dust into the upper atmosphere and this dust would act as a barrier to solar radiation. Her letter, published in *Peace News*, was reprinted with concern in the *South Australian Farmer* before being cited by *Tribune*.[14]

Lucy was still unprepared for the four days she spent in Hiroshima. She spoke to a group of young people in Perth on her return about how deeply moved she had been by what she saw there.

> We can only talk about atomic war. But when you actually see the imprint of a man's shadow in the stones of Hiroshima, you know what the Japanese people experienced and why they say never again.[15]

Jessie's notes, incorporated later into a Peace conference speech, documented the meetings she and Lucy had with survivors of the Hiroshima blast – people who had lost everyone, were scarred physically and emotionally for life and had been marginalised by Japanese and later Allied governments for embodying inconvenient truths. These survivors told them that before the Imperial surrender, there was already a strong popular opposition to the continuation of the war.[16]

In early December 1954, as soon as Lucy had reached their next stop, in New Delhi, she wrote to Alley about her experiences in Japan, where she 'found the Japanese people very firm in their resolve for peace'. Lucy explained that she had met a Chinese Government representative, Madame Li The-Chuan, who attended a huge meeting in Kyoto where Lucy saw 'a most enthusiastic crowd' receive Madam Li very well. 'There is a growing feeling of friendship for China in Japan', Lucy assured Rewi. The Peace movement was of most interest to Lucy, who told Rewi about the Japanese signature campaign against the hydrogen bomb. '20,000,000 signatures have been gathered already by the women, so they mean to stop the bomb if they can.' While this was a hopeful sign, Lucy was disturbed by 'the cancer of the American occupation', which she believed had led to widespread corruption, prostitution and gambling.[17]

---

14   *Tribune* (Sydney), 27 October 1954, 3.
15   Clipping annotated *Tribune* 10 August 1955, in Lucy Godiva Woodcock ASIO file, Vol. 1, f 194, A6119, 2030, NAA.
16   Jessie Street, 'My interview with the victims of Hiroshima and Bikini', Typed notes, Jessie Street Papers, MS 2683/4/1271, NLA.
17   Lucy Woodcock to Rewi Alley, 3 December 1954, Rewi Alley Papers, MS-Papers-6533–307, NLNZ.

A little later in December, Lucy reported to the NSW Peace Council about the Japanese women's Peace campaign and their meeting with the Lucky Dragon survivors:

> Miss Woodcock says that over 20 million Japanese have signed a petition for the outlawing of the Hydrogen Bomb. With Mrs Street she had visited the 22 surviving Japanese fishermen who were injured by the Bikini explosion last March. One died and the others remain in hospital. Miss Woodcock said that the men greatly appreciated the Australians' visit.[18]

Lucy believed that trade unions were crucial in building that Peace movement. She told young people in Western Australia that unions in Japan and India were playing most important roles. As *Tribune* summarised her speech:

> Herself an old Trade Unionist with ACTU experience, she went to the Unions in every country she visited. She emphasized particularly the work of the unions in India and Japan. 'Japanese rearmament is being held up by a great people's movement against war and the unions are in the thick of it', she said.[19]

Yet Lucy reported to the United Associations of Women that she found the conditions of women in Japan troubling. She was impressed that equality was written into the constitution and that there were 41 women in the *Diet*, but was concerned that these goals of equality were not met in practice. Women working in Japanese factories were forced to take three days unpaid 'sick leave' for menstruation. Lucy 'advised them to go in a body and demand pay for the enforced sick leave'. In schools, Lucy continued, there were no cleaners, so women teachers – not male! – had to stay behind to do the cleaning. Lucy was happy to find that the general secretary of the teachers' union was a woman,[20] but her main concern was about the general neglect of education. Lucy believed that this too was due to the influence of the large numbers of US troops there in the country, which led to the prioritisation of their needs and the widespread existence of 'child immorality'.[21]

---

18   *Tribune* (Sydney), 21 December 1954, 2.
19   *Tribune* (Sydney), 10 August 1955.
20   UA *Newsheet*, October 1955, 3. 'The Diet' is the national bicameral legislature of Japan.
21   *Tribune* (Sydney), 10 August 1955.

Lucy had more background for the last leg of their journey, in India, where Jessie had been born, where Elsie Rivett's sister had been working and about which there had been regular reports in the Teachers Federation journal *Education*. Having written her letters to Rewi Alley and the Peace Council about the Japanese experiences, Lucy spent three weeks with Jessie in and around the capital, Delhi, where they met with women activists, including Anasuya Gyan Chand, a leader in the newly formed National Federation of Indian Women (NFIW), who was an educator from the western state of Maharashtra. One of the few photographs of the visit shows Jessie, Lucy and Anasuya taken at the Red Fort.

Then Lucy and Jessie began visiting communities and particularly working people in Uttar Pradesh, the state in which Delhi was located. Lucy later recounted an experience that had moved and inspired her. At Amritsar, in the north-west towards the Pakistan border, she and Jessie had spoken to 25,000 textile workers, both men and women. They asked to meet with women workers and had been taken 'to one of the back streets, where they talked to 400 women who were amazed that a white woman should be anxious to meet them'. Lucy explained that she and Jessie had 'brought a message about how women could help themselves', to which 'the response of those women of Amritsar was most inspiring'.[22] Typically, it was Lucy who wrote about this visit in her report to the UA, rather than Jessie whose accounts had focused more on leadership meetings.

Yet while reporting on the strength of Indian unions, Lucy was uneasy about the conditions women workers faced in India. She felt that much of the 'development' she was being shown in the 'new India' was 'only a façade'.[23] She and Jessie were with Dr Andrea Andreen, the medical doctor from Sweden who was well-known as a Peace activist and prominent member of the Women's International Democratic Federation (WIDF). Lucy wrote to Rewi:

> India needs [the] co-operative movement and she needs help of a positive nature! I am writing for all three of us because we think of what the Sandan [Shandan] experiment could do here … The contrast between China and India is most marked.[24]

---

22 UA *Newsheet*, September 1955, 4.
23 Lucy Woodcock to Rewi Alley, 3 December 1954, Rewi Alley Papers, MS-Papers-6533–307, NLNZ.
24 Ibid.

Figure 11.3: Lucy, Jessie Street and Anasuya Gyan Chand, Maharashtrian NFIW leader and cooperative advocate, in Lodhi Gardens, New Delhi, 1954.
Source: Courtesy of National Library of Australia, Jessie Street papers, MS 2683, Series 11, Box 30, folder 4.

This is particularly interesting as an insight into Lucy's attention in all things to education – in this case, she saw cooperatives as a means to deliver training for justice in employment, both industrial and agricultural, as well as efficient development, like the Shandan Bailie cooperative school with which Rewi Alley was involved in China.

Lucy and Jessie had expected to be involved in other speaking events, but some state-level officials opposed their strongly left-wing messages. Jessie appealed to Prime Minister Nehru who interceded and they found officials more cooperative after that.[25] Lucy was nevertheless sceptical about Nehru. She told a meeting of the Union of Australian Women in May 1956 that although Nehru was proceeding with plans for socialism, 'they cannot be a success because he himself is a millionaire several times over'.[26]

25 W.R. Crocker, Aust High Commissioner, to Sec External Affairs, 6 December 1954, Jessie M.G. Street ASIO file, f 29, A6119, 363, NAA; NSW Teachers Federation ASIO file, Vol. 3, ff 54–56, A6122, 2477, NAA, referring to discussions at a national teachers meeting held in Canberra, May 1958.
26 Lucy Godiva Woodcock ASIO file, Vol. 3, ff 17–18, A6119, 2032, NAA.

After leaving Delhi on 6 December, they travelled to Nagpur to stay with Mithan Lam, the barrister who had come to Australia in 1946. Jessie spoke at the Rotary Club about her background in India and her work for Peace. Both Jessie and Lucy spoke to tertiary students and staff at the Shri Binzani City College, explaining the world movement for Peace and praising India's role in international peacekeeping, in particular the 'Five Principles'. These were (1) mutual respect for each other's territorial integrity and sovereignty, (2) mutual non-aggression, (3) mutual non-interference in each other's internal affairs, (4) equality and cooperation for mutual benefit, and (5) peaceful co-existence. Articulated first in the World Peace Council, these principles had been debated among emerging decolonising nations, becoming by late 1954 associated particularly with Nehru and Chou En Lai.

Jessie was reported as saying that 'Asia must give the lead to the world on the path of peace' by frustrating the plan of those (implying the United States) who would have 'Asians fighting Asians'. Lucy, described as an 'eminent educationalist', warned that the world was 'drifting to a dangerous misunderstanding' that would bring in its wake the use of 'heinous weapons of mass destruction'. As always, however, Lucy advanced solutions. She insisted that the way to avert this grave threat was not the amassing of arms but 'the conquest of poverty and ignorance'.[27]

Spending time with Mithan Lam in Nagpur gave Lucy and Jessie more insight into the split in the Indian women's movement. Lucy had met Kapila Khandvala and Mithan herself in Australia in 1946, when they visited as representatives of the All India Women's Conference (AIWC), established in 1927 in Poona. This active and energetic body had been grappling with major problems facing Indian women, but it represented predominantly northern and western India. In some ways, the AIWC elite and middle-class membership mirrored that of the earlier Australian feminist organisations like the AFWV.

By 1953, however, some AIWC members, including Kapila, had come to feel that the AIWC had not addressed the needs of working women – professionals like nurses and teachers or industrial and agricultural workers. These AIWC members broke away to form the NFIW, which was, in many respects, comparable to the Union of Australian Women,

---

27 Cuttings from *Hitavada* (*The People's Paper*, Nagpur), 9 December 1954, 11 December 1954, in Jessie M.G. Street ASIO file, Vol. 4, ff 31–32, A6119, 363, NAA.

formed in 1951. Communist Party of India (CPI) members made up a substantial proportion but not all of the membership of the new Indian break-away body, although all the members of both Indian and Australian organisations were left-wing. Anasuya, for example, was never in the CPI nor was Kapila Khandvala, although she was strongly sympathetic to socialism. Both took leadership roles in the NFIW. Anasuya became the first NFIW secretary (with CPI member Hajrah Begum) in 1954 and then its president in 1957.

Both the UAW and the NFIW accused earlier feminist groups of addressing only the concerns of middle-class women and tried to solve this by turning attention onto working-class women.

As a unionist, Lucy had built her initial alliance in 1932 with the United Associations of Women (UA), a middle-class feminist organisation whose founder, Jessie Street, was a member of the Australian political and economic elite. Yet as Lucy demonstrated, by also becoming a member of the UAW when it formed in 1950, there was much in common between the UA and the UAW. The predominantly professional women in the UA, particularly after they split with the older and more conservative feminist groups like the AFWV, were sympathetic to the same economic and legal goals as the UAW.

Many of the Indian women who decided to remain with the AIWC were similar to those in the UA – professionally trained women including Mithan Lam. One woman who remained in the AIWC but retained close relationships with women in the new NFIW was Rameshwari Nehru. Similarly, in Australia, Lucy continued to hold office in the UA, as well as holding her membership of the UAW, keeping in contact with UAW groups, attending many UAW meetings and certainly publicising issues through the professional UAW publicity structure such as its journal *Our Women*. In the same way, in India, Mithan Lam in the AIWC and Kapila Khandvala in the NFIW remained in contact with each other. These contacts were important in later years when they each became president of their respective organisations, Mithan of the AIWC, from 1961 to 1962, and Kapila of the NFIW, from 1962 to 1967.

After Nagpur, Lucy and Jessie travelled to Madras on the south-east coast of India for the All-India Peace Congress. This region, however, was very different, culturally and politically, to the north. The configurations of both the Peace and the women's movements were probably surprising for Australians, who were more familiar with women's politics in northern India. In both movements, India was widely respected for its active role at the United Nations in negotiating a ceasefire in the Korean conflict and the appointment of a woman, Vijaya Lakshmi Pandit, to head its diplomatic mission to the United Nations. Australia's conservative Menzies Government had openly supported the British in Malaya, but the Peace movement in Australia had sent a 'Friendship Letter' with a thousand signatures to the 1954 All-India Peace Congress. Lucy and Jessie probably expected that international relations, including those with Australia, would be a major theme of the Peace Congress.

Figure 11.4: Jessie Street, Lucy and Padma Narasimhan, Madras women's activist, (possibly) during the Madras Peace Conference, 25 December 1954.

Source: *Jessie Street: Documents and Essays*, edited by Heather Radi (Broadway, NSW: Women's Redress Press Inc., 1990), p. 248. Courtesy of National Library of Australia, Jessie Street papers, MS 2683, and Women's Redress Press Inc.

In fact, the major Indian newspaper in Madras, *The Hindu*, viewed the Peace Congress entirely in terms of India's own interests and as having only male participants of any significance. Relations with Pakistan were its overriding concern.[28] *The Hindu*'s only photograph of the congress shows the foreign visitors, most of whom were women, seated behind the male Indian speakers on the podium – but none of the international visitors were named.[29] The news pages of the paper were dominated by two issues: the venue of the Afro-Asian Summit, as the location in Bandung, Indonesia, had not been decided; and the concerns about Indians in Malaya and their relationship with nominally independent Malayan authorities.[30] The only mention of Australia was in Indonesia's demand that, due to Australia's unwelcome constraints on Indonesian fishing in contested waters, Australia should not be invited to the Summit.[31]

---

28 *Hindu*, reviewed from Wednesday 29 December 1954 to Monday 3 January 1955.
29 *Hindu*, 31 December 1954, 10. Indian newspapers of the period used far fewer photographs than did those in the West.
30 *Hindu*, 2 January 1955, (Editorial page).
31 *Hindu*, 24 December 1954, 4; 27 December 1954, 3.

There was, however, a strong contingent of women participating from the NFIW. The Peace Congress was written up far more extensively in its journal, *Women's News*, than in mainstream Madras newspapers like *The Hindu*. The article in *Women's News* was similar in tone to the reports of two other Australian delegates to Madras, Marion Hartley and Andrew Hughes, both of whom had missionary backgrounds in India and were active in the Australian Peace movement.[32] It was notable that Hartley and Hughes aligned Australia with Asia, as did the *Women's News*: its article was titled 'Asians Will Stand with Asians', a theme continued in the text. This was in contrast to the position taken in *The Hindu*, in which Indonesian hostility positioned Australia with European colonisers. Jessie and Lucy met the NFIW women activists in Madras and had a photograph taken with one Madras activist, who is probably Padma Narasimhan, a social worker who continued to be active in Madras over many decades.[33] In all the coverage – from the *Women's News* through the Hartley and Hughes reports and Lucy's own speeches after her return – it was India–China unity that was stressed. Australia was a part of this Asia, but its central pillars were India and China, along with the 'Five Principles' they had endorsed.

The women with whom Jessie and Lucy had less contact were the southern Indian women who had taken a different activist path to the AIWC or NFIW. These were the women involved with the most influential movement in South Indian politics and overseas Tamil populations, the Self-Respect Movement led by E.V. Ramasamy (known to his followers as Periyar, meaning 'elder' or 'wise one'). This movement connected gender inequality directly to caste, class and racial inequalities.[34] The Theosophical Society, based in Madras, had brought many strongly feminist European women to India, including Margaret Cousins, but they remained committed to the AIWC. It was, however, the multidimensional

---

32   *Women's News* (NFIW Journal) 2, no. 7 (February 1955): 4, held in Sarla Sharma's personal collection, Delhi; Andrew Hughes, *Tribune* (Sydney), 23 February 1955, 9; Marion Hartley, *Asia Awakes: Return to India* (Melbourne: Australian Peace Council, c. 1955). Another Australian report by delegates from South Australia was George Hutchesson and Edna Hutchesson, *Venture in Goodwill* (Moonta, South Australia, 1955) published initially as a series of articles in the *SA Farmer*.
33   Image shown here scanned from Heather Radi, ed., *Jessie Street: Documents and Images* (Broadway, NSW: Women's Redress Press, 1990), 248. Original, with date in annotation on reverse, was misplaced in the Jessie Street papers and has not yet been located.
34   V. Geetha, 'Periyar, Women and an Ethic of Citizenship', *EPW* 33, no. 17 (1998): WS9–WS15; V. Geetha and S. V. Rajadurai, *Towards a Non-Brahmin Millennium: From Iyothee Thass to Periyar* (Kolkata: Samya, 2007).

equality imagined by the Self-Respect Movement that drew many strong southern Indian women to it, including Dalits, who were not attracted to the doctrines of the AIWC. In its article, the NFIW *Women's News* tried to acknowledge the role of activist women from Dalit and backward castes by emphasising the speeches by sweeper women (a job undertaken by 'lower castes') at the conference as well as textile and peasant women workers.[35]

Despite the constrained coverage in *The Hindu*, the Peace Congress was presented as a major event. There were around 1,400 delegates attending the conference, around 40 per cent of them being industrial or agricultural workers or students. During the procession through Madras on the final day, up to 200,000 people marched through the city.[36]

Lucy sent a report to the NSW Peace Council about the Madras Peace conference, but she offered little to the UA about the conditions of women in Tamil Nadu. She appears to have been on more familiar ground in her analysis of working conditions and education in the north.

The final leg of their Indian journey was reassuring – Lucy and Jessie flew to Bombay, on 4 January 1955, and spent most evenings with Kapila Khandvala and her partner, C.M. Trivedi, at Nellville in Santa Cruz.[37] Kapila was able to fill them in on the developments in education in Bombay City. One of the photographs taken there with Lucy and Jessie includes the family of Reba Lewis. She was an American writer and Kapila had introduced her to the school system she was consolidating in Bombay. Such international contacts, including the book Reba later wrote about Bombay and its education system, were strategies that Kapila used repeatedly to gain support for what was then considered her unconventional approach to education.[38] She had pioneered progressive education in public schools prior to Independence. After Partition in 1947, when thousands of refugees came into Bombay, she ensured they were able to access education for their children. While Kapila could not singlehandedly dismantle the caste system, despite opposing it, she was able to bring caste and religious groups into contact with each other when she initiated regular gatherings, where all of the city's schools

---

35   *Women's News* 2, no. 7 (February 1955): 4, held in Sarla Sharma's personal collection, Delhi.
36   Andrew Hughes, 'India and Asia United, Say Aust Delegate', *Tribune* (Sydney), 23 February 1955, 9; Hartley, *Asia Awakens*; *Women's News* 2, no. 7 (February 1955): 4.
37   Jessie Street, Appointments Diary, 1955, MS 2683, Series 1, File 45, Box 6, NLA.
38   Reba Lewis, *Three Faces Has Bombay* (Bombay: Popular Book Depot, 1957).

came together to celebrate Maharashtrian festivals, both traditional and contemporary. Kapila's close friend Mulk Raj Anand (also a Peace Assembly attendee) participated in these performances and readings with the children and their families. During the 1952 Family Planning conference in Bombay, Lucy organised for her friend Lotte Fink to meet with Kapila. Kapila introduced Lotte to the city and area facilities for women's health and education. Later, Lucy invited Lotte to speak to the UA about her trip to Bombay and the work in 'Family Spacing'.[39]

This trip to Asia was immensely important for Lucy. It added the weight of experience to the vision for an end to prejudice about which she had been speaking since the 1930s. However impressed she was by developments in the Soviet Union, Lucy felt that the decolonising world was the way of the future. The final paragraph in the UA *Newsheet* report of Lucy's speech about her journey in Asia said:

> that her travels has shown her that once women are conscious of their destiny, progress must follow. Women are coming together as they never have before on many matters – on the welfare of children, on women's status and on peace. She has come home full of inspiration, of hope and a desire to arouse Australian women to get ahead with the job they must do.[40]

The following chapter, 'Peace and Prejudice', traces the impact that Lucy's experiences in Asia had on her work back in Australia.

---

39 Lotte's letters have been transcribed by her daughter Ruth Latukefu and are cited here courtesy of Ruth. Letters, each written in Bombay, and dated 26 November 1952, 5 December 1952 and 11 December 1952; UA *Newsheet*, June 1953, 4.
40 UA *Newsheet*, October 1955, 4.

Figure 11.5: Visiting Kapila Khandvala in Bombay, 1955.

From left, the elder Lewis son is obscured, then Lucy, C.M. Trivedi (Kapila's partner), then Jessie, Richard Lewis and Kapila, with younger Lewis son in front of her.

Source: Courtesy of National Library of Australia, Jessie Street papers, MS 2683, Series 11, Box 30, folder 4. Photo taken by Reba Lewis.

12

Peace and Prejudice

Lucy stayed in Europe for some time after her visit to India, speaking at the Commonwealth Countries League about the education of women in New South Wales, as a delegate for the United Associations of Women (which still called the organisation the British Commonwealth League).[1]

As the finale to her trip, Lucy attended the World Assembly for Peace in Helsinki in June 1955.[2] The 31 Australian delegates who attended brought with them a petition signed by over 200,000 Australians calling for the banning of nuclear weapons and the destruction of existing stocks.[3] Held in Finland, the Assembly brought together representatives from China, India, Japan, Burma, Indonesia and Vietnam. Jessie Street spoke about the importance of the United Nations in offering a platform for negotiated resolutions of conflicts. Lucy was among the Australians there who issued a statement published by the NSW Peace Council, endorsing the overall conclusions of the Assembly.[4] They prioritised total nuclear disarmament, negotiated resolution of conflicts and an end to partitions, like those in Korea and Vietnam. They argued that the recent Bandung meeting in April 1955 had given a model for Europe. Its 'Five Principles

---

1   Lucy Godiva Woodcock ASIO file, Vol. 1, f 203, A6119, 2030, NAA. This sheet is the flyer for the Peace Council in Western Australia advertising Lucy's speaking engagements in Perth immediately after her return, in August 1955, close to Hiroshima Day, the commemoration of the dropping of the first atomic bomb.
2   Ibid.
3   *Peace* (NSW Peace Council), no. 2, May 1955; no. 3, June 1955; no. 4, July 1955; no. 5, August 1955.
4   *Peace*, no. 5, August 1955, 4.

of Peaceful Coexistence' – first framed in an even earlier meeting between Jawaharlal Nehru and Chou En Lai, then rebadged by Sukarno as *Pancha Sila* – could form the basis for universal peaceful coexistence:

> India, recently freed from colonial domination, has demonstrated the importance of such freedom in the special position it occupies in Asia in the struggle to safeguard the peace. The clear and obvious fact [is] that in Asia and Africa, peace and national sovereignty are indissolubly linked.[5]

When Lucy reached Australia by sea, she arrived in Perth in time for Hiroshima Day, the commemoration of the atomic blasts in Japan in 1945. Although she spoke at a number of venues, including delivering a sermon at the Wesley Church, the Western Australian Education Department refused her permission to speak at any schools. ASIO had been following her travels in Asia and Europe, compiling a file on her activities, which was apparently used against her almost before she set foot ashore.[6]

After a busy series of talks in Perth, Lucy returned to Sydney and began a period of frenetic activity. She plunged into organising a Sydney conference for 'Peace and Co-existence' with the NSW Peace Council – to be held in inner-city Sydney on 26 and 27 November 1955.[7] It aimed to contribute to the formulation of an Australian policy for peaceful coexistence through two strategies: friendly diplomatic, cultural and commercial relations with all countries and arms reduction with a refocus on using atomic power for peaceful purposes.

Lucy was inspired by the advances in women's rights in emerging, decolonising nations while the Peace movement also looked to this new Asian world to find strategies for Peace. The Afro-Asian conference had taken place at Bandung in April (1955) and the Peace movement in Australia and elsewhere argued that the Bandung concept of 'non-aligned nations' should be the immediate basis for planning for peace in Europe and around the world. Bandung's Five Principles stressed non-interference in others' internal affairs and respect for each other's territorial unity, integrity and sovereignty, thus enabling cross-cultural and transnational cooperation between newly independent, non-aligned nations. The goal

---

5   Ibid.
6   Lucy Godiva Woodcock ASIO file, Vol. 3, A6119, 2032, NAA.
7   *Tribune* (Sydney), 12 October 1955, 3; 2 November 1955, 2.

of the Sydney conference in November was to demonstrate Australians' commitment to this concept of non-alignment and to consider the strategies for developing policies of Peace.

Bill Morrow, a Queensland unionist and former ALP senator, became the NSW Peace Council Secretary in 1954 after travelling in China and the Soviet Union. He remembered Lucy as a stalwart of the movement. Along with Morrow himself, Bill Gollan (a teacher and Communist Party of Australia member) and Elsie Wakefield (a Hunter River organiser for the CPA), Lucy became one of the regular speakers for the Peace Council from the time of her return from overseas in 1955:

> These people made their time available whenever and wherever a speaker on peace was requested. They spoke at large public gatherings – some in the Sydney Town Hall – where police and plainclothes photographers were always present to get a record of what was said and to whom. There were smaller gatherings in country towns, church halls or private houses.[8]

Bill Morrow preferred to talk to the miners and other unionists, but Lucy and the others would speak anywhere.

Lucy was a frequent speaker at a series of local preparatory meetings for the Peace Council conference for Peace and Co-existence, which she was organising during 1955. One such local meeting was at Chatswood in early November, when Lucy spoke alongside scientist Richard Makinson (Rachel's husband) and architect Maurice Edwards.[9] Notably, Lucy shared a platform with the Christian minister Neil Glover and the Peace Council's Frank Nieass at a 'Friendship with Asia' meeting at Ashfield Congregational Church.[10] Lucy's own networks in the Chinese Australian community may have been a part of this Peace Council work.

---

8   Audrey Johnson, *Fly a Rebel Flag: Bill Morrow, 1888–1980* (Ringwood, Vic.: Penguin, 1986), 256–57.
9   *Tribune* (Sydney), 16 November 1955, 2.
10 *Tribune* (Sydney), 23 November 1955, 2.

Figure 12.1: Helsinki Peace Conference, June 1955, program cover.
Source: Melbourne University Archives, Special Collection on the Peace movement, 1980.0172 AND 1980.0068, Box 6, folder 3.

On 16 November, at the height of this Peace movement planning activity for the late November conference, Lucy took on the role of convenor of the first Women Workers' Conference, initiated by the World Federation of Trade Unions (WFTU), and to be held in Vienna in June 1956.[11] The WFTU, like the women's body, the Women's International Democratic Federation (WIDF), was seen by the West as aligned to the Soviet Union – and was often accused of being a 'communist front'. It had suffered from the same Cold War polarisation that had split the Australian union movement. Lucy's role involved awareness-raising, encouraging unions to elect their delegates and then coordinating the fundraising, to cover fares. Her calls to union activists to plan and raise funds for delegates were frequently mentioned in the pages of *Tribune*.[12]

The Peace and Co-existence conference was not advertised in any of the mainstream newspapers, but information was locally disseminated in Peace movement circles and it went ahead with around 330 delegates on 26 and 27 November 1955.[13] In line with the theme of coexistence and the example of Bandung, the conference motions laid stress on international support, with messages from India and Italy, and had called for a withdrawal of Australian troops from Malaya, and for globalised, free and unimpeded trade with all countries, regardless of political or religious affiliation.[14] Bill Morrow placed particular stress on global networks opposing nuclear weapons, reporting that 300,000 Australians had signed the World Appeal against Atomic War. The conference voted to broaden the membership of the NSW Peace Council, in recognition of the organisational problems facing the isolated, state-based Peace movements and launched plans for a nationwide Peace conference to coincide with the Olympic Games in 1956.

***

While Lucy's attention was focused on these activities, her close friend and union ally Sam Lewis faced a major problem. Lucy had known Sam since the 1920s and had worked closely with him in the Federation and elsewhere since the mid-1930s. Teachers had been expressing concerns through the Federation for some years about increasingly unruly playground behaviour. The union argued this was related to the rising pressures on the education

---

11 *Tribune* (Sydney), 16 November 1955, 2.
12 *Tribune* (Sydney), 23 November 1955, 11; 14 December 1955, 10; 18 January 1956, 12; 15 February 1956, 10; 18 April 1956, 11.
13 *Tribune* (Sydney), 30 November 1955, 2; 7 December 1955, 2.
14 *Tribune* (Sydney), 7 December 1955, 2.

system as postwar migration was unaccompanied by parallel rises in resources, infrastructure or teacher training. Consequently, there was a strong Federation campaign, led by Sam Lewis, for increased staffing and better resources to allow teachers to deal constructively with such situations.

It was ironic, then, that Sam lost his temper with a student at Newtown Boys' Junior Technical High and slapped him across the face. There were suggestions that the boy, who had a troubled past, had abused Sam with a racist slur, denigrating his Jewish background. To make the slap even worse, the boy only had one eye. Lewis's defence that he had hit the boy on the other side of his head did nothing to placate his understandably angry parents. Yet this was so out of character for Lewis that many teachers, including the Newtown headmaster, defended him.[15] Harold Wyndham, then Director of Education, launched a formal investigation, which concluded that Lewis had been subject to extreme provocation and given his longstanding satisfactory record, a formal caution would suffice.[16]

After this decision, the Public Service Board made an unprecedented intervention. It reopened the case and ordered Lewis to be transferred to Bankstown Boys, a more distant suburban school.[17] This exacerbated the NSW Teachers Federation's ongoing concerns over the shadowy role of the Public Service Board. The power the board held to sit in judgement over teachers had been visible in the case of Beatrice Taylor in 1933 (see Chapter 5). The board had since then been increasing its control over education decision-making and teacher conditions.[18] The Federation was particularly concerned about teachers on the Left like Lucy because Harry Heath, the right-wing teacher who had won the Federation presidency from Lewis in 1952, had unexpectedly become a member of the board. Heath defeated Lewis a second time in 1954, but abruptly left the presidency in 1955 when offered a position on the Public Service Board. All of this made the intervention of the board in the matter of Sam Lewis in December 1955 seem even more sinister.

---

15   Prof. Bob Carr, former premier of NSW, who had been taught by Sam Lewis at Matraville High in 1963, said in his experience Lewis had never physically disciplined a student and it would have been uncharacteristic for him to have done so. Pers. comm., 24 November 2017.
16   *SMH*, 25 November 1955, 11 December 1955; *Canberra Times*, 2 December 1955; *Tribune* (Sydney), 18 January 1956, 12.
17   *SMH*, 20 January 1956; A.D. *Spaull*, 'Teachers and Politics: A Comparative Study of State Teachers' Organizations in Victoria and New South Wales Since 1940' (PhD thesis, Monash University, 1972).
18   Bruce Mitchell, *Teachers, Education and Politics: A History of Organisations of Public School Teachers in New South Wales* (St Lucia: University of Queensland Press, 1975), 175–79.

Over the summer of 1955–56, Lucy wrote *The Lewis Case and You*, published in April 1956.[19] Although she had previously reiterated her opposition to gender and racial discrimination, Lucy did not mention the racist abuse Lewis might have suffered, nor did she defend his physical violence although she emphasised that it was uncharacteristic. Instead, her book pointed out that the Public Service Board was a danger to all citizens since its administrative, legislative and judicial powers were not open to legal review. It operated as an opaque and punitive arm of government: an exercise of secret power. Lucy summed up:

> In the Public Service Board the State has created an instrument of government violating the accepted principles of democratic social organization. These are the principles which we teach as being fundamental to the 'democratic way of life' and for which century-long struggles have been fought.[20]

Lucy brought the very charges against this NSW Government system that were then, ironically, being laid against the Soviet Union. She was an advocate of open and honest debate. Her view of democracy demanded that government action be transparent and open to the law – the Public Service Board was violating that fundamental principle of democratic governance. Lucy's argument was lucid and cogent, including photographs that showed not only the arid playgrounds of a working-class school but also, beyond the school fences, the backyards of street after street of working-class inner-city housing. In Lucy's view, the problems of discipline in schools were a reflection of the fact that the schoolyards were not isolated from the rising and intolerable pressures on the working-class communities in which their children lived. She believed that teachers should be heard on the questions of better resources for working-class parents and for education in general.

***

Through that summer, Lucy decided to formalise her role in the United Associations of Women, becoming vice president in February 1956. This allowed her to speak with the authority of the UA in her continued campaigning for equal industrial, legal and social rights for women. She continued to speak regularly for the Peace movement, on call, as Bill Morrow

---

19 *Tribune* (Sydney), 13 June 1956, 11.
20 Lucy Godiva Woodcock, *The Lewis Case and You* (Sydney: self-published with donations, 1956), 27.

remembered, on subjects such as nuclear disarmament and non-alignment 'anywhere and anytime'. From February 1956, she began attending peak trade union conferences and events as a UA representative. She became a frequent presence in the UA *Newsheet*; she had much in common with the editor, Vivienne Newson, who was a committed Peace activist and drew on Lucy increasingly to summarise the industrial dimensions of a number of the Equal Pay and education issues. Lucy brought an economic and political analysis to the pages of the *Newsheet*, which had not been present before. As well as her own views, she was able to call for contributions from the women she had become close to in the union movement, particularly Flo Davis in the Hotel, Club and Restaurant Employees' Union.[21]

***

Another border that Lucy helped to bridge was that between Aboriginal and non-Aboriginal activists. The Aboriginal-Australian Fellowship (AAF) was formed in March 1956.[22] As Beverley Bates remembered, Lucy had already worked in Erskineville with Aboriginal children and their parents. She knew Pearl Gibbs, the activist from Brewarrina, who had been heavily involved in the Aborigines Progressive Association with Bill Ferguson and Jack Patten and in the planning of the Aboriginal-only Day of Mourning in 1938. Pearl wanted to develop an organisation that would involve both Aboriginal and non-Aboriginal people and discussed it with Faith Bandler, born in Tweed Heads from a South Sea Island background and married to a German migrant who had fled Nazism.

We have important insights into this process from a recorded interview with the late Faith Bandler in 2016, quoted here extensively as there are no other sources. Faith recalled that, when Pearl first discussed a new organisation with her, Pearl had said:

---

21   UA *Newsheet*, April, May and June 1956.
22   The history of this organisation has become confused by biographer Bruce Mitchell who thought its title included 'evangelical' and was some sort of Christian body. (See Mitchell, 'Woodcock, Lucy Godiva (1889–1968)', *Australian Dictionary of Biography*, National Centre of Biography, The Australian National University, adb.anu.edu.au/biography/woodcock-lucy-godiva-9172/text16197, published first in hardcopy 1990, accessed online 14 February 2012.) As will be very clear from the memories of AAF co-founder Faith Bandler and member Jack Horner – and indeed from Lucy's own background – it definitely had *no* Christian affiliations!

> We've got to get something going. And we don't want any of those churches in it or any of those trade unions, or Liberal party, Communist party, Labor party. We've got to keep them all out. But it will be a fellowship of black and white.[23]

Pearl approached Lucy to assist with organising. After years in the union movement, Lucy was very good at chairing meetings – as Sam Lewis and others have recalled, Lucy managed meetings with tact and humour but also with ruthless efficiency! Jack Horner said:

> Lucy Woodcock, a retired primary school principal who had encouraged mature-aged Aboriginal people to attend the Cleveland Street Evening School, was a popular recruit among black and white members alike … When it was thought there were enough interested parties to form the new group, Pearl Gibbs arranged for the first official meeting to be held at Woodcock's small flat in George St Sydney in March 1956.[24]

As Faith Bandler explained:

> So there was a woman by the name of Lucy Woodcock. She was the President of the Teachers Federation. And also I think President of one of Jessie Street's organisations for feminism. The United Association of Women. Lucy lived in George Street where the Regent Hotel is now. She was on the first floor there … Well at that stage I guess she was in her 60s.
>
> She was a woman who knew how to conduct a meeting.
>
> And how! And she would rule with an iron rod. (laughs)
>
> So Pearl knew Lucy very well and Lucy offered her flat for a meeting for the fellowship. Because Pearl had been around Sydney coming and going for a long time. She knew what feminism was about. Anyhow, Pearl said, 'Lucy's going to chair this meeting.' Most undemocratic I must say! (more laughter) So, we all got into Lucy's flat.
>
> Now by this time the La Perouse people had come good. Pearl had said to them, 'Now we don't want any churches and we don't want any political parties. And that's it. Nobody's going to dominate

---

23   Faith Bandler, interview with Carolyn Craig, 2016, SLNSW, amplify.sl.nsw.gov.au/transcripts/mloh307-0001-0010-s001-m, accessed 1 January 2019.
24   Jack Horner, *Seeking Racial Justice: An Insider's Memoir of the Movement for Aboriginal Advancement, 1938–1978* (Canberra: Aboriginal Studies Press, 2004), 18–19.

this organisation'. Well they thought this was good, you know? They didn't want to be told what to do. They wanted to make the decisions.

So, Lucy said, 'Order please. Order!'

And there was silence and … Lucy said, 'Look if you've got an organisation you have to give it a name.'

Well Muir [Holburn] was there so one of the first things on the agenda was that we should find a name for the organisation and this is fresh in my memory as though it all happened yesterday. Muir said, 'Let's call it…' he said, 'I have been thinking about this and I thought we should include the word fellowship'. And he went on to speak about the foundings of the Fellowship of Australian Writers and how fellowship brought people together and we want to bring the black and the white people together and let's call it fellowship. Well there was agreement that that word could be used.

And then we all went on and I said, I would suggest that we call it the Aboriginal Australian Fellowship. And the [Aboriginal] tram driver said, bowed his head and said, 'No. Don't use that word. Don't use that word.'

And Lucy said, 'Which word is it you're referring to?' He said, 'That word'.

She said, 'Is it Australian?' And he said, 'No, the other one'.

'Aboriginal is it?'

He said, 'Mm, what we'll get is "Abos". They'll call us "Abos." We've had enough of that'.

But the people from La Perouse said: 'And what's wrong with it?' You know? They put up a battle and so [he] saw the light and accepted it.

And it's my opinion that [because] that organisation was formed to have a title that included that word – Aboriginal – it contributed to the dignity of the Aboriginal people of New South Wales.

> More and more people began to come out and say I'm Aboriginal. I found that meeting very moving because I had never in fact fully realised how … what it was like to be an Aboriginal person.[25]

The AAF began its activities with a series of public meetings and included many teachers in its membership. Faith's family remember that she spoke about and with Lucy Woodcock often, in particular because of her contact with teachers and the Federation.[26]

***

Lucy had maintained her work as the convenor of the Australian contingent to the WFTU Women Workers' Conference, which had been planned for Vienna in early June. Cold War politics intervened, however, forcing the conference to be moved to Budapest, Hungary, and held later in June. Lucy herself did not attend, explaining to Rewi Alley in her letters to him at the time that she had been travelling from Sydney to London with her sister Beth, her grazier husband Fred Cowley and their two children, Janet and Tom, over June, arriving in London only in early July and remaining there till January 1957.[27] At least four Australian women attended, all active unionists and all in the Communist Party, including Kath Williams and Esther Taylor who had been sponsored by Lucy and Flo Davis. Although she had not attended, Lucy was certainly aware of the high tension that the Australians had felt in Budapest in July, a precursor to the Hungarian uprising of October and the invasion by Soviet troops in November.[28] In January 1957, Lucy wrote to Rewi Alley that 'there is much confusion in Australia over the Hungarian situation' and significantly did not reveal her own position.

Lucy spent much of the second half of 1956 showing her sister and her family around London, but she also delivered a paper to a seminar on women and work, organised by Jessie Street and the Six Point Group, which was held in association with a much larger British trade union conference in Brighton in August. Like her previous contributions to the *Newsheet*, Lucy's paper to the 'Women and Work' seminar focused on the themes of

---

25 This extended quotation is a lightly edited extract from Faith Bandler, interview, 2016.
26 Dr Lillon Bandler, pers. comm., 2016.
27 Lucy Woodcock to Rewi Alley, 14 July 1956; 31 January 1957; Rewi Alley Papers, MS-Papers-6533-307, NLNZ. Beth was Lucy's only surviving sister – another, who had lived with Lucy's mother in Enmore, had died some years earlier. We do not know the location of Beth's property.
28 *Tribune* (Sydney), 18 January 1956, 18 April 1956; Eric Aarons, 'Remembering and Reflecting: 1956', *The Hummer* 3, no. 10 (Winter 2003), www.labourhistory.org.au/hummer/vol-3-no-10/1956-aarons/.

Equal Pay and education for girls. These were Lucy's ongoing interests but she again crossed boundaries. British conditions dominated the conference but Lucy insisted on comparing them to Australian conditions. In the *Newsheet*, she highlighted a warning for Australians in the talk by Miss B. Harrison, the Tobacco Workers' Union representative, who explained that, although women's wages had risen in the United Kingdom, the continuing classification of jobs into 'men's work' and 'women's work' meant that the margins between men's and women's take-home pay had not reduced. In terms of education, Lucy reported that Australians should reject the model of some regional British educational authorities that had limited the number of girls who could enter secondary schools because girls were performing better than boys in entrance exams. Furthermore, like the conditions Harrison had pointed out in the tobacco industry, Lucy warned that the hierarchies of teacher employment in British education had been perpetuated, even though the British claimed that 'equal pay' was being brought in by installment. So the outcome would be the same inequalities: there would always be jobs – the higher paid ones – which were classified as 'men's work' and so would simply never be offered to women teachers. While these examples would bring no joy to Australian women, Lucy could also report more hopefully on the slowly rising number of British women able to practise their professions in law, architecture, science and diplomacy.[29]

During this time in London, although Lucy saw Jessie at some events, she was most occupied with union networks in the UK, and following up on her attendance at the Brighton trade union conference.[30] But she also tried to follow British news about the treason trial in the United States of friends of Rewi Alley, the journalists J.B. and Sylvia Powell and Julian Schuman, the former editors of the *China Monthly*, an American magazine published in Shanghai until 1952. Writing to Rewi early in October, Lucy expressed her fears that the trial of the Powells and Schuman would replicate that of the Rosenbergs.[31]

Lucy was also following Australian politics, even from the United Kingdom. She expressed her relief to Rewi that the expulsion of extreme anti-communists from the Australian Labor Party late in 1954 had finally borne fruit in another Peace Assembly, just held in Australia in September

---

29   UA *Newsheet*, October 1956, 1–2.
30   Lucy Woodcock to Rewi Alley, 1 September 1956, Rewi Alley Papers, MS-Papers-6533-307, NLNZ.
31   Lucy Woodcock to Rewi Alley, 18 October 1956, Rewi Alley Papers, MS-Papers-6533-307, NLNZ.

1956, when – without the constraining conditions imposed by the presence of the anti-communist 'Groupers' – many continuing members of ALP had felt free to attend. Lucy was finally confident, she told Rewi, that the 'Grouper influence of which I wrote earlier is definitely on the wane'.[32] Optimistic as ever, Lucy wrote to Rewi a year later, still following the American court cases like those against the Powells and Schuman, that 'it would appear that the days of witch hunting are drawing to a close'.[33]

Lucy remained in Europe, returning to Australia in April 1957, although Jessie Street had returned earlier, in January 1957. In February and March, Lucy had travelled to the Soviet Union with Elizabeth Mattick, the researcher to the Teachers Federation in the early 1950s.

Figure 12.2: Teachers Federation executive group, c. 1953.
Standing from right of image: Harry Norington, Lucy Woodcock, Elizabeth Mattick and Sam Lewis (in glasses, looking forward), next to whom stood Harry Heath (tall man with striped tie, in glasses, looking directly at camera), who had defeated Lewis as president.
Source: NSW Teachers Federation archives, undated photograph P8552.

---

32 Lucy Woodcock to Rewi Alley, 1 September 1956; 18 October 1956, Rewi Alley Papers, NLNZ; Paul Strangio, 'Australian Politics Explainer: The Labor Party Split', *The Conversation*, 18 April 2017, online at theconversation.com/australian-politics-explainer-the-labor-party-split-74149, accessed 4 January 2019.
33 Lucy Woodcock to Rewi Alley, 16 July 1957, Rewi Alley Papers, MS-Papers-6533-307, NLNZ.

As she had been in China, Japan and India, Lucy was again particularly interested in the education system and how it worked for girls. She wrote up her observations about the system in the USSR, based on conversations with teachers and visits to some city schools, in two articles for *Friendship*, the journal of the Australia–Soviet Friendship Society. She was interested in the economic priority given to education, which ensured that there were adequate schools and equipment for school children, as well as high-quality training for teachers. She contrasted this with the lack of funds for education and teacher training in New South Wales, as well as the lack of adequate equipment in new schools, which had to be found through extensive parent and teacher fundraising.

She was also positive about the after-hours 'Pioneer Palaces', which provided a range of recreational and cultural activities. These appeared similar to those in the Children's Library and Club in which Lucy was involved in Erskineville.

Lucy inquired particularly about the examination system, which consisted of a sequence of internal testing carried out by the class teacher in younger years, with the goal of equipping the children to pass the tests rather than using the tests to rank the students. The external test was the matriculation at the end of the 10th year and a good record throughout school was necessary for a university stipend. All education was coeducational and women were strongly represented in the professions and trades.

What Lucy found most interesting, however, was not the infrastructure but the high level of enthusiasm among students wherever she went. Forty years earlier, there had been few schools and low literacy, but now there was higher literacy and widespread interest in attending schools. This, she felt, was the greatest achievement of the Soviet system – engendering enthusiasm for learning.

She was careful not to comment where she could not make personal observations – she had not actually visited a teacher training institution so could not say what it was like. And while she observed equality for women in wages and promotion, she did not have firm data on the promotion of women to positions of responsibility, although she observed many women in charge of schools. She recognised the reluctance of many Australian teachers to consider Soviet educational approaches:

> Teachers in Australia may not agree with the pattern of education in Russia. I could only attempt to get essential detail, gleaned from teachers while I was there, but you feel that in the 40 years of Soviet rule, impetus has been given to a tremendous network of educational establishments that are part of the life of the people … Sputnik I and Sputnik II are not accidents or lucky hits, but are one of the direct results of the educational activity of the Soviet Union.[34]

In her second article, which focused more on teachers' conditions and training, she reiterated:

> You may not believe in the Russian way of life, but as a teacher, one must be aware of the changes occurring in other parts of the world. The teacher cannot work in isolation because he is educating pupils not only for the present but for the future so his horizons must be forever expanding, otherwise his work stagnates.[35]

Lucy made clear in this article that, despite advances in science like the Sputnik satellites, it was the 'outstanding performance in education of the millions of Russian men and women that is without parallel'.[36]

Her views would have been met with caution in Australia. Some members of the Communist Party of Australia, like Helen Palmer and the group who formed around the journal *Outlook*, had left the party after the Soviet intervention in Hungary in November 1956. Neither Lucy nor Jessie, who had been active 'fellow travellers', distanced themselves irretrievably after 1956.[37] Lucy – as she so often did – maintained a non-aligned position, speaking to the Australia–Soviet Friendship Society in May 1959, alongside other UA office bearers Jessie Street, Millicent Christian and Muriel Tribe, in a forum titled 'The life and interests of Soviet women based on the personal recollections of Australian citizens'.[38]

Yet Lucy was not unaffected by the tensions and eventual split within the CPA, and it had an impact on the Peace Council. The biography of Bill Morrow, then secretary of the NSW Peace Council, covers this period and

---

34 'They Have Made People Value Education', *Friendship* 2, no. 3 (March 1958): 8 (four pages illustrated).
35 'The Soviet View on Education…', *Friendship* 2, no. 4 (April 1958): 15.
36 Ibid.
37 Lucy Woodcock to Rewi Alley, 31 January 1957, Rewi Alley Papers, MS-Papers-6533-307, NLNZ.
38 Lucy Godiva Woodcock ASIO file, Vol. 2, A6119, 2031, NAA.

its complexities. As Morrow had recorded, Lucy had been a frequent and reliable speaker for the council. Lucy had become close to Carl and Susie Heins, political refugees from the Nazis, since Susie was Jewish. They were both active in the Peace movement and were affiliated with both the CPA and the Australian Labor Party – despite such 'double card holding' being disallowed by ALP rules. In their case, although the Heins's affiliations were known, they were overlooked by their supportive ALP branch.

The NSW Peace Council was loosely connected to the Victorian body, the Australian Peace Council. The Peace Assembly was established in September 1956 to bring together all interested parties. Eventually, in February 1958, the NSW Peace Council, which was reputed to be influenced by the Communist Party, merged with the Assembly. This merger was fostered enthusiastically – if somewhat ironically – by the CPA members of the Assembly, who felt it would allow the Peace movement to be more popular because it would be perceived as less 'political'. As a result, however, Carl and Susie Heins were pushed out, eventually resigning as the CPA members of the new body felt they were 'too political'.[39]

Lucy wrote to Susie and Carl Heins in October 1958:

> I have been very worried about rumours that I have heard about the way you and your husband have been treated by [the] Peace Assembly. I for one thoroughly appreciate the warm-heartedness, generosity and width of vision both of you had concerning this all-important matter of Peace. I know how sincerely interested both of you were and I know also how much you helped others.[40]

Nevertheless, Lucy did not withdraw from the Peace movement. She remained committed to the long struggle, continuing to talk about Peace to all manner of 'groups', including those who had very conservative positions like the Esperanto organisation, as she told Rewi Alley in a number of letters, and appeared on the platform of major Peace rallies in 1960 and 1962.[41] She was unfailingly available, as Bill Morrow appreciatively remembered, despite feeling daunted by the enormity of the task, as she wrote to Rewi in 1962:

---

39 Johnson, *Fly a Rebel Flag*, 266–73, outlines the conflict and then quotes Lucy's letter in full to Susie and Carl Heins, 273.
40 Ibid., 273.
41 Lucy Woodcock to Rewi Alley, 23 May 1957; 15 August 1961; 16 December 1961; 2 March 1962; 19 December 1963; Rewi Alley Papers, MS-Papers-6533-307, NLNZ.

> It seems a long time since I have written to you but time just flashes by as you become so much involved in this vital struggle to preserve the peace and security of the world. Things are such a tangle here that the ingenuity of men has been taxed to their utmost to promote goodwill.[42]

Appearing with her in so many of the rallies at which she spoke were her long-time political allies, who displayed a range of political affiliations: the Anglican priest and co-operative teacher the Reverend Alf Clint, the communist teacher Bill Gollan and the ex-ALP unionist Bill Morrow.[43]

* * *

This chapter has discussed Lucy's years of activism after her first trip to Asia. The impact can be seen throughout her work once she returned to Australia. It is clear in her enduring role in the Peace movement – in all her speeches thereafter, she frequently referred to her first-hand experience in Japan, along with her personal interactions with Chinese, Japanese and Indian Peace workers. It is just as clear in her commitment to industrial and gender justice as well as her recognition of the importance of decolonisation and self-determination as a way to combat racism in Australia as well as overseas. The following two chapters – 'Uniting Women' and 'Bringing the World Back Home' – trace the varied ways that Lucy brought the world back home to Australians during the last decade of her life.

---

42   Lucy Woodcock to Rewi Alley, 2 March 1962. Rewi Alley Papers, MS-Papers-6533-307, NLNZ.
43   *Tribune* (Sydney), 18 May 1960, 12; 2 May 1962, 2.

13

Uniting Women

Lucy did not ever abandon her vision of a world where borders were unnecessary but she made only one more trip overseas, a brief second visit to China in 1964 with four other women on the invitation of the People's Republic of China's National Women's Council. With her Peace movement commitment unshakeable, she put much of her considerable energies into showing Australians that they did not have to be isolated or fearful. She invited them to recognise that they belonged in a region where emerging nations were offering visions of new and peaceful worlds. Rewi Alley had written to her in 1955:

> Dear Lucy,
>
> … your letters are grand to have, giving one a sense that things are being done constructively … You have done a fine job, Lucy, in getting around and bringing the word back home again …[1]

In fact, what Lucy went on to do was bring the *world* back home.

This was a time, however, when very new movements were emerging in women's politics. Lucy was by this time elderly and, however sympathetic she might have been to the goals of these new movements, she seemed to be from a different era. Many of the activists who in the 1960s were young women, just beginning to take part in politics, knew Lucy's name and remembered her being in figurehead roles, but few of them knew anything about her life or her passions. Lucy commented on this sense

---

1 Rewi Alley to Lucy Woodcock, 17 October 1955, from Lucy Woodcock's papers in the care of Kit Edwards.

of distance as she reflected on age – as we will see in these final chapters. When we look at her practical actions, we see her sustained energy and participation, often as speaker and always as an organiser, chairperson and letter writer. But at the same time, we see her carefully avoiding taking the limelight. Nevertheless, Lucy not only contributed to the causes she had been fighting for over her long life, but took steps to link the struggles in Australia with those taking place internationally.

Our final chapters trace the different ways that Lucy tried to show Australians that they could be global citizens not island hermits. This chapter explains her multifaceted role as president of the United Associations of Women (UA) where she was spokeswoman, strategist, journalist and campaigner. The next chapter considers both her public role as president of the New South Wales International Women's Day (IWD) committee and her more low-key role as mentor and tutor to Sydney's Chinese-background community and students.

The most familiar strategy for Lucy was the one discussed in this chapter, as the president of the United Associations of Women (UA). This position was closest to the role she had taken in the union, where she had been in an organisational structure where she could call on alliances and trusted colleagues built up over a number of years. We can see her role in the UA through her articles in the UA *Newsheet*, which were about the transnational networks around movements for industrial justice, to raise the status of women, for progressive education and, from 1961 onwards, for peace.

Both the situations we look at in the following chapter were less familiar for her. First, in her role in IWD, Lucy was embroiled in the internal tensions dividing both the Communist Party in Australia and the Australian Labor Party. At the same time, there were new developments in Aboriginal politics and in the Peace movement that all became entangled in IWD. Lucy felt more at home in her tutoring work after years in inner-city public education, but now she was engaging with new groups, which meant she had to deepen her knowledge about Chinese Australians and Chinese-background international students. She learned that some things were very different but that others were depressingly the same.

As always, however, Lucy's busy life meant that no single body of source materials ever told the full story. For this chapter on the UA, the archival and published records we draw on are the UA *Newsheets*; the press reports

– most of which are from the CPA newspaper *Tribune* as the mainstream press ignored the left-wing and, particularly, peace activities of the time – and the records of ASIO, the secret service observers, from the files on Lucy herself, the Teachers Federation and the Union of Australian Women (UAW), as well as those of other individuals like Sam Lewis.

Yet at the same time, Lucy was active in IWD and was tutoring. We can see the differing coverage in each source by looking at just one short period of a few months in 1960. The ASIO reports covered her IWD events – although they assumed they were organised by the UAW, which the government regarded as a 'communist front'. So the ASIO reports detailed the visiting Chinese speakers and the Australia–China Society reception on 10 May, as well as the major Peace rallies in Victoria and New South Wales on 18 May where Lucy spoke at Lithgow. The ASIO agents reported in great detail all the speeches at the UAW National Conference from 27 May to 2 June.

The CPA newspaper reported somewhat differently. *Tribune* covered IWD events and followed the Chinese speakers' travels, but did acknowledge that many organisations were involved, including the UA. *Tribune* also reported the Peace rallies. On the same page, and unlike ASIO, *Tribune* mentioned an education conference. Its report on the UAW conference, however, did not detail the activists' speeches in the very useful way that ASIO did.

Only Lucy, however, writing in the UA *Newsheet*, reported extensively on the large national conference on education on 21 May 1960. She explained that it had been attended by representatives of parents' and citizens' groups and mothers' clubs as well as teachers from each state and had been held at the Leichhardt Stadium. Yet, neither in Lucy's pieces nor the rest of the *Newsheet* was there any mention of the Peace rallies on 18 May nor the UAW conference at the end of the month, at both of which Lucy had spoken.

So each type of resource offers a different view of Lucy's roles in the UA and the IWD committee from 1957 to around 1964. But for the low-key interactions Lucy was having at the same time with the Chinese-background communities and students, there are no published or government records. The very few sources include some of Lucy's letters to Rewi Alley from 1954 to 1965, as well as personal memories and some glimpses in the few papers that Lucy kept.

***

Earlier chapters have traced Lucy's steps as she formed a strategic alliance with the UA in 1932 to build the campaign against the legislation forcing the dismissal of women teachers who married.[2] She had, as well, built a strong friendship with the UA's Jessie Street, despite significant class differences. A visiting speaker to the UA, Dorothy Crabb, commented in September 1961 that the UA was an organisation 'of erudite professional women', which seems to have well described the UA.[3] Despite Street's leadership, its members were not the elite and affluent women of Jessie's class, but rather were working professionals, many of them university-educated, some with families and some unmarried. More teachers joined after Lucy became active, and there were many members of the Business & Professional Women's Club (B&P Club), in both urban and rural businesses. Although these women may have been landowners, it was their interest as working farmers that the *Newsheets* addressed.

The UA monthly *Newsheets* are a rich source for learning about the many campaigns of the women's movement, some of which were very close to Lucy's heart. Rather than tracing all of them, however, this chapter will focus on the campaigns that demonstrate the transnational nature of Lucy's inspiration. The UA *Newsheets* allow us to see far more about how Lucy worked than the brief notes of motions and votes in the Teachers Federation journal, *Education*. At the UA Lucy worked month by month beside Vivienne Newson, the fellow Peace activist and *Newsheet* editor. Lucy, however, increasingly wrote many of the entries herself, either signing them with her initials 'LGW' or her full name or writing under the headline 'The President's Diary' or 'The President Writes' (or 'Reports' or 'Reflects'!).[4] Despite the significant proportion of teachers in its membership, Lucy and Vivienne were writing for a different audience than the men and women teachers and unionists to whom Lucy had previously been directing her comments.

Through the pages of the *Newsheets* until the early 1960s, Lucy can be seen focusing on three issues: first and most extensively, it was Equal Pay and opportunity for all women, whether married or single, working

---

2 *Married Women (Lecturers and Teachers) Act 1932* (NSW).
3 UA *Newsheet*, September 1961, 4.
4 The UA reports have been read in detail from 1950 to 1956 inclusive. The *Newsheets* came out at the beginning of each month, usually four or six close-typed A4 pages, with half-page feature articles, and then shorter items.

class or middle class; then equality of access to leadership and board positions; and, underpinning it all, access to education for women, including apprenticeships for all forms of trades, with special attention to those in rural and agricultural fields. From 1961, activities of the Peace movement came to be a more regular and extensive topic in the *Newsheets*. Tenacious and relentless, Lucy wrote dozens of letters on all these topics to politicians, unionists and public servants, inside and outside Australia, responding to polite dismissals with still more letters. She used the media increasingly, being heard frequently on radio talk shows like Eric Baume and many ABC debates and formal discussions.[5]

Prior to Lucy's assumption of executive roles (vice president in 1956, then president in 1957 till her death in 1968) the UA had few speakers who were not from and speaking about Australia, even after the Peace campaigner Vivienne Newson returned from overseas to become *Newsheet* editor in 1953. What overseas speakers and information there were in the *Newsheets* came largely from the United Kingdom and Europe and seem to have been dependent on Jessie Street. The *Newsheets* occasionally contained colourful letters from Jessie about her travels, like that in August 1950, which detailed a tour with Kapila Khandvala around her city of Bombay, but these described Indian working people and villagers as exotic and needy, while Jessie positioned herself as the sympathetic but distanced Westerner.[6] This positioning was quite different, as will be clear below, from that which Lucy made in her references to the workers in these emerging nations.

With Lucy's assumption of executive roles, the absence of international news changed quickly. Before long there was someone talking about Asia or international issues (e.g. about Russia) for at least one of the four weekly luncheons announced in each monthly *Newsheet*. Lucy ensured there was information about the communist countries as well as about those in what was regarded as 'the West'. Just in 1962,[7] as an example, speakers included women from – or speaking about – Ceylon and the USSR in February; the Netherlands, Norway and Europe in March; Japan

---

5 Virginia Madsen, 'Innovation, Women's Work and the Documentary Impulse: Pioneering Moments and Stalled Opportunities in Public Service Broadcasting in Australia and Britain', *Media Information Australia* 162, no. 1 (2016): 19–32.
6 UA *Newsheet*, August 1950, 2. Such letters were unusual in the context of Jessie's autobiography too, which focused on the top-level meetings Jessie had with politicians and diplomats. Her own and her later biographers' selectivity has perhaps narrowed the impression of the range of her interactions.
7 UA *Newsheets*.

and Scotland in April; South Africa and Apartheid, India and Europe in May; Antarctica, France/UNESCO and Australian Aboriginal conditions in June; the South Pacific with two speakers in July; speakers from the Women's International League for Peace and Freedom (WILPF) conference in August; Japan and the US in September; Rhodesia (Zimbabwe), Japan and the UK in October; and the US in November. International news became a regular and distinct part of each monthly issue, gleaned from overseas press – gathered perhaps by the Open Door International or the Women's International Democratic Federation (WIDF) – but with particular attention to the 'new nations' of Africa and Asia, as well as to Russia. Over 1962 again, there were news items about advances for women in the US, Italy and Canada in March; USSR, US, United Arab Republic and the Philippines in April; Malaya and Greece in May; Pakistan, Egypt and the UK in June; Cuba, India and the UK in July; Nyasaland in August; Sierra Leone, the Philippines and, from the Open Door International, a long article about Brazil, Uruguay, Argentina and Peru in September; from Denmark, Switzerland, US, UK, Canada, Kenya and Japan in October; Indonesia in November; and there were speakers foreshadowed from Iran and Malaya for the New Year (published in May 1963). The speaker from Rhodesia in October was not from the minority white governing group. Instead, the UA was addressed by Mrs Godsiang Gaobepe, who was in Australia on a UNESCO scholarship. Lucy chaired Mrs Gaobepe's session on the subject 'Through an African Woman's Eyes'.[8]

Perhaps this was a product of the times: by the early 1960s, travel was cheaper and easier and women were travelling more widely. Yet these entries in the UA *Newsheet* in the 1960s echoed closely Lucy's article immediately after her retirement:

> Women in other parts of the world, during a few short years, have achieved an equality far greater than we have. We owe these women a debt.[9]

This was the way that Lucy had begun her active contribution to the UA and it was to be characteristic of all her *Newsheet* entries on industrial justice and the status of women, up to and including those in the last months of her life. The only way they changed was that it became clearer that when she said 'other parts of the world' she was referring to the

---

8   UA *Newsheet*, October 1962, 4.
9   UA *Newsheet*, March 1954, 1–2.

decolonising nations. What was notable in all of her entries was that Lucy's goals for future equality were all measured by the newly won equality of women in the constitutions of so many of these emerging nations in the decolonising world. The way that Lucy positioned decolonising women was very different from the exotic but needy role in which Jessie Street had placed them in 1950, however much Street admired their questions. Instead of describing them as needy, Lucy took quite a different stance. She was looking to the new nations of Asia and Africa as the models to show Australians the way to reach equality in gender as well as racial terms.

Equal Pay

Lucy's large body of *Newsheet* writing about Equal Pay shows best the many dimensions of her activism. Her transnational vision was entangled with every level of this work.

She had to face a rising issue for both men and women – particularly outside teaching – which was automation. She had long campaigned against the classification into 'men's' and 'women's' work: from the late 1950s, automation was eroding any rationale about physical strength that had earlier been given for this distinction. As she memorably said in 1960: 'Women have to teach men that automation knows no sex!'[10]

Lucy's *Newsheet* responses to her opponents were often shaped by satire and humour as she pointed out the flaws in their arguments. But at times her anger was visible at the continued dismissal of women's claims. She lashed out at misogynist politicians and trade union leaders who feared women's equality.[11] She actively promoted women's organisations that were putting the case for working in industries like meat processing,[12] and she castigated the leaders of their unions who refused to listen to their women members. Trade union leaders had *never* been criticised in the UA *Newsheets* in the period before Lucy's formal roles, but she was not reluctant to name and shame the men who tried to hold back the industrial tide. Mr F. Lovett, secretary of the Broken Hill Shop

---

10   UAW Second National Conference 27 May – 2 June, 28 May 1960, Lucy Godiva Woodcock ASIO file, Vol. 2, f 194, A6119, 2031, NAA.
11   UA *Newsheet*, August 1958, 1. Under Lucy's signature, Premier Cahill was condemned for lagging on fulfilling his promises on equal pay. Lucy wrote: 'Mr. Cahill may be remembered as the Premier who had a vision, but lost the will to implement it, because of the pressure behind the scenes of men who fear equality.'
12   UA *Newsheet*, February 1958, 3.

Assistants' Union, came repeatedly to her attention. He withdrew union membership from and tried to have their employers sack 22 women shop assistants in Broken Hill because they were married. Although the law forcing the dismissal of women teachers who married had been repealed in 1947, the 'marriage bar' had remained in place in many industries, and, despite the Boyer Report recommending change in 1958, this rule did not end in the Commonwealth Public Service until late in the 1960s.[13] The UA *Newsheet* published extracts from Mr Lovett's 1959 speech to a compulsory Conciliation Court hearing, where he stated that:

> For the most part, married women employees were economically a menace – a threat to stability and a help-mate to depression … And we can't lose sight of the fact that, in the main, working wives spend their earnings on the wrong things.[14]

Lucy responded as UA President in a letter to the editor of the *Sydney Morning Herald*. The paper, however, did not publish it, so the UA *Newsheet* did:

> The Four Freedoms of the UN Charter guarantee the right of women to work; the ILO and the ACTU affirm this right. The present situation in Broken Hill, which has been caused by a fall in world prices for the commodity which Broken Hill supplies, calls for some positive approach to the problem, not the negative one of selecting a group and denying them rights enjoyed by all other members of society.[15]

Yet, in 1967, Lovett was still demanding that married women be forced to resign as shop assistants, arguing they should never have been 'allowed' to join the Clerks' and the Town Employees' unions. Once again, and only six months before her death, Lucy responded, scathingly pointing out:

> what the isolation of male unionists can do to their thinking and how backward they can become in relation to modern trends in the community … This attitude of 'allowing' women to belong to

---

13   Extract from the *Report of the Committee of Inquiry into Public Service Recruitment*, 1958 (Boyer Report), Australian Government Public Service Commission, www.apsc.gov.au/publications-and-media/current-publications/apsc-news/thumbnails/boyer-report, accessed 2 January 2019.
14   UA *Newsheet*, August 1959, 2.
15   Ibid., 2–3.

> their appropriate union contravenes the basic principles of trade unionism. The word is 'the right' – not a privilege, to be extended to them by their fellow male workers.[16]

The Barrier Industrial Council complained that Lucy's attack was unjustified because the employment situation in western NSW was so marginal that married women had to give way to unmarried girls or all the young people would leave for the city. Lucy agreed that this was a real problem but insisted that the way to solve it was to work with government and industry to develop new enterprises, *not* to marginalise and then attack a segment of working people.[17]

Lucy attended peak union meetings, like the Australian Council of Trade Unions (ACTU) and the NSW Trades and Labor Council, reporting back to the UA membership, explaining the issues and the strategies. The situations were always complex and Lucy's union experience and economic background were important resources previously inaccessible to the UA. Prior to Lucy's active role, the UA had expressed support for equal pay but had never included details of disputes or industrial laws, referring to 'a factory' and 'a union' without any names or context.[18] Even if industries were identified, the laws governing job classification and margins were never discussed.

Again, Lucy's presence changed all that. To explain the complexities of industrial conditions, Lucy patiently wrote concise and accessible 500-word pieces for issue after issue of the *Newsheet* to show how the classification of jobs as either 'men's work' or 'women's work' had always been a way to undermine women's as well as men's pay. She explained, too, how the use of 'protective legislation', which seemed to be about taking care of women's needs, was in fact usually a way to discriminate against them by paying lower wages while avoiding charges of discrimination. All of this, plus the persistent obstacle of 'margins' for alleged skills, needed to be considered in the complex tangle of reforms needed to reach equality. Given the increasing concern over automation, she spent a great deal of time in 1961 explaining the issues around the recently imposed graphic arts award, which had just been overturned by an appeal to the Industrial Court. The issue turned on the rising use of high technology in many industries. Due to new printing equipment, the court had initially

---

16   UA *Newsheet*, September 1967, 1.
17   UA *Newsheet*, October 1967, 1.
18   UA *Newsheet*, July 1950, 1. This strike in 'a factory' is a good example.

reclassified some jobs as 'women's work', thus increasing the work available to women but reducing the newspaper proprietors' wages bill and cutting out men's jobs. Lucy pointed out that this was exactly the situation where the classification of work as 'male' or 'female' was damaging to the employment of all workers, men and women. Her solution was to raise women's wage rates and to remove sex classifications altogether, so there was a simple rate for the job, no matter who did it. The court's action was challenged by the Graphic Arts union, which won its appeal. Lucy counted this as a victory although it did not raise women's wages – it just meant that the battle to do that continued!

Lucy's accessible articles and her quoted letters, along with editor Vivienne Newson's 'news' items, had allowed UA members to follow the industrial issues around women's work far better than before. Lucy brought into view, in this way, the sequence of hope and disappointment between the first ACTU Conference on Equal Pay in 1958 and the third in 1961. The account of this long campaign in the UA *Newsheet* showed the strategies Lucy used to be effective in supporting fellow activists during long struggles – a quality that must have been extremely important throughout her union career but had not been visible in the pages of the Federation journal *Education*.

As the UA *Newsheet* described this long campaign, first, in an apparent response to the 1958 ACTU conference, the NSW Premier gave a promise in April to legislate for equal pay, a major shift from the federal government's insistence that it would leave the issue up to the Industrial Courts. But, after months of prevarication, when the legislation finally appeared in November, it did little more than address an anomaly that had crept in during the Depression, so it simply meant that women's wages were raised slightly – from 67 to 75 per cent of men's. Nevertheless, it was a small step along the way, and Lucy's reports to the UA always offered positive interpretations by pointing out that even minor improvements would form the basis for more advances in the future.

After three years of high-level campaigning by national unions as well as women's organisations, with deputations to Prime Minister Menzies and wide publicity, there was to be a National Equal Pay Week, in March 1961, organised by the ACTU, to be observed in every state.[19] The recession of 1961 was beginning to hit unskilled women workers and married women

---

19 UA *Newsheet*, May 1961, 1–2.

hardest, so it became increasingly urgent that equal pay was achieved. Lucy had of course been campaigning all her working life for Equal Pay, but she went along enthusiastically to many events representing the UA, often with her old friend and fellow unionist Betty Dunne, then treasurer of the UA and a clerk who had been active in the Public Sector Association. The climax was to be a two-day ACTU seminar that was expected to produce practical strategies to achieve pay equality. Instead, the delegates heard nothing more than calls for more inquiries and surveys and for 'gentle persuasion'.

Lucy's exasperation was visible in her report to the UA:

> The discussions might have been new in 1938, but not in 1961. The winds of change, that blow so strongly in newly emancipated countries, have not reached the ACTU and its members. It is still bogged in the rituals of the past, still concerned with preserving orthodox procedure in its approach to equality; with establishing a Women's Bureau, instead of pressing for the inclusion of a clause ensuring the equality of women in the Constitution, which is in process of revision, and of making the issue of Equal Pay for the Sexes a live election issue for the forthcoming State and Federal elections.
>
> Once roused, women – half of Australia's populations – could bring about the ratification of ILO Conventions Number 100 and 111 and could change the attitude of the Government on this issue of equality. If they use 'persuasion' it will be 2000 AD before Australia catches up with the new Nations within the Commonwealth on this vital question of giving its women equality.[20]

Yet this anger was not Lucy's contribution to the seminar. Betty Dunne, although herself frustrated by the way women were given so little time to speak, added this postscript:

> As the curtain was about to fall on the 1961 Seminar, our Chairman, Miss Lucy Woodcock, rose, and in the five minutes at her disposal, gave a most stirring speech on the reasons why women will be denied social justice until equal pay and sex equality are established facts and not something to debate.

---

20 Ibid., 1.

> It was a climax to two days of frustration, and gave a fresh breath of hope that so many of the delegates and observers had come to the Seminar to hear.[21]

Just as she did in this UA report, each time Lucy explained the complexities of Australian state or federal industrial law, she pointed to the decolonising new nations as inspiration for the ways their constitutions were enshrining equal pay and civil rights for women. Lucy was not a romantic about these new nations – her reports about women's conditions in India, Japan, China and the Soviet Union were all alert to the disappointments and failures in some of those grand constitutional promises. But nevertheless, the equality of women with men as citizens had at least been recognised as a foundational principle of these new states. It is ironic today, then, that Lucy's frustrated reference to the year 2000 looks sadly optimistic!

Lucy saw the UA as a vehicle to intervene directly at the international level through the International Labour Organization (ILO) whereas previously she had acted through the education unions. Lucy frequently demanded that the government endorse ILO Convention 100, on Equal Remuneration (1951), and Convention 111, on Discrimination in Labour Conditions (1958). To this, too, the federal Menzies Government had repeatedly sidestepped the issue by saying it had to be left to the Industrial Courts. However, Lucy pointed out to the UA membership, just as frequently, that these two ILO conventions held a major contradiction, by retaining 'protective' labour exemptions to 'discrimination'. Lucy nevertheless welcomed the announcement that the ILO would hold an Asian conference in Sydney in November 1962, offering UA hospitality to the women she assumed would be among the overseas visitors 'because of the importance of the roles which Asian women are playing in the development of their countries, we hope there will be many women in the various delegations.' There was to be disappointment, although this was hardly a surprise. There were few women apparently in attendance, although Lucy persisted with the offer until the last moment.[22] Nevertheless, by the following year (1963) there was to be a conference on 'Women Workers in a Changing World' that was to reflect the rising concern and focus on automation that removed questions of physical strength from sex classifications. Lucy as always responded strongly, arguing that this was an important discussion

---

21　Ibid., 2.
22　Conference to be November 28–December 8 1962, UA *Newsheet*, April 1962, 3; October 1962, 2; December 1962, 1.

to be held and must result in more pressure to fulfil equality in pay rates – removing discrimination by having one rate for the job. She took the opportunity to write again to the Australian Government and Opposition, asking if their parties would ratify ILO Conventions 100 and 111 – only to be told by Menzies and Calwell that they would not commit before the coming election but would decide later.[23]

Status of women

Although less extensive than her writing on industrial issues, Lucy's input to the *Newsheets* on the status of women bore the same approach of drawing on the lessons of the decolonising world as the benchmark of progress. She focused her attention less on the questions of property and divorce that had filled the UA *Newsheet* before 1954 and more on the presence of women in leadership roles. Her concern was visible in every issue with mentions of her numerous letters to the various heads of government and ministries about boards of all sorts, from the Public Service Board, her old bête noir, to the boards of hospitals, the Anglican Board of Missions and universities. At the same time, she called for open access for women to all jobs, from judges to taxi drivers, garbage collectors and drovers, as well as to civil responsibilities like jury duty on equal terms and conditions, including compulsory service, as men.

Often she used humour, satirising the Australian Institute of Management that had a conference in 1962 about secretaries as the 'Right Hand of Management' but had failed to include any secretaries – or indeed any women at all – among its speakers.[24] She was more blunt with British journalist Anthea Goddard, who had written seriously that 'women have won absolutely nothing from equality'. Lucy called her views 'ludicrous', turning to the decolonising world to define progress:

> The 20th Century, significant for scientific advancement, is also important for its recognition of the rights of people – men and women. The freeing of the colonial people and the partial economic emancipation of women are features that are now realities …
>
> The emergence of women in 65 countries to equal political rights is a reality that will take some organisation to destroy. Women are needed as first class citizens, intelligently sharing and participating

---

23 UA *Newsheet*, October 63, 2; November 1963, 4.
24 UA *Newsheet*, July 1962, 2–3.

> in guiding destinies of mankind. Woman's former status as a second class citizen, classed with minors, criminals and lunatics, allowed her no scope even to 'act, subtly as consultant' …
>
> As a journalist, enjoying equality with male journalists, we were surprised that you should give so much of your valuable time to report such a stupid movement …[25]

Lucy had a particular concern about the councils and governing bodies of universities. She had herself sat on the Senate at the University of Sydney in 1942 as a graduate representative, which reflected the interest she had – along with the Teachers Federation – in the way universities controlled the curricula in secondary schools. The questions she raised as UA President had expanded, however, to point out the rising numbers of women students at universities. Lucy herself had completed two degrees – the hard way – as a night student while working a full-time job. She wanted more women's voices to be heard to represent those students, but she also wanted better provision for the retraining of women in mature age to allow them to meet the needs of a changing workplace and to return to work after child-rearing.[26] Just as they had been throughout, Lucy's examples of women's competence were consistently drawn from the decolonising world: from the role of Mrs Pandit at the UN in 1953 and Lakshmi Menon as both Deputy Minister for Foreign Affairs with Nehru and President of the All India Women's Conference in 1958, to Mrs Sumati Morarjee of Bombay becoming managing director of the Scindia Navigation Company, to the 1966 election of Indira Gandhi as Indian Prime Minister.[27] It was a sustained theme in all her writing that the constitutional guarantees of gender equality built into the constitutions of new nations had allowed women to demonstrate already their capacity, skills and determination in such responsible leadership roles.

Education

Lucy's writings on education and Peace in the *Newsheets* took a slightly different approach – she saw these two movements as collaborations and partnerships, in which the goals were still far off for everyone but that the best strategies to get there would be friendship and mutual learning. She remained convinced, however, that there was much that people in

---

25   UA *Newsheet*, September 1962, 2.
26   UA *Newsheet*, May 1958, 2; July 1958, 1.
27   UA *Newsheet*, May 1958, 4; October 1962, 3; February 1966, 1.

Australia could learn from their neighbours in the decolonising countries and it should be to these close neighbours that Australians should look for partnerships.

Lucy had always been active at the state, federal and international levels in organising by teachers – she had co-founded the NSW Teachers Federation, had served as president of the Federated State School Teachers' Association in 1931 and been an office holder in the NSW NEF since 1937. Particularly since her time in rural schools – from Eden to Cessnock and then to Grafton – as well as being aware of her sister Beth's life on a grazing property, Lucy had been aware of the presence of girls in agriculture and in the technical trades. There were UA members who were rural famers as well as those who were teachers and unionists, and those rural women were receptive to Lucy's sustained interest in making technical and vocational trades training along with agricultural science and skills available to women. Lucy was just as consistent in her criticism about the diminishing numbers of girls studying sciences and maths at schools, blocking them from scientific careers, including agriculture and medicine. As UA President, she demanded that this problem be addressed at all levels. Girls – and their families – were simply making logical judgements about their future prospects, Lucy argued. If they chose these careers, they faced few job opportunities ever being offered to women, and those that were offered had pay that was never equal to those of male colleagues and in which there were no chances of promotion. So, she asked, why should they choose these careers?[28]

As well as access to the sciences and mathematics at universities, Lucy argued for an increased number of apprenticeships that would allow training in the workplace and through community cooperatives. This linked her strongly to the international. Not only were cooperatives a central part of Rewi Alley's work and teaching practice in China but Alf Clint, Lucy's fellow Australian Peace activist, was a pioneer of cooperatives in Papua New Guinea (PNG) and among Aboriginal people in Australia. Clint had given luncheon lectures to the UA members about his PNG work before Lucy's time and she brought him back to talk about cooperatives among Aboriginal people in rural Australia as well as about his work in the Peace movement. Building networks as always, Lucy kept Rewi informed about the formation of Alf's cooperative education hostel, Tranby, in Glebe in 1957.[29] Many of the Indian women

---

28 For example, ibid., March 1961, 3; November 1961, 2; July 1962, 2; November 1962, 2.
29 Lucy Woodcock to Rewi Alley, 16 July 1957, Rewi Alley Papers, NLNZ.

with whom Lucy was in touch were, like Anasuya Gyan Chand, long-time activists in the development of cooperatives in India. The Indian cooperatives had involved agricultural workers generally, and large-scale cooperatives had been favoured by the post-Independence government in rural areas. But cooperatives had also been utilised among women seeking economic independence through craft work and the All India Women's Conference (AIWC) had been closely involved. Furthermore, cooperatives had been an approach also developed among Adivasi, the 'Tribal' or Indigenous peoples of various areas across India, who had often converted to Christianity as a political statement to extract themselves from local power structures. It had then been through Christian or Christian socialist networks, like that to which Alf Clint was affiliated, that they had become involved in the international cooperative movement.

All of this talk of cooperatives also of course raised the spectre of communism, which Lucy had had to struggle with in her career as a teacher and unionist. The UA had made a significant stand in 1954 when Lucy's presence at the Stockholm Peace Conference had been challenged by the Australian Federation of Women Voters (AFWV). The UA had taken decisive steps to endorse Lucy's contribution, despite the accusations that the Peace movement was communist-led, and then, to make its message clear, the UA had disaffiliated from the AFWV. On Lucy's return to Australia and the organisation, she felt more strongly supported by the remaining members of the UA to pursue her goals of gender justice in education as well as in the workplace, but was nevertheless cautious in leading the UA members beyond the middle ground.

At the national level on education, Lucy was actively involved as UA representative, but also as a former president, with the conference held by the Australian Teachers' Federation in Canberra in 1958. Despite Lucy's careful approach to polarising Cold War politics, ASIO kept her under surveillance and took notes on her contributions to the debate. The security officer was, however, more interested in her informal conversations with teachers from Western Australia and other states about education policy, union matters, other delegates and, in particular, her impressions of her trip to Soviet Union schools.[30] Lucy herself was apparently mostly concerned about passing on to her fellow delegates the fact that she had

---

30   20–21 May 1958, NSW Teachers Federation ASIO file, Vol. 3, f 54, A6122, 2477, NAA.

been prevented from speaking to schoolchildren or in schools about her experiences in Japan, China and India when she returned through Western Australia in 1955.[31]

Lucy took a similar role in the UA on education as she had done in industrial matters, explaining the technicalities and the politics in short, accessible articles. She did this in February 1962 when the Wyndham reforms were announced.[32] She explained how they would work but she also pointed out some concerns, so that *Newsheet* readers could take an informed look at how the reforms operated in the schools they knew, able to recognise improvements but be alert to potential problems. At the same time as she was writing these explanations to the UA readers, she was also attending union meetings and had a particular interest in the training of teachers. The Assistant Teachers group was, of course, where her career had begun and this had been one of her early organising roles in the Federation. Strong training of teachers had been a major part of her appreciation of the Soviet education system and she had been a consistent advocate of more resourcing and better planning in order to increase teacher training. So she took a very active role, through the pages of the *Newsheet*, in a campaign to ensure that when trainee teachers were offered government Teachers' College scholarships, they became automatically employees of the Education Department, receiving the same industrial benefits that members of the Teachers Federation received.[33]

In some respects, her continuing involvement in NSW education beyond the demands of one particular school allowed Lucy to reflect on her previous positions. While headmistress at Erskineville, which in 1932 had been one of the first schools to have the new 'Opportunity Classes' selected from primary schools on the basis of IQ testing, Lucy had distinguished IQ testing from the university-controlled exams that she had so bitter opposed. She had been supportive of the way the primary school Opportunity Classes worked at Erskineville, where she felt the selection process grouped children of comparable abilities and allowed additional time for the type of creative, exploratory activities advocated by progressive educators. But when in 1943 the IQ test was introduced as a way to select for high schools, Lucy had been far more critical.

---

31 Ibid.
32 UA *Newsheet*, February 1962, 3.
33 UA *Newsheet*, June 1962, 2–3.

Her views did not appear in the pages of the *Newsheet* but were part of an interview she did in 1959 for the UAW journal *Our Women*. There she pointed out that the IQ test was primarily a measure of reading. At this time, a wider range of media including television was available. So the capacity to read text was not the only means of communication required. Instead, critical skills in reading images and sound were also increasingly needed. She felt that 'the IQ should never be regarded as a final determining factor and should be the servant, not the master, of the educational system'. She argued that the role of schools was to *teach* so that children who may have low IQ scores at one stage would, with highly trained and well-resourced teaching, later produce first-class work.[34]

At the international level, Lucy worked by bringing the UA into the network of the New Education Fellowship, which already had a close link to the NSW Teachers Federation. The NEF had taken up the challenge of decolonisation and was a very different organisation in composition than it had been in the 1930s. It had been accused of leaning towards communism and had lost American funding because of the accusation, but the NEF continued to bring educators together across political borders.[35] Its 1962 conference in Sydney was titled 'The Winds of Change in Education' and it had speakers from the US, the UK, India and the Philippines on 'the changing relationships between East and West and need for understanding'. Lucy was frustrated, however, because the conference was poorly attended. This was largely, in her view, because it had been necessary to hold it in the school holidays as the NSW Education Department would not give teachers any leave if they wished to attend. The departments in Western Australia and South Australia supported the NEF by guaranteeing such leave for conferences, but 'NSW resists such liberal ideas so the vital messages were given to "enthusiasts only"'.[36] The low attendance may, however, have reflected a decrease in teacher involvement with the NEF – its appeal in Australia seems to have been declining in this period.[37]

---

34 September–November 1959, cited in Lucy Godiva Woodcock ASIO file, Vol. 2, f 137, A6119, 2031, NAA.
35 Christopher Clews, 'The New Education Fellowship and the Reconstruction of Education: 1945 to 1966' (PhD thesis, Institute of Education, University of London, 2009), 52, 83–122.
36 UA *Newsheet*, October 62, 3.
37 Margaret White, 'Traversing Personal and Public Boundaries: Discourses of Engagement in New Education, 1930s to 1980s', *Paedogogica Historica* 43, no. 1 (2007): 151–63, doi.org/10.1080/00309230601080634.

A new development was much more evident in the speakers at the UA luncheons – this was the presence of Colombo Plan students who were coming in increasing numbers into the Australian university system. Lucy met a number of them through the UA meetings and elsewhere. She took an increasing interest in them, seizing the opportunity it gave her to learn more about them and their countries at the same time as she offered them her educational skills.

Peace

The *Newsheets* had *not* reported at all on the major Peace rallies in 1960. Lucy had been heavily involved in organising the metropolitan conference, and then spoke at Lithgow; yet, apart from a reference to the Black Sash movement in South Africa (March 1961) where women protested against apartheid, there was no mention in the *Newsheets* up to 1961 of women taking direct action of any sort and certainly not about the Peace movement. The absence of this topic is more remarkable given the intensity of Lucy's concern during 1956 and 1957 in her letters to Rewi Alley about the atomic testing occurring at the Maralinga range. She was deeply angered by the exorbitant expense of the tests, about the 'huge preparation and much money going up in smoke that could help ordinary people'.[38] She believed, like many others, that the unusually wet conditions in Australia and elsewhere during the 1950s must be caused by the impact of the many atomic explosions occurring.[39] 'The H-Bomb', she wrote to Rewi, 'is very real and people are beginning, too late, not just to wake up but to do things.'[40]

Although it is not clear why the *Newsheet* issues were silent on this theme until 1962, it may have been the lengthy after-effects of the 1955 split in the Australian Labor Party – when anti-communist members formed the Democratic Labor Party. Although the split allowed continuing ALP members far more freedom to take part in organised Peace movement activities, the repercussions went on for some years, as Lucy commented to Rewi Alley in 1957.[41]

---

38 Lucy Woodcock to Rewi Alley, 14 March 1956, Rewi Alley Papers, NLNZ.
39 Lucy Woodcock to Rewi Alley, 14 March 1956, 14 July 1956, Rewi Alley Papers, NLNZ.
40 Lucy Woodcock to Rewi Alley, 16 July 1957, Rewi Alley Papers, NLNZ.
41 Lucy Woodcock to Rewi Alley, 11 December 1957, Rewi Alley Papers, NLNZ.

There were other reasons, however, which made the year 1962 very different: the Menzies Government had again supported the testing of nuclear weapons perilously close to Australia. In April, the *Newsheet* carried the UA protest over the government's approval of the UK decision that its colony of Christmas Island (Kiritimati) should be a bomb test site.[42] It was as if this had given Lucy the platform she needed to launch the UA headlong into her Peace campaigning.

In the April issue, too, the *Newsheet* reported on the trial of demonstrators against the NATO airbase from which the H-Bomb could be launched, as well as discussing a disarmament conference being held in New York. It included extensive discussion of the US Women Strike for Peace movement, which had written to President Kennedy in protest over nuclear weapons. The June *Newsheet* carried further news about US citizens protesting at the continued presence of US troops in Vietnam, and the UA – that is, Lucy – wrote to the Women Strike for Peace movement to support it:

> The organized force of women throughout the world is a most important factor in the preservation of peace and in Australia, women are becoming much more interested in all aspects of this great problem.[43]

Lucy had not, however, moved to campaigning fully in the UA *Newsheets*. There was no mention at all in the *Newsheets* of a large rally held in Sydney's Trocadero at the end of April 1962 to call for an end to all nuclear tests.[44] Lucy was on the speakers' platform with Alf Clint, Bill Gollan and Bill Morrow, on behalf of the Peace Committee. What the UA did do was ask the heads of all the Christian Churches to make the Easter sermons and masses of their clergy centre on 'the quest for Peace, the banning of Nuclear Tests and Total Disarmament'.[45]

The August *Newsheet* then heavily publicised the WILPF conference to be held in Sydney later in the month and quoted a British Peace activist, Jacquetta Hawkes, co-founder of the Campaign for Nuclear Disarmament

---

42   UA *Newsheet*, April 1962, 1. Note this was Kiritimati Island, in the UK colony of the Gilbert and Ellice Islands, now part of the Republic of Kiribati.
43   UA *Newsheet*, June 1962, 2.
44   *Tribune* (Sydney), 2 May 1962.
45   UA *Newsheet*, May 1962, 2.

(CND), calling for the banning of all forms of war.[46] The *Newsheet* went on to quote the UK feminist magazine *Women Speaking*, which cited the Canadian Peace activist Helen Tucker:

> It is time that the embarrassed shuffling-off of women's opinion ended and that they – and all men – realized that they have a powerful role to play in the salvation of mankind. Taking a cue from the Black Sash movement in South Africa, we wish, with Mrs Tucker, President of *Voice of Women*, that women might find the resources to picket the Geneva Conference and keep the delegates sitting until, like the Cardinals at a Papal election, they reach agreement.[47]

The speakers at the UA luncheons began to include regularly people who spoke on the Peace movement, like Agnes Stapledon (October 1962), president of the UK section of WILPF, on the recent WILPF conference in Sydney along with Lucy's colleagues on the Peace Council, including Alan Walker (May 1962) and Bill Morrow (September 1962). In October, too, the *Newsheet* published a report on the WILPF conference and the UA wrote to ALP Opposition parliamentarian Tom Uren asking him to convey its protest at plans to install two US bases on Australian soil as they were a threat to world peace.[48] In November, Lucy quoted the chief Australian delegate to the UN in an article headed 'Australia Joined Other Non-Nuclear Powers in Demanding an Early Ban on Atomic Testing'. It continued:

> The chief Australian delegate, Sir James Plimsoll, told the UN main Political Committee that major Powers should agree immediately to stop all tests which caused radioactive fallout.[49]

Lucy wrote on behalf of the UA to congratulate Plimsoll and the government but attacked Senator Nancy Buttfield (Liberal, South Australia), who had purported to be 'putting the woman's point of view' in minimising the dangers of radiation and atomic warfare. The UA instead approved of Senator Dorothy Tangney (ALP, Western Australia), who had supported the nuclear test ban and argued that face-to-face communication between peoples of opposing states was the best strategy for peace.[50]

---

46   UA *Newsheet*, August 1962, 4. See Jacquetta Hawkes, *Women Ask Why? An Intelligent Woman's Guide to Nuclear Disarmament* (London: Campaign for Nuclear Disarmament, 1962).
47   UA *Newsheet*, August 1962, 4.
48   UA *Newsheet*, October 1962, 2.
49   UA *Newsheet*, November 1962, 2.
50   Ibid.

The Peace movement became a sustained presence on the *Newsheet* pages – with at least one article and one speaker each month through 1963 – with rising anxiety and widening support as the Vietnam War escalated and the threat of nuclear testing loomed ever closer to home. By October 1963, it had become clear that not only were the British and the United States undertaking the testing of H-Bombs, but the French were planning to test a hydrogen bomb on their South Pacific colonial territories.[51] In the first issue of 1964, along with the news items about Burma, Ceylon, Uganda and Japan, the *Newsheet* reported that Jean Richards would speak on 20 February to the UA about the Quakers' petition to persuade French President de Gaulle to reverse this plan. The ALP Labor Women's Organising Committee conference, held on 22 and 23 February, condemned the French plan to test H-Bombs and stressed the urgency of implementing ALP policy for a nuclear-free zone in the South Pacific. At the same time, over 50 Australian women 'prominent in public and professional life' had signed a petition that called on de Gaulle to call off the tests.[52] Lucy and Elsie Rivett were both signatories, but it was to be the last public task that they shared – Elsie died in May.

After 1963, the *Newsheet* took a more cautious approach to overt politics. It may have been the impact of the Sino-Soviet rift, about which Lucy expressed concern in her letters to Rewi late in 1963.[53] Outside the UA, Lucy maintained her own commitment to the Peace movement, speaking and actively campaigning until her death. But the *Newsheet* no longer took such an activist position as it had in 1962 and '63. While the issue of French testing in the South Pacific remained, along with peace and decolonisation, the *Newsheets* focused more on individual women like the teacher and activist Helen Joseph (1905–1992) who consistently spoke against apartheid in South Africa.[54] Certainly, there were still individual speakers on international peace, like Phyl Latona in August 1964, and international racial conflicts, like Margaret Brink in March 1964. In relation to racism inside Australia, the UA also invited individuals to speak on the themes, like Charles Perkins and Faith Bandler, rather than taking part in actual campaigning. There was, however, little mention of the eventual tests at Mururoa Atoll beginning in 1966, of the massacres

---

51 UA *Newsheet*, October 1963, 1.
52 *Tribune*, 26 February 1964.
53 Lucy Woodcock to Rewi Alley, 19 December 1963, Rewi Alley Papers, NLNZ.
54 Ameen Akhalwaya, 'Helen Joseph, Obituary', *Independent*, 28 December 1992, www.independent.co.uk/news/people/obituary-helen-joseph-1565649.html, accessed 2 January 2019.

in Indonesia in 1965–66 in which Gerwani was destroyed nor of the Six-Day War in the Middle East in June 1967. Yet the speakers at the UA luncheons in 1967 notably included both those giving the Israeli view (in August) and those giving the Palestinian view (in September) of the conflict.

The UA sustained the pressure on its focal issues like Equal Pay and opportunity for women, continuing to demand better recognition of nursing as a professional career, but it developed many of its themes to meet changing times. Automation became an issue in the *Newsheets* and the UA raised those needs of working women that would ensure equal access to work, like adequate high-quality childcare and support for single mothers, along with removal of the punitive treatment of unwed mothers in society generally as well as in the workforce. The presence – or absence – of women on boards was a constant theme, with major attention directed at the structures of the new Macquarie University, which the UA – and Lucy directly – argued should address the needs of women to retrain as mature-aged students in order to return to the workforce. This pressure was probably one of the more successful aspects of the UA work, and, like the question of training of childcare workers, it linked to Lucy's long commitment to women's education.

Her role as president continued and Lucy contributed many hours particularly to the *Newsheet*, as Vivienne Newson recalled in her moving tribute to Lucy after her death in February 1968. Lucy not only wrote hundreds of letters, but also was always ahead of deadlines to contribute articles and reports, Newson recalled. But more than this, she was drawn into the tedious work of dealing with rising rents, remodelling to fit the UA work into smaller premises and negotiating with landlords and tradesmen over the changes.

Newson recalled what working with Lucy had been like:

> When she related interesting incidents from her crowded, vital life, we would press her to write her memoirs, but, inevitably, her great generosity left her a prey to all who came to her for assistance with various projects or for her wise counsel and sympathy, so that, in the end, all her waking moments were filled – alas! – to the exclusion of her memoirs.[55]

---

55   UA *Newsheet*, April–May 1968, 2.

14

Bringing the World Back Home

Beside her major commitment to the United Associations of Women (see Chapter 13), Lucy took two further approaches to crossing Cold War borders and we discuss them both in this chapter. One was very public: she focused on the links between working women across the world through International Women's Day (IWD). The second was lower profile: Lucy began tutoring Chinese-background students, from Australia and overseas. Lucy's role as president of the New South Wales IWD organising committee was harder than her role in the United Associations of Women (UA). In the IWD committee, she had moved out of the familiar structures of teachers' unions and into the complex worlds of left-wing Labor and Communist Party politics in a time of high tension. After the anti-communist Democratic Labor Party had been formed in 1955, more ALP members had become active in the Peace movement. But anti-communism remained strong within unions. The women's movement was gaining greater recognition within the Communist Party, but, at the same time, there was rising conflict over the Soviet role in Hungary, Krushchev's 'secret' speech and the widening rift between the USSR and China. Lucy had many allies and close friends, like Freda Brown, among the women organisers in the CPA, who were caught up in these conflicts.

Lucy was still strongly based in the union movement although she was, by this time, far to the Left of many Teachers Federation colleagues. She had bitterly opposed the Teachers' Anti-Communist League, formed in 1946 and, in the wider union movement, the anti-communist activists known as the 'Groupers', who had formed 'Industrial Groups' within unions to challenge what they saw as rising communist control. The 'Groupers' had formed the nucleus of the Democratic Labor Party in 1955 and continued to take a major role in Australian union and parliamentary politics, as Lucy discussed in her letters to Rewi Alley.[1] On the other hand, because she was not in the CPA, her tireless efforts in IWD were given little space in the pages of the *Tribune* (the CPA newspaper), which instead gave greater coverage to accounts about IWD activity by women who were members of the CPA.

In the same period, rapid changes were occurring in the Aboriginal movement through the mobilisation of the Aboriginal-Australian Fellowship (AAF) and the upsurge of the Civil Rights movement in the United States. In the Peace movement, the internal divisions in the CPA and ALP were of major significance along with the intensification of the conflict in South Africa and the war in Vietnam. The IWD events each year reflected these underlying tensions as well as emerging issues and new movements, making their planning and implementation challenging exercises. Lucy tried to use the IWD role to strengthen regional networks through friendship and reciprocity.

In the second approach we see Lucy employing in her later life, she worked at a far less public level. She turned the broad transnational visions of her IWD work into concrete reality in the close personal relationships she was forming with the women and young people of the Asian and Australian Chinese communities in Sydney. She became increasingly interested in offering her skills and knowledge to young people in Australia for university studies in an industrial climate where exploitation disadvantaged them and where the cultural climate was poisoned by the continuing hostility of the 'White Australia' and anti-communism. The scattered evidence shows that Lucy was building on her lifetime of committed unionism as well as her skills in teaching by returning to her greatest strength, one-on-one tutoring, to support students from Australia and overseas.

International Women's Day

We know less about Lucy's role in the IWD committee than about her work in the UA, but her IWD work provides an interesting counterpoint to her UA work. In IWD, Lucy was working in a context of tensions within both the Labor Party and the Communist Party. She was nevertheless

---

1   Lucy Woodcock to Rewi Alley, 18 October 1956, 11 December 1957, Rewi Alley Papers, MS-Papers-6533–307, NLNZ.

among unionists, a familiar environment. The IWD secretary until 1962 was Audrey McDonald, then a young member of the Clerical Workers' Union. When Audrey took leave for the birth of her son, her role as secretary was filled by Sylvia Harding, who also continued as the secretary of the Union of Australian Women (UAW).

During the early 1950s, IWD was observed on 8 March with local gatherings of women's rights activists and strong support from the Communist Party, an emphasis on industrial rights, sometimes a concert and always a commemoration of earlier women's struggles. Lucy had been involved in IWD activities since at least 1941 and, during the 1957 events, although Lucy was overseas, she became president of the United Associations of Women. Her time abroad probably made her more aware of the IWD celebrations in Europe. For IWD in Sydney in 1957, activist women in the CPA like Lucie Barnes and local unionists spoke at factories and also at large gatherings of women with guests of honour, including Elsie Rivett, with whom Lucy continued to work on peace and women's rights issues. In the months following her return to Australia, Lucy took on the role of president of the New South Wales organising committee for IWD.[2]

In 1958, the first year in which Lucy had taken a leadership role, the IWD events had an expanded vision. It was the 50th anniversary of the 1908 strike by the New York garment-maker unionists that had so inspired later IWD commemorations. The Sydney committee held an exhibition of arts and crafts at a major Sydney department store, Anthony Hordens, to which women from America, Italy, Pakistan, Israel, Germany and Spain contributed creative sewing and fabric work as well as floral arrangements. There was also a film evening at the UA rooms. Lucy opened the exhibition with a speech emphasising the international character of the event, drawing on various themes she championed, including the importance of meeting women from other lands and learning more about each other through personal relationships:

> It is one day of the year when women of all nationalities, all creeds, all colours, can tie their activities round friendship and mutual understanding among women of all nations. Friendship and mutual understanding are factors of immense importance in promoting peace and goodwill among people wherever they may live and whatever government they may live under.[3]

---

2   *Tribune* (Sydney), 6 March 1957, 8; 13 March 1957, 9.
3   *Tribune* (Sydney), 26 February 1958, 8; 3 March 1958, 11. Sadly, there was no mention of the films shown.

Celebrations were held in all capital cities and in the coastal industrial sugar-harvesting regions like Townsville and Cairns, where the unions, the UAW and the CPA were strong. The Women's Christian Temperance Union and the National Council of Women, both conservative bodies, were just as involved, holding events in Perth, Adelaide and Brisbane.[4]

In 1959, the focus on local women's achievements continued with the Brisbane IWD Committee coordinating the national events. A more transnational vision was suggested by the NSW IWD Committee when it circulated a letter endorsing the Women's International Democratic Federation (WIDF) call for immediate cessation of nuclear tests, banning of all nuclear weapons and for disarmament.[5] Interestingly, the NSW IWD Committee under Lucy altered the WIDF appeal slightly – the original was couched in maternalist language, appealing to women in their child-bearing capacity. The NSW endorsement was instead focused on a more straightforward and universal call for nuclear disarmament, based on a vision of global citizenship.

In 1960, the NSW IWD Committee had the daunting responsibility of coordinating the national events on the 50th anniversary of the first IWD celebration. In honour of the occasion, major international input was planned for a large Sydney meeting at Town Hall. The president of the All China Women's Foundation, Mrs Chao Feng, was to come with her interpreter, Miss Tai Yi-Feng, and also the distinguished Indonesian journalist Mrs Rusijati to speak on Gerwani, the Indonesian women's movement.[6] The New Theatre would present dramatic sketches and there would be musical items. Lucy's view was that the whole event was focused on peace, in support of the WIDF call made in October for a Women's Assembly for Disarmament. *Tribune* reported on the IWD preparations in February:

> This new hope raised by disarmament proposals and the part Australian women can play in making it a reality will feature prominently in Sydney's 50th Anniversary celebrations, Miss Lucy Woodcock, President of the IWD Committee, told *Tribune*.

---

4 *Tribune* (Sydney), 19 March 1958, 10.
5 *Tribune* (Sydney), 4 March 1959, 2.
6 UA *Newsheet*, March 1960, 1.

> The function to be held at the Assembly Hall, Sydney, on March 8, will celebrate the achievements of NSW women in their long battle for equal rights and status, Miss Woodcock said.

> 'The achievements of the past have their significance now and for the future. Women have always been profoundly interested in peace and are even more so today. The oneness of women in the fight for peace is becoming more and more recognised by women all over the world, including Australia.'[7]

At the last minute, however, the plans were thrown into disarray by federal government visa restrictions. The Chinese women arrived too late for the Sydney meeting but went on to Newcastle, Brisbane and far north Queensland. The Sydney meeting was large and imposing in any case. Lucy wrote a special historical introductory speech that was widely quoted, especially her view that the women's movement had a long, inclusive history. Lucy's historical overview was presented by the actress Nellie Lamport, a staunch feminist herself, who had been prominent in IWD events in earlier years. It opened with a celebration of Aboriginal women and a recognition of convict women 'who came to this country against their will'.[8]

Lucy then flew to meet the Chinese delegates in Brisbane – where she did three radio interviews – and accompanied them to Townsville and Rockhampton for an IWD event that the local press called 'the most representative and best function of its kind ever held there'. They all flew back to Sydney where Lucy introduced them and the Indonesian journalist Mrs Rusijati, who had eventually been able to enter the country to begin her speaking tour,[9] to the NSW Trades and Labor Council. Finally, Lucy took the Chinese women to a reception in their honour hosted by the Australia–China Society and the Chinese Youth League early in April, before they flew home.[10]

---

7   *Tribune* (Sydney), 3 February 1960, 3.
8   *Tribune* (Sydney), 9 March 1960, 12.
9   *Tribune* (Sydney), 30 March 1960, 9; 6 April 1960, 10.
10 Lucy Godiva Woodcock ASIO file, Vol. 2, f 166, A6119, 2031, NAA.

Lucy reported to the UA about the North Queensland meetings in terms that were different from the *Tribune* account, which had quoted the local press as calling the events 'the most successful and most representative events of its kind ever held there'.[11] In Lucy's report, she took the opportunity to explain the industrial situation of the far north Queensland towns and point out the cooperation between the various women's organisations including the unionists' wives' committees. She was impressed by 'the keen interest taken by many young women in public affairs. It was most stimulating to find that so many of the speakers at the meetings I addressed were young and very vital'. Her warmest praise, however, was directed to Mrs Shirley Cairns, from the Aboriginal Advancement Committee in Brisbane:

> One of the finest, most invigorating speeches I heard in Queensland was given by a young Aboriginal woman, Mrs. Shirley Cairns, of Brisbane. She took for her subject 'These are the Rights of My People.'[12]

Lucy's interest in Aboriginal politics reflected the rising tempo of Indigenous activism since the formation of the AAF in which she had taken a role since 1956.[13] One notable event occurred during the visit of the American singer and activist Paul Robeson with his wife, Eslanda, in November 1960. In an informal meeting organised by both the Peace Council and the AAF, Robeson viewed two films about Western Australia that moved him so much that he declared he would come back to Australia to take up the campaign for full Aboriginal citizen rights.[14] One was a problematic film shown under various names around activist circles in the early 1950s, purporting to show Aboriginal poverty in Warburton.[15] The other was the short film *People of the Pindan* (made as a pilot to raise funds for a longer film) about the successful Yandiyarra mining cooperative in the Pilbara, set up by the many Aboriginal pastoral workers who had gone on strike in 1946 against exploitative conditions.

---

11   *Tribune* (Sydney), 30 March 1960, 9.
12   UA *Newsheet*, April 1960, 2.
13   Lucy attends annual NSW State Conference AAF, 15 November 1961, Lucy Godiva Woodcock ASIO file, Vol. 2, f 251, A6119, 2031, NAA.
14   Ann Curthoys, 'Paul Robeson's Visit to Australia and Aboriginal Activism, 1960', in *Passionate Histories: Myth, Memory and Indigenous Australia*, eds Frances Peters-Little, Ann Curthoys and John Docker (Canberra: ANU E Press, 2010), 163–84, doi.org/10.22459/PH.09.2010.08.
15   Faith Bandler, interview, 2016.

One of the people involved in organising this event and who hoped to produce the longer version of the second film was Helen Hambly, a member of the CPA. Helen, and others who became close to Aboriginal communities in New South Wales, felt they received little support from the Communist Party, which was more interested in remote 'traditional' Aborigines than in the complex conditions and aspirations of colonised Aboriginal people in the south-eastern states.[16]

The IWD events of 1961 and 1962 demonstrated this tension. In 1961, the Russian pianist Tatyana Nikoley was the visiting guest at an IWD luncheon at which the Reverend Alf Clint spoke of Aboriginal conditions, focusing on heavily settled south-eastern Australia and particularly on the cooperative organisations run by Aboriginal communities in east coast areas.[17] On the other hand, *Tribune* emphasised remote-area conditions, focusing on Aboriginal women as 'wards of the state' in the Northern Territory during its IWD coverage.[18]

Aside from the tensions around Aboriginal issues, Lucy's IWD events also continued the theme of Equal Pay, a cause Lucy had championed over many years. On 11 March 1961, ASIO reported that Lucy had chaired a meeting of the IWD committee on equal pay at Federation House. As ASIO summarised her speech:

> She had given her life to fighting for the rights of women. Started in 1919 and still going in 1961. Some progress; need for solidarity of women. Assistance of IWD. Need for women to get together; instanced that the first teachers' meeting at Federation House, where David Jones now stands, very few enthusiasts, but grown to the mighty Teachers Federation. Need for women to join trade unions.[19]

---

16 Con O'Clerkin, activist on South Coast, NSW, pers. comm. to Heather Goodall, 1977–78; Helen Hambly, interviews with Heather Goodall, conducted 1989; Curthoys, 'Paul Robeson's Visit to Australia'.
17 Re Union of Australian Women, 8 March 1961, Lucy Godiva Woodcock ASIO file, Vol. 2, ff 220–21, A6119, 2031, NAA; UA *Newsheet*, March 1961, 1.
18 *Tribune* (Sydney), 15 March 1961, 12.
19 International Women's Day Committee forum, 11 March 1961, Lucy Godiva Woodcock ASIO file, Vol. 2, ff 222–26, A6119, 2031, NAA.

Figure 14.1: Lucy at International Women's Day outdoor rally with Enid Hampson (Union of Australian Women, in striped dress) with Tom Wright (Sheet Metal Workers Union) speaking, IWD 1962 at Wynyard Park.
Source: Courtesy of Audrey McDonald.

In 1962, the issues came much closer to home. There was a rally, chaired by Lucy, in Wynyard Park where the key guest – Mrs Boney, an Aboriginal woman from Coonamble – spoke about Aboriginal women's struggles in NSW for equality, decent housing and access to town services. She was supported by Helen Hambly, the CPA and AAF member, who had been involved in the films shown to Paul and Eslanda Robeson.[20] The theme of IWD that year was 'Women's Right to Security – a question of our happiness and wellbeing', and Mrs Boney spoke about the challenges she had faced trying to raise seven children in a tin shed on the Reserve with no house and no running water because of local racism and the lack of any state government interest.[21]

The UA *Newsheet* in 1962 focused on the Equal Pay conference on 28 March, chaired by Flo Davis from the Hotel, Club and Restaurant Employees' Union, who argued for an end to calls for 'Equal Pay for Equal Work'. Instead, she asserted, there should simply be no classification into men's work and women's work, just a rate for the job. By this time, Lucy was pressing for more than overall equal pay. She was now demanding that questions of racial prejudice needed to be addressed at work places. As evidence of the first steps in the shift she was calling for, Lucy argued that airline companies were training Aboriginal girls to be air hostesses, while 'the teaching service, too, is recruiting people of all nationalities, irrespective of colour'.[22] Equal Pay, she said, necessitated equal access to jobs and an end to racial discrimination.

Three women from the USSR – one an educationalist, one a judge – whose visas had eventually been granted for a limited stay of 14 days, were among the international visitors to IWD. Women's organisations struggled to ensure their mobility and one of the women suffered a motor vehicle accident in Brisbane soon after she arrived. The other two, however, made it to Sydney and were welcomed by Lucy to a conference on 13 March at the Russian Social Club. According to ASIO, Lucy 'referred to International Women's Day and said how gratifying it was to

---

20 Helen Hambly, interviews with Heather Goodall, 1989. Helen and her husband, Sidney Lloyd Hambly, were two of the eight shareholders of Marngoo films, 1960, which produced *People of the Pindan*, about the Pilbara Strike. Helen was a member of the CPA and the AAF. Ann Curthoys, 'Paul Robeson's Visit to Australia'.
21 *Tribune* (Sydney), 14 March 1962, 11.
22 UA *Newsheet*, April 1962, 3.

have such capable and brilliant women representatives of the USSR to be present in Australia at this time'. In return, the Soviet women conveyed a message from women of the USSR calling for peace.[23]

Audrey McDonald, secretary of the NSW IWD Committee from the mid-1950s until 1962, remembered Lucy as a dedicated and hard-working activist, but one who did not easily share her feelings with others. After the birth of her son, Audrey was surprised to receive an unexpected and warm note from Lucy that congratulated her and thanked her for the 'valuable contribution you yourself made to the success of IWD' and hoped that her baby son might learn 'your perseverance and splendid cooperation'.[24]

Lucy continued her formal role of president of the International Women's Day committee after 1962 but her presence is rarely seen in the pages of *Tribune*, which, as noted earlier, continued to focus its coverage on the members of the CPA who participated in the IWD events in the key cities in each state where it was celebrated. There were international guests – Geeta Mukherjee, for example, came in 1965 for the Third National Conference of the UAW. She had strong connections to the Indian Communist Party and so was most often photographed and profiled with UAW and CPA members like Freda Brown.[25] Lucy, however, seems to have been active throughout 1962 in the Australian Women's Charter of which again she was the chairperson. The Charter held a major conference in Sydney on 15–16 June 1962. Lucy remarked that the goal of the Charter meeting was 'winning equal rights and opportunities for women'. She was again thinking of the decolonising world as a model for the Australian Charter movement. In her view, much had been won in these new nations, pointing to 'a need to break through in the Western World'.[26]

***

---

23   Visit to Sydney by Soviet Women, 20 March 1962, Lucy Godiva Woodcock ASIO file, Vol. 3, ff 24–25, A6119, 2032, NAA.
24   Lucy Woodcock to Audrey McDonald, 25 May 1962, courtesy Audrey McDonald.
25   See photograph, Freda Brown, Geeta Mukherjee, Enid Hampson and Beth Evans, Third National UAW Conference, *Tribune*, 18 September 1963. UAW Files, AU NBAC Z236, NBABL.
26   Re Australian Women's Charter, 29 June 1962, Lucy Godiva Woodcock ASIO file, Vol. 3, ff 33–36, A6119, 2032, NAA.

It is hard to remember that, in this period of intense activity, Lucy was ageing: by 1962 she was 73. The pages of the UA *Newsheet* began from 1960 to record stories of loss. Lotte Fink died in June 1960 and Rosine Guiterman died barely a month later.[27] Beatrice Taylor by this time was crippled with arthritis and others whom Lucy knew well passed away over the next months. At the same time, the UA reported the deaths of many suffragettes or marked the anniversaries of others who had passed away years ago. In September 1961, Jess Rose died – she had been a foundation member of the Assistant Teachers' Association. Lucy referred to her as a hero of the struggle for Equal Pay: 'She was tireless working in the cause of equality and though dogged by ill health, she still kept going, giving generously of her time, energy and money to the cause of equality.'[28]

The centre of gravity of the women's movement shifted in the early 1960s and such deaths increased the weight on those who remained. In April 1962, Betty Dunne, Lucy's activist colleague over many years, died suddenly. Betty, a staunch member of the Public Service Association, had worked hard to gain real pay rises for women union members. Over the years, Betty's politics had not moved to the left as Lucy's had done, but Lucy had learned to make allowances. She told friends in 1958 that there were some things she felt she could not say in front of Betty.[29] But she relied on Betty throughout her activist life in the unions and the women's movement, often travelling with her, and she appreciated Betty's wit and her insights in tight political corners. Lucy wrote in the *Newsheet*:

> Betty and I were fellow students in Economics at Sydney University. Throughout almost 40 years we remained close friends. She was an active member of this Association and Treasurer for two years. She represented the UA on the Status of Women Committee and at various Conferences on Equal Pay … Her unselfish work for her fellows will long be remembered. A fitting tribute was paid to her at the funeral, by a colleague. He told Mrs Alting, 'I was a better man for having known Betty'.[30]

---

27   This terrible sequence of losses could explain the unusual ASIO observation of 31 October 1960 'Lucy Woodcock does not look well' It is the only entry on the page – all other words have been redacted. Lucy Godiva Woodcock ASIO file, Vol. 2, f 18 of 140, A6119, 2031, NAA.
28   UA *Newsheet*, July 1960, 4; August 1960, 4; October 1961, 2.
29   Re Canberra Education Conference, 13 June 1958, NSW Teachers Federation ASIO file, Vol. 3, ff 53–56, A6122, 2477, NAA.
30   UA *Newsheet*, May 1962, 3.

There was some respite from the deaths early in 1963. Jessie Street had retreated to the North Coast – to write – but returned to Sydney often, keeping up to date with UA matters and offering support and the cash needed for practical necessities, like the soundproofing that helped the UA cope with new accommodation and tighter spaces. It was getting harder and harder for Lucy to maintain her frenetic activity. Then, in May 1964, Elsie Rivett died. Lucy had lost the people to whom she was closest.

***

Lucy kept busy. A week before Elsie died, Lucy was a witness with Alec Robertson at the wedding of her friend, the unionist poet Denis Kevans on 13 March. A few weeks later, Lucy paid tribute to Jessie when she came to Sydney for her 75th birthday celebrations in late May. Lucy maintained her letter-writing for the UA, sending Vivienne Newson copy for the *Newsheet* until the last weeks of her life. And she made one more overseas trip.

Figure 14.2: Lucy on delegation to China late in 1964 as guest of the National Chinese Women's Council.
Leader of the delegation Kath Williams seated third from the right.
Source: Lucy Woodcock papers, held by Kit Edwards, personal collection.

In August 1964, Lucy was in China again as a guest of the National Women's Federation of the People's Republic of China. She was part of a delegation of five women trade unionists, led by Kath Williams, who was an Equal Pay advocate from Melbourne and who later left the CPA to join the China-line CPA (Marxist-Leninist).[31]

On her return, Lucy reported to the Australia–China Society, as well as the UA. Her verbal report was recorded in the staccato style of the ASIO agent secreted in the Australia–China Society meeting:

> I went to China as the guest of the Federation of Chinese women with a group of Australian women. I was impressed with Canton. It is a clean city and I saw no hungry people there. In Peking I looked at Child Study Groups, schools etc and studied the universal education system they have. It is compulsory education as we know it. I saw no evidence of aggression towards the USSR. I saw a Defence Budget in operation, easily as defence happy as Holt's Budget. The Revolutionary People's Government want to unite the Chinese people with pride and complete unity into a whole Socialist nation. I am convinced that China wants peace above all. Massive new and modern buildings in all cities. 100 broadcasting stations on the Mainland. Education needs Western History and other text books. The structure of Specialised Universities of Iron and Steel is filled with erstwhile part time students who have qualified to enter these important special universities. The Chinese realize, as we do, that agriculture is the back-bone of a Nation's strength.[32]

In her written report to the United Associations, Lucy focused on women's access to education in China and its positive consequences. Women were high-ranking provincial politicians and filled senior roles in the University of Iron and Steel. There were women she met who were engineers and scientists. She wrote:

> In the professions of geology, mining, road and railway engineering the women of China are now well established and have done extremely well – but Australia continues to deny women the right of entry to many of these fields.[33]

---

31 Zelda D'Aprano, *Kath Williams: The Unions and the Fight for Equal Pay* (North Melbourne: Spinifex Press, 2001). The China-line Communist Party was the smallest of those to emerge from the Sino-Soviet split in Australia and is usually referred to by its initals as 'CPA ML'.
32 Aust China Society meeting, 2 September 1964, Lucy Godiva Woodcock ASIO file, Vol. 3, ff 113–14, A6112, 2032, NAA.
33 UA *Newsheet*, September 1964, 1.

Person to person: Internationalism in close focus

Alongside her work in the UA and the IWD committee, Lucy had continued to speak to many groups of all political complexions about her hopes for peace, stressing that shared knowledge and personal friendships were essential steps on the way. She reinforced this with her observations of China from her visit in 1954 and her continuing involvement with the Australia–China Society, having become close friends with the NSW secretary, Dr Cecil English, who had spent time with Rewi Alley in China.[34] She was interested not only in China itself, but also in Australians of Chinese background in Sydney and in the Chinese-background students who were coming increasingly under the Colombo Plan. In 1959, she wrote to Rewi Alley that she had begun tutoring young Chinese men from Singapore – and it was characteristic that although they had probably come to Australia for tertiary study, she was concerned first about gaining them industrial justice.

She wrote to Rewi, in April 1959, in apology for a delay in writing to him:

> Then I have taken on a task of teaching some of the young Chinese here from Singapore etc, some elementary English. Many of these lads are employed in our cafes and because they cannot speak English, have to put up with many things that they should not have to endure in their work.[35]

Rewi Alley himself came to Australia in the following year, 1960, when Lucy organised for him to give a talk at Teachers Federation House and was able once more to enjoy his companionship.[36] Lucy began to offer tutoring to some of these young Chinese Singaporeans and news that she was available for tutoring circulated by word of mouth, bringing her

---

34 Lucy Woodcock to Rewi Alley, 11 December 1957, 3 April 1959, 22 December 1962, Rewi Alley Papers, MS-Papers-6533–307, NLNZ. The Australia–China Society was later to become the Australia–China Friendship Society. Dr Cecil Hampshire English was a secretary of the NSW group in the late 1950s and early 1960s, although records are scarce from this period. Lucy, who was also on good terms with English's mother, wrote to Rewi in her 3 April 1959 letter about English: 'His heart is still in China'.
35 Lucy Woodcock to Rewi Alley, 3 April 1959, Rewi Alley Papers, MS-Papers-6533–307, NLNZ.
36 Clipping from *Tribune*, 13 April 1960, 10 on reception for Rewi Alley, Australia–China Society, 10 April 1960, Lucy Woodcock included in Lucy's ASIO file, with ASIO officer's report, Vol. 2, p. 173, A6119, 2031, NAA.

a modest but steady stream of students. By 1963, Lucy wrote to Rewi that her students now included young women as well as young men. And their interests had extended beyond the industrial conditions they faced:

> I have been so busy with my Chinese boys and girls that I haven't had time to write. So many of them have attempted the leaving certificate or other Uni exams that I have [been] flat out doing my best to get them through the barriers to enable them to get some good training, hoping that they will return after they have qualified to help in building the homeland.[37]

Among her non-Asian students was Kit Edwards, who became her student around 1964. Lucy was on good terms with the owners of the small shops and pubs around her upper George Street flat. Kit's family had a store in the building next to Lucy's, which had originally been a bespoke shoemaking concern but gradually came to include various tailored items. Kit was a teenager when his family approached Lucy to tutor him for his matriculation exam. He was her student through the later part of 1964, striking up a friendship with her and dropping in often over the next few years when he was at university, and then when he became a teacher himself. Kit enjoyed the wide-ranging conversations he had with Lucy, and has fond memories of afternoons spent in her flat, chatting about his studies and asking her about her life in the way, as he laughs about it today, of an inquisitive teenager. While Lucy remained just as private about her personal life and just as humble with him as she was with others, Kit recalled her emotional reaction to a piece of poetry he was studying, which recounted a soldier's experiences of war. Lucy had told him about her brother's death in World War I; he felt that the grief he saw in her at that instant reflected her enduring sadness over her brother's death and that this had motivated her lifelong pacifism.

During this time, one of Lucy's friends from the Peace movement, Janice Crase, introduced Lucy to her son Antony Symons, an artist who painted portraits in oils. Around 1965, he painted Lucy's portrait, as she sat in the streaming sunlight near the large eastern window of her flat overlooking Circular Quay. This is Kit's enduring memory of her, a strong figure but also an elderly woman. The portrait depicts her dozing in the sunlight waiting for her students, her hands twisted with arthritis but, as Kit

---

37 Lucy Woodcock to Rewi Alley, 19 December 1963. Rewi Alley Papers, MS-Papers-6533–307, NLNZ.

remembers, she would instantly snap alert when he or another student arrived. The portrait hangs now in Kit's home, high above a bookshelf, in pride of place, looking down across his own sunlit dining room.

Figure 14.3: Portrait of Lucy in the sunny sitting room of her George Street flat, overlooking the Quay, Sydney Harbour.

Painted in this flat by Antony Symons, c. 1965. Portrait now owned by Kit Edwards, who was tutored by Lucy in this sitting room during this time.

Source: Courtesy Kit Edwards, photograph Heather Goodall.

Kit did not meet Lucy's other students, but Lucy mentioned some of them to his parents in the weeks before his successful matriculation exam. His parents had sent her a gift to thank her for her attention to Kit, whom she knew as Chris. She wrote back saying how much she had enjoyed getting to know 'a lad of his ability' and how sure she was that he would do well in his exams:

> The path is not easy these days for unfortunately, people teach subjects not growing lads, and this is so apparent in the lads who come into the flat [as her students]. However we have had some great successes this year. One boy, Joseph Yong, has just been in to tell me that he is now BE (Chemistry). Another has passed his 5th year medicine and another got one of those 4th year special Commonwealth Scholarships, so tell Chris that I think the success cycle will hold.[38]

Kit visited Lucy in the last weeks of her life when she was ill in hospital. He found her weak but lucid and eager to hear how his studies were going. Her last words to him were an encouraging command: 'Finish that degree!'[39]

After her death, Kit was able to rescue the small bundle of papers that she had chosen to keep along with some of her books. The papers contained some further references to the Asian students she had been teaching. One was a card sent from Hong Kong in 1965, by someone called George who promised to look up the families of her former students who lived there. Another was an undated card from a student called Moy Hor, who had gone to Adelaide. They and Lucy must have talked about possible tensions in what sounds like a new town for them.

The letter read:

> Dear Miss Woodcock,
>
> I am sorry to cause you so much troubles. I found everything would be all right if only I had my bankbook. I like Adelaide, no hostility so far. I hope to tour Adelaide this afternoon,
>
> best wishes,
> Moy Hor.

---

38   Lucy Woodcock to M. and P. Edwards, undated, estimated to have been sent late in 1964, courtesy of Kit Edwards.
39   Kit Edwards, interview with Heather Goodall, 30 November 2017.

It was only after Lucy's death that Kit met the Chinese students she had taught. They came to her funeral, with tears and tributes. This was so striking that it was highlighted in the Teachers Federation obituary for Lucy. Their contributions to Lucy's funeral highlighted a whole dimension of her community involvement, far beyond the individual students whose studies she had supported. As was her custom, Lucy had become involved in the community, supporting education for all and reaching out particularly to women and girls.

The Teachers Federation tribute to Lucy included this special section on her involvement with the Chinese and Asian communities, told through the testimonies given at her funeral. There is no byline for this article, but it is included here almost in full as there is so little other information about this informal set of relationships. The *Education* obituary read:

A Tribute from the Chinese Community

> Few will miss Lucy Woodcock more than members of Sydney's Chinese community, by whom she was loved and respected. Always a champion of the poor and oppressed, Miss Woodcock's interest in China dates back a long way and she took a passionate interest in their long struggle to win emancipation and human dignity.
>
> A staunch supporter for the new socialist China from its inception, Lucy was associated with the formation in Sydney of the Australia China Society. Right until her end she took a continuing and well-informed interest in China's efforts to build a new life …
>
> Lucy extended this interest and support for China to Chinese living here (perhaps because they also labored under an extra handicap) so much so that she came to be regarded as a guardian angel by the Chinese and Malayan students. She spent an enormous amount of her time helping them with their English, coaching them in their general studies, assisting them to get jobs in their vacation, battling to have them admitted to university and aiding them in their problems with the immigration authorities. Nor did she confine this assistance to students from overseas, but also helped Chinese workers here, from café or market garden, and their children, with their English and all their other problems.
>
> Perhaps typical of her indignation at injustice and her determination and courage is an incident that happened a few years ago. A Chinese girl had come here as a wife for the son of

> a family who rigidly followed the old feudal traditions, making the girl work for the family and keeping her a virtual prisoner forbidden to have contact with anyone outside the family.
>
> At last, an appeal was made to Lucy for help in solving the problem. Promptly, with a group of other women she want to the house and 'liberated' the girl there and then, taking her out of the house. With the feudal tyranny thus broken, the young couple set up house on their own and now have a young and happy family.
>
> Truly the tears that were shed by the Chinese girl at the funeral came from the hearts of the Chinese community.

The World Education Fellowship (formerly the New Education Fellowship) also published an obituary which pointed to Lucy's border-crossing role:

> Lucy became known as one of our fearless fighters for enlightened and progressive education, for human rights and social justice – especially for children and for women – and for international friendship and world peace. Those who knew her well will never forget her immense power as a fighter for people and causes needing a champion and her compassion and concern for children in every land. She was a true internationalist and was especially concerned to support and help migrants to Australia.[40]

Lucy's friendship with the Robinovitz family in 1911 had set her on a course of fighting for justice, which led, both to her assistance for Jewish refugees fleeing Nazism and, later on, to her support for Chinese-background Australians, Singaporeans and Malayans fighting racial discrimination and economic exploitation in Australia. As always, Lucy saw education not for its own sake, but as a strategy to foster gender equality, transnational understanding and peaceful border crossings.

---

40   World Education Fellowship: NSW Section, *News Bulletin*, April 1968, 1–2.

Legacy

15

Young in Hope

This last chapter will address themes raised in earlier chapters and then return to finish Lucy's story with some of her own words.

Biography as method

This book has demonstrated for us the strengths of biographical method. Following one person's life has allowed us to pull together the threads from diverse movements and see some of the interconnections between them. In Lucy's life, this means her work with Jewish refugees in the 1930s and her work with Chinese Australians and students in the 1960s can be understood in terms of her commitments to economic justice, education, feminism and peace. This quality of intersecting movements has not been shown in studies of one movement or another, which characteristically focus on what differentiates movements rather than what draws the same person to more than one. Nor do movement studies shed light on those who do not seek the limelight for themselves. Those people who do the hard back-room work but do not tell their own story in some other way are also neglected. But following one person's life allows an insight into how various movements overlapped and diverged, who was in all and who was in only one, how all were influenced by wider political currents.

Limits of memory: Ageing and sexual orientation

This book has also, however, demonstrated that there are limits to memory and personal experience as we try to use oral history to investigate the people of the past. Two important factors have limited people's insights into Lucy's life. The first is that ageing separated her from many of those she worked with in her later life. The women who were young activists during the 1960s knew her only as a 70-year-old who filled what seemed to be figurehead roles. They have proved to have very little understanding of her long, active and passionate life.

Figure 15.1: Lucy Woodcock with Sam Lewis, Ethel Teerman Lewis and a friend at Sam's farewell event.
Source: NSW Teachers Federation archives, undated photograph P7579.

The second is that Lucy herself may have limited what people could know about her. She had faced the constraints of living an unconventional life – living as a single woman and possibly in same-sex relationships – in a time and culture when 'spinsterhood' and same-sex relationships were both condemned. She was a senior teacher, so she faced the judgemental attitudes not only of her fellow activists but of her state employer as well as those of colleagues and parents. She was intensely guarded about her private life. The people who have proved to have most insight have been those people who came to know her as teacher, and who then developed a friendship with her through that earlier one-on-one interaction.

Transnational vision

Throughout this book, Lucy's global vision has been repeatedly demonstrated. In her interests, her knowledge and her vision for the future she looked far beyond the borders of Australia for her goals and admired examples of achievement. This imaginative transnationalism had been evident from her earliest career in her awareness of the wider world. Characteristically, Lucy demonstrated a critique of the Europe of racist and religious pogroms and of 'tradition' – which she regarded as a deadweight. Her vision became more engaged with women of Asia, probably from her involvement with the New Education Fellowship from 1937 and certainly from 1946. She saw the decolonising countries as leading the way towards the recognition of civil and economic gender equality – of women as citizens. For Lucy – it was as *global* citizens. Yet while she saw the decolonising countries as inspirational in gender equality, she saw Asia and Africa as equal partners, rather than as distant leaders, in the as-yet unfinished project they all shared of the quest for progressive education and for international peace. Her view went far beyond nationalism or the celebration of any one nation state. Instead, hers was a vision in which cultural differences were recognised and respected, but where borders posed no barriers. It was a vision of a world where peaceful negotiation and mutual understanding would resolve conflict. This was the vision that inspired all her campaigns till the end of her busy life.

Gender, travel and activism

Yet Lucy – even as a single professional woman – was still dependent on her employment to sustain not only herself but, for many years, an aged mother. Family networks could be important too for safety and security, but Lucy had none that would assist her even in Britain, and certainly none outside the Anglophone world. So, for reasons of income, safety and – in the Cold War – state intervention, travel for her was seldom possible.

This was just as much a difficulty for her as it might have been for women of her limited means who were the carers of children. It was even less possible for working women to travel, and the few who did were those, like Betty Reilly and others, who could find occasional organisational funds for conferences.

The means of transnational mobility that were available to working-class men, such as seafaring or military service, were largely unavailable to women in the period of Lucy's lifetime. Women might travel as the wives of mobile men, whether merchants or migrants, but otherwise employment was necessary. The cross-border employment available to lower middle-class women in the period of Lucy's life, 1889 to 1968, was sometimes as nurses but most often as teachers. In this lay the importance of education in offering some structures by which women might become mobile across borders. While early mobility in this role might be associated with Christian missionary work, as it was with Eleanor Rivett, there were others who travelled in association with other institutions, such as another focal subject of our project, Leonora Gmeiner, who was recruited by Theosophists to teach in India in the 1920s. Lucy Woodcock was able to use teaching exchange in 1927 to structure her year in London.

This period in the early twentieth century saw the expansion too of new political organisations with international networks, notably the Communist Parties but also the international governance bodies like the International Labour Organization (ILO) and the League of Nations, with both of which Lucy interacted. Each of these – the political networks and the governance networks – circulated information around the circuits of an expanding press and cable infrastructure, relaying both news and opinions around the globe. By mid-century, radio, film and the new air transport were, as Lucy was very aware, intensifying the circulation of images, ideas and people.

Even with her limited access to overseas travel through much of her life, Lucy took all opportunities available to her to learn about and interact with international networks. Whether it was through migrants like the Robinovitz family, refugees like the Fink family, through conference attendees like Kapila Khandvala and Mithan Lam or through students like those she was tutoring in the 1960s, Lucy learned through all of her friendships to develop her knowledge of and interaction with networks that stretched far beyond Australian shores. Letters remained for her a crucially important means of communication and learning. Her long and warm correspondence with Rewi Alley gave her insights of his experiences at the same time as it allowed her to clarify her own. She was able to maintain contact with Kapila Khandvala as well as with Jessie during her long periods in London, and through them made new friendships like that with Reba Lewis in 1956.[1]

Transnational identity, knowledge and imagination are both shaped by gender and change over time. While Lucy was not one who took political action in places outside Australia, she brought all her knowledge and experience of the transnational world into the visions she had for Australia's future.

Legacies: Equal Pay 1963

Lucy made an enormous and sustained contribution to the campaign for Equal Pay for all women, across Australia, in all areas of work. She began campaigning on behalf of teachers in the earliest days of the NSW Teachers Federation from 1918. Then, from 1932, when the NSW Government legislated for the dismissal of women teachers who were married, Lucy opened up another front on that score too, which was only won when the Act was rescinded in 1947. As well as her work at the state level, Lucy had continued to work at the national level for teachers. This meant she

---

1   Lucy Woodcock to Rewi Alley, 14 March 1956, Rewi Alley Papers, MS-Papers-6533–307, NLNZ.

was acutely aware of the continuing discriminatory attitudes to married women in all states and, at times, among women unionists as well as men. So it was a very long campaign, and when Lucy made her first speech to the United Associations of Women (UA) in 1954 she made that point:

> No-one knows better than I do how long it takes to achieve reforms. For 30 years, the Teachers Federation has fought for equal pay, but it was not until 1952 that the women teachers' pay was raised from 80% to 85% of the male rate.[2]

In 1963, the strategic incremental increases in women teachers' wages led to parity with men. Lucy hailed it as a victory, assessing the achievement as worth fighting for. Nevertheless, she made it very clear that she regarded it as only a small step along the way. She wrote for the UA:

> The next step is the implementation of the principle in all avenues of employment. This will not take 50 years, for the winds of change have brought many new factors into the situation: (1) public opinion has changed; (2) the attitude of male trade unionists is different; (3) women themselves are – numerically – more active; (4) the wholesale recognition of the principle in the newly developing countries.[3]

She pointed out the other battles still to be fought, including 'protective' discrimination, but continued:

> Equality of opportunity will be the hardest nut to crack for there is resolute resistance to women as equal partners in world affairs. When women sit in on the policy-making conferences of all nations, then it may be said that the opportunities for women are equal. A long view, indeed![4]

Lucy was as always generous in giving most credit to those women – the 'Brave Souls' – who had been her colleagues in this long struggle.

> The first champions of equality are often forgotten – and yet they are so worthy of remembering! Among them were Miss Elizabeth Fordyce, Miss Rose Symonds, Miss Edith Symonds, Miss Margaret Swann, Miss Rebecca Swann, Miss Effie Macintosh, Miss Jess Rose – these and many others carried on the fight.[5]

---

2   UA *Newsheet*, March 1954, 1.
3   Ibid., February 1963, 4.
4   Ibid.
5   *WA Teachers' Journal*, May 1963, 106; *Our Women* (UAW), March–May 1964, 26.

She added even earlier names to these when she wrote again in 1964: Anne, Kate and Belle Golding, Dame Mary Gilmore, Bertha Lawson and many others.

She wrote again about the way the world had changed to recognise the justice of the call for Equal Pay:

> The world itself after World War II changed in its attitude to women. Newly emerging independent nations wrote equality into their Constitutions. The UN Status of Women Commission was established. The Australian Council of Trade Unions and the International Labor Organisation interested themselves in the claims of women … The year 1963 brought partial victory, but much still remains to be done to ensure full recognition of women in the community.[6]

The Union of Australian Women offered her this tribute in 1960, republished in the UA *Newsheet*:

> A graceful tribute has come to our president from the Union of Australian women, who wrote to thank her for her outstanding contribution in the fight for Equal Pay and for the many years she has spent in untiring work in the interests of women.[7]

Working-class schools and public education

Another important area of her legacy is her sustained commitment to progressive education in working-class schools. As senior vice president over many years in the NSW Teachers Federation and with her refusal to leave Erskineville Public School, Lucy was a fearless advocate for working-class communities. She demanded better food and unemployment relief during the Depression, better housing in the community's existing location and good-quality, highly resourced education for all working-class children – boys as well as girls, Aboriginal and immigrant children as well as locally born – and facilities for lifelong learning for mature women as well as men. Lucy's commitment to progressive education was always engaged with her socialist economic analysis and commitment to working-class communities. In 1962, a speaker from the Teachers Federation addressed the UA and said of Lucy:

---

6 *Our Women* (UAW), March–May 1964, 26.
7 UA *Newsheet*, July 1960, 4.

> During her long career as a teacher, Miss Woodcock had been a shining light, not only to her fellow teachers, but to all the children who had been her pupils over the years. An inspiration to all who worked with her, she would always be remembered by the Teachers' Federation for her forthrightness and courage, in the face of all opposition.[8]

The recognition of Lucy's energy and courage was a theme of the speeches at the Teachers Federation when Lucy retired in 1953. Then Federation President Harry Heath, the anti-communist campaigner (who had opposed Lucy's tenure), said that she had 'immense energy'. Lucy's tenacious activity – perhaps a sign of her determination and commitment rather than any innate 'energy' – was demonstrated many times over throughout her life. She attended countless meetings, wrote hundreds if not thousands of letters for many organisations, made speeches, took part in deputations to state and federal politicians and was a delegate to many conferences.[9]

Yet, as she herself said, 'I am very good at giving but not at taking'. She made sure that the schoolchildren at Erskineville had enough to eat and warm clothes – and shoes – to wear in the winters of the Depression. But she never took credit or sought the limelight. Nor did she ever put herself into the headlines deliberately – but if she ended up there, she never took a backward step! Rather than the spotlight, she preferred to make practical, real progress – real change.

The NSW Minister for Education R.J. Heffron spoke at the Federation retirement dinner where he paid tribute to Lucy's courage and intelligence. He knew her, as he admitted, 'from the other side of the table' as a committed unionist. Yet he commented many times on how much courage it had taken to do the things she had done – to stand up for the Federation, to study for her degrees at night school, to demand equal pay, to insist on decent housing and childcare for working-class mothers and to defend older sisters' rights to school and training.[10]

---

8   Ibid., March 1962, 1. Sheila Cleary, Leading Equal Pay advocate, Teachers Federation.
9   Transcript of speeches from Lucy Woodcock's Teachers Federation Farewell, on her Retirement in December 1953. UAW Files, Extracts *Education*, 3 February 1954, 2, AU NBAC, Z236, NBABL.
10   Ibid.

Visions of a teacher's role: As courageous – and constructive – leader

Sam Lewis, her friend and close ally on the Federation, spoke warmly at this dinner about her many tenacious campaigns, and pointed out how fine a negotiator she was – and how widely respected. She was, he explained, the only person in the Federation who would be listened to by all sides with attention and respect. He reserved perhaps his greatest praise for her work for peace:

> She championed the cause of world peace when peace was being treated as a dirty word. She has dared to work so that the children of Erskineville, Australia and the world should live free from war and pestilence.[11]

Lucy herself stressed leadership – she used the word many times in her short speech in response – insisting that this was the teachers' responsibility. She had said this in Kempsey in 1940 when she spoke to a large gathering of North Coast teachers at a regional Federation conference.[12] Again, at her 1953 Federation farewell, she spoke directly to all teachers:

> You are leaders! You are the people who make the way forward, not the way backwards. You should take the lead and keep the lead … As a teacher, I have never retreated from public life! Teachers must lead if they are going to get something for education![13]

She had taken risks to lead on so many issues because, she explained, 'I have retained my fundamental conviction of the worth of the common man. I have believed in him fully … I know he can do mighty things if given a chance!'[14]

---

11 UA *Newsheet*, April–May 1968, 2.
12 *Macleay Chronicle*, 16 October 1940, 2.
13 Transcript of speeches from Lucy Woodcock's Teachers Federation Farewell, on her Retirement in December 1953. UAW Files, Extracts *Education*, 3 February 1954, 2, AU NBAC Z236, NBABL.
14 Ibid.

Figure 15.2: Opening of the Lucy Woodcock Hall, Erskineville Public School. Heather Goodall with Kit Edwards, 2016.
Source: Helen Randerson.

View from today?

Given the breadth of Lucy's activism, it is unhelpful to look at her work from the perspective of any one 'movement', but it is important to realise how she foreshadowed many contemporary activist trends. Her championing of economic justice for women was rewarded with some success during her lifetime, with the final stage in the incremental granting of 'equal pay' in 1963 in the New South Wales Public Service.[15] Lucy had not wanted gradualist approaches – she had often said that there should be immediate change rather than incremental advances. But she was also such a practical and determined leader, with a view to the long struggle, that she always sought to recognise the most minor of successes and plan pragmatic ways to develop them further. There is no doubt that the continuing struggle for gender justice could draw strength from Lucy's multifaceted legacy.

A consummate negotiator and strategist, Lucy was nevertheless uncompromising in her defence of working-class communities and public education. Similarly, the demands Lucy made for a recognition of decolonisation and an end to racism have been partially recognised in the developments of feminist theory – towards socialist feminism

---

15   Lucy Woodcock, 'Brave Hearts Led Bid for Equality', *Our Women*, March–May 1964, 26.

and intersectionality – where Lucy would undoubtedly have felt more comfortable than she did with many of the more right-wing, racially hierarchical and bourgeois of the feminist organisations with which she made alliances.

While she did not identify the 'personal as political' in the ways that the emerging women's liberation movement was doing in the later 1960s, Lucy had nevertheless made sustained demands for recognition of women's rights to personal safety and dignity. She had campaigned, with Lotte Fink and others, for sexual safety for women, for sexual education for all schoolchildren and for safe and freely accessible contraception. She had insisted women should have equality of access with men in all hotels, with no more humiliating 'ladies lounges' and, in the hotels in the bohemian community where she chose to live, she and others had made that a reality. And, in the pages of the UA *Newsheet*, she demonstrated repeatedly that women had the right and the capacity to embrace complex economic and legal arguments affecting their employment, lifestyle and legal conditions.

Where she did not act in any public way was to challenge the pressures on women to live a heterosexual domestic life. Her deep silence on her own personal choices was a successful protective shield throughout her lifetime, but it was the one area where she perhaps chose self-protection rather than risk.

Young in hope …

But by the 1960s, Lucy herself had recognised how great a gulf age was creating between herself and the younger activists. She wrote about a demonstration and forum held by the Trainee Teachers' Association in 1962. These were young teachers who had in Lucy's early career been thrust into the classrooms with no training and called 'Assistant Teachers'. In 1962 they were receiving better training but little recognition. Lucy had enjoyed supporting their demands and was humbled by their interest.

> At the Town Hall Meeting, I was particularly impressed with the high quality of the speeches made by the students, especially by the young women. Miss Cathy Bloch and Miss Sally Kerr helped tremendously to lift the tone of the meeting. I felt very proud of these young women and others; for so long there have been regrettably few women to take up the challenge.

> The invitation of the young people for me to take a seat on the platform was a gracious tribute to someone whom so few knew but who was as young as they were in the hopes and aspirations of the students to achieve their objectives.
>
> L.G. Woodcock[16]

Perhaps Lucy's defining qualities were her warmth as well as her courage and tenacity, suggested in the caricature of her speaking at the Teachers Federation, so the microphone is gasping, 'What? Again?'

Lucy closed her final speech to the Teachers Federation by telling the members how much she had relished her time with the union:

> I, with you, have shared in that great work.
>
> It has been a very happy time and I have enjoyed every moment of it.
>
> I have enjoyed the fights very much indeed!
>
> And I think we have done a lot together.[17]

---

16   UA *Newsheet*, June 1962, 2–3.
17   Transcript of speeches from Lucy Woodcock's Teachers Federation Farewell, on her Retirement in December 1953. UAW Files, Extracts from *Education*, 3 February 1954, 2, AU NBAC Z236, NBABL.

Bibliography

Archives

Organised by collections and their holding bodies

All India Women's Conference (AIWC) Delhi and Bombay

- Annual Reports
- Office Files
- *Roshni*

Erskineville Public School Archives

Granville Historical Society

- Granville Guardian

Kapila Khandvala College, Bombay

- Photographs, portraits

National Archives of Australia (NAA)

ASIO files

- Ellen Grace Reeve
- Jessie M.G. Street
- Lucy Godiva Woodcock files, Volumes 1 to 3 (NAA)
- Samuel Phineas Lewis
- Teachers Federation

National Federation of Indian Women (Delhi)

- Archives
- Images

National Library of Australia (NLA)

- Jessie Street Papers

National Library of New Zealand (NLNZ)

- Alley, Rewi, 1897–1988: Papers / 1 Inward correspondence – Lucy Woodcock, 1954–1965, MS-Papers-6533–307

Nehru Memorial Museum and Library, Delhi

- *The Hindu*

New South Wales Teachers' Federation Library

- Images
- Archives

Noel Butlin Archives of Business and Labour (NBABL)

- Betty Reilly Papers, AU NBAC N188
- NSW Teachers' Federation files, AU NBAC T15
- UAW files, AU NBAC Z236

Social Networks and Archival Context (SNAC), University of Virginia Library

- International Peace Campaign (various archives, catalogued in SNAC, including Swathmore College Peace Collection)
- Khandvala, Kapila. Speech in session titled 'Lessons from the Far East'. Program, Third Annual Conference on Militant Pacifism, War Resisters League, NY, 6–8 May 1932. Swathmore College Peace Collection, War Resisters League 1923–1994, Records, SERIES A: 1923–1949, Subseries IV, Conferences, Box 9.

State Library of NSW (SLNSW), including the Mitchell Library

- Creative Leisure Movement
  - Correspondence
  - Photographs
- International Women's Day, NSW Committee
- NSW Peace Council papers – 'Peace'
- Rivett Family Papers (Collection of Elizabeth Long: Bib ID: 4922528)

- United Associations of Women
  - Newsheets
  - Annual Reports
  - Correspondence

Theosophical Society Archives, Adyar, Tamil Nadu

- *Stri Dharma*, journal of the Women's Indian Association
- Women's Indian Association Annual Reports

University of Melbourne Archives: Special Collections (UMA/SC)

- Campaign for International Cooperation and Disarmament (CICD) papers, Boxes 49 ('1950s') and 52, 3/88 ('Australian Convention for Peace and War, 1953'). UMA/SC
- *Meanjin* files, Boxes 187 (A.C. Jackson) and 274 (Folder 2: Australian Convention on Peace and War). UMA/SC
- Records of the Victorian Peace Council, Box 6, Folder 3, UMA/SC

Personal Collections (photographs, papers, clippings, objects)

- Beverley Bates
- Kit Edwards
- Judith Emmett
- Phyllis Johnson
- Ruth Fink Latukefu
- Audrey McDonald
- Sarla Sharma

Newspapers

- *Advertiser* (Adelaide)
- *Advocate* (Tasmania)
- *Age* (Melbourne)
- *Albury Banner and Wodonga Expres*
- *Argus* (Melbourne)
- *Australian Worker* (Sydney)
- *Barrier Daily Truth* (Broken Hill)

- *Barrier Miner* (Broken Hill)
- *Bega Budget*
- *Biz* (Fairfield)
- *Cairns Post*
- *Canberra Times*
- *Catholic Press* (Sydney)
- *Cessnock Eagle and South Maitland Recorder*
- *Courier* (UNESCO)
- *Courier Mail* (Brisbane)
- *Daily Advertiser*
- *Daily Mercury* (Mackay, Qld)
- *Daily News* (Perth)
- *Daily Standard* (Brisbane)
- *Daily Telegraph* (Sydney)
- *Dubbo Liberal and Macquarie Advocate*
- *Education: The Journal of the NSW Teachers Federation*
- *Evening News* (Sydney)
- *Friendship*
- *Glen Innes Examiner*
- *Hebrew Standard of Australasia*
- *Hindu*
- *Hitavada* (The People's Paper)
- *Illawarra Mercury*
- *Independent*
- *Kalgoorlie Miner*
- *Labor Daily* (Sydney)
- *Land* (Sydney)
- *Lithgow Mercury*
- *Macleay Chronicle*
- *Maitland Daily Mercury*
- *Maitland Weekly Mercury*
- *Mercury* (Hobart)
- *Morning Bulletin* (Rockhampton)
- *Murrumbidgee Irrigator* (Leeton)
- *New Horizons*
- *Newcastle Morning Herald and Miners' Advocate*

- *Newcastle Sun*
- *News* (Adelaide)
- *News Bulletin*
- *Newsheet* (UA)
- *Northern Miner* (Charters Towers, Qld)
- *Northern Star* (Lismore)
- *Our Women* (UAW)
- *Peace* (now held in SLNSW) launched April 1955.
- *Peace News*, NSW Peace Council newsletter, 1954 to early 1955
- *Pix* (Sydney)
- *Queensland Times* (Ipswich)
- *Register* (Adelaide)
- *Roshni* (AIWC)
- *Singleton Argus*
- *Smith's Weekly*
- *South Coast Times and Wollongong Argus*
- *South Western Advertiser*
- *Stri Dharma* (Women's Indian Association journal)
- *Sun* (Sydney)
- *Sunday Times*
- *Sydney Morning Herald* (*SMH*)
- *Telegraph* (Brisbane)
- *The Abo Call*
- *Townsville Daily Bulletin*
- *Tribune* (Sydney)
- *Truth*
- *WA Teachers' Journal* (also *Bulletin*)
- *Wellington Times*
- *West Australian* (Perth)
- *Windsor and Richmond Gazette*
- *Women's News* (NFIW)
- *Workers' Weekly*
- *World Education Fellowship*, NSW Section, *News Bulletin*

Interviews

Conducted by authors

- Clare Anderson, 2013, Heather Goodall
- Lillon Bandler, email correspondence and meetings, Heather Goodall
- Beverley Bates (née Langley), 1 September 2016, with Heather Goodall, Devleena Ghosh and Helen Randerson, audio recording and notes
- Cathy Bloch, phone interview and email correspondence, Helen Randerson
- Kit Edwards, 30 November 2017, interview with Heather Goodall, Hardy's Bay, audio recording, notes and scans
- Judith Emmett (née Mitchell), 2017, with Heather Goodall, phone conversations, letters
- Helen Hambly, 1989, with Heather Goodall
- Phyllis Johnson, 10 May 2007, Heather Goodall
- Ruth Fink Latukefu, 3 September 2015, with Heather Goodall, audio recording, notes, photographs
- Jean Lewis, email correspondence and meetings, Heather Goodall
- Audrey McDonald, 2013, 2015, with Heather Goodall, notes, scans, letters
- Marie and Ken Muir, November 2017, conversation with Heather Goodall, photograph identification, Pyrmont
- Sarla Sharma, 28 November 2012; 14 February 2013; 18 January 2014, interviews with Devleena Ghosh, assisted by Heather Goodall, Subarta Singh and Helen Randerson, audio recordings, notes, photographs, scanned documents

Conducted by others

- Faith Bandler, Interview, with Carolyn Craig, 2016, SLNSW: amplify.sl.nsw.gov.au/transcripts/mloh307-0001-0010-s001-m
- Ruth Fink (Latukefu), Interview, April 2010, with April Garner, held in NLA
- Former pupils Erskineville Public School, interviewed by Sean Macken, digital video, 10 February 2013
- Kathleen Rachel Makinson, 1 March 1997, interviewed by Dr Ragbir Bhathal, Australian Women Scientists – Oral History Project, NLA
- Queenie Symonds 1987, interviewed by Brenda Factor in the NSW Bicentennial oral history collection [sound recording]. Held NLA, (Session 1 of 2, 42:47–43:45). nla.gov.au/nla.obj-216364926/listen?searchTerm=Woodcock%20jewish%20refugees, accessed 15 October 2017

Reports

Australia. Royal Commission into British Nuclear Tests in Australia. *Report of the Royal Commission into British Nuclear Testing in Australia*. Canberra: Australian Government Publishing Service, 1985.

Mazumdar, Vina. 'Women's Participation in Political Life in India'. Report for UNESCO Meeting of Experts on Participation of Women, SS–83/CONF.620/8. Paris: UNESCO, 1983.

National Planning Committee of Congress (India). *Woman's Role in a Planned Economy*, Report of the Sub-Committee (on women). Bombay: Vora, 1948. (Subcommittee set up in 1938 and submitted report 1940, not published until 1948.)

NSW Heritage Reports on 16–20 Rochford St and Children's Library, Erskineville.

Publications

Aarons, Eric. 'Remembering and Reflecting: 1956', *The Hummer* 3, no. 10 (Winter 2003), www.labourhistory.org.au/hummer/vol-3-no-10/1956-aarons/.

Allen, Margaret. 'Eleanor Rivett (1883–1972): Educationalist, Missionary and Internationalist'. In *Founders, Firsts and Feminists*, edited by Fiona Davis, Nell Musgrove and Judith Smart, 45–63. Australian Women's Archives Project. Melbourne: eScholarship Research Centre, University of Melbourne, 2011. Also at www.womenaustralia.info/leaders/fff/pdfs/rivett.pdf.

Allport, Carolyn. 'Left Off the Agenda: Women, Reconstruction and New Order Housing'. *Labour History*, no. 46 (1984): 1–20. doi.org/10.2307/27508642.

Australian Women's Charter Conference. *Australian Woman's Charter, 1946–1949: Which Comprises the Resolutions Adopted by the Australian Women's Charter Conference*. Sydney: Australian Women's Digest, no date, c. 1949.

Australian Women's Conference. *Australian Woman's Charter, 1943: Which Comprises the Resolutions Adopted by the Australian Women's Conference for Victory in War and Victory in Peace, November 19–22, 1943*. Sydney: Australian Women's Conference, 1943.

Bandler, Faith and Len Fox. *The Time Was Ripe: A History of the Aboriginal-Australian Fellowship, 1956–69*. Chippendale: Alternative Publishing Cooperative, 1983.

Banton, Michael. 'UNESCO Statements on Race'. In *Encyclopedia of Race, Ethnicity and Society*, edited by Richard T. Schaefer, 1099–100. Los Angeles, London: Sage, 2008. doi.org/10.4135/9781412963879.n450.

Barcan, Alan. *Radical Students: The Old Left at Sydney University*. Carlton, Vic.: Melbourne University Press, 1998.

Benjamin, Rosemarie. 'The Story of the Theatre for Children'. Typescript play, c. 1949, held online by Victorian Library, digital.slv.vic.gov.au/dtl_publish/pdf/marc/3/2125895.html.

Berger, Stefan and Sean Scalmer, eds. *The Transnational Activist: Transformations and Comparisons from the Anglo-World since the Nineteenth Century*. Palgrave Studies in the History of Social Movements. New York: Springer, 2017. doi.org/10.1007/978-3-319-66206-0.

Blakeney, Michael. *Australia and the Jewish Refugees, 1933–1948*. London: Croom Helm Australia, 1985.

Brady, Anne-Marie. *Friend of China: The Myth of Rewi Alley*. Abingdon: Routledge Curzon, 2002.

Brehony, Kevin J. 'A New Education for a New Era: The Contribution of the Conferences of the New Education Fellowship to the Disciplinary Field of Education, 1921–1938'. *Paedagogica Historica* 40, nos 5 & 6 (2004): 733–55. doi.org/10.1080/0030923042000293742.

Burgmann, Verity. 'Rosa, Samuel Albert (Sam) (1866–1940)'. *Australian Dictionary of Biography*, National Centre of Biography, Australian National University, adb.anu.edu.au/biography/rosa-samuel-albert-sam-8264/text14475, published first in hardcopy 1988, accessed online 13 May 2016.

Campbell, Craig. '*Education for Complete Living* (1938)'. In *Dictionary of Educational History in Australia and New Zealand*, 18 March 2014. dehanz.net.au/entries/education-complete-living-1938/.

Carter, Barbara. 'The Peace Movement of the 1950s'. In *Better Dead than Red: Australia's First Cold War 1945–1959*, edited by Ann Curthoys and John Merrit, 58–73. Sydney: Allen and Unwin, 1986.

Cavanagh, Michelle. *Margaret Holmes: The Life and Times of an Australian Peace Campaigner*. Sydney: New Holland Press, 2006.

Chanin, Eileen. 'Hinder, Margel Ina (1906–1905)', *Australian Dictionary of Biography*, National Centre of Biography, The Australian National University, adb.anu.edu.au/biography/hinder-margel-ina-18079, published online 2016, accessed 3 January 2019.

Clews, Christopher. 'The New Education Fellowship and the Reconstruction of Education: 1945 to 1966'. PhD thesis, Institute of Education, University of London, 2009.

Cole, Anna, Victoria K. Haskins and Fiona Paisley. *Uncommon Ground: White Women in Aboriginal History*. Canberra: Aboriginal Studies Press, 2005.

Coltheart, Lenore, ed. *Jessie Street: A Revised Autobiography*. Sydney: Federation Press, 2004.

Cunningham, K.S., ed. *Education for Complete Living, the Challenge of Today: The Proceedings of the New Education Fellowship Conference Held in Australia, August 1 to September 20, 1937*. Melbourne, London, Edinburgh: Melbourne University Press with Oxford University Press, 1938.

Curthoys, Ann. 'Paul Robeson's Visit to Australia and Aboriginal Activism, 1960'. In *Passionate Histories: Myth, Memory and Indigenous Australia*, edited by Frances Peters-Little, Ann Curthoys and John Docker, 163–84. Canberra: ANU E Press, 2010. doi.org/10.22459/PH.09.2010.08.

Curthoys, Barbara and Audrey McDonald. *More than a Hat and Glove Brigade: The Story of the Union of Australian Women*. Sydney: Union of Australian Women, 1996.

Cusack, Dymphna. *A Window in the Dark*. Edited by Debra Adelaide. Canberra: National Library of Australia, 1991.

Cusack, Dymphna. Foreword to Winifred Mitchell, *50 Years of Feminist Achievement: A History of the United Associations of Women*. Sydney: United Associations of Women, no date, c. 1980.

Dalton, Les. 'Politics of the Australian Peace Movement, 1930s to 1960s'. In *Centre for Dialogue Working Paper Series*, no. 2011/1. Melbourne: La Trobe University, 2011.

Damousi, Joy. *Women Come Rally*. Melbourne: Oxford University Press, 1994.

D'Aprano, Zelda. *Kath Williams: The Unions and the Fight for Equal Pay*. North Melbourne: Spinifex Press, 2001.

Davis, Lynne. 'Jessie Street and War-Time Child Care'. *Lilith* 6 (1989): 33–49.

Day, Robert, Lucy Woodcock and Muriel Heagney. *Are Women Paid Men's Rates?* Sydney: The Workers' Trust, 1942.

Deery, Phillip. 'The Sickle and the Scythe: Jack Blake and the Communist Party "Consolidation", 1949–1950'. *Labour History*, no. 80 (2001): 215–23. doi.org/10.2307/27516780.

Deery, Phillip. 'Menzies, the Cold War and the 1953 Convention on Peace and War'. *Australian Historical Studies* 34 (2003): 248–69. doi.org/10.1080/10314610308596254.

Deery, Phillip. 'Shunted: Ian Turner's "Industrial Experience", 1952–53'. *The Hummer* 4, no. 2 (2004): 18–29.

Deery, P. and D. Jordan. 'Fellow-Travelling in the Cold War: The Australian Peace Movement'. In *The Past Is Before Us. Refereed Proceedings of the Ninth National Labour History Conference*, edited by Greg Patmore, John Shields and Nikola Balnave, 115–23. Sydney: Australian Society for the Study of Labour History and University of Sydney, 2005.

Deery, Phillip and Craig McLean. '"Behind Enemy Lines": Menzies, Evatt and Passports for Peking'. *The Commonwealth Journal of International Affairs* 92, no. 370 (2003): 407–22. doi.org/10.1080/0035853032000111125.

Docker, John. *Australian Cultural Elites: Intellectual Traditions in Sydney and Melbourne*. Sydney: Angus and Robertson, 1974.

Forbes, Geraldine. 'The Politics of Respectability: Indian Women and the Indian National Congress'. In *The Indian National Congress: Centenary Highlights*, edited by D.A. Low, 54–97. Bombay: Oxford University Press, 1988.

Frances, Rae. 'Authentic Leaders: Women and Leadership in Australian Unions before World War II'. *Labour History* 104 (2013): 9–30.

Freeze, ChaeRan Y. and Jay M. Harris, eds. *Everyday Jewish Life in Imperial Russia: Select Documents, 1772–1914*. Lebanon, New Hampshire: Brandeis University Press, 2013.

Geetha, V. 'Periyar, Women and an Ethic of Citizenship'. *Economic and Political Weekly* 33, no. 17 (1998): WS9–WS15.

Geetha, V. and S.V. Rajadurai. *Towards a Non-Brahmin Millennium: From Iyothee Thass to Periyar*. Kolkata: Samya Press, 2007.

Godden, Judith. 'Rivett, Elsie Grace (1887–1964)'. *Australian Dictionary of Biography*, National Centre of Biography, The Australian National University, adb.anu.edu.au/biography/rivett-elsie-grace-8514/text14385, published first in hardcopy 1988, accessed online 18 November 2018.

Goodall, H. *Invasion to Embassy: Land in Aboriginal Politics, 1770–1970*. St Leonards: Allen and Unwin, 1996.

Griffin, Cheryl. 'A Biography of Doris McRae, 1893–1988'. PhD thesis, Department of Education Policy and Management, University of Melbourne, 2005.

Griffiths, P. 'Women and the Communist Party of Australia, 1920–1945'. Honours thesis, Macquarie University, 1998.

Groenewegen, Peter Diderik. *Educating for Business, Public Service and the Social Sciences: A History of the Faculty of Economics at the University of Sydney, 1920–1999*. Sydney: Sydney University Press, 2009.

Hartley, Marion. *Asia Awakes: Return to India*. Melbourne: Australian Peace Council. c. 1955.

Haskins, Victoria. *One Bright Spot*. London: Palgrave Macmillan, 2005.

Hawkes, Jacquetta. *Women Ask Why? An Intelligent Woman's Guide to Nuclear Disarmament*. London: Campaign for Nuclear Disarmament, 1962.

Hemmings, Ray. *Children's Freedom: A.S. Neill and the Evolution of the Summerhill Idea*. New York: Schocken Books, 1973.

Henry, Margaret. 'Flowering, Fading and Facing the Facts: World Education Fellowship in Queensland – 1970 to 2005'. *New Horizons* 114 (2007): 2–6.

Horne, Julia. 'The "Knowledge Front", Women, War and Peace'. *History of Education Review* 45, no. 2 (2016): 151–67. doi.org/10.1108/HER-01-2016-0004.

Horner, Jack. *Vote Ferguson for Freedom*. Sydney: Australian and NZ Book Company, 1974.

Horner, Jack. *Seeking Racial Justice: An Insider's Memoir of the Movement for Aboriginal Advancement, 1938–1978*. Canberra: Aboriginal Studies Press, 2004.

Hutchesson, George and Edna Hutchesson. *Venture in Goodwill*. Moonta, South Australia: published initially as a series of articles in the *SA Farmer*, 1955.

Irvine, R.F. *The Midas Delusion*. Adelaide: self-published, printed by Hassell Press, 1933.

Jacobs, Margaret. *White Mother to a Dark Race: Settler Colonialism, Maternalism and the Removal of Indigenous Children in the American West and Australia 1880–1940*. Lincoln: Nebraska. 2009.

Jennings, Rebecca. *Unnamed Desires: A Sydney Lesbian History*, Clayton, Vic.: Monash University Publishing, 2015.

Johnson, Audrey. *Fly a Rebel Flag: Bill Morrow, 1888–1980*. Ringwood, Vic.: Penguin, 1986.

Johnson, Penelope. 'Gender, Class and Work: The Council of Action for Equal Pay and the Equal Pay Campaign in Australia During World War II'. *Labour History*, no. 50 (1986): 132–46. doi.org/10.2307/27508787.

Jordan, Douglas. 'Conflict in the Unions: The Communist Party of Australia, Politics and the Trade Union Movement, 1945–1960'. PhD thesis, Victoria University, 2011.

Jordan, Douglas. *Conflict in the Unions: The Communist Party of Australia, Politics and the Trade Union Movement, 1945–60*. Sydney: Resistance Books, 2013.

Kennedy, Priscilla. *Portrait of Winifred West*. Sydney: The Fine Arts Press, 1976.

Khandvala, Kapila. 'Education, International Understanding and Peace'. In *Education for International Understanding: Selected Addresses to the International Education Conference Held In Australia from 31st August to 12th October, 1946*, edited by Rupert Best, 113–16. Adelaide: New Education Fellowship, 1948.

Kirkpatrick, Peter. *The Sea Coast of Bohemia: Literary Life in Sydney's Roaring Twenties*. St Lucia: University of Queensland Press, 1992.

Lake, Marilyn. 'Feminism and the Gendered Politics of Anti-racism, Australia 1927–57: From Maternal Protectionism to Leftist Assimilation'. *Australian Historical Studies* 29, no. 110 (1998): (online).

Lake, Marilyn. *Getting Equal: The History of Australian Feminism*. St Leonards: Allen and Unwin, 1999.

Lake, Marilyn. *Faith: Faith Bandler, Gentle Activist*. St Leonards: Allen and Unwin, 2002.

Larsson, Yvonne. *The World Education Fellowship: Its Origins and Development with Particular Emphasis on NSW, the First Australian Section*. Working Paper 16. London: Australian Studies Centre, Institute of Commonwealth Studies, University of London, 1987.

Lawn, Martin. 'Reflecting the Passion: Mid-century Projects for Education'. *History of Education* 33, no. 5 (2004): 505–13. doi.org/10.1080/00467600 42000254497.

Lewis, Reba. *Three Faces Has Bombay*. Bombay: Popular Book Depot, 1957.

London School Masters' Association. *Equal Pay and the Teaching Profession*. London: The Association, c. 1924.

McCallum, David. *The Social Production of Merit: Education, Psychology and Politics in Australia, 1900–1950*. London: Falmer Press, 1990.

McFarlane, B.J. 'Irvine, Robert Francis (1861–1941)'. *Australian Dictionary of Biography*, National Centre of Biography, The Australian National University, adb.anu.edu.au/biography/irvine-robert-francis-6800/text11763, published first in hardcopy 1983, accessed online 14 May 2016.

McIntyre, John. 'Theatre For Children and the Freudian Influence – A Guest Posting'. Online at Christine Brest Vickers' blog, *Freud in Oceania*, 2014. freudinoceania.com/2014/09/11/theatre-for-children-and-the-freudian-influence-a-guest-posting-from-dr-john-mcintyre/.

McIntyre, John. 'Rosemarie Benjamin and the Theatre for Children', 2013. www.artpages.com.au/Theatre_for_Children/McIntyre_Theatre%20for%20Children.pdf.

Macintyre, Stuart. 'Women's Leadership in War and Reconstruction'. *Labour History*, no. 104 (2013): 65–80. doi.org/10.5263/labourhistory.104.0065.

Mackinnon, Alison. *Women, Love and Learning: The Double Bind*. Bern: Peter Lang, 2010. doi.org/10.3726/978-3-0351-0113-3.

Mackinolty, Judy. 'To Stay or to Go: Sacking Married Teachers'. In *In Pursuit of Justice*, edited by Judy Mackinolty and Heather Radi, 71–72, 140–147. Sydney: Hale and Iremonger, 1979.

McLeod, Julie. 'Educating for "World-Mindedness": Cosmopolitanism, Localism and Schooling the Adolescent Citizen in Interwar Australia'. *Journal of Educational Administration and History* 44, no. 4 (2012): 339–59.

McLeod, Julie and Katie Wright. 'Education for Citizenship: Transnational Expertise, Curriculum Reform and Psychological Knowledge in 1930s Australia'. *History of Education Review* 42, no. 2 (2013): 170–84.

McNamara, Clarice. 'Summer School of Leadership, Newport, NSW'. *New Horizons*, Autumn 1940, 15.

Madsen, Virginia. 'Innovation, Women's Work and the Documentary Impulse: Pioneering Moments and Stalled Opportunities in Public Service Broadcasting in Australia and Britain'. *Media Information Australia* 162, no. 1 (2016): 19–32.

Malherbe, E.G., ed. *Educational Adaptations in a Changing Society: Report of the South African Education Conference held in Capetown and Johannesburg in July, 1934, Under the Auspices of the New Education Fellowship*. Capetown-Johannesburg: New Education Fellowship, 1937.

Maynard, John. *Fight for Liberty and Freedom*. Canberra: Aboriginal Studies Press, 2007.

Milner, Lisa. *Swimming Against the Tide: A Biography of Freda Brown*. Adelaide: Ginninderra Press. 2017.

Mitchell, Bruce. *Teachers, Education and Politics: A History of Organisations of Public School Teachers in New South Wales*. St Lucia: University of Queensland Press, 1975.

Mitchell, Bruce. 'Woodcock, Lucy Godiva (1889–1968)'. *Australian Dictionary of Biography*, National Centre of Biography, The Australian National University, adb.anu.edu.au/biography/woodcock-lucy-godiva-9172/text16197, published first in hardcopy 1990, accessed online 14 February 2012.

Mitchell, Susan, ed. *The Matriarchs: Twelve Australian Women Talk about Their Lives*. Ringwood, Vic.: Penguin, 1987.

Mitchell, Winifred. *50 Years of Feminist Achievement: A History of the United Associations of Women*. Sydney: United Associations of Women, no date, c. 1980.

Moore, Deirdre. *Survivors of 'Beauty': Memoirs of Dora and Bert Birtles*. Sydney: Book Collectors Society of Australia, 1996.

Moore, T. 'Australia's Bohemian Tradition'. PhD thesis, History, SOPHI, University of Sydney, 2007.

Nelson, George and Robynne Nelson. *Dharmalan Dana: An Australian Aboriginal Man's 73-Year Search for the Story of His Aboriginal and Indian Ancestors*. Canberra: ANU Press, 2014. doi.org/10.22459/DD.04.2014.

Newman, Sally. 'Silent Witness? Aileen Palmer and the Problem of Evidence in Lesbian History'. *Women's History Review* 11, no. 3 (2002): 505–30. doi.org/10.1080/09612020200200333.

North, Marilla. 'Dympha Cusack and the Hunter: A Reciprocal Impact'. In *Radical Newcastle*, edited by James Bennett, Nancy Cushing and Erik Eklund, 144–51. Sydney: NewSouth Publishing, 2015.

O'Brien, John Michael. 'The NSW Teachers Federation, 1957–1975'. PhD thesis, University of Wollongong, 1985.

O'Neill, Steve. *Development of Federal Industrial Powers*. Background paper no. 33. Canberra: Commonwealth of Australia, Parliamentary Library Research Service, 1993.

Paisley, Fiona. *Glamour in the Pacific: Cultural Internationalism and Race Politics in the Women's Pan-Pacific.* Honolulu: University of Hawai'i Press, 2009. doi.org/10.21313/hawaii/9780824833428.001.0001.

Paisley, Fiona. 'The Spoils of Opportunity: Janet Mitchell and Australian Internationalism in the Interwar Pacific'. *History Australia* 13, no. 4 (2016): 575–91. doi.org/10.1080/14490854.2016.1249273.

Palmer, Helen. *An Australian Teacher in China.* Sydney: Teachers' Sponsoring Committee, NSW Peace Council, 1953.

Phelan, Gloria. *Women in Action in the Federation: A Series of Articles.* Sydney: NSW Teachers' Federation, 1981.

Radi, Heather, ed. *Jessie Street: Documents and Essays.* Broadway, NSW: Women's Redress Press, 1990.

Ranald, Pat. 'Feminism and Class: The United Associations of Women and the Council of Action on Equal Pay in the Depression'. In *Worth Her Salt: Women at Work in Australia*, edited by Margaret Bevege, Margaret James, Carmel Shute, 270–85. Sydney: Hale and Iremonger, 1982.

Ranald, Pat, 'Women's Organisations and Communism'. In *Better Dead than Red: Australia's First Cold War, 1945–1952*, edited by A. Curthoys and J. Merritt, Vol. 2, 41–57. Sydney: Allen and Unwin, 1986.

Raza, Ali, Franziska Roy and Benjamin Zachariah, eds. *The Internationalist Moment: South Asia, Worlds, and World Views, 1917–39.* New Delhi, Thousand Oaks, London, Singapore: Sage, 2015. doi.org/10.4135/9789351507994.

Roe, Michael. *Nine Australian Progressives: Vitalism in Bourgeois Social Thought 1890–1960.* St Lucia: University of Queensland Press, 1984.

Rowse, Tim. *Nugget Coombs: A Reforming Life.* Cambridge: Cambridge University Press, 2005.

Russell, Lani and Marian Sawer. 'The Rise and Fall of the Australian Women's Bureau'. *Australian Journal of Politics and History* 45, no. 3 (1999): 362–75.

Saha, Panchanan. *Rajani Palme Dutt: A Biography.* Kolkata: Biswabiksha, 2004.

Salt, Annette. 'Women of the Northern Coalfields of NSW'. *Labour History*, no. 48 (1985): 44–53.

Sanders, Anne. 'Burgmann, Ernest Henry (1885–1967)'. In *Inner Worlds: Portraits & Psychology*, edited by C. Chapman, 134–37. Canberra: National Portrait Gallery, 2011.

Schedvin, C.B. 'Rivett, Sir Albert Cherbury David (1885–1961)'. *Australian Dictionary of Biography*, National Centre of Biography, The Australian National University, adb.anu.edu.au/biography/rivett-sir-albert-cherbury-david-8512/text14381, published first in hardcopy 1988, accessed online 31 January 2013.

Sekuless, Peter. *Jessie Street: A Rewarding but Unrewarded Life*. St Lucia: University of Queensland Press, 1978.

Shorten, Ann R. 'The Legal Context of Australian Education: An Historical Exploration'. *Australia New Zealand Journal of Law Education* 1, no. 1 (1996): 2–32.

Simic, Zora. 'A New Age? Australian Feminism and the 1940s'. *Hecate* 32, no. 1 (2006): 152–72.

Simic, Zora. 'Butter not Bombs: A Short History of the Union of Australian Women'. *History Australia* 4, no. 1 (2007): 07.1–07.15.

Spaull, A.D. 'Teachers and Politics: A Comparative Study of State Teachers' Organizations in Victoria and New South Wales Since 1940'. PhD thesis, Monash University, 1972.

Stevens, Joyce. *A History of International Women's Day in Words and Pictures*. [Pennington, SA]: IWD Press, 1985. Online: www.isis.aust.com/iwd/stevens/joyce.htm, accessed December 2017.

Stevens, Joyce. *Taking the Revolution Home – Work Among Women in the Communist Party of Australia, 1920–1945*. Melbourne: Sybylla Cooperative Press, 1987.

Street, Jessie M.G. *Truth or Repose*. Sydney: Australasian Book Society, 1966.

Sullivan, Martin. 'Taylor, Beatrice Mary (1893–1982)'. *Australian Dictionary of Biography*, National Centre of Biography, The Australian National University, adb.anu.edu.au/biography/taylor-beatrice-mary-15677/text26875, published first in hardcopy 2012, accessed online 18 November 2018.

Sullivan, Martin. 'Lewis, Samuel Phineas (Sam) (1901–1976)'. *Australian Dictionary of Biography*, National Centre of Biography, The Australian National University, adb.anu.edu.au/biography/lewis-samuel-phineas-sam-10825/text19205, published first in hardcopy 2000, accessed online 6 October 2015.

Summy, Ralph and Malcolm Saunders. 'The 1959 Melbourne Peace Congress: Culmination of Anti-communism in Australia in the 1950s'. In *Better Dead than Red: Australia's First Cold War: 1945–1959*, edited by Ann Curthoys and John Merritt, 74–98. Sydney: Allen and Unwin, 1986.

Symons, Beverley. 'Muriel Heagney and the Fight for Equal Pay During World War Two'. *The Hummer* 3, no. 1 (Summer 1998–99): 1–13.

Theobald, Marjorie R. *Knowing Women: Origins of Women's Education in Nineteenth-Century Australia*. Cambridge: Cambridge University Press, 1996.

Theobald, Marjorie R. 'And gladly teach? The Making of a Woman's Profession'. In *Women Teaching Women Learning: Historical Perspectives*, edited by Elizabeth Smyth and Paula Bourne, 65–85. Toronto: Innana Publications, 2006.

Theobald, Marjorie and Donna Dwyer. 'An Episode in Feminist Politics: The Married Women (Lecturers and Teachers) Act, 1932–47'. *Labour History*, no. 76 (1999): 59–77. doi.org/10.2307/27516628.

Turner, Ian. 'My Long March'. *Overland* 59 (Spring 1974): 23–40.

Wadia, Avabai B. *The Light Is Ours: Memoirs and Movements*. Regents Park, UK: International Planned Parenthood Federation, 2001.

Ward, Chloe. 'Activism without Discrimination'. In *The Transnational Activist: Transformations and Comparisons from the Anglo-World since the Nineteenth Century*, edited by Stefan Berger and Sean Scalmer, 227–56. Palgrave Studies in the History of Social Movements. New York: Springer, 2017.

Watras, Joseph. 'The New Education Fellowship and UNESCO's Program of Fundamental Education'. *Paedagogica Historica: International Journal of the History of Education* 47, no. 1–2 (2011): 191–205.

White, Margaret. 'The New Education Fellowship: An International Community of Practice'. *New Era in Education* 82, no. 3 (2001): 71–75.

White, Margaret. 'Traversing Personal and Public Boundaries: Discourses of Engagement in New Education, 1930s to 1980s'. *Paedogogica Historica* 43, no. 1 (2007): 151–63. doi.org/10.1080/00309230601080634.

Whitehead, K. 'The Spinster Teacher in Australia from the 1870s to the 1960s'. *History of Education Review* 36, no. 1 (2007): 1–17. doi.org/10.1108/08198691200700001.

Whitehead, K. 'Exchange Teachers as "Another Link in Binding the [British] Empire" in the Interwar Years'. *Social and Education History* 3, no. 1 (2014): 1–24.

Whitehead, Kay and Stephen Thorpe. 'The Function of Age and the History of Women's Work: The Career of an Australian Teacher, 1907–1947'. *Gender and History* 16, no. 1 (2004): 172–97. doi.org/10.1111/j.0953-5233.2004.332_1.x.

Whitehead, Kay and Judith Peppard. 'Transnational Innovations, Local Conditions and Disruptive Teachers and Students in Interwar Education'. *Paedagogica Historica* 42, nos 1 & 2 (2006): 177–89. doi.org/10.1080/00309230600552112.

Women's Propaganda Committee for Combined Women's Teachers' Association of New South Wales. *Justice vs Tradition*. Sydney: Epworth Press, 1925.

Woodcock, Lucy Godiva. Foreword to Helen Palmer, *An Australian Teacher in China*. Sydney: Teachers' Sponsoring Committee, Australian Peace Council, 1953.

Woodcock, Lucy Godiva. *The Lewis Case and You*, April. Sydney: self-published with donations, 1956.

Author Biographies

Heather Goodall is a historian and Professor Emerita at the University of Technology Sydney. She is the author of *Invasion to Embassy: Land in Aboriginal Politics in NSW* (1996) and *Beyond Borders: Indians, Australians and the Indonesian Revolution, 1939–1950* (2018). She has co-authored and co-edited a number of volumes on environmental history (2006, 2009, 2017) and collaborated with Indigenous authors Isabel Flick and Kevin Cook on their autobiographies (2004 and 2013).

Helen Randerson is a Sydney-based researcher whose interests have focused on inner-city areas as places of radical activity including their industrial and trade union histories. She is the author of 'The Red with the Green Thumb' in *Dirty Secrets: Our ASIO Files* by Meredith Burgmann (2014) and co-author with Max Solling of 'Forest Lodge' for the *Dictionary of Sydney* (2018).

Devleena Ghosh is Professor of Social and Political Sciences at the Faculty of Arts and Social Sciences at the University of Technology Sydney. She is the author of *Colonialism and Modernity* (with Paul Gillen, UNSW Press, 2007) and editor of *Women in Asia: Shadowlines* (Cambridge Scholars Press, 2012), *Water, Sovereignty and Borders in Asia and Oceania* (with Heather Goodall and Stephanie Hemelryk Donald, Routledge, 2009) and *The Cultures of Trade: Indian Ocean Exchanges* (with Stephen Muecke, Cambridge Scholars Press, 2007). She has also published widely in the areas of environmental and gender studies in South Asia.

Index

Aboriginal activists 127, 167, 175, 183, 248
Aboriginal-Australian Fellowship (AAF) 59, 61, 63, 168, 284, 288, 291
    Lucy's role in AAF formation 249–251
Aboriginal people 7, 14, 127–129, 130, 167, 175, 203, 260, 273, 287, 288–289, 291, 310
    Indian views (1946) about 179
    Lucy's pupils and families 31, 63–64, 71, 122
    Peace Conference and Aboriginal people 211–213
    Urban Aboriginal conditions 165, 175
    Women's movement, contradictory views about Aboriginal people 151–152, 161, 164–165
    Woman's Charter (1946) 182–183
Aborigines Progressive Association 248
Aborigines Protection Board 127
activism of Aboriginal Australians 127
    campaign for full citizens' rights 175
    see also Day of Mourning
All-India Peace Congress, Madras 235–238
All India Women's Conference (AIWC) 156, 234
    break-away National Federation of Indian Women 234–235
    Cooperatives, AIWC role in 274
    Indian Women's Charter 169–170, 173–175
    parallels with United Associations of Women 235–238
    representatives visit 1946 177–186
Alley, Rewi 256, 259, 261
    Australian visit (1960) 296
    biography 12–13
    cooperatives 228, 232–233
    Lucy's correspondence with 83, 92, 146, 230, 251–253, 255–256, 284, 296, 308
    Lucy's meeting with (1954) 12, 228–229
    Peace Movement 256–257, 273, 277
    sexual orientation 13
    Sino-Soviet rift 280
Anand, Mulk Raj 239
Anderson, John 24–25
Anderson, Rev. N. St Clair 203, 224
Andreen, Andrea 232
Andrews, C.F. 195
Arundale, George 66
Atlantic Charter (1941) 154, 159, 163, 184

atomic bombing of Japan 86, 223, 229–230, 242
atomic testing 279–80
   British testing, Australia 146, 179, 212, 223, 277
   French testing, Mururoa Atoll 280
   US testing, Marshall Islands 218, 224
      Bravo H-bomb Bikini Atoll (1954) 224, 231
      Lucky Dragon survivors 231
atomic weapons 179, 184, 198, 218, 229
   move to outlaw 230–231, 241
Australia–China Society 261, 287, 295, 296, 300 (later the Australia–China Friendship Society 226)
Australia First movement 127, 128
Australia–New Zealand Congress for International Cooperation and Disarmament 75–76
Australia–Soviet Friendship Society 254, 255
Australian Atomic Energy Bill 203
Australian Chinese community 51, 284
Australian Convention on Peace and War (1953) 75, 203, 210–214
   publication of findings in *Convention Record* 212, 214
Australian Council for Educational Research 113
Australian Council of Trade Unions (ACTU) 92, 267, 310
Australian Federation of Women Voters (AFWV) 219, 220–221, 225, 274
Australian Fellowship of Writers 117, 186
Australian Labor Party (ALP) 7, 8, 10, 92, 252, 253, 256, 260, 276, 277
Australian Peace Council 199, 256

Australian Security Intelligence Organisation (ASIO) 118, 135, 146, 219, 220, 227, 242, 261, 274, 289, 291, 295
Australian Teachers' Federation (ATF) 11, 45, 49, 62, 98, 101, 104, 133, 137, 149, 189–190, 198, 274
Australian Woman's Charter (1943) 159–165, 169
Australian Woman's Charter (1946) 170–172, 175–186, 292
   call for close relationships between world powers 184
   call to outlaw atomic weapons 184
   conference (1946) 175–181
   conference outcomes 188
   charter clauses 181–184
   contradictory recommendations on Aboriginal people 182–183
Australian Workers' Union 127

Bandler, Faith 59, 248–249, 280
Bandung Conference 241, 242
Baracchi, Guido 24
Barnes, Lucie 285
Barton, E.C. 58
Baume, Eric 263
Bavin Government 90, 91, 93
Beeby, G.S. 92
Bendeich, Sam 92
Benjamin, Rosemary 36, 108, 116, 117, 120
Bennett, Mary 151, 161, 164
Bertie, Charles 70, 71
Bickerton, Max 228
Birtles, Bert 109
Birtles, Dora 25, 109–110, 123
Blake, J.D. 206–207
Bland, F.A. 22
Board, Peter 19
Bocking, Zillah 82, 137
Bodenweiser, Gertrud 117
bohemianism 6, 7, 9, 13, 14, 23, 24–26

Boney, Mrs 291
Boomla, Kitty (Ketayun) 156
Broken Hill Shop Assistants' Union 265–266
Brown, Freda 219, 283, 292
Brown, Lee (now Rhiannon) 177
Brown, Norman 44
Boys' Town initiative at Engadine 118
Burgmann, Bishop Ernest Henry 136
Business & Professional Women's Club (B&P Club) 260
Byk, Hilde 120

Cairns, Shirley 286
Campbell, Craig 118
Campbell, Persia 35
Carnegie Corporation of New York (CCNY) 113
Cecil, Robert 128
Cessnock 41, 42, 44, 45, 46, 48, 50, 61
    coalminers' strike 41–43
Cessnock Citizen's Relief Committee 43
Cessnock Public School 43–51
Chakravartty, Renu 156
Chapman, Geoff 210
charter, concept of 154
Chaudhuri, Pramila (née Bannerjee) 66
childcare 111, 167, 311
    Kindergarten Union 148
    Sydney Day Nurseries Association 148
    wartime childcare 147–149
child endowment 35, 46, 47–48, 51, 52, 62, 84, 146–147
Children's Library and Craft Movement
    Erskineville 68–76
    Phillip Street 71
    Surry Hills 23, 68–69
    Woolloomooloo 71

China 33, 51, 92, 115, 123, 151, 201, 202, 233, 254, 296
    All China Women's Foundation (later Federation) 286
    India–China unity 237
    Industrial Co-operative Movement (CIC) 228
    Japanese invasion of 51–52, 176
    Lucy's attempted travel to (1952) 201–202
    Lucy's travel to (1954) 226–229
    Lucy's travel to (1964) 259, 295–295
    Sino-Soviet rift 280, 283
    Western puritanism embraced after 1949 13, 228
    women in 270, 295, 300
Chinese-background students 296–300
Chinese Youth League 287
Chou En Lai 234, 242
Christesen, C.B. 210–211
Christian, Millicent 255
Christian Socialists 123
Clerical Workers' Union 285
Clint, Rev. Alf 136, 203, 208, 219, 257, 274, 278, 289
Clubbe, Phyllis 66
Cold War 8, 29, 168, 169, 170, 172, 176, 181, 207, 245, 283, 307
Collocott, Rev. E.E.V. 216
Colombo Plan 215, 277, 296
colonialism 5, 33–34, 211–212
    anti-colonial movements 154, 176
    decolonisation 167, 190–191
    international campaign for decolonisation 175
Combined Women Teachers' Association of NSW 33
Committee for the Care of the Child in War Time 148
communism 23, 170, 220, 274, 276
    anti-communism 7, 113, 200, 283, 284
    fear of 168

Communist Party of Australia (CPA) 10, 11, 24, 90, 93, 97, 118, 128, 146, 207, 243, 255
Communist Party of India (CPI) 235
Conference 'Education for a Progressive, Democratic Australia, Sydney' (1938) 50
Cooper, Ada 211
Cooper, William 211
Cot, Pierre 128
Council for Action on Equal Pay (CAEP) 103–105, 153, 164–165, 167, 176
Country Women's Association 31
Courier (UNESCO) 199
Cousins, Margaret 154, 237
Crabb, Dorothy 262
Crase, Janice 297
Creative Leisure Movement 70, 133
Crowley, Grace 23
Cunningham, Ettie 32, 92
Currey, C.H. 96
Curtin, John 151, 153, 165
Cusack, Dymphna 50

Dalton, Nora 61
Darlington Public School 23, 30, 35, 41, 61, 203
Davies, William 91–92
Davis, Flo 147, 248, 251, 291
Day, Robert L. 104, 165
Day of Mourning 127, 128, 129, 175, 248
Dazaud, Christiane 191
Deamer, Dulcie 25
Democratic Labor Party (DLP) 277, 283, 284
Depression
    1890s 19
    1930s 22, 41, 50–52, 61, 68, 71, 78, 89, 98, 107, 112
Dick, N.H. 55
Dickie, Rev. Alf 220
Domestic Workers' Association 95

Drummond, D.H. 48, 49–50, 51, 96–97, 136
Duguid, Phyllis 151
Dunne, Betty 269

Easter Rebellion in Ireland 154
Eden, NSW 17–19
education 9
    'child-centred' education 36–37, 65, 71, 112, 160, 163, 189, 208
    Dewey experiential learning 66
    differences between primary and secondary education 27
    'educability' 114
    importance of physical environment 55–57
    influence of psychology as a discipline 113
    IQ testing 114–115, 121, 122, 160, 163
    Lucy's aims for education 67, 79, 100, 123–124, 133, 146
    need for curriculum changes 65
    opportunity classes 85, 114, 160
    peacetime reconstruction, role in 146
    progressive education 65, 66, 68, 160
    research into 113, 116, 138, 163
    sex education 149
    teaching 27
        for Peace 118–119
        role in expansion of European colonialism 2
        teachers seen as above industrial workers 97
    teaching strategies
        emphasis on discussion and free exchange of views 138
        use of theatre as teaching aid 36, 76, 84, 108, 116
    UNESCO work in 'Fundamental Education' 189
    vocational training for girls 81

Education (journal) 115
Education Charter (1952) 200
Educational Workers' League (EWL) 91
Edwards, Kit 12, 297, 298, 299, **313**
Edwards, Maurice 204
Eldershaw, Flora 22
Elkin, A.P. 129, 149
Ellison, Una F. 104
employment 5, 22, 78, 79, 86, 92, 105, 150, 153, 233, 267, 307, 309, 314
    gender equality in 22
    high unemployment in Erskineville 46, 53, 82
    married women 90, 91, 92, 93, 94, 95, 98, 150–151, 262, 267
    pay cuts 90, 93, 104
    rates of pay 78, 79
    Subsidised Apprenticeship Scheme for Unemployed Youths 82
    unemployment relief 310
    women 182, 182, 185
English, Cecil 296
Ensor, Beatrice 66, 75, 112, 116
equal rights for women 3, 26, 152, 162, 287, 292
    access to education 160, 172, 188, 261, 295
    Equal Pay 31–32, 94, 97, 153, 181, 281, 308–310
    Equal Pay for Equal Work 20, 31, 32, 34, 89, 291
Equal Rights International (USA) 152
Erskineville
    Depression, effect on 54
    poor state of housing 53, 55
Erskineville Public School 54–57, 60–67, 76–78, 84, 86
Erskineville YWCA Girls Club 68
Evatt, Clive 102, 161
Evatt, H.V. ('Bert') 22, 163
Exchange Teachers' Club 37

fascism 109, 129, 198
    anti-fascist movements 122, 123
federal Arbitration Court 101
federal Arbitration system 22, 98
federal government
    Aboriginal people, failed referendum 165
    Border control (passports, immigration) 123, 136, 161, 201, 219, 287
    Cold War, anti-communism 208, 219
    education 137
    industrial laws 42, 268, 269, 270
    International relations, peace and war 199
    malnutrition, school children 49
    reconstruction, postwar 159
    sesquicentenary (1938) 127
    social services 149
Federated Clerks' Union 102
Federated State School Teachers' Association (FSSTA) (1924–1937) 11, 78, 79, 82, 89, 98–99, 101, 102, 104, 120, 133, 273
    Lucy as first woman President (1932) 45, 49
Feminist Club 175
Feng, Chao 286
Ferguson, Bill 127, 175, 248
Finey, George 24
Fink Latukefu, Ruth 59, 110, 120–123, 152
Fink, Lotte 110–111, 120–123, **125**, 149, 152, 161, 177, 202, 239, 293, 314
Fink, Siegfried (Friedel) 111, 120
Fink, Thomas 110, 122
Fizelle, Rah 6, 23, 60, 203
Fordyce, Elizabeth 90, 309
Frensham school 66, 108, 118

Gandhi, Indira 272
Gandhi, Mohandas 5, 155, 157, 176
Gaobepe, Godsiang 264
gender discrimination 4, 20, 25–26, 31, 33–34, 94, 96, 97, 99, 100, 151, 167, 170, 223, 267
    gendered constraints on women 13, 27
    opposition to 172, 188, 199, 214, 247, 271
    single women stigmatised 27
Gerwani (*Gerakan Wanita Indonesia*, or Indonesian Women's Movement) 281, 286
Gibbs, Pearl 59, 61, 64, 128, 129, 164, 175, 248–249
Gilmore, Dame Mary 218, 310
Glover, Rev. Neil 219, 243
Gmeiner, Leonora 307
Golding, Annie 19–20, 310
Golding, Belle 310
Golding, Kate (later Dwyer) 31, 310
Goldschmidt family 111
Goldstein, Vida 51
Gollan, Bill 219, 243, 257, 278
Gollan, Marie 130, 147
Gordon, L.A. 139
Greville, Henrietta 218
'Groupers' ('Industrial Groupers' associated with DLP) 253, 283–284
Guiterman, Rosine 293
Gyan Chand, Anasuya 232, **233**, 235, 274

Hambly, Helen 291
Hampson, Enid **290**, 292
Harding, Sylvia 285
Harford, Lesbia 24
Harris, Thistle 198
Harrison, B. 252
Hartley, Marion 237
Harvester Judgement (1907) 47

Haley, Father A.N. 219
Heagney, Muriel 103
Heath, Harry 30, 216, 246, 311
Hebrew Standard of Australasia 124
Heffron, R.J. 86, 201, 216, 217, 219, 311
Heins, Carl 256
Heins, Susie 256
Henry, Margaret 117
Hermes 26
High Court 101
Hill, Ted 207
Hinder, Eleanor 151
Hinder, Frank 23
Hinder, Margel 23
Home Service Company 95
homosexuals, difficulties of 10, 13, 228
Horner, Jack 31, 64, 249
Hornibrook, P.E. 118
Hotel, Club and Restaurant Employees' Union (HCRE) 147, 248, 291
Hu Shih 115
Hughes, Andrew 237
Hughes, John 103, 104
Hungary (1956) 251, 255, 283

India 241, 254, 263–264, 270, 276
    Amritsar massacre 154
    Australian teachers in 5, 66, 68, 108, 196, 307
    cooperatives as a means to deliver training in 233, 273–274
    disadvantage of women in 33, 157, 270
    equal rights in 173, 270, 272
    exclusion, White Australia 7
    'Five Principles of Peaceful Coexistence' 234, 237, 242
    food shortages 184
    independence movements 157
    Independent India post-1947 202
    India–China unity 237

INDEX

Indian women's movement 9, 14, 156, 173–189, 234, 270
  Lucy's travels to 4, 14, 225, 230, 232–239
  Peace movement 8, 241–242
  possibilities offered by social change 14
  Theosophy 116, 154, 155, 164, 307
  trade unions 178, 232
  see also Women's Indian Association (WIA)
Indian National Congress 169
Indian Women's Charter of Rights and Duties (1946) 167, 169, 170, 171, 173–175
Industrial Workers of the World (Wobblies or IWW) 24, 25
Institute of Pacific Relations 113, 115
International Federation of Teachers' Associations (IFTA) 189
International Labour Organization (ILO) 270, 307
International Peace Campaign (IPC) 128, 129, 131, 132, 197
International Teachers Charter 172, 190
International Women's Day (IWD) 9, 76, 161, 260, 283, 284–287, 291–292
Irvine, R.F. 6, 22, 23, 27–29, 55, 91
  forced resignation 28
Irvine, Ysobel 6, 23, 29
Isaacs, Susan 116, 117

James, Shadrack 211–212, 214
James, Thomas 211
Japan 8, 157, 218, 225, 227, 228–231, 241, 254, 257, 270, 275
  invasion of China 51–52, 176
Jewish refugees 110, 112, 152, 301, 305
  difficulty in gaining entry to British dominions 111
  émigré Jewish networks 117
  interest in innovative education 112
  see also refugees
Johnson, Florence 93
Johnson, Phyllis 97
Julian Ashton's Art School 23

Kanuga, Vidya (later Munsi) 156
Kay, John (Kurt Kaiser) 117
Kelly, Caroline Tennant 128, 129, 130, 131, 175, 183
Kent-Hughes, Margaret 90
Kevans, Denis 294
Khandvala, Kapila 170, **171**, 177–178, 181, 183, 184–186, 198, 202, 214, 234–235, 238, **240**, 263, 308
Khandvala, T.C. 177

Labor Women's Organising Committee 280
Lady Gowrie Pre-school Child Centre 53, 68
Lam, Mithan 170, **171**, 172, 177–179, 180–81, 183, 184, 185–186, 198, 214, 234–235, 308
Lamport, Nellie 287
Lang, J.T. 91, 92, 98, 188, 220
Lang Labor Government 93, 95
Lange, D. 204
Langley, Beverley (now Bates) 60, 63–64, 71, 79, 108, 141, 196
Latukefu, Sione 122
Lawson, Bertha 310
League of Nations 114, 115, 128, 130, 131, 132, 154, 159, 168, 307
Left Book Club 119
Lewis, Reba 238, 308
Lewis, Sam 11, 22, 23, 45, 59, 109, **133**, 146, **187**, 216, 220, **253**, 261, **306**
  Conference 'Education for a Progressive, Democratic Australia' (1938), Coordinator 132, 135–139

343

Educational Workers' League
(EWL) 91, 102
Equal Pay, consistent support for
105, 187, 208
married women, opposition to
forced retirement 96, 146
Public Service Board, conflict
with 245–247
tribute to Lucy 12, 29–30, 87,
217, 312
UNESCO 198, 200
Li The-Chuan 230
Lindsay, Jack 22, 24
Littlejohn, Linda 151
London County Council 36, 37, 65,
108
Lovett, F. 265–266
Lucas, Ruth 90
Luxton, Joan 36

Mackinnon, Malcolm 37
Makin, Betty 52–54, 59, 62, 67, 81,
141
Makinson, Rachel 156, 179, 184, 243
Makinson, Richard (REB) 156, 243
Malayan students 300
Malherbe, E.G. 114
Martin, Mary 25
Matheson, Mary (Doris May Rivett)
68–69, 75
Matthias, Betsy 25
Mattick, Elizabeth 22, 253, **253**
McDonald, Audrey 285
McDougall, Bonnie 83
McFarlane, Bruce 23, 28
McGuinness, Alfred 96, 101
McNamara, Clarice 93, 117, 139,
146, 147, 219
Meanjin (journal) 210
Medworth, Frank 187
Mehta, Hansa 170
Men's Assistants' Association 91
Mitchell, Judith (later Emmett) 60,
82

Morrow, Bill 219, 243
Mukherjee, Geeta 292

Narasimhan, Padma 237
National Council of Jewish Women
(NCJW) 110, 123, 152, 161
National Council of Women (NCW)
35, 130, 204, 286
National Federation of Indian
Women (NFIW) 232, 234–235,
237, 238
National Women's Peace Conference
129–130
Nazi Germany
New Education Fellowship and
Nazism 129
persecution of Jewish people 110,
111, 152
teachers' awareness of rise of
108–110, 129
Nehru, Jawaharlal 233, 234, 242, 272
Nehru, Rameshwari 235
Nelson, Edna (Edna Ryan) 36
New Education Fellowship (NEF) 9,
55, 61, 65–66, 95, 146, 172, 189,
196, 223, 276, 306
Conference 'Education for
Complete Living' (1937)
115–116
Australian Press response 1937
118
Conference 'Education for
International Understanding'
(1946) 116, 179–180, 198
cultural receptiveness and
cosmopolitanism 153
familiar to European refugees 112
India 276
innovative educational approaches
66
Newson, Vivienne 12, 248, 262, 268,
281, 293
New Zealand 13, 18, 37, 111, 115,
227

Newth, H.G. 110
Newth, Nan 110
Nikoley, Tatyana 289
Noble, R.B. 139
non-aligned movement, Bandung Conference 241–243
Norington, Harry (Hal) 187
NSW Education Department 27, 35, 51, 102, 128, 201, 276
NSW Government 43, 69, 82, 90, 247, 308
NSW Peace Council 75, 119, 198–202, 216, 218–221, 223–239, 241–257
NSW Public Service (Salaries Reduction) Act 1930 90
NSW Teachers' Association 20
NSW Teachers Federation 9, 41, 49, 58, 60, 82, 89, 92, 102, 145, 148, 163, 172, 189, 308
   Cessnock branch 43
   Combined Women Teachers' Association of NSW 33
   Conference 'Education for a Progressive, Democratic Australia' (1938) 127–143
   Conference on Education (1958) 274–276
   discipline, corporal punishment 246
   Equal Pay and Equal Status Committee 20, 31–34, 90, 104–105
   formation (September 1918), Lucy's role 19, 21–22, 29, 273
   Lucy's elected positions in the Union
      Vice President (1925, 1933) 35, 96
      Senior Vice President (1934–1953) 11, 49, 103–104, 129, 133, 136–137, 146, 215, 217, 310
      Delegate, Interstate Teachers' Conference (1925) 47, 32
      Delegate, NSW Trades and Labor Council (TLC) 186, 206, 217, 267, 287
      Delegate, Australian Council of Trade Unions (ACTU) 231, 266, 267–269
      Delegate, Asia-Pacific Peace Conference, Peking (1952) 200–202
   malnutrition, among children of unemployed 48, 50, 52
   married women teachers dismissal 94–96, 98
   New Education Fellowship 115–118
   Peace Group 129–132, 150, 197–199, 208
   UNESCO Charter of Education (including Teachers' and Youth Charters) 190–192
   Windsor and Richmond Branch 100
NSW Trades and Labor Council (TLC) 186, 206, 217, 267, 287
NSW Women Assistant Teachers' Association 19, 91

O'Harris, Pixie 203
Open Door International (ODI) 221, 225, 263
Opie, Mrs 183
Owen, Rev. J.E. 208

Paddison, Alf 91
Palmer, Aileen 123
Palmer, Helen 123, 201, 202, 225, 255
Palmer, Nettie 123, 201
Palmer, Vance 123, 201
Pandit, Vijaya Lakshmi 218, 236
Parker, Margaret 201
Parramatta Historical Society 31
Patten, Jack 127, 175, 248
Peace movement 7, 157, 195–220, 234–239, 241–257

Peace News 224, 230
People of the Pindan 288
Phelan, Gloria 86
poverty 78, 86, 159
    Cessnock 41–45
    Erskineville 76–87
    housing conditions 53–55
    hunger 41–52
    overcrowding 41, 42, 52, 61
    rural poverty 45
Powell, J.B. 252
Powell, Sylvia 252
Prichard, Katherine Susannah 24, 130, 183
Public Service (Salaries Reduction) Amendment Act 1931 93
Public Service Association 132, 293
Public Service Board 102, 129, 246, 247, 271
pupil-teacher 17, 18, 19, 30

racism 130, 247
    Australian anti-Semitism 111, 130
    Australian racism 51, 257
    eugenics 34, 114
    European racism and persecution 4, 107
    experience of the East End Jewish community 108
    prejudice against Aboriginal people 130
    racial discrimination 110, 161, 167, 291
        opposition to 172, 188, 199, 214, 247, 301
    'racial hygiene' used to justify eugenicist measures 114
    'scientific' testing to identify class and racial 'educability' 114
Ramasamy, E.V. 237
Ravenscroft, Mona 147
Reading, Fanny 110, 111, 120, 123, 152, 161, 176
Reeve, Ellen Grace 189, 198, 208

refugees 4, 7, 51, 108–112, 117, 120, 123, 152, 176, 238, 256, 301, 308
Reilly, Betty 11, 307
Rich, Ruby 110–111
Rischbieth, Bessie 130
Rivett, Rev. Albert 68, 195, 196
Rivett, David 22, 196
Rivett, Eleanor 157, 232, 307
Rivett, Elsie 68, 69, 70, **70**, 123, 195, 208, 280, 285, 294
Robeson, Paul and Eslanda 288, 291
Robertson, Alec 294
Robinovitz, Isaac 18
Robinovitz family 17, 18–19, 108, 110, 140, 223, 301, 308
Rockefeller Foundation 113
Rosa, Sam 24, 25
Rose, Jess 89, 90, 120, 131, 196, 293, 309
Rosenberg, Ethel 202–203, 252
Rosenberg, Julius 202–203, 252
Ross, Hettie 89, 90, 91, 93, 146
Rothbury 42, 44
Rourke, E.J. 96
Rusijati, Mrs 286, 287
Russia 4, 7, 18, 66, 81, 110, 135, 136, 176, 255, 263, 264, 289
Russian Social Club 291

Salvation Army 131, 179
Sastri, V.S. Srinivasa 115
Sawtell, Michael 127
Sayle, Murray 86
Schuman, Julian 252
Seidler, Max 123
Seidler, Rose 123
Self-Respect Movement 237–238
Sharkey, L.L. (Lance) 207
Six Point Group 225, 251
Smith's Weekly 140, 141
South Australian Farmer 230
South Western Advertiser 148

Soviet Union (USSR) 8, 81, 101, 135, 153, 184, 203, 225, 239, 243, 245, 247, 253, 254, 255, 263, 264, 270, 274, 283, 291–292, 294
Spanish Civil War 109
Spender, P.C. 22
Stevens, Bertram 96
Street, Jessie 5, 102, 165, 186, **226**, **227**, **233**, **236**, **240**, 251, 252, 253, 265, 308
    Aboriginal people 151–152, 249
    alliance with unions and Lucy 94–97, 147
    biography 8, 158, 225
    Charter, role in 159–162, 169–182
    class differences from Lucy 225, 262
    travels with Lucy, (1954–1955) 223–240
    USSR 135–136, 255
    United Associations of Women, leadership role in 95, 262–263
    United Nations 241
    writing retreat, North Coast 294
Students' Representative Council (SRC) 210
Sutton, Harvey 48–49
Swann, Margaret 31, 90, 309
Sydney Girls' High 46, 49, 122
Sydney Morning Herald 75, 96, 148, 266
Sydney University Economics Society 35
Sydney University Women's Graduates Association 35
Symonds, Queenie 17
Symonds, Rose 90, 309
Symons, Antony 297

Tai, Yi-Feng 286
Taylor, Beatrice 32, 89, 90, 91, 92, 102, 146, 217, 246, 293
Taylor, Don 217
Taylor, Esther 251
Teachers' Anti-Communist League 283
Teachers' Charter, 1950 167
teachers' organisations seen as industrial unions 6
Teerman, Ethel Caroline (later Lewis) 11, 45, 136, 208, 220, **306**
    Educational Workers' League 91
    Peace Committee, NSW Teachers Federation 128–132, 197
    retirement, forced on marriage 139, 146, 150, 198
Teerman, Ethel Nelson 42–45
Teerman, Jack 42, 43, 44
The Century 220
The Hindu 236, 237, 238
Theosophy 66, 95, 112, 116, 123, 157
    strong bases in India and Ceylon 116
    Theosophical Society, Adyar, Madras 154, 237
Tribe, Muriel 255
Tribune 84, 212, 227, 284, 288
Trivedi, C.M. 177, 238
Truth 25, 129
Tsurumi, Yusuke 115

UA Newsheet 260–265, 293, 310, 314
    changed emphasis under Lucy's presidency 262–265
        Apartheid and anti-racism 273, 276–280
        civil rights 271–277
        economics, Equal Pay and unions 265–271, 291
        Peace 277–281
UN Commission on the Status of Women 169
UNESCO 167, 169, 172, 187, 188–189, 190–191, 192, 197, 199, 200, 219, 223
UNESCO Charter on Education, 1946 172

UNESCO Teachers' Charter, 1947–54 167
  principle that racial and gender discrimination were linked 172
union publications
  Common Cause 25
  Labor Daily 25
United Associations of Women (UA) 102, 122, 154, 156, 165, 241, 247, 248, 255, 284, 296
  Aboriginal people 127, 248
  alliance with Teachers Federation 94–98
  Anti-racism 151–3
  Asia and Peace trip, Lucy's Reports (1954–1955) 221–239
  Australian Woman's Charter (1943, 1946) 167–193
  childcare, wartime 147
  China, visit (1964) 295, 296
  Cold War, UA break with AFWV (1954) 216–220
  Equal Pay 103–104, 309–310
  International Women's Day 283–294
  Lucy as Vice-President (1956) 247–248
  Lucy as President (1957–1968) 9, 247, 259–281
  married women's employment 94–98, 145, 151
  Newsheet 12, 22, 248
  see also UA Newsheet
  Six Point Group, UK 251–252
Union of Australian Women (UAW) 218, 225, 233, 234–235, 261, 276, 285, 286, 292, 310
United Kingdom (UK) 2, 8, 36, 37, 49, 66, 108, 112, 114, 154, 156, 158, 189, 252, 263, 264, 276, 278, 279
United Nations (UN) 154, 169, 183, 184, 214, 236, 241
  UN General Assembly 218

United States (US) 110, 113, 114, 154, 176, 177, 189, 203, 218, 224, 234, 252, 276, 280, 284
University Settlement 30, 35
USSR 254, 263, 264, 283, 291, 292, 295

Walsh, L.A. 139
Watson, Phoebe 93
Watton, Virginia 63, 71
Wells, H.G. 23
West, Winifred 66, 108, 120, 158
White Australia policy 151
  challenges to 3, 7
Williams, Kath 251, **294**, 295
Witton, Emil 123
Witton, Hannah 123
women
  Australian and Indian women 9
  blocked from leadership positions 104
  family planning 61, 63, 149, 162, 167, 202
    ignored in Australian Women's Charter 182
  gendered racial and religious equality 172
  ignored in postwar reconstruction 181
  jingoism taught to children by mothers 118–119, 130, 197
  prejudice in Education Department 97
  professional career available 27
  single women stigmatised 27
  women's movement(s) 11, 127, 153
Women Assistant Teachers' Association 19, 91, 94
Women Teachers Guild 98
Women's Christian Temperance Union 286
Women's Forum for Social and Economic Reconstruction 147

Women's Indian Association (WIA) 154–155, 169
Women's International Democratic Federation (WIDF) 169, 170, 232, 245, 264, 286
Women's International League for Peace and Freedom (WILPF) 157–158, 264, 278–279
Women's International Zionist Organisation (WIZO) 110–111
Women's News 236–238
Wood, Bill 211
Woodcock, Lucy Godiva (1889–1968)
    awards 75, 216
    employment
        pupil-teacher 17–19, 30
        assistant teacher 6, 17, 19, 29, 32, 41, 43, 45, 90
        exchange teacher, London (1927) 35–37, 65, 108, 156, 189, 307
        headmistress (Mistress of Girls) 45, 54, 59, 60, 65, 68, 84–86, 90, 120, 121, 133, 201, 215, 217
    family
        Beth (sister) 251, 273
            children 251
            Cowley, Fred (husband) 251
        Janet (née Howieson) (mother) 21
        Richard (brother) 83
        Thomas (brother) 21, 195, 297
        Thomas (father) 17, 21
    offices held
        Council for Action on Equal Pay (CAEP) Co-Chair (1942–1948) 103, 153
        Federated State School Teachers' Association, President (1932) 45, 49, 93–94, 98–101
        International Women's Day, NSW Committee, President (1958–1968) 283–295
        New Education Fellowship co-founder, President (1937–1938) 66–67, 116–117, 136
        New Education Fellowship, Vice President (1939–1968) 152–153, 178–181, 196, 198, 276, 301
        NSW Teachers Federation, Vice-President (1932–1933) 35, 96
        NSW Teachers Federation, Senior Vice-President (1934–1953) 11, 49, 103–104, 129, 133, 136–137, 146, 215, 217, 310
        United Associations of Women, Vice-President (1956) 247–248
        United Associations of Women, President (1957–1968) 9, 247, 259–281
        University of Sydney Senate, Graduate representative (1942–1944) 139–141
    private life
        bohemianism 6, 24, 60
        reticence about 9–10, 12–14, 297
    publications
        Justice Vs Tradition (1925) 33–34
        The Lewis Case and You (1956) 245–247
    retirement (1953) 216
        honoured by the United Associations of Women 218

release from control by NSW Department of Education 218
tributes 86–87, 216–17
schools
Eden (1910–1911) 17–20, 124, 140
Darlington (1921–1927) 23, 30, 35, 41, 61, 203
Cessnock (1929) 43–57
Grafton (1930–1932) 45, 81, 89, 92, 109, 273
Erskineville (1933–1953) 41–87
speeches and articles on
cost of war, diversion of funds from education (1938) 56–57, 118–119, 134–135, (1943) 159–162, 197, (1947) 199, (1949) 85, (1952) 200, (1953) 75, 210, 215–216, 234
decolonising countries, leading on women's rights (1954) 224, 230, 264, (1961) 269–270, (1964) 310, (1966) 272.
'Education and Creative Expression', Sydney (1940) 117
'Education for the Future', Wollongong (1938) 56
'Living in the Slums', radio (1939) 55
prejudice (1933) 99–101, (1938) 119, 130, 135, (1953) 212, 214, 215–216, (1962) 291
World Appeal against Atomic War 245
World Conference of Women Workers (1956) 245, 251
World Education Fellowship (WEF, formerly the NEF) 66, 116, 301
World Federation of Trade Unions (WFTU) 169, 245
World Fellowship of Faiths 158
World War I 5, 7, 14, 21, 27, 42, 68, 110, 128, 132, 141, 157, 195, 297
World War II 4, 7, 105, 145, 167, 195, 201, 223
employment of married teachers 145
entangling of race and gender issues postwar 167
globalising impact 115
increased pressure on working-class women 147
postwar political environment 167
rise of nationalist movements postwar 168–169
vision of a new world 168, 172, 223, 310
worsening situation for women 145
Wright, S.E. 204
Wright, Tom **290**
Wyndham, Harold 65, 246, 275

www.ingramcontent.com/pod-product-compliance
Lightning Source LLC
Chambersburg PA
CBHW061255230426
43665CB00036B/2929